State and Local Governments

Murray S. Stedman, Jr.

Temple University

Winthrop Publishers, Inc.

Cambridge, Massachusetts

Library of Congress Cataloging in Publication Data

Stedman, Murray Salisbury
  State and local governments.

  Includes bibliographical references and indexes.
  1. State governments. 2. Local government—United
States. I. Title.
JK2408.S85   320.4'73   75-30711
ISBN 0-87626-841-6

©1976 by Winthrop Publishers, Inc.
   17 Dunster Street, Cambridge, Massachusetts 02138

10   9   8   7   6   5   4   3   2   1

Contents

Preface

The decline in the authority and prestige of the national government has resulted in a renewed interest in the roles of state and local governments. The issue is not really one of liberalism or conservatism; these terms have become largely irrelevant. Rather, the lines are drawn between those who favor centralization and those who favor more decentralization. This book, which adopts a decentralization perspective, attempts to illustrate and to explain the increasing importance of state and local governments in the lives of America's citizens.

The degree of my indebtedness to others is enormous: to other writers whose works are cited in the text and in the chapter notes; to colleagues in the Department of Political Science at Temple University; to Robin Garrison for handling the bulk of the typing; and to Doris Shinn for keeping the volume of traffic under control. I would also like to take this occasion to recognize the specific contribution of a former graduate student at Temple University, Robert J. Piccone, whose research on problems of metropolitan reorganization served as the basis for Chapter 12.

Thanks are also due to Professor David C. Saffell of Ohio Northern University for his preparation of the key terms and items for discussion in each chapter and also for his comments on the text. I am also greatly indebted to Professor William G. O'Hare, Jr., of Salem State College for his many constructive suggestions which greatly improved the final manuscript. My long-time friend James J. Murray III, president of Winthrop Publishers, Inc., served as a most effective coordinator of the entire project. I should also like to express my appreciation for the assistance of his very able staff.

Finally, I am happy to acknowledge the many contributions

of Eve Stedman, my wife. She helped in every stage of the preparation of the book, and expertly prepared the index.

M.S.S.

1

The Importance of State and Local Politics

Key Terms

Conversion: In systems analysis, refers to the internal decision-making process of changing inputs into outputs.

Hortitherapy: Rehabilitation of the physically and mentally handicapped, as well as criminals, through work with one's hands in a garden.

Inputs: In systems analysis, represents requests from society for government action. Distinguished as *supports* (do more of the same) and *demands* (change or expand present policies).

Outputs: In systems analysis, the end result of the conversion process—the policy decisions produced by government decision makers in the form of statutes, ordinances, court decisions.

Participatory democracy: Concept connected with the New Left in America. Stresses decentralization permitting local groups to govern themselves and urges active participation in politics.

Performance review: In the budgetary process, this concept refers to the gathering of statistical information, such as man-hours worked, to determine how much, if any, money should be spent for specific operations.

Political culture: Fundamental beliefs of a group of people regarding political activity, the nature of the

1

political process, and the role that individuals play in the process.

Roles: In systems analysis, refers to expected behavior of individuals and groups in particular situations.

Systems analysis: A framework for understanding how government operates. Two characteristics of all systems are interdependence of parts and a boundary which separates the system from its environment.

Trade-off model: Compromise arrangement to give recognition to the needs of both industrial development and environmental control.

Tweed Ring: Those who surrounded William Tweed, a notable late-nineteenth-century leader (boss) of Tammany Hall in New York City. As a political society, Tammany Hall was notorious for its corruption.

Voucher model: Educational program in which the state makes a receipt (a voucher) available to parents who then can use it to pay for their children's education in either private or public schools.

Zero-base budgeting: Process of justifying all expenses in an annual budget, rather than accepting in large part the continuation of existing programs.

The meeting place was Seattle; the time was the first week of June 1974; and the chief participants were the governors of the fifty states, their advisors, and their consultants. The occasion was the four-day National Governors' Conference.

To put it mildly, the governors were in a condition of euphoria. The conditions which account for this feeling are somewhat complex: Watergate, a lack of confidence in the national government, the vastly improved status of state treasuries, the refusals of then President Nixon and Vice President Ford even to attend.

Though in the past top federal officials had normally attended similar conferences, on this occasion a White House domestic counselor, Kenneth R. Cole, Jr., and the Secretary of Health, Education, and Welfare, Casper W. Weinberger, were dispatched to represent the federal government. Both of them were low-voltage speakers who maintained even lower profiles.

They were clearly outshone by Senator Edward M. Kennedy of Massachusetts, the most visible of President Nixon's numerous adversaries.

As a *New York Times* columnist put it: "The larger sense of this Governors' Conference, confident to the point of cockiness, is that the states have recovered political leadership from a general collapse in Washington."[1] Academic speakers before the conference stressed two themes: first, that the states had taken the initiative, vis-à-vis the federal government, in administration and in innovation; second, that in a world undergoing decentralization almost everywhere, some of the strongest leaders were governors of American states.

Examples of the second point were still fresh in the minds of the governors, as well as of the public at large. During the early months of 1974, the country had been confronted with both the theory and the fact of a large-scale strike by independent truckers. Because of its snowballing tendency, the strike threatened massive industrial disruptions and increased unemployment and inconvenienced nearly everyone. The hero of the hour was Milton J. Shapp, the governor of Pennsylvania (and a former trucker himself). Governor Shapp moved into a Washington hotel and negotiated a settlement between the truckers and their customers (having mostly to do with the price of diesel oil used by the truckers), and the agreement lasted. In short, for virtually a week, while the White House busied itself with Watergate-related matters and was therefore incapable of decisive domestic action, the governor of one state moved in, filled the vacuum, and took over the formulation of public policy in a highly critical area. Regardless of partisan affiliations, the other governors were proud of the successful effort of Governor Shapp.

But there were, of course, more general advances that the governors could and did cite. Daniel J. Evans, governor of Washington and chairman of the conference, prefaced his official report with these words: "During much of this century, and particularly since the onset of the Great Depression, most political scientists and many public leaders viewed state government as a reluctant, timid, and fading force in the federal system. In 1965 one Senator remarked that in the not too distant future, 'The only people interested in state boundaries will be Rand-McNally.' "[2]

All of this, Governor Evans continued, was now obsolete. A new era began, he stated, when the federal government accepted the principle of revenue sharing—a practice that had

President Ford meets with eastern governors. Across table from left are Governors James Longley of Maine, Ella Grasso of Connecticut, Michael Dukakis of Massachusetts, and Milton Shapp of Pennsylvania. The president is at lower right. (Wide World Photos.)

taken place for many decades between state governments and local subdivisions. Moreover, the states had taken the lead, through court actions, to release funds for economic development and other purposes that had been "impounded" by the Nixon Administration.

The governor and the conference referred to four broad areas of change and progress in state government. Though the details of these developments will be dealt with later in this book, it is worth citing the areas themselves at this time. The following summary is quoted directly from the report of the Governors' Conference:[3]

> *Funding.* Fifteen years ago the states could not afford to provide the level of service demanded of them; most of them had to rely on weak, narrow-gauge revenue systems that depended more on "nuisance" taxes than on more broadly based courses. Most of the states have changed that condition with the politically courageous adoption of income and sales taxes and more than five hundred rate hikes. Half the states now produce at least 60 percent of their combined state-local tax revenues, and many states

are now assuming more of the obligations of local governments or helping to fund them.

Organization. In 1960 most states had outmoded structures that constitutionally tied the hands of the Governor in cumbersome executive organization, impeded legislatures in effectively tackling the public's business and made it difficult for the judiciary to assure justice with dispatch. Since then the number of Governors with a four-year term has increased from 34 to 43. The number of legislatures that meet annually has risen from 19 to 33, and states with major elements of a unified judiciary have increased to 31. Nine states have adopted new constitutions, four have made extensive revisions in their existing charters, and over the past decade 18 states have comprehensively reorganized their executive branches.

Ongoing services. States have always been responsible for major ongoing domestic services such as education, welfare, health and transportation. But only with improved fiscal systems and streamlined structures have they been able to cope with the steadily increasing demands for such services. In the last fiscal year, states spent a total of $90 billion from their own sources on domestic services—a startling jump from $15.8 billion in fiscal 1954. In fiscal 1971, the states spent more than $17 billion on local schools, more than $12 billion on welfare and health, nearly $10 billion on highways—just from their own revenue resources.

Current issues. The political, social and economic diversity of the states is producing innovative responses to some of the most urgent problems and issues of the day. More than half the states took significant action on campaign finance or government ethics in 1973. States were the first to react with practical programs to deal with the energy crisis—more than a quarter of them established some form of gasoline rationing, and nearly half implemented their own energy conservation plans. States also pioneered the idea of consumer protection agencies, and now every state has established such a body. Since 1970, while Congress debated the issue, 11 states have enacted some form of no-fault auto insurance, and eight have extensively modified their auto insurance codes. In a different context, practically every state has taken some action on land-use planning, and a number have taken still other innovative measures in environmental protection.

The preceding paragraphs, then, represent a mid-1970s appraisal by the governors of the progress made by the fifty states of the Union in the last two decades. Some of the merits of the governors' specific claims will be examined at appropriate points in succeeding chapters. What is beyond debate is that the states, and their subdivisions, have provided and continue to provide a large number of absolutely vital functions and services to the American people.

THE STUDY OF STATE AND LOCAL GOVERNMENT

Even before political science became a separate discipline by breaking away from departments of history, individual scholars had studied state and local government with considerable care. For example, the best studies of the Tweed Ring were made by historians with a perspective on the current, while the best studies of oligarchical state political organizations were made at one time by overseas visitors such as De Tocqueville and Ostrogorski, whom we could today classify as sociologists.

But in the last thirty or forty years, the most intensive and continuing studies have been conducted by political scientists. A major contribution toward clarification of the status of these studies was made by Charles O. Jones in a contribution to a book entitled *Political Science and State and Local Government*, published by the American Political Science Association in 1973.[4]

The basic question which political scientists raise is whether politics makes any difference at all in the policy outputs of state and local governments. To some this question itself may seem surprising, but it has given professional students of government and administration an endless amount of difficulty and soul-searching.

Concentrating purely on studies of the last decade, Jones found that there had been three major—and conflicting—emphases in the works he surveyed. First, there was the assumption that political variables—such as party composition in the legislature and the nature of the party system—do matter. Jones cites V. O. Key, one of the giants of modern empirical political science, as being a member of this camp. For example, Key speculated on the possible effects of the then dominant one-party factionalism in the South on public policy as enacted by legislatures and councils.

According to Jones, a second and subsequent belief was

that the socioeconomic variables were the most important factors in the determination of policy outputs. For example, it has been and is contended that the general income of a region has more to do with public support for education than does action inside the legislature. Jones cites Thomas R. Dye, a leading scholar in the field, as an advocate of this position.

But a third major emphasis has emerged more recently, one which Jones himself appears to accept. He states: "It appears now, in a third phase, that state and local scholars may be in the process of rediscovering a role for politics in policy."[5] He then proceeds to refer to a number of studies which have appeared since 1970, and the weight of the evidence is fairly heavy, if not overwhelming.

On the other hand, Jones is somewhat ambiguous as to the utility of the policy process approach. After an intensive review, he concludes that ". . . taken as a whole the policy process articles also tend to open many more doors than they close. Perhaps that is the fate (or function) of the political scientists."[6]

What does this add up to for a student of state and local politics? The Jones analysis is a warning that the study of state and local government is not an applied science, and may never become one. Extremely able scholars, examining the same evidence but often using different techniques, continue to arrive at varying conclusions when they deal with the question of the relationship between political variables and policy outputs. The general view taken in this book is presented in the following section, with the understanding that it is not to be confused with Sacred Writ.

THE SYSTEMS APPROACH TO POLITICS

In 1953, David Easton brought out an important book entitled *The Political System.*[7] The book is complex and not always easy reading, but its central thrust is clear. Easton proposes that political processes be considered interrelated parts of a total system. As with an organism, what happens in one part of the system affects the other parts.

At about the same time, the International Social Science Research Council, with the help of Unesco, was reexamining critically the traditional method of teaching comparative politics. At first, the subject had been treated on a country-by-country approach, a sort of Cook's tour. Subsequently, the prevailing method was to handle the various countries by comparing the institutions of each; for example, French, British, and German political parties in one chapter, and the parliaments of the same countries in another chapter. While this represented a considerable advance over the earlier method, it still failed to achieve a truly comparative technique of analysis.

In the spring of 1954, a Unesco-sponsored conference met in Florence, Italy, with the objective of encouraging the development of comparative politics through a systemic approach. Because the conference was high level, widely attended, and brilliantly led, it was influential. The writings of those who attended the conference almost immediately began to reflect the acceptance of the systems approach in the study of comparative politics among nations.

Thanks to the widespread interest in Easton's approach to a national political system, and thanks also to the widespread use of the systems approach in comparative politics between nations, the idea of applying the same general mode of analysis to the study of state, provincial, and municipal politics quickly took root. Although different writers employ different models, some general observations about systems analysis may be offered.

When one uses the term *system*, it is clear that interdependence of parts is implied, as well as some kind of boundary between the particular system (political, religious, economic) and its social environment. It also is implied that systems are made up of "roles"—judges, legislators, lobbyists, and so on—and not merely of individuals. These roles interact at numerous points in the system.

It is customary when defining the boundary between political and other systems to utilize three phases: inputs, conversions, and outputs. Inputs are thought of as demands and supports. For example, a demand might be to extend a service, while a support might be payment of taxes or obeying the law. To put the matter differently, demands usually affect policies or objectives, while supports provide the resources necessary to make it possible for a political system to achieve its goals. Conversion refers to the process of decision making within the system—for example, the making of statutes, court decisions, or the orders of administrative agencies. Outputs are the end result of the process, the expression of public policy—for example, in taxes or provisions for education.

As David C. Saffell has noted, the systems framework is a

"useful approach rather than a true theory."[8] Nonetheless, it
provides insight into how any particular government operates, it
makes possible meaningful comparisons, and it is useful in
suggesting general insights into political processes. Figure 1.1
suggests some of these possibilities.

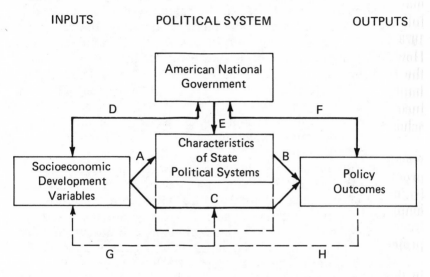

| INPUTS | POLITICAL SYSTEM | OUTPUTS |

Examples:

Examples:	Examples:	Examples:
urbanization	constitutional framework	educational policy
industrialization	partisanship	health and welfare policy
income	party competition	housing policy
adult education	political participation	tax levels
	apportionment system	law enforcement
		transportation policy
		civil rights
		division of state–local
		responsibilities

Figure 1.1
A model for the analysis of state political systems.
Source: Thomas R. Dye, *Politics in States and Communities.*
Englewood Cliffs, N.J.: Prentice-Hall, 1973. Reprinted by permission.

For example, the systems approach draws attention to the
importance of social and economic differences among the states.
The per capita income, as an illustration, stood at $4,156 for the
nation as a whole in 1971. But the distinctions among the fifty
states were substantial. Even within New England, the Connecticut per capita income was $4,995 in 1971, and for Maine the

figure was $3,375. The lowest total in the nation was found in Mississippi: $2,788. The highest per capita income was recorded in New York, at $5,000. In addition to Connecticut, the incomes in Alaska ($4,875) and in Hawaii ($4,738) were also well above the national average.

Obviously comparisons can be made in other areas, and it is easy to guess at some relationships, however indirect they may be. For example, for the states we have mentioned, the following per pupil expenditures were made in public schools in 1973: New York, $1,584; Alaska, $1,473; Connecticut, $1,241; Hawaii, $1,055; Maine, $840; Mississippi, $689. At the bottom of the list were Arkansas, with $651, and Alabama, with $590. The implication is that there is some relationship between per capita income and per capita expenditures for the education of public school students.

The individual states may be compared in scores of other ways: in terms of urbanization, manufacturing, farm areas and products, crime rates, health statistics, forest lands, housing units, motor vehicles, highways and railroads, employment and unemployment rates. One of the most obvious, and one of the most interesting, of the indices is population. Figure 1.2 shows the projected population changes from 1973 to 1990.

Although the states have a very high degree of uniformity in their constitutional frameworks, their socioeconomic environments differ considerably. The same observation may be applied to their political systems. Clearly, the strength of the Democratic and Republican parties varies among the states. In some states there is domination by a single party; in some there is genuine competition between the major parties. Some governors may succeed themselves; others may not. In some states regionalism appears to be a stronger factor than party loyalty in choosing members of the state legislature. Conflicts may occur along any number of lines: liberal versus conservative; city versus rural; labor versus management; one interest (for example, truckers) versus another (for example, railroads).

THE SETTINGS OF STATE POLITICS

Historical circumstances have had a profound impact upon state politics. The settlement of New England by English Nonconformists produced a different outlook than that existing in Maryland, where Catholicism was the religion of the reigning

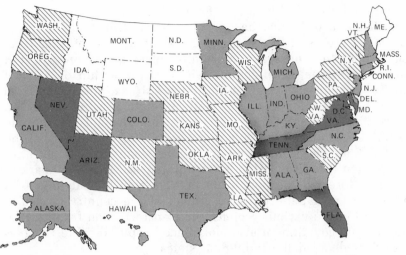

■ States gaining more than 25%   ☒ States gaining less than 15%
□ States gaining from 15% to 25%   ☐ States losing population

	1973 Population (in thousands)	1980 Population (est. in thousands)	1990 Population (est. in thousands)	Change, 1973–1990		1973 Population (in thousands)	1980 Population (est. in thousands)	1990 Population (est. in thousands)	Change, 1973–1990
Alabama	3,539	3,747	4,090	Up 15.6%	New Jersey	7,361	8,080	8,923	Up 21.2%
Alaska	330	333	391	Up 18.5%	New				
Arizona	2,058	2,226	2,701	Up 31.2%	Mexico	1,106	1,055	1,131	Up 2.3%
Arkansas	2,037	2,087	2,271	Up 11.5%	New York	18,265	19,352	20,946	Up 14.7%
California	20,601	22,403	24,982	Up 21.3%	North				
Colorado	2,437	2,586	2,890	Up 18.6%	Carolina	5,273	5,736	6,465	Up 22.6%
Connecti-					North				
cut	3,076	3,358	3,710	Up 20.6%	Dakota	640	579	563	Down 12.0%
Delaware	576	627	707	Up 22.7%	Ohio	10,731	11,651	12,609	Up 17.5%
D.C.	746	750	750	Up .5%	Oklahoma	2,663	2,762	2,993	Up 12.4%
Florida	7,678	8,926	10,978	Up 43.0%	Oregon	2,225	2,335	2,537	Up 14.0%
Georgia	4,786	5,147	5,907	Up 23.4%	Pennsyl-				
Hawaii	832	848	979	Up 17.7%	vania	11,902	12,649	13,416	Up 12.7%
Idaho	770	708	738	Down 4.2%	Rhode				
Illinois	11,236	12,091	13,056	Up 16.2%	Island	973	1,032	1,115	Up 14.6%
Indiana	5,316	5,784	6,364	Up 19.7%	South				
Iowa	2,904	2,913	2,993	Up 3.1%	Carolina	2,726	2,819	3,122	Up 14.5%
Kansas	2,279	2,228	2,281	Up .1%	South				
Kentucky	3,342	3,609	3,982	Up 19.2%	Dakota	685	655	648	Down 5.4%
Louisiana	3,764	3,744	3,937	Up 4.6%	Tennessee	4,126	4,557	5,191	Up 25.8%
Maine	1,028	972	992	Down 3.5%	Texas	11,794	12,167	13,580	Up 15.1%
Maryland	4,070	4,473	5,275	Up 29.6%	Utah	1,157	1,160	1,310	Up 13.2%
Massachu-					Vermont	464	482	519	Up 11.9%
setts	5,818	6,267	6,876	Up 18.2%	Virginia	4,811	5,295	6,135	Up 27.5%
Michigan	9,044	9,743	10,645	Up 17.7%	Washing-				
Minnesota	3,897	4,119	4,553	Up 16.8%	ton	3,429	3,550	3,806	Up 11.0%
Mississippi	2,281	2,328	2,450	Up 7.4%	West				
Missouri	4,757	5,071	5,439	Up 14.3%	Virginia	1,794	1,832	1,845	Up 2.8%
Montana	721	670	665	Down 7.8%	Wisconsin	4,569	4,737	5,013	Up 9.7%
Nebraska	1,542	1,499	1,557	Up 1.0%	Wyoming	353	331	334	Down 5.4%
Nevada	548	616	761	Up 38.9%					
New									
Hamp-					UNITED	209,851		246,039	
shire	791	843	919	Up 16.2%	STATES		223,532		Up 17.2%

Note: Population estimates by U.S. Census Bureau assume birth rates will remain near recent levels.

Figure 1.2
Projected population change, 1973-1990.
Source: U.S. Bureau of the Census.

Calvert family. Florida was a Spanish territory until 1819, and the Hispanic influence has recently been strengthened by the arrival of scores of thousands of Cubans who are refugees from Castro's Cuba. There are substantial elements of French civil law in Louisiana, a reflection of its past ownership by France; the Texas civil law system still carries a strong inheritance from Spanish law in, for example, matters relating to the family. In short, the political culture of each state depends on unique historical circumstances. Figure 1.3 serves to remind us that the United States grew in quantum regional leaps. It was not until 1917, when the Virgin Islands were purchased from Denmark in order to forestall the possibility that German U-boats might be based there, that the physical growth of the country ceased.

Within the various regions, the transformation from territorial to state government also took place in spurts. Table 1.1 gives historical data on the individual states.

RECENT INNOVATIONS IN STATE GOVERNMENT

One of the themes of this book is that state governments, after a long period of inaction, are once again in motion. The states operate under a number of obvious con-

Figure 1.3
Regional growth of the United States.
Source: U.S. Bureau of the Census, *U.S. Census of Population*, 1960.

straints. After all, in many ways they are dependent upon the federal government, and they have little control over the national, let alone the world, economy. Yet with all these limitations, there has been in recent years very substantial movement. Since there may be some reader skepticism on this point, the following paragraphs, drawing once again from the National Governors' Conference of 1974, will attempt to document the assertion.[9] This will be done under ten general headings, with specific references to specific states.

New Departures in Administration

Administrative restructuring of state government is a continuing process. What is essentially new is the increasing sense of public accountability that underlies current restructuring. At the same time, modern management methods are being adopted to improve the quality and cost factors of the services that are rendered. The following are some examples:

Wisconsin has undertaken a state government productivity program. The idea is to improve efficiency and simultaneously lessen the demands on the taxpayer.

New York has endorsed a method called "performance review." Already, positive results have been claimed in the operation of the welfare system, and the next target is the educational system.

Texas has established a centralized information system. It is service-oriented and uses modern data processing methodology and other modern management tools to improve state services.

Tennessee, like Texas, has adopted a variety of modern management techniques. These have already resulted in substantial savings.

South Dakota added an innovation to the reorganization process when, in 1973, it became the first and the only state to restructure its executive branch by a single executive order of the governor.

Georgia has become the first state to adopt "zero-base" budgeting. Under this concept, every dollar requested for expenditure during the next budget period must be justified, including current expenditures that are to continue. At the same time, the state merged the budgeting and planning functions.

Nebraska divided the state into natural resource districts based on river systems. This did away with hitherto

Table 1.1
States: Settled, Capitals, Entry into Union, Area, Rank

State	Settled*	Capital	Entered Union	Extent in Miles		Area in square miles			Rank In Area
				Long	Wide	Land	Inland Water	Total	
Ala.	1702	Montgomery	1819, Dec. 14	330	200	50,708	901	51,609	29
Alaska	1784	Juneau	1959, Jan. 3	(A)900	800	566,432	19,980	586,412	1
Ariz.	1848	Phoenix	1912, Feb. 14	390	335	113,417	492	113,909	6
Ark.	1785	Little Rock	1836, June 15	275	240	51,945	1,159	53,104	27
Cal.	1769	Sacramento	1850, Sept. 9	770	375	156,361	2,332	158,693	3
Colo.	1858	Denver	1876, Aug. 1	390	270	103,766	481	104,247	8
Conn.	1635	Hartford	1788, Jan. 9	90	75	4,862	139	5,009	48
Del.	1638	Dover	1787, Dec. 7	110	35	1,982	75	2,057	49
Dist. Col.	...	Washington	...	...	...	61	6	67	51
Fla.	1565	Tallahassee	1845, Mar. 3	460	400	54,090	4,470	58,560	22
Ga.	1733	Atlanta	1788, Jan. 2	315	250	58,073	803	58,876	21
Hawaii	...	Honolulu	1959, Aug. 21	...	...	6,425	25	6,450	47
Idaho	1842	Boise	1890, July 3	490	305	82,677	880	83,557	13
Ill.	1720	Springfield	1818, Dec. 3	380	205	55,748	652	56,400	24
Ind.	1733	Indianapolis	1816, Dec. 11	265	160	36,097	102	36,291	38
Iowa	1788	Des Moines	1846, Dec. 28	300	210	55,941	349	56,290	25
Kan.	1727	Topeka	1861, Jan. 29	400	200	81,787	477	82,264	14
Ky.	1774	Frankfort	1792, June 1	350	175	39,650	745	40,395	37
La.	1699	Baton Rouge	1812, Apr. 30	280	275	44,930	3,593	48,523	31
Me.	1624	Augusta	1820, Mar. 15	235	205	30,920	2,295	33,215	39
Md.	1634	Annapolis	1788, Apr. 28	200	120	9,891	686	10,577	42
Mass.	1620	Boston	1788, Feb. 6	190	110	7,826	431	8,257	45
Mich.	1668	Lansing	1837, Jan. 26	400	310	56,817	1,399	58,216	23
Minn.	1805	St. Paul	1858, May 11	400	350	79,289	4,779	84,068	12
Miss.	1699	Jackson	1817, Dec. 10	340	180	47,296	420	47,716	32
Mo.	1735	Jefferson City	1821, Aug. 10	300	280	68,995	691	69,686	19

	Settlement*	Capital	Statehood							
Mont.	1809	Helena	1889, Nov.	8	580	315	145,587	1,551	147,138	4
Nebr.	1847	Lincoln	1867, Mar.	1	415	205	76,483	744	77,227	15
Nev.	1850	Carson City	1864, Oct.	31	485	315	109,889	651	110,540	7
N.H.	1623	Concord	1788, June	21	185	90	9,027	277	9,304	44
N.J.	1664	Trenton	1787, Dec.	18	160	70	7,521	315	7,836	46
N.M.	1605	Santa Fe	1912, Jan.	6	390	350	121,412	254	121,666	5
N.Y.	1614	Albany	1788, July	26	320	310	47,831	1,745	49,576	30
N.C.	1650	Raleigh	1789, Nov.	21	520	200	48,798	3,788	52,586	28
N.D.	1766	Bismarck	1889, Nov.	2	360	210	69,273	1,392	70,665	17
Ohio	1788	Columbus	1803, Mar.	1	230	205	40,975	247	41,222	35
Okla.	1889	Oklahoma City	1907, Nov.	16	585	210	68,782	1,137	69,919	18
Ore.	1811	Salem	1859, Feb.	14	375	290	96,184	797	96,981	10
Pa.	1682	Harrisburg	1787, Dec.	12	300	180	44,966	367	45,333	33
R.I.	1636	Providence	1790, May	29	50	35	1,049	165	1,214	50
S.C.	1670	Columbia	1788, May	23	285	215	30,225	830	31,055	40
S.D.	1856	Pierre	1889, Nov.	2	380	245	75,955	1,092	77,047	16
Tenn.	1757	Nashville	1796, June	1	430	120	41,328	916	42,244	34
Texas	1691	Austin	1845, Dec.	29	760	620	262,134	5,204	267,338 (B)	2
Utah	1847	Salt Lake City	1896, Jan.	4	345	275	82,906	2,820	84,916	11
Vt.	1724	Montpelier	1791, Mar.	4	155	90	9,267	342	9,609	43
Va.	1607	Richmond	1788, June	26	425	205	39,780	1,037	40,817	36
Wash.	1811	Olympia	1889, Nov.	11	340	230	66,570	1,622	68,192	20
W. Va.	1727	Charleston	1863, June	20	225	200	24,070	111	24,181	41
Wis.	1766	Madison	1848, May	29	300	290	54,464	1,690	56,154	26
Wyo.	1834	Cheyenne	1890, July	10	365	275	97,203	711	97,914	9

The Original Thirteen States—The 13 colonies that seceded from Great Britain and fought the War of Independence (American Revolution) became the 13 original states. They were Massachusetts, Rhode Island, Connecticut, New Hampshire, New York, New Jersey, Pennsylvania, Delaware, Maryland, Virginia, North Carolina, South Carolina, and Georgia.

* First permanent settlement.

† Changes in land and water area between 1960 and 1970 are the results of the construction of dams and reservoirs.

(A) Aleutian Islands and Alexander Archipelago are not considered in these lengths.

(B) Total area of Texas reduced 1 sq. mile by Chamizal boundary solution between U.S. and Mexico, 1963.

arbitrarily bounded subdivisions. The theme is one of regionalization along natural lines.

Initiatives in State Planning

Substantial progress in state planning was reported at the Governors' Conference. Planning is a tricky concept. Operationally, the present trend is to obtain, or try to obtain, partnerships among agencies at all levels of government. It also involves a process whereby conflicting claims may be reconciled. Six states and Puerto Rico have been experimenting in an effort to improve their planning procedures.

New Mexico has revitalized its State Planning Office into an effective instrument for the coordination of programs throughout the state. In an era which sometimes uses the idea of decentralization as an ideological goal, this is an interesting development.

Arizona has developed a so-called trade-off model by which hard data are collected in an effort to equate the differing demands of industrial development and environmental safeguards.

Delaware now uses its State Planning Office in a new kind of strategy called "Delaware Tomorrow." A feature of the plan is vastly increased citizen input in the process of long-range development.

Utah has established substate Regional Planning Districts. The idea is to formalize partnerships between state and local governments.

Puerto Rico has approached the problem by setting up a permanent system of Governor's Workshops. Through this mechanism it is expected that increased coordination among agencies will be achieved.

Kansas has established in the governor's office an Office of Policy Review and Coordination. Its particular responsibility is to advise the Governor and the legislature on environmental problems.

Land Use and Environment

One of the most difficult problems facing the American states and the country as a whole is how to improve the environment in the face of demands that standards be relaxed because of the energy crisis. Federal environmental standards are being relaxed, but many of the states have demonstrated innovative ways of coping with environmental deterioration. In many respects, some of the state governments have been far more imaginative and thoughtful than the federal government. Some illustrations are given here:

Vermont has been one of the leading states in taking broad but precise measures to maintain its attractive environment and its quality of life. It has insisted on developmental guidelines and controls. For example, it has declared war on that highway litterbug, the billboard.

Colorado has developed a comprehensive plan to protect its different regional environments. It is attempting to direct growth and development from a statewide perspective.

Florida, which has traditionally suffered from a history of unchecked development, has adopted a whole package of legislation designed to prevent further misuse of the land. Whether these laws will accomplish their purpose of course remains to be seen. But Floridians have become remarkably environment conscious in the last few years.

Alaska has established a Regional Profiles program to collate data on its six major regions as a basis for future land-use planning and development. Given the impending oil boom in the north of Alaska, the necessity for some kind of environmental planning is obvious.

Oregon for some years has been in the avant garde of environmental protection. It achieved considerable fame and admiration when it became the first state to require cash deposits on cans containing beer and soft drinks to reduce solid waste litter.

Hawaii, already considerably overdeveloped in many areas, has undertaken a program to safeguard its remaining coastal resources with a system of trails to interlink and preserve them for the benefit of the entire citizenry.

New Responses to the Energy Crisis

While the primary response to the energy crisis should come from the federal government, that response has not to date been particularly forceful. This may, of course, change, but in the meantime several of the states have taken actions that are worth noting. Of the many states which have reacted, the following five are singled out for special attention:

Montana, or at least its governor and legislature, would like to develop a new land-use ethic. The problem has been made acute by the realization that in eastern Montana at least 43 billion tons of strippable low-sulphur coal are buried beneath the plains. One response has been the passage in 1973 of a very strong surface reclamation law. Other measures undoubtedly will be taken.

North Dakota, primarily an agricultural state, faces the dilemma of energy or food. The problem here is lignite, which lies just underneath the soil and which can easily be converted into fuel gas. The dilemma has not been resolved.

Maine has been battling for years to prevent a potentially massive buildup of oil refineries from deteriorating its splendid coastline. It has drafted defensive legislation to prepare for spill damage and to control the location of any refineries.

Kentucky belatedly has been taking steps to protect its environment in the fact of large-scale, ruthless, and destructive strip mining of its vast coal deposits. It remains an open question whether the legislature can, in fact, control the coal companies. Meanwhile, large sections of the mountain part of the state have been devastated, probably forever.

Wyoming, a much more progressive state than Kentucky, has been experimenting in revegetating, reclaiming, and renewing the quality of lands subjected to open-cut mining. Whether these efforts will be successful continues to be the subject of lively controversy between the mining interests and the environmentalists.

Economic and Rural Development

In the past, the principal developmental emphasis of state governments was industrial. This concern still remains important to state officials, but it has been broadened to include, in many cases, a social commitment as well. It is difficult to assess the depth of this commitment unless one is extremely familiar with the workings of particular state governments. But the claims put forth by the governors are impressive.

Mississippi has approached the problem by devising an elaborate system for combining public and private equity to create business opportunities for the disadvantaged. While attempting to diversify the economy and deemphasize the former importance of "King Cotton," the state has sought to do so in a social context.

Rhode Island faced a crisis when the federal government, in an economy move, closed down several naval bases. The state responded by trying to encourage new industries to enter the state. It also embarked upon manpower retraining programs.

Louisiana faced an entirely different type of problem: how to protect its environment in the face of offshore oil drilling. The answer was to found a Superport Authority, which was given substantial planning powers.

Alabama, using its revenue-sharing funds, proceeded to build badly needed rural water systems. Service was provided to some 50,000 persons in rural areas previously without public water service.

North Carolina, often a pioneering state, proceeded to develop a unique rural health program as a basis for rural renewal. In doing so, the state drew heavily on the resources of the great universities in the state. A new health delivery system was developed with a combination of area health education centers and rural health clinics.

Human Services and Welfare Systems

The states have been under strong pressure to balance welfare caseloads and the resulting taxloads. One way to do this has been to streamline and coordinate the delivery of much-needed services. New approaches have also been undertaken in rehabilitation, help for the elderly, and housing. Some state-by-state illustrations are cited as follows:

Minnesota has stressed the improvement of management in the state supervision and the local delivery of a broad range of human services.

Arkansas, on the other hand, has emphasized improved coordination in this general area of service. The point has been to improve state-local relations.

California, under the leadership of its former governor, Ronald Reagan, embarked upon a large-scale (and controversial) welfare reform program. The aim was to achieve a comprehensive system and at the same time to reduce the tax burden.

West Virginia used a different approach. It set up a selective verification system to establish quality control over the welfare caseload, with the goal of maximizing the return on welfare tax dollars.

Indiana tried another method, seeking a more equitable balance between high standards of determining need and the traditionally low level of benefits actually paid out.

South Carolina, in another field, pioneered in applying "hortitherapy" to the rehabilitation of the mentally retarded, drug abusers, public offenders, the blind, and the underprivileged. "Hortitherapy" is defined as the use of horticultural appeal and methods for improvement of physical and mental well-being. For example, the Menninger Foundation in Kansas has used gardening therapy ever since it opened its doors.

Pennsylvania has adopted a variety of programs to help senior citizens, especially programs relating to tax relief and free or subsidized transportation.

Guam's territorial government has undertaken a low-cost housing program by combining grants with loans. The program is intended not only to produce more homes but to enable low- and moderate-income people to become owners of homes.

Child Care Services

All the fifty states engage in child-care services, and all have been criticized from time to time for treating children more as commodities than as persons. But at least three states have been taking a consciously humane view toward children.

Illinois has demonstrated that it regards itself as an advocate of disadvantaged children. It has done so by "humanizing" its services for children, primarily through the Department of Children and Family Services.

Idaho has shown a special concern for the needs of preschool children. This is an important subject on which few hard data have been collected. Idaho is in the process of collecting and studying such data.

Missouri has extended its state educational system to include training and guidance for its handicapped children. While other states also include provisions for handicapped children within their educational systems, Missouri appears to have tackled the problem more thoroughly than most other states.

Educational Services

One of the basic problems in education is to achieve a balance between limited tax resources and the mounting educational requirements. There has been a good deal of innovation in meeting this challenge. Here are some illustrations of recent state actions:

New Hampshire has been testing a "voucher model," with the objectives of aiding parents and providing an alternative to the traditional public school pattern of education. Under this plan the state makes a receipt (a voucher) available to parents, who then can use it as cash to pay for their children's education in either private or public schools. While this model raises constitutional questions, it has the merit of innovation and experimentation at a time when the public schools are under tremendous criticism.

Iowa has devised a state School Foundation Plan. The basic idea is to equalize the tax burden among school districts.

Maryland, in a somewhat related move, has chosen to assume the costs of local public school building construction. The goal is to relieve the tax load on local communities and also to effect significant savings.

Nevada has enlarged the public school curriculum to include drug abuse education. The obvious objective is to warn students of the dangers of drug addiction and, it is hoped, to discourage the use of harmful drugs.

Oklahoma has pioneered in extending its state educational services to elements of the prison population. Instead of merely punishing inmates, the objective is to retool them for useful roles once they have been released from prison.

American Samoa founded a community college in 1970. Open throughout the year, the college now has an enrollment of more than one thousand students. Some 35 percent of the students are more than 30 years of age.

Transportation Systems

Historically, transportation systems were developed independently of each other and, even if publicly subsidized, under private ownership. The result has been a confusing jumble. At least two states have recently been engaged in comprehensive planning in this field.

Michigan is in the process of formulating what could become a truly comprehensive statewide transportation system. This involves railroads, buses, and ships. It is interesting that the center of America's automobile industry should be taking the initiative in this area.

Ohio has set up what it calls the Action Plan. Still in its initial stage, the plan, when and if fully effective, will coordinate transportation of all kinds, including aviation and pipeline systems. Citizenship participation is built into the Action Plan.

The State and the Individual

In this broad area, many states have taken dramatic steps; Illinois and Connecticut, for example, have adopted the idea embodied in the Napoleonic Code that sexual acts between consenting adults constitute a private, not a state, matter. There are many other illustrations. The Governors' Conference drew attention to the following:

> *Washington* has developed a program to encourage and support volunteer services to state and local agencies. In other words, the principle of volunteerism has been aided and abetted by the state. A kind of "participatory democracy," involving thousands of citizens, has been one of the results.
>
> *Connecticut* has developed an unusual system for responding and responding immediately to citizens' inquiries and needs in its state Information Bureau, established in 1973. According to then-Governor Thomas J. Meskill, the effect was to bring citizen and state government into a closer relationship.
>
> *Massachusetts* has taken steps to defend the citizen's privacy against possible infringement by the growing computerized federal data systems. In a number of actions, Massachusetts refused to turn over to the FBI and HEW certain data unless adequate safeguards concerning the individuals' rights to privacy were guaranteed. In defense of this policy, then-Governor Francis W. Sargent declared: "It is often said that information is power. Centralized information is centralized power. It is time to return some of that power to the states; the personal privacy and individual rights of our citizens depend upon it."[10]

THE VITALITY OF THE STATES

Ten or fifteen years ago, many careful scholars of American government were prepared to dismiss state governments as more or less dysfunctional appendages of the American political system. Today that perspective has nearly been reversed. Disillusionment with the national government is at or near an all-time high. The federal government bears the

onus of disastrous Asian wars, recession, inflation, and unemployment. Its integrity is under constant question. It very
often seems to be in a condition of paralysis. The president and
Congress, as James MacGregor Burns has put it, are normally in
a state of "deadlock."

No one, of course, would contend that the state governments have an unblemished record. Taken as a whole, the
record is spotty. But there has been, and there continues to be, a
kind of experimentation and diversity which the federal government simply does not display. The action has shifted in the 1970s
from Washington to state capitals. It is for this reason that there
has been something of a renaissance in the scholarly and jour-
nalistic examination of state governments, and the study of state
political systems has become important.

In the following chapters, we examine the structure and
operations of state governments and the relationships of such
governments both to their own subdivisions and to the national
government. In doing so, we follow the general systemic approach outlined earlier in the present chapter.

Items for Discussion

1. Considering what has happened since the
1974 National Governors' Conference, was the governors' optimism justified?

2. What are some of the economic, political,
and social consequences that can be expected by 1990 as a result
of state population changes?

2. Considering your own state, describe how
pre-Civil War events have affected politics in the twentieth century.

4. What recent innovations in your own
state's government can you add to the list in the text?

5. Can you make a case for the proposition
that the states, during the past twenty-five years, have been
more innovative than the national government?

Chapter Notes

1. Christopher Lydon, in the *New York Times*, 6 June 1974.

2. *The State of the States in 1974* (Washington, D.C.: National Governors' Conference, 1974), p. 1.

3. *Ibid.*, pp. 6–7.

4. Charles O. Jones, in *Political Science and State and Local Government* (Washington, D.C.: American Political Science Association, 1973), pp. 27–54. Jones's essay is entitled: "State and Local Party Analysis: A Review of Progress."

5. *Ibid.*, p. 37.

6. *Ibid.*, p. 43.

7. David Easton, *The Political System* (New York: Knopf, 1953).

8. David C. Saffell, *The Politics of American National Government*, 2nd ed. (Cambridge, Mass.: Winthrop, 1975), p. 13.

9. *Innovations in State Government, Messages from the Governors* (Washington, D.C.: National Governors' Conference, 1974).

10. *Ibid.*, p. 374.

2

The Place
of the States
in the Federal Union

Key Terms

Articles of Confederation: Approved in 1776, ratified in 1781, replaced by the Constitution in 1789. The central government under the articles was weak, with a single legislative branch, and the states retained strong independent authority.

Commonwealth: In the case of Puerto Rico, indicates a position in which Puerto Ricans are citizens of the United States, have a resident commissioner in the House of Representatives, but are not liable for federal taxation. A kind of halfway position between independence and statehood.

Cooperative federalism: Middle ground of state-federal cooperation which avoids the extremes of centralization of power or unworkable decentralization.

Due process of law: Limits government by giving individuals protection against arbitrary deprivation of life, liberty, or property (see the Fifth and Fourteenth Amendments).

Dual federalism: Situation in which states and the national government are believed to have separate areas of authority and each is supreme in its own area; discarded since 1937 by the Supreme Court in favor of the doctrine of national supremacy.

Equal protection of the laws: Requires that

states may not arbitrarily discriminate against persons (Fourteenth Amendment).

Executive privilege: The power of the president to refuse to produce information sought by the other two branches of government.

Extradition: The return by one state to another of a person accused of committing a crime in the second state.

Federalism: Governmental system in which two or more governments exercise power over the same people at the same time.

Full faith and credit clause: Obligates states to honor the civil proceedings (divorces, wills, contracts) of other states (Article IV, Section 1).

Impoundment: Power of the president to refuse to spend money that has been appropriated by Congress.

Implied powers: Authority of the national government based on inference from those powers specifically delegated to it in the Constitution. A means by which the national government has strengthened and broadened its authority.

Nationalists: Those who believe the Constitution is to be interpreted liberally to allow broad exercise of power by the national government.

New Federalism: Nixon administration concept of decentralization by returning power to the states and local governments.

Privileges and immunities: Places restrictions on states in their dealings with United States citizens, e.g., cannot restrict the right to travel. Because of vagueness and uncertain judicial interpretation, has been of limited use (see Article IV, Section 1, and Fourteenth Amendment).

Republican government: One that operates through elected representatives of the people; distinguished from a pure democracy in which the people govern directly.

States' righters: Those who view the Constitution as a compact drawn up between the states and the national government in which the states reserved for themselves substantial authority.

Unitary government: Form of government in which all power rests with the central authority, as in Great Britain; thus local governments do not have independent powers as in a federation.

At a time when memories of the Bicentennial celebration are fresh in everyone's mind, it is perhaps worth recalling that some of the thirteen original states—for example, Virginia and Massachusetts—are themselves nearly twice as old as the Union. Or, for those historically inclined, it may be noted that Spanish America was originally colonized a good deal earlier than English America. Ponce de León, moving from his base in Puerto Rico, "discovered" Florida in 1513, and subsequently the Spaniards established the earliest permanent settlement, St. Augustine, in 1565. During the American Revolution, Florida, then under British rule, was the only Loyalist British province south of Canada. In the West, notably what is now California, Arizona, and New Mexico, there were numerous additional, if somewhat later, permanent settlements founded by the Spanish. Viewed in this perspective, the period of two hundred years celebrated by the Bicentennial of 1976 represents about half of the history of Europeanized North America.

As the Bicentennial also made clear, the American Revolution did not begin, except in a very technical sense, on 4 July 1776. For at least a decade prior to the issuance of the Declaration of Independence, it was clear to many perceptive observers on both sides of the Atlantic that the relationship between Britain and the colonies was coming under increasing stress. In a constitutional sense, as Professor Henry Steele Commager has remarked, the problem was how to accommodate a situation in which the central government was unitary, while the colonies had, in many respects, become accustomed to a high degree of self-autonomy. For instance, for all practical purposes both Connecticut and Rhode Island had become self-governing entities within the British Empire long before the Revolution took place. The failure of the British government to solve this constitutional dilemma made some kind of a clash inevitable, as Benjamin Franklin had repeatedly warned his friends in London.

On the other hand, once the War of Independence had begun, it lasted interminably. It was, in fact, very much of a civil war. Had the colonists been united, they could have won the war in a year, as Samuel Eliot Morison and Henry Steele Commager, along with other historians, have pointed out. But loyalist sympathy was so strong, and apathy was so widespread, that the final scene of the drama did not come until the conclusion of the Peace of Paris of 3 September 1783.

From the governmental point of view, the war was conducted under the authority of a unitary Congress built up of blocs of state delegates. On 7 June 1776 Richard Henry Lee had moved that Congress appoint a committee to draft articles of confederation among the several states. As with the conduct of the war, delay was also typical of the plan for confederation. Ratification by all of the states was required, and it was not until 1781 that the Articles of Confederation went into effect.

They contained, as it turned out, some substantial defects. For example, the articles did not give Congress control over taxation and trade, and they failed to provide for a federal executive or judiciary. In brief, the Congress could do little unless the states permitted it to act. A kind of general disillusionment set in, and the country began to experience severe internal pressures which the Congress could not handle. Eventually, as almost always happens, a thermidorean reaction—a sort of counterrevolution—took place. People needed a sense of order and security. The Constitutional Convention of 1787 was the response to this need. The new Constitution was ratified by the requisite number of states in 1788, and the Congress of the Confederation set the first presidential election for 4 March 1789, and then dissolved. Thus began the new Union.

STATE POWERS UNDER THE CONSTITUTION

As every textbook on civics records, normally with approbation, the federal government possesses only enumerated powers. The reference is usually to those powers of Congress defined in Article I, Section 8 of the Constitution. There is often little or no attention paid to the last clause of the section, the sleeper clause, which gives to Congress the power ". . . to make all laws which shall be necessary and proper for carrying into execution the foregoing powers, and all other powers vested by this Constitution in the Government of the United States, or in any Department or Officer thereof." It was from this clause that the "implied powers" doctrine was derived. As interpreted by Chief Justice John Marshall, a nationalist rather than a states' rights proponent, the clause considerably broadened federal authority in a number of fields.

Commenting on another aspect of the problem in *McCulloch v. Maryland* (1819), Marshall stated the opinion of the Supreme Court:

This government is acknowledged by all to be one of

enumerated powers. The principle that it can exercise only the powers granted to it . . . is now universally admitted. But the question respecting the extent of the powers actually granted is perpetually arising, and will probably continue to arise, as long as our system shall exist.

In other words, the chief justice was saying that the boundary line between what the federal government may do and what the states may do will shift constantly. His prediction has been borne out by history.

The interpretation of Article II, relating to the powers of the president, has also changed since 1788. The result has been the creation of doctrines such as "impoundment" of appropriated funds, "executive privilege," and "war powers" that the Founding Fathers (with the possible exception of Alexander Hamilton) never dreamed of.

Nonetheless, in order to allay fears concerning the possible development of a potentially tyrannous central government, the first Congress added to the Constitution (as part of the Bill of Rights) the Tenth Amendment, which reads as follows:

> The powers not delegated to the United States by the Constitution, nor prohibited by it to the States, are reserved to the States respectively, or to the people.

The Tenth Amendment has not been favorably treated by the courts, which have found it redundant, unnecessary, and a statement of the obvious. On the other hand, Article VI of the Constitution has real teeth in it. Section 2 reads:

> This Constitution, and the laws of the United States which shall be made in pursuance thereof; and all treaties made, or which shall be made, under the authority of the United States, shall be the supreme law of the Land; and the judges in every State shall be bound thereby, any thing in the constitution or laws of any State to the contrary notwithstanding.

Given these powers, plus the doctrine of implied powers, plus the nationalistic interpretations of the formative Marshall Supreme Court, one might wonder exactly what powers the states today actually possess. The answer, in general, is that the states continue to have numerous, residual, and undefined powers. The states tax; they borrow money; they make and administer civil and criminal law; they have very broad powers over health, welfare, and morals; they control public education; they share in the administration of social security and related programs; they charter corporations; they regulate the suffrage; they make the laws that apply to their subdivisions, i.e., local government; and they regulate trade within the state. The list could be lengthened considerably, but the point is that the states have a great deal of scope and variety with respect to the use of the powers given them under the Constitution.

Indeed, the states continually have been increasing their activities. The states have a great reservoir of powers which they to a large extent still have not tapped. On occasion, the governments of individual states have set patterns which the federal government belatedly has accepted, as, for example, in the various agricultural measures taken in North Dakota in the 1920s. Many of them were later adopted by the Franklin Roosevelt Administration in the mid-1930s. Depending on the state, numerous other examples will readily come to mind in the areas of health insurance, automobile insurance, pension benefits, wage-and-hour legislation, and workmen's compensation.

ASPECTS OF FEDERAL AND STATE RELATIONS

The original thirteen states became members of the Union by ratifying the Constitution, the last holdouts being North Carolina and Rhode Island. Under the Constitution, Congress is given the power to admit new states, subject to the proviso that no state may be erected within the jurisdiction of any other state, or created by the merger of two or more states or parts of states, without the consent of the legislature of each concerned state.

The admission of states has occurred in spurts. After New Mexico and Arizona were admitted in 1912, no new states were admitted until 1959, when Hawaii and Alaska were granted admission. Under a constitution which became effective in 1952, Puerto Rico has had the status of a "commonwealth" within the United States. This provides both a substantial amount of home rule for the island and relief from certain federal taxes.

Once admitted to the Union, a state has the same rights and privileges of any of the original thirteen states. Strangely enough, this question did not come before the Supreme Court until 1911 in the case of Coyle v. Smith. Congress, in its 1906 enabling act granting statehood to Oklahoma, had imposed these restrictions upon Oklahoma: the new state capital should be located at Guthrie and would not move from that place before 1913, nor could the state appropriate any unnecessary monies for public buildings. The agreement was ratified by the voters of the state at the time when the new constitution was adopted, and, thus committed, Oklahoma entered the Union. But in 1910 the legislature passed a bill, initiated by the people, providing that the state capital should forthwith be moved to Oklahoma City and appropriating $600 thousand for public buildings. This was obviously in violation of the "irrevocable" agreement which the state had made.

In upholding the right of a state to move its capital, at its discretion and in violation of its agreement with Congress, the Supreme Court enunciated a very important doctrine: there is political equality among the states. A new state is the equal of any of the original thirteen. The Court concluded:

> Has Oklahoma been admitted upon an equal footing with the original states? If she has, she, by virtue of her jurisdictional sovereignty as such a state, may determine for her own people the proper location of the local seat of government. She is not equal in power to them if she cannot . . . .
>
> To this we may add that the constitutional equality of the states is essential to the harmonious operation of the scheme upon which the Republic was organized. When that equality disappears we may remain a free people, but the Union will not be the Union of the Constitution.

There are certain reciprocal duties of the nation and of the states. For its part, the nation has an obligation to guarantee to every state a "republican" form of government (although the term republican is not defined in the Constitution). It also has the duty to protect each state against invasion and, by proper application by the state government, against domestic violence. This can mean federalizing a state's national guard or, as in the case of Central High School in Little Rock, Arkansas, sending in the 82nd Airborne Division to protect the access of students to school.

On the other hand, a state has an obligation not to secede from the Union. The definitive case on the subject is Texas v. White (1869). The facts of the case are of some intrinsic interest. In 1850 the United States gave the state of Texas $10 million in 5 percent bonds in settlement of certain boundary claims. Half of these were held in Washington; half were delivered to the state and made payable to the state or bearer redeemable after 31 December 1864. Texas, of course, joined the Confederacy, and during the war used some of the bonds, which were not endorsed, for the purchase of military supplies. After the war Texas sued in the Supreme Court to get the bonds back. It also wanted to enjoin White and others from presenting the bonds for payment. But the Court could take jurisdiction only if Texas were a state within the meaning of Article III. Texas was still unrepresented in Congress, and White took the position that by secession she had ceased to be a state and could not sue.

But the Court held that secession was constitutionally impossible. Texas had never ceased to be a state in the Union. Chief Justice Chase, on behalf of the Court, declared: "The Constitution, in all of its provisions, looks to an indestructible union, composed of indestructible states." The Court accordingly took jurisdiction in the case and decided that Texas was entitled to recover the bonds.

CONSTITUTIONAL LIMITATIONS ON THE STATES

The states are limited in what they may do both by the provisions of the original Constitution and by various amendments. Most of the limitations in the original Constitution are found in Section 10 of Article I:

(1) No State shall enter into any treaty, alliance, or confederation; grant letters of marque and reprisal; coin money; emit bills of credit; make anything but gold and silver coin a tender in payment of debts; pass any bill of attainder, ex post facto law, or law impairing the obligation of contracts, or grant any title of nobility.

(2) No State shall, without the consent of the Congress, lay any imposts or duties on imports or exports, except what may be absolutely necessary for executing its inspection laws: and the net produce of all duties and imposts, laid by any State on imports or exports, shall be for the use of the Treasury of the United States; and all such laws shall be subject to the revision and control of the Congress.

(3) No State shall, without the consent of Congress, lay any duty of tonnage, keep troops, or ships of war in time of peace, enter into any agreement or compact with another State, or with a foreign power, or engage in war, unless ac-

tually invaded, or in such imminent danger as will not admit of delay.

Some further comment on some of these provisions, as well as others found in the amendments, is intended to bring the question of constitutional limitations on the states into sharper focus.

Impairment of Contracts

The impairment of contract clause is intended to prevent a state legislature from passing a law applicable to pre-existing contracts that would make it impossible or more difficult for a party to the contract to enforce against the other party the obligations due him under the contract. Included are not only contracts between individuals but also those in which a state, one of its subdivisions, or a corporation may be a party. In the famous Dartmouth College case (1819), the Supreme Court held that a charter granted the college in 1769 by the English Crown was a contract within the meaning of the federal Constitution. Thus the state of New Hampshire could not by legislation unilaterally alter the original charter of the college.

The Fourteenth Amendment

The most important limitations placed upon the states by the amendments to the Constitution are found in the first section of the Fourteenth Amendment. It reads as follows:

> All persons born or naturalized in the United States, and subject to the jurisdiction thereof, are citizens of the United States and of the state wherein they reside. No state shall make or enforce any law which shall abridge the privileges or immunities of citizens of the United States; nor shall any state deprive any person of life, liberty, or property, without due process of law; nor deny to any person within its jurisdiction equal protection of the laws.

The purpose of the section defining citizenship was to override the decision of the Supreme Court in the Dred Scott case (1857), in which the Court tried, obviously unsuccessfully, to settle the slavery question once and for all. The following sections are designed to protect various rights, and each will be commented on separately.

The Privileges and Immunities Clause. The Court first came to grips with the meaning of this clause in the Slaughterhouse Cases, decided in 1873. Under the clause, certain independent butchers had challenged the constitutionality of a Louisiana statute that gave a monopoly of the slaughterhouse business in New Orleans to one company. But the Court construed the clause to mean that any right the butchers might have was a right conferred by the state; that is, such a right could not be sustained under the privileges and immunities clause, which affected United States citizenship.

Over the years, the Court has retained this narrow interpretation of the clause. As a result, the clause has had little or no effect on state action. Nor, for that matter, has it affected national action very much. About the only right a citizen has under the clause is to ask the American ambassador or consul for help when in difficulties encountered abroad.

The Due Process of Law Clause. This clause provides that no state shall deprive any person of life, liberty, or property without due process of law. Although this sounds simple, it is in fact extremely complex. In the first place, it repeats with regard to the state governments what is stated about the federal government in the Fifth Amendment. This idea goes back to Jefferson, who took it from John Locke. As subsequently interpreted, the term *person* was very broadly interpreted by the Supreme Court. The word includes citizens and aliens alike, and corporations as well as natural persons. It is to be noted that the due process clause limits only the states; it does not act as a restraint upon the actions of the national government or of individuals. The prohibition against interference with life, liberty, or property is, of course, qualified. The states take property every moment, in the form of taxes; they infringe on the liberties of individuals by an enormous penal system; they seize land under the power of eminent domain. All of these things constitutionally may be done if the *requirement of due process is observed.*

It is easy to understand why this clause has been the subject of more litigation than any other restriction the Constitution imposes on the states. Over the decades, there have developed two major aspects of the process, one procedural, the other substantive. For example, on the procedural side, certain standards must be observed in criminal proceedings. Or, as another illustration, adequate notice must be given that a hearing will be held.

On the substantive side, the due process clause has served as a very strong check, even an obstacle, upon state and local governments and their agencies. At stake have been personal as well as property rights. Practically speaking, all the famous rights in the First Amendment have now been absorbed into the due process clause of the Fourteenth Amendment.

Equally broad interpretations have occurred in the area of property rights. Anyone who follows state regulation of public utilities is aware that the courts are one of the principal, often the principal, arenas of action. For example, due process means that a utility is entitled to a "reasonable" rate of return. Ultimately, the courts will determine what is "reasonable."

The Equal Protection of the Laws Clause. A provision of the Fourteenth Amendment, noted earlier, holds that no state shall deny to any person within its jurisdiction the equal protection of the laws. What the Radical Republicans, who wrote the amendment, had in mind was to ensure against discrimination on the grounds of race. In practice, the Supreme Court simply did not enforce this clause of the amendment in the manner intended by its framers. For example, in the landmark case of Plessy v. Ferguson (1896), the Supreme Court upheld as valid a Louisiana statute which required segregation of the races in railway coaches. What was important, the Court said, was that the accommodations accorded the two races, though separate, be "equal." This doctrine, the factual basis of which was always more myth than established truth, was officially overthrown in the famous school case, Brown v. Board of Education of Topeka (1954). The new interpretation, i.e., that separation per se resulted in inequality, was extended from education to other fields in the next few years.

In the various reapportionment cases, beginning with the Tennessee case of Baker v. Carr (1962), the Court gradually has extended the meaning of the equal protection clause to include the principle of "one man, one vote" in state and congressional elections. We shall consider this question in the chapters on legislative bodies.

INTERGOVERNMENTAL TAX IMMUNITY

Very early in the history of the Union, the courts adopted the position that neither the federal government nor the states could tax the instrumentalities of the other. The controlling case was *McCulloch* v. *Maryland* (1819), which concerned a Maryland statute under which that state taxed bank notes issued by the Baltimore branch of the Bank of the United States, a federal corporation. McCulloch, the cashier of the branch in Baltimore, issued notes without complying with the state's tax law, and this precipitated the action by Maryland to recover penalties.

The case is important for two reasons, the first of which we have already touched upon. It established beyond any doubt the doctrine of implied powers. Chief Justice Marshall, on behalf of a united Court, while admitting that the Constitution did not give Congress the power directly to charter a bank, declared that this power could reasonably be implied from other powers specifically given to Congress.

It is the other aspect of the case which relates to intergovernmental tax immunity. The second question, Marshall said, is this: "Whether the state of Maryland may, without violating the Constitution, tax that branch?" He then proceeded, in a fairly rambling way, to discuss the importance of the taxing power in general. Without it, there is no government. Then, closing in on the quarry at hand, he asserted in thunderous words:

> The great principle is, that the Constitution and the laws made in pursuance thereof are supreme; that they control the Constitution and laws of the respective states, and cannot be controlled by them. From this, which may be almost termed an axiom, other propositions are deduced as corollaries, on the truth or error of which and on their application to this case, the cause has been supposed to depend. These are, 1. That a power to create implies a power to preserve. 2. That a power to destroy, if wielded by a different hand, is hostile to, and incompatible with, these powers to create and preserve. 3. That where this repugnancy exists, that authority which is supreme must control, not yield to that over which it is supreme. . . .

The chief justice then acknowledged that both the federal government and the states possess powers of taxation. But some common sense, under the Constitution, must be applied. "That the power to taxing it [the federal government] by the states may be exercised so as to destroy it, is too obvious to be denied." But this would in itself be unconstitutional. A tax on the operations of a federal instrumentality, in this case the Bank, is as unconstitutional as would be a tax on the federal government itself. "We are unanimously of opinion that the law passed by the Legislature of Maryland, imposing a tax on the Bank of the United States, is unconstitutional and void."

As one might have expected, the doctrine is today not quite so ironclad as it sounds. For example, in 1938 and 1939 the Court held that salaries paid by state and local governments are subject to the federal income tax. Also, it held that the state and local governments could tax the incomes of resident federal officers and employees. On the other hand, interest from state and municipal bonds is still not taxed by the federal government. Yet, income from state-operated businesses, such as liquor stores, is not exempt from federal taxes. But federal property and activities were and continue to be considered exempt from state taxation. In brief, the Supreme Court continues to maintain the doctrine of intergovernmental tax immunity. But it has narrowed the application of the doctrine since the original Bank of the United States case.

FEDERALISM

As every schoolchild knows, a basic principle of the American political system is federalism. Yet there are many varieties of federalism existing in the world. The principle may be approached historically, in which case various leagues in ancient Greece may serve as the starting point, or more recently, from the obvious mercantile advantages accruing to the Hanseatic League.

Modern federalism, however, really begins with the American Constitution of 1787, and our discussion will be limited largely to American federal experience. At the outset, several things are evident. The old style of federalism, which was a legal concept, is dead. The new style is really intergovernmental relations, and it is very much alive. It stresses interdependence and the sharing of functions. The sharing of functions is most dramatically shown in the growth of the federal grants-in-aid system. But, as we shall see in a later chapter, revenue sharing is an alternative to that system.[1]

The old style of federalism received a fatal blow with the outcome of the Civil War. At the very least, some constitutional questions about the nature of the Union were presumably settled forever. But there developed, under the Fourteenth Amendment, a kind of "dual federalism" which had two main threads:

each government, federal or state, was supreme in its area of responsibility and, curiously, some areas of life were simply off limits to any government at any level. An example of this was the inability of both the federal government and the states to regulate child labor because of the tendency the Supreme Court had developed to assert that the subject was outside the range of regulation by *any* government. Similar problems developed regarding wage-and-hour legislation, health standards for employees, and other concerns. Happily, this brand of states' rights federalism did not survive the new interpretations made by the Supreme Court in the late 1930s and early 1940s.

Since this reversal in thinking about the nature of federalism, the emphasis has been on what has come to be called "cooperative" federalism. The emphasis is on running programs, not on passing statutes. This is not to say that there are no problems remaining; there are. As Michael Reagan has brilliantly pointed out, there is a crisis of "fiscal federalism"—the two sides in the game are simply a fiscal mismatch.[2]

Another leading contemporary scholar of federalism, Daniel J. Elazar, agrees that there is a crisis in federalism and asserts that the crisis is due in part to confusion as to what federalism is all about. There is no single, consistent modern theory of federalism. Thus, the "New Federalism" of the Nixon Administration was based on a supposedly highly centralized federal government which would decentralize functions within it. But, Elazar declares, this hierarchical model does not in fact exist. If you want to decentralize power, you had better begin by centralizing it. For this and other reasons, Elazar was extremely critical of the "New Federalism" approach.[3]

Under the old states' rights style of federalism, who gained? The following groups would seem to qualify: slave owners in the prewar South, and plantation owners in the postwar South; eastern and northern corporation interests; highly organized interest groups.

Under the old style, who lost? These groups would seem to qualify: the black population, whether in the North or the South; working-class groups; small farmers; any groups that stood a chance of bettering themselves by a change in the status quo. The justification for this last statement is that federalism is inherently legalistic, and excessive legalism would seem in most cases to lead to a course of delay and inaction. In this connection, it is notable that for the first few editions of the significant reader on American government—*Basic Issues of American*

Democracy by Hillman M. Bishop and Samuel Hendel—the problem of segregation in American society was considered under the rubric of "federalism."[4] More recent editions have treated the two topics independently. But federalism has been blamed in large part for the widespread maintenance of racialism even after the passage of the post-Civil War amendments to the Constitution. The approach taken today is, of course, that racial problems are national in scope and must be dealt with wherever possible on a national basis. It is also admitted that this may not always be possible, as in the case of school busing inside northern cities.

The Cases For and Against Federalism

No responsible scholar has seriously contended that federalism in America should be sacrificed in favor of a unitary state. Rather, the disagreements have centered on spheres of activities, the sharing of programs and personnel, and the possibility of more regionalization. One of the best analyses ever made of the arguments for and against federalism was that by Paul Studenski and Paul R. Mort.[5] The paragraphs which follow are based largely on their study.

The case for decentralization (or federalism in general) is said to rest on the following pillars:

1. Local control, by promoting local unity and a sense of neighborhood responsibility, brings about a sense of self-reliance.

2. This type of control also tends to bring about a close adaption of public services to local needs.

3. Local control also is said to promote freedom and responsible government. This idea has been developed at great length by many writers in this country.

4. Local control also is believed to promote socially beneficial intercommunity competition; for example, if New York builds the Erie Canal, Pennsylvania then builds a Pennsylvania Canal (with portage over the Allegheny Mountains watershed). Or, if there is a New York Central Railroad, then it follows that there must be a Pennsylvania Railroad. And so on.

5. Local control is said to encourage experimentation and innovation, and therefore, in the long run, the whole country gains from the pioneering efforts of a few farsighted leaders and communities or states.

6. Finally, it is held that the national government's workload is reduced because details of local administration may be handled locally. Underlying this belief is a widespread distrust of national bureaucracies in democratic countries.

According to the same authorities, Studenski and Mort, the case against decentralization (or federalism) is based on the following contentions:

1. The result of extreme decentralization is an inefficient and uneconomic management of local affairs. There is said to be duplication, overlapping of functions, and insufficient awareness of or responsiveness to social problems.

2. Decentralization, it is charged, may result in local autocratic rule by petty officials and powerful minority groups. In short, it is difficult to achieve change in the political arena.

State Forestry conservation crews clean up spillage from offshore oil well leakage in Santa Barbara, California. The Supreme Court now has ruled that regulation of offshore oil drilling is a federal, not a state, matter. (Wide World Photos.)

Even state-wide and national trends may be resisted for years, with no adverse effects at the polls.

3. A third alleged shortcoming of decentralization—and it constitutes a very serious charge—is that it produces national and regional disunity and organization. For example, a small unit may, in effect, possess a veto power over what larger units desire. This is nowhere more evident than in the continual voting down of proposals for metropolitan government by local governments which feel their own powers—and the jobs they control—would be reduced.

4. Decentralization is said to result in extreme inequality in standards of public service and protection of civil rights throughout the country or region. It is hard to see how anyone can quarrel with the first part of this proposition, for example, in aid to the blind or to those on welfare. With regard to the second part, a degree of nationalization of civil rights began in the early 1950s, and it continues to maintain support. To put the matter bluntly, one's life chances are considerably better if one is born in Connecticut than in Mississippi.

5. Given a proper balance between local and national interests, it is contended that a strong central government will unify the nation, with beneficial results. This is said to be especially true in the realm of civil rights, equal employment opportunities, and the promotion of national symbols and ideals.

The Case Against Federalism. In the discussion to this point, a kind of political accounting has been occurring. One column has listed the benefits of federalism and the other, its liabilities. In real life, few Americans approach the question with such a high degree of balance and composure. This was pointed out by the distinguished political scientist the late Franz L. Neumann in an analysis, first appearing in 1955, of American and German federalism.[6]

Neumann begins his analysis by noting that the theoretical argument for federalism "revolves around the potential of political power for evil." If power is centralized, it follows, according to Lord Acton and others, that it will be abused. Everyone agrees that this is a possibility.

But it is the second assumption of the federalists that troubled Neumann. This is the widely held belief that a federal state per se increases individual freedom. Even though many Americans cherish this thought—or profess to do so—Neumann can find nothing in American or German history to support the contention.

Going even further, Neumann challenges the conviction that "federalism is necessary for democracy." The evidence from the Weimar Republic is inconclusive on this point. For example, Bavaria—the most states'-rights-conscious land—was the most reactionary; Prussia, the most democratic. In the United States, on the other hand, the actions which have infringed the most on civil liberties have always been taken by the state governments. Were he writing in the 1970s, Neumann would have little difficulty in reconfirming his thesis.

Neumann concludes that it "seems impossible to attribute to federalism, as such, a value; or to assert that the federal state—as contrasted to the unitary state—enhances political and civil freedom by dividing power among autonomous territorial subdivisions." Surely other students of comparative democratic governments, after examination of such unitary states as the United Kingdom and the Scandinavian countries, would for the most part agree with Neumann's judgment. In short, federalism has no necessary connection with freedom.

INTERSTATE RELATIONS

The Founding Fathers were well aware that inevitably there would be causes for friction among the different states. In various ways, they sought to minimize these frictions. They also realized that people would move from one state to another and that in such a case their interests deserved protection. The following is a summary of the leading provisions to accomplish these ends.

The Right to Move

The right to move from one state to another might, on its face, be deemed a "privilege and immunity" of a citizen of the United States within the meaning of the Fourteenth Amendment. But, as we have seen, that clause is virtually inoperative. The right to move from one state to another—in this case, from Oklahoma to California—was finally asserted by the Supreme Court in *Edwards* v. *California* in 1941 (314 U.S. 160). At stake was the constitutionality of a California "anti-Okie" law, a Depression-born statute designed to keep the destitute from migrating to California. The California law was struck down on the grounds that it was offensive to the interstate commerce clause.

Full Faith and Credit

This clause of the Constitution has been interpreted to mean that court records, vital statistics, and other official records of one state must be accepted by another state. If New York state says Jones was born on a certain date, Texas officials will assume that the document is correct. On the other hand, certain divorce actions have been challenged, usually on the ground that the residence requirements of a particular state have been self-serving. The allegation is that very short residence requirements exist to encourage the local divorce business, which is true. There is also the rather interesting international law question as to whether a "quickie" divorce obtained in, for example, the Dominican Republic would be valid if challenged in the courts of, say, Ohio.

Extradition

Here the Constitution provides for the return of fugitives who evade local capture by crossing state lines. The relevant provisions are as follows:

> A person charged in any state with treason, felony, or other crime, who shall flee from justice, and be found in another state, shall on demand of the executive authority of the state from which he fled, be delivered up, to be removed to the state having jurisdiction of the crime.

While this seems clearly mandatory, the Supreme Court has interpreted "shall" in the above provision to be permissive in character. Usually the fugitive is returned in a routine manner, either after a hearing or after having waived a hearing. But on several famous occasions fugitives have not been returned and there is no way of forcing a governor to take action if he or she is disposed not to do so. The most famous cases concern blacks who have escaped from southern "chain gangs" who have received sympathy in the northern press and who have been permitted to remain in the state to which they fled. But there have been other cases—for example, so-called mercy killings—in which public opinion has been on the side of the fugitive, thus making extradition politically unpopular.

Interstate Competition

The tendency among states to favor local rather than out-of-state businesses takes many forms. Historically, New Jersey and Delaware have, through low fees, encouraged corporations to be incorporated in their respective states. Some states offer long-range property tax advantages for migrating corporations, which explains in part why so much of the textile industry has moved from New England to the South. One of the most ludicrous examples occurred in the state of Rhode Island during the Depression. In an effort to encourage the Rhode Island dairy industry at the expense of out-of-state producers, the legislature passed a statute requiring that all out-of-state milk, before being placed on the counter for sale, be colored pink. Quite predictably, the statute was declared to be invalid as a patent infringement of the interstate commerce clause of the Constitution.

But there are numerous other examples. States require new residents to take out new automobile licenses and plates. They vie with each other in residential requirements for licenses to practice medicine, to practice law, and to teach. Some states require that a course be given in the history of the state, thus encouraging attendance of would-be teachers at that state's colleges of education. The states try very hard to come up with trucking regulations which differ from those of neighboring states, for example, with regard to permissible weight loads, width, and height. Generally, the competition is most ferocious during periods of recession or depression. When you start to see slogans on bumper stickers which say, "Buy Indiana products," you can conclude that times are tough. On a nation-wide basis, this mood is, of course, both uneconomic and self-defeating.

Interstate Cooperation

On the other hand, there are pressures working toward interstate cooperation. The Constitution allows states to enter into agreements with one another, subject to the consent of Congress. Some of the principal advocates of such cooperation are administrative officials themselves. For example, almost all law enforcement officers were in favor of the Crime Compact of 1934, now subscribed to by all the states.

An interesting question is whether interstate compacts, taken as a whole, perform a function of national integration that would otherwise be missing. A 1973 study by Susan Welch and Cal Clark suggests that the answer is yes.[7] The same study also identified four general trends in the recent making of interstate compacts: (1) compacts have become increasingly popular; (2) a large proportion of them have become national in scope; (3) there has been a steady increase in service compacts; and (4) on the other hand, there has not been recently any great upsurge in contracts which establish permanent regulatory machinery.

Uniform State Law

In addition to compact arrangements, states may achieve some uniformity, especially in restricted areas, by the passage of uniform state laws. The National Conference of Commissioners on Uniform State Laws was established as long ago as 1892. Since then, the conference has agreed on more than one hundred proposed laws. The conference has been supported by many business interests, as well as by the American Bar Association.

There are many illustrations of the process at work; for example, all the states have adopted uniform laws on negotiable instruments, stock transfers, and warehouse receipts. In other cases, a proposed law may be adopted by some, but not by all, of the states. In addition, even if the wording of a law is identical in the statutes of certain states, court interpretation or administrative actions may mean that the operations of the statutes in practice are not really uniform. But all would agree that the conference has been a move in the right direction.

The Council of State Governments

No discussion of interstate relations would be complete without at least a brief reference to the role played by the Council of State Governments. It was formed in 1925 to help state officials share common experiences and compare notes. The council both conducts research and helps in the formation of legislative drafts. *State Government*, its monthly publication, helps to keep officials and observers informed of important recent developments. In addition, the council has developed several spin-off specialized organizations, for example, the Governors' Conference (previously referred to), the American Legislators' Association, the Conference of Chief Justices, and the National Association of Attorneys General. Through this elaborate set of organizations, it is possible for agents of competing states to understand each other's problems and often to arrive at a common proposed policy. For each fiscal year, the council publishes *The Book of the States*. This invaluable volume contains basic statistical data on each of the states, as well as the results of elections, summaries of important laws, and new constitutional developments.

A Note on Cakes

From the preceding analysis, it is clear that the relationships between the federal and state governments are not neat, tidy, logical ones. Rather, they are, as Morton Grodzins puts it, "chaotic . . . the multitude of governments does not mask any simplicity of activity. There is no neat division of functions among them."[8]

Grodzins points out that Americans have been brought up to think of government in terms of three layers—federal, state, and local—in the manner of a "layer cake." But in fact—and the findings of his famous seminars at the University of Chicago amply bore this out—virtually all governments are involved in virtually all functions. Using a metaphor which was to become famous, Grodzins said, with the layer cake analogy in mind:

> A far more realistic symbol is that of the marble cake. Wherever you slice through it you reveal an inseparable mixture of differently colored ingredients. There is no neat horizontal stratification. Vertical and diagonal lines obliterate the horizontal ones, and in some places there are unexpected whirls and an imperceptible merging of colors, so that it is difficult to tell where one ends and the other begins.[9]

AMERICAN FEDERALISM IN THE THIRD CENTURY

The Advisory Commission on Intergovernmental Relations (ACIR) was created by Congress in 1959 to monitor the operation of the American federal system and to recommend improvements. ACIR is a permanent national bipartisan body representing the executive and legislative branches of federal, state, and local governments as well as the public.

In 1974, ACIR looked into its crystal ball and came out with specific recommendations to strengthen the workings of the federal system. The commission-made "checklist of agenda items" may be summarized under the following five general headings:

1. To revitalize local government:

States should clarify the legal powers of general purpose local governments and authorize them to determine their own internal structure.

States should discourage nonviable units of local government through a number of available devices.

States should help local governments cope with area-wide problems by facilitating county consolidation.

States should facilitate regional coordination.

The federal government should move further to avoid aid programs that encourage special districts and to strengthen regional and metropolitan review of local grant applications.

States should deal with the problems of inner-city alienation by authorizing major urban governments to create neighborhood "subunits."

2. To build stronger states:

The institutional framework of state government should be modernized to permit a more positive role in the rapidly expanding sphere of domestic governmental affairs.

Where states have acted responsibly, the federal government should allocate funds directly. Where states have not done so, the funds should go directly to localities.

States should pay part of the bill for urban development, housing code enforcement, mass transit, and other major urban functions.

States should adopt a shorter ballot, give reorganization authority to the governor, develop improved and interrelated planning and budgeting processes.

3. To achieve balanced growth and housing opportunity:

There should be a national urbanization policy.

State housing legislation should provide financial assistance for low- and moderate-income housing and should assure access to housing without discrimination.

State urbanization policies should complement the national policy. States should bring order out of chaos in building codes.

States should actively oversee local zoning.

4. To streamline and humanize the administration of justice:

States should upgrade police personnel practices and expand their supportive services to local law enforcement agencies. They should also provide better police protection in rural areas, create specialized striking forces, and clarify intrastate extraterritorial police powers.

The states should strengthen the power of the attorneys general to coordinate the activities of local prosecutors.

Every state should adopt a unified court system.

States should expand their administrative and supervisory authority over corrections and systematize the various corrections activities. Rehabilitation and training should be stressed.

5. To restore fiscal balance in the federal system:

Federal revenue sharing should be continued and strengthened.

Congress should provide new federal aid through block grants.

The federal government should assume financial responsibility for the dependent children assistance program and Medicaid, and continue the welfare takeover begun in 1972 when the adult categories were federalized.

State government should assume the predominant share of the costs of elementary and secondary schools, thus fostering equality of educational opportunity and releasing the property tax for other purposes.

States should come out more strongly for high-quality, high-yield tax systems, placing a greater reliance on progressive income taxes and strong sales taxes.

States should overhaul the local property tax to make it equitable and productive and assure its fair administration. At the same time, the states should provide protection for the elderly and the poor against excessive property tax burdens.[10]

These, then, are the highlights of the recommendations of the ACIR for action during the coming years. As Robert E. Merriam, the chairman of the commission, observed: "The purpose of this brief summary is to highlight the ACIR agenda, hopefully as a guide to help in unravelling our terribly complex system, and as a help in sorting out our often confused thinking about it." Merriam also warned readers of the report—officials and public alike—that intergovernmental relations are never static; they are always in a state of flux. In the following chapters, we shall examine some of the institutions that affect and are affected by these relationships and the forces behind them.

Items for Discussion

1. What do you think the Tenth Amendment means today?

2. Is the United States likely to add any new states in the near future? What might they be?

3. Review the confusion and complexity which results from fifty different states having the freedom, in large part, to control such matters as taxes, divorce, and age-of-majority laws. Should a "reasonable" system allow these conflicting laws to continue?

4. Have we been successful since 1968 in decentralizing American government? In what areas do you believe that greater state and local authority is needed?

5. Rather than cooperate, what actions are taken by states to compete against each other?

Chapter Notes

1. See the excellent discussion of this in Michael D. Reagan, *The New Federalism* (New York: Oxford University Press, 1972).

2. *Ibid.*, p. 33.

3. Daniel J. Elazar, "Authentic Federalism for America," Vol. 62, No. 9, *National Civic Review* (Oct. 1973), pp. 474–478.

4. The first edition of *Basic Issues of American Democracy* by Hillman M. Bishop and Samuel Hendel appeared in 1948 (New York: Appleton-Century-Crofts). The most recent edition is that of 1975.

5. Paul Studenski and Paul R. Mort, *Centralized vs. Decentralized Government in Relation to Democracy* (New York: Bureau of Publications, Teachers College, Columbia University, 1941).

6. Franz L. Neumann, "Federalism and Freedom: A Critique," in A. W. Macmahon, ed., *Federalism: Mature and Emergent* (New York: Doubleday, 1955), pp. 45–49.

7. Susan Welch and Cal Clark, "Interstate Compacts and National Integration: An Empirical Assessment of Some Trends," Vol. 26, No. 3, *The Western Political Quarterly* (Sept. 1973), pp. 475–484.

8. From Morton Grodzins, "Centralization and Decentralization in the American Federal System," in *A Nation of States* (Chicago: Rand McNally, 1963), pp. 1–23. Citation at p. 1.

9. *Ibid.*, pp. 3–4.

10. *American Federalism: Into the Third Century* (Washington, D.C.: Advisory Commission on Intergovernmental Relations, May, 1974). Checklist agenda items are from pp. 35–39.

11. *Ibid.*, Preface.

3

State Constitutions

Key Terms

Amendment: Change in or addition to a constitution. Amendments to state constitutions are much more prevalent than are amendments to the United States Constitution.

Bill of rights: Provisions in state constitutions, patterned after the United States Constitution, which contain a listing of individual rights which cannot be infringed upon by the government.

Constitutional government: Principle of limited government under a written or unwritten contract (constitution). The constitution assigns the powers and duties of government agencies and establishes the relationship between the people and their government.

Distributive article: Part of state constitutions which separates power among the legislative, executive, and judicial branches.

Popular initiative: Means by which citizens can propose legislation or constitutional amendments through petitions signed by the required number of registered voters.

Popular referendum: Gives the voters the opportunity to approve or reject amendments to state constitutions; also used frequently to allow voters in local elections to act on such measures as spending money for public schools.

Ratification: Formal voter approval of action taken by state legislators or by members of a constitutional convention who have proposed amendments to the state constitution.

Revision: A major change in a constitution

or a complete rewriting. Most often done by a constitutional convention whose members are selected to revise the basic state law.

Democratic theorists have always pointed out that the basic characteristic of constitutional government is that it is in various ways limited government. Certain substantive areas may be declared beyond the reach of the government, for example, the regulation of religion. Or certain procedural safeguards may be provided. A safeguard of this type is the universal prohibition against ex post facto laws, that is, making an activity or deed retroactively illegal.

In addition to such limitations—which are intended to protect the basic liberties of the citizen—all constitutions give at least a general outline of the structure and powers of the government in question. Most Americans have at least a broad understanding as to how the United States Constitution affects the structure and powers of the national government. And, as noted before, that same Constitution places limitations upon the powers which the state governments may exercise.

Each of the fifty states has its own constitution. As we shall see, there are certain similarities; for instance, each adopts the same tripartite separation of powers—executive, legislative, and judicial—as is found in the national Constitution. On the other hand, the state constitutions differ in many substantial ways. To begin the analysis of these problems, we shall start with a look at the earliest constitutions, and then we will examine more recent trends and developments.

EARLY CONSTITUTIONS

When the break between the English colonies in America and the mother country took the form of armed rebellion, it became obvious at once that the royal charters under which the provinces had been governed would require change. Therefore, between 1776 and 1780, new fundamental laws or constitutions were formulated in all of the thirteen original states with two interesting exceptions: in Connecticut and Rhode Island, with a few changes of nouns and adjectives in strategic places, the colonial charters, which had conferred substantial powers of self-government, remained in effect for many years. In Connecticut, the first constitution was drafted in 1818; in Rhode Island, the same step was taken in 1843, spurred on by Dorr's Rebellion, basically an effort to enlarge the suffrage.

By today's highly legalistic standards, the method of creating the earliest state constitutions would be considered most irregular. Usually, the legislature simply formulated a document and submitted it to the electorate for acceptance or rejection. However, the Massachusetts constitution of 1780 was framed by a convention of delegates chosen for the sole purpose of creating a constitution. In turn, the convention submitted the document to the people for approval or rejection. This was to become the generally accepted model: the election of delegates to a constitutional convention, with its effectiveness made contingent upon a favorable vote of the electorate.

When we contrast the early state constitutions with those in effect today, several differences are outstanding. The first is the length of the documents themselves. In the 1770s, with a war on their hands, the constitution writers tended to be brief. Usually the constitutions did not exceed five thousand words. The modern-day record was held by Louisiana, whose constitution, until shortened in 1974, contained with its 536 amendments about 255 thousand words. But there may be a trend toward curtailment of length. The newest constitutions, those of Alaska and Hawaii, run to only about twelve thousand words each.

Another important distinction between the earlier and the modern constitutions is the weights assigned to the executive and the legislative branches of government, respectively. Because of their colonial experiences, the framers of the earlier constitutions were distrustful of executive power and put their faith in elective legislative bodies. On such bodies the early framers placed few restrictions. But the powers of the governors were severely restricted. Faith in unlimited legislative bodies eroded rather quickly, and constitutions were amended, especially during the middle part of the nineteenth century, to limit legislative powers. This mood in part explains the extraordinary number of amendments which were tacked onto the original constitutions. In effect, these amendments restricted the sphere of legislative activity. The restrictions were most apparent in money matters, such as taxation, spending, and borrowing of funds.

Another significant difference between the ancient and modern state constitutions lies in the way they treat the question of who may vote. The importance of the question is hard to exaggerate. It was especially crucial in the constitutional convention of New York state in 1821. The central question was whether voters for the state senate should be required to meet a property qualification. It was conceded that the lower house should be popularly elected without such a qualification.

On each side, the debate was conducted with a brilliance seldom equaled in this country. On behalf of a property restriction for those allowed to vote for the state senate, Chancellor James Kent observed:

> The Senate has hitherto been elected by the farmers of the state—by the free and independent lords of the soil, worth at least $250 in freehold estate, over and above all debts charged thereon. The governor has been chosen by the same electors, and we have hitherto elected citizens of elevated rank and character. Our assembly has been chosen by freeholders, possessing a freehold of the value of $50, or by persons renting a tenement of the yearly value of $5, and who have been rated and actually paid taxes to the state. By the report before us, we propose to annihilate, at one stroke, all those property distinctions and bow before the idol of universal suffrage.[1]

The chancellor concluded:

> The apprehended danger from the experiment of universal suffrage applied to the whole legislative department, is no dream of the imagination. It is too mighty an excitement for the moral constitution of men to endure. The tendency of universal suffrage, is to jeopardize the rights of property, and the principles of liberty.[2]

The leadership of the opposition to Chancellor Kent rested in the persons of P. R. Livingston, John Cramer, and David Buell, Jr. Of these speakers, perhaps the most effective was Buell, who accused Chancellor Kent of drawing lessons from European history which, Buell said, were inapplicable to the United States.

In the end, the new constitution did away with the property requirement. The result, of course, was profoundly to democratize the electorate of New York state by bringing about what in effect amounted to universal male suffrage.

CONTEMPORARY CONSTITUTIONS

Even though modern constitutions vary a good deal in their details, it is customary to group their principal provisions in three general categories: (1) a bill of rights, (2) provisions concerning structures, powers, and procedures of the state government, and (3) the provisions for amendment and revision. Also, there is usually a rather high-sounding "preamble," stating in general language that the basic idea is to further the safety, liberty, and prosperity of those who live within the state's boundaries. General information on state constitutions is given in Table 3.1.

The Bill of Rights

Today, much of what appears in the Bill of Rights has been made redundant because the United States Supreme Court has, in effect, nationalized the protection of civil liberties. It has done so through a broad interpretation of "liberty" which is protected against state interference under the due process clause of the Fourteenth Amendment. But until modern times, the Bill of Rights in the national Constitution was held to apply only against the national government. Therefore, it was deemed necessary that the commonly accepted civil liberties be spelled out by the state constitutions in order to protect such liberties from infringement by the state.

Especially in the older constitutions, one set of rights is basically a reiteration of those rights which the colonists believed they were entitled to as the "rights of Englishmen." These are rather general in character, as one would surmise.

But a more important set of provisions lists the rights of individuals, some of which are quite specific. In this category are included such concepts as religious freedom, freedom of the press and of speech, the rights of those accused of criminal acts, and property rights.

Governmental Structure, Powers, and Procedures

Usually following the bill of rights, state constitutions have a so-called distributive article. This provides for three distinct divisions of government: the executive, the legislative, and the judicial. The idea is that each of the three departments shall never exercise powers given to one of the others. The titles and

Table 3.1
General Information on State Constitutions

State or other jurisdiction	Number of constitutions	Dates of adoption	Effective date of present constitution	Estimated length (number of words)	Number of amendments Proposed	Number of amendments Adopted
Ala.	6	1819; 1861; 1865; 1868; 1875; 1901	1901	106,000	497	326
Alaska	1	1956	1959	12,000	12	11
Ariz.	1	1911	1912	18,500	141	77
Ark.	5	1836; 1861; 1864; 1868; 1874	1874	40,170	(a)	53
Cal.	2	1849; 1879	1879	68,000	667	392
Colo.	1	1876	1876	40,190	147(b)	53(b)
Conn.	4	1818(c); 1965	1965	7,959	5	4
Del.	4	1776; 1792; 1831; 1897	1897	22,000	(a)	83
Fla.	6	1839; 1861; 1865; 1868; 1885; 1968	1969	21,286	15	10
Ga.	8	1777; 1789; 1798; 1861; 1865; 1868; 1877; 1945	1945	500,000	1,016	767
Hawaii	3	1950; 1958; 1968	1968	11,904	41	38
Idaho	1	1889	1890	22,280	125	85
Ill.	4	1818; 1848; 1870; 1970	1971	17,500	0	0
Ind.	2	1816; 1851	1851	11,120	52	29
Iowa	2	1846; 1857	1857	11,200	41	36(d)
Kan.	1	1859	1861	14,500	93	65(d)
Ky.	4	1792; 1799; 1850; 1891	1891	21,500	47	20
La.	10	1812; 1845; 1852; 1861; 1864; 1868; 1879; 1898; 1913; 1921	1921	256,000	749	498
Me.	1	1820	1820	20,000	143	123(e)
Md.	4	1776; 1851; 1864; 1867	1867	37,300	199	160
Mass.	1	1780	1780	36,000	115	97
Mich.	4	1835; 1850; 1908; 1963	1964	19,867	13	6
Minn.	1	1858	1858	20,080	186	100
Miss.	4	1817; 1832; 1869; 1890	1890	25,742	106	37
Mo.	4	1820; 1865; 1875; 1945	1945	33,260	52	37
Mont.	2	1889; 1972	1973	11,250	0	0
Nebr.	2	1866; 1875	1875	19,975	238	164

State	No.	Dates of constitutions	Effective date of present constitution	Estimated number of words		
Nev.	1	1864	1864	17,270	117	70
N.H.	2	1776; 1784(f)	1784	12,200	135(f)	61(f)
N.J.	3	1776; 1844; 1947	1947	16,030	23	17
N.M.	1	1911	1912	26,136	185	88
N.Y.	5	1777; 1822; 1846; 1849; 1894	1894	47,000	249	172
N.C.	3	1776; 1868; 1970	1971	17,000	5	5
N.D.	1	1889	1889	31,470	(a)	90
Ohio	2	1802; 1851	1851	30,000	195	110
Okla.	1	1907	1907	63,569	196	85
Ore.	1	1859	1859	23,000	284	143
Pa.	4	1776; 1790; 1838; 1873; 1968(g)	1873; 1968	24,750	9	6
R.I.	1	1843(c)	1843	21,040	79	42
S.C.	6	1776; 1778; 1790; 1865; 1868; 1895	1895	45,740	430	417
S.D.	1	1889	1889	24,000	161	82
Tenn.	3	1796; 1835; 1870	1870	15,150	34	19
Texas	5	1845; 1861; 1866; 1869; 1876	1876	54,000	343	218
Utah	1	1896	1896	20,990	103	60
Vt.	3	1777; 1786; 1793	1793	7,600	200	44
Va.	6	1776; 1830; 1851; 1868; 1902; 1970	1971	8,000	2	2
Wash.	1	1889	1889	26,930	103	61
W. Va.	2	1863; 1872	1872	22,970	74	42
Wis.	1	1848	1848	17,966	127	98(d)
Wyo.	1	1889	1890	23,170	67	36
Am. Samoa	2	1960; 1967	1967	5,000	9	5
P.R.	1	1952	1952	9,338	6	6

(a) Data not available.
(b) Information only available from 1912 to present.
(c) Colonial charters with some alterations, in Connecticut (1638, 1662) and Rhode Island (1663), served as the first constitutions for these states.
(d) Amendments nullified by Supreme Court. Iowa: three on procedural grounds; Kansas: one; Wisconsin: two.
(e) One adopted amendment will not become effective until the Legislature enacts further legislation.
(f) The constitution of 1784 was extensively amended, rearranged, and clarified in 1793. Figures show proposals and adoptions since 1793.
(g) Certain sections were revised by limited convention.
Source: The Book of the States, 1974–75, p. 23.

terms of the principal officers are then spelled out, and it is specified how they may be removed from office.

The limitations are most explicit concerning the legislative branch which, as we saw, the ordinary voters began to distrust during the nineteenth century. On the other hand, it is a mistake to think that the three departments constitute watertight compartments. As is the case with the federal government, many of the powers are in reality shared between or among the three departments. There is often, in addition, a good deal of overlap.

Because it is easier to add to a constitution than to take from it, some of the provisions of some state constitutions appear downright humorous. For instance, the California constitution limits the power of the legislature on setting time limits on wrestling matches. In the Georgia constitution, there is a provision offering a reward of $250 thousand to the first person to strike oil in that state. The constitution of Louisiana proclaims Huey Long's birthday an annual holiday.

Besides making frequent amendments necessary, what is the political importance of these and other constitutional restraints upon state power? Duane Lockard, who has written widely on the subject, explains:

> Substantially, the reason the complexity is important is that it allots an advantage to some contestants in the political process and a handicap for others. By inviting litigation the wealth of detail plays into the hands of those who want to prevent a particular law from going into effect, and although a legislative majority may have approved it, and the governor's signature may be authentic, there are always possibilities that the courts can be persuaded to invalidate a law on grounds that some minute aspect of constitutional procedure was not properly complied with. If so, dissenters to the law may carry the day, and the legislation be cancelled, for it may be impossible to mount once again the necessary peak of interest that pushed through the legislation in the first place. At least, delay of from one to two years is likely since reenactment must wait until the next legislative session.[3]

In short, highly detailed and lengthy constitutions strengthen the position of conservative interest groups, increase the role of the courts, and reflect the strength of organized interest groups in the state at the time of adoption of the constitutions or amendments.

Provisions for Amendment and Revision

The people who wrote the early state constitutions had no delusion that their creations would survive unscathed throughout eternity. That being the case, they provided means whereby changes could be made in a responsible and orderly manner as social and economic conditions made changes inevitable. The problem is to balance stability with flexibility, an obviously difficult one.

In general, most state constitutions today provide for two alternative methods of change. It is customary to distinguish between two types of alteration of a constitution, amendment and revision. An amendment means the making of either a single, specific change or a relatively small number of changes. On the other hand, a revision implies at a minimum the overhauling of the document, and at a maximum its total rewriting. As one might imagine, this distinction is sometimes not very clear-cut in actual practice. But it gives us a typology which is useful for general analysis.

Proposing Amendments. There are two steps in the amending process: the proposal of an amendment and its ratification. Though in New Hampshire amendments as well as revisions may be proposed only by convention, in other states two methods of proposal are used. These are legislative proposal, and proposal by popular initiative. The general processes by which these methods are handled are discussed below. For any particular state, an interested person should consult the constitution of that state, or a summary of the constitutions as analyzed, for example, by the League of Women Voters or some other civic organization.

Except for New Hampshire, every state permits the state legislature to propose amendments to the state constitution. In most of the states, only the incumbent legislature (including both houses, except in Nebraska which is unicameral) must act on a proposal. Yet some thirteen states require approval by two succeeding legislatures. The thought behind this requirement is to assure deliberate consideration of the proposal over a prolonged period, and to permit the proposed amendments to become issues in the election at which the second legislature is chosen. In practice the effect has usually been to delay ratification.

The variation in the vote required in the legislature for

proposing amendments is considerable. In some eighteen states, a simple majority of each house is required. In nineteen states, the required vote is two-thirds of the members. And in the remaining seven states, the requirement is three-fifths. There are various combinations and permutations in the requirements of interest only to lobbyists and other specialists.

Some thirteen states provide the second method of proposing amendments: the use of the popular initiative. Under this plan, voters may put forth proposals by petition for provisions which they think are desirable but on which the legislature has not acted. The number of voters needed to sign such a petition varies, as would be expected, from state to state. It is usually set as a certain percentage of the votes cast in the last election for a designated state officer, usually the governor. The use of this method is not, as is often believed, confined to California and other western states. For example, it is also employed in Michigan, in Missouri, in Ohio, and in Massachusetts, among other nonwestern states.

Ratifying Amendments. The ratification of proposed amendments is handled through a popular referendum in all states except Delaware, where approval by two successive legislatures is all that is needed. The process is usually a relatively simple one, but some states have managed to complicate it needlessly. Normally, the vote required to approve an amendment is merely a majority of those voting on the amendment, but in a few states, including Minnesota, Mississippi, and Oklahoma, the requirement is a favorable vote by a majority of those voting in the election. Where this method is used, an amendment may be defeated even if more votes are cast in favor of it than against it.

Frequency of Amendment. The frequency of amending state constitutions varies greatly. At one extreme stands Tennessee, whose constitution was unamended from its adoption in 1870 until 1953. At the other extreme is the Louisiana constitution of 1921, which managed to accumulate 536 amendments before the whole document was redrafted in 1974. In those cases in which a constitution has been amended almost annually, many of the amendments are really to be conceived of as special-purpose legislation. Especially in Georgia and South Carolina, many amendments represent an attempt to deal with local governmental matters through the process of constitutional revision. No one has yet come up with a logical defense of this practice; it appears to rest entirely on ingrained custom.

Revision by Convention. No matter how well a constitution is kept up to date through amendments, there comes a time when it may be desirable to go over the entire document and redraft it entirely. Every state has accepted the philosophy that a new constitution should be written by a special body popularly elected for that purpose. As a practical matter, legislatures are not by their nature well adapted to drawing fundamental charters. It seems possible to persuade very able people to serve as members of constitutional conventions. This is not, unfortunately, always the case with members of the legislatures, some of whom are highly undistinguished.

In terms of procedure, the usual method in calling for a convention is for the legislature, by resolution, to submit to the voters the question of whether to hold a convention at all. If the answer is in the affirmative, the actual calling for a convention is issued by the legislature in the form of a statute. Interestingly, the Jeffersonian philosophy that a constitution should be revised

Legislators meet in the assembly chamber at the Montana Constitutional Convention in Helena. (Time-Life Picture Agency.)

at regular intervals has been accepted by some states. For example, the constitutions of Maryland, Missouri, New York, Ohio, and Oklahoma require that the question of calling a constitutional convention be submitted to the voters every twenty years.

The best way to study an actual convention is to attend one. The next best is to make use of case studies prepared by qualified observers. In this respect, a review of the 1974 Louisiana convention by Cecil Morgan is instructive. Morgan, a National Municipal League former president, was a member of the Louisiana Constitutional Revision Commission. The summary which follows is taken from an article he prepared on the subject.[4]

On 20 April 1974 the people of Louisiana approved the work of the Constitutional Convention of 1973–1974. The new constitution, to take effect at midnight, 31 December 1974, received 360,980 affirmative and 262,676 negative votes. This represented an electoral turnout of fewer than 37 percent of eligible voters. The heaviest majorities in favor of the proposal were in New Orleans and the adjoining parishes of Jefferson, Plaquemines, and St. Bernard. Some thirty-six of the sixty-four parishes gave majorities against it.

As a group, the convention delegates prided themselves on their "independence." The goal was to write a document which ordinary people could understand—a "people's constitution." According to Morgan, ". . . strangely enough the final document gives evidence of a degree of accomplishment along these lines. Rephrasing of familiar language is certainly not legalistic. And in a number of specifics it is easy to see how the layman could understand the new provisions, but the lawyer could not. Consequently there will inevitably be much judicial interpretation to follow in the years ahead."[5]

On the other hand, no matter how hard the delegates tried to be amateurs, of necessity they were forced to consult with experts and specialized associations on specific matters. The views of the National Municipal League, the League of Women Voters, and the Committee for a Better Louisiana had an impact on the final document. Also felt were the lobbying efforts of the AFL-CIO, such other organizations as the NAACP, and such movements as that for women's liberation.

As was pointed out earlier, the new constitution is far shorter than the one it superseded; it runs to a very respectable 35 thousand words. The reduced portion consists mostly of legislation that was eliminated in drafting the new document. This came to 62 percent of the old document, or about 158 thousand words. It was provided that a special session of the legislature be held in October 1974 to reenact, this time as legislation, those portions of the old constitution that were absolutely vital to the management of the state.

Very powerful political figures in the state supported ratification of the new constitution, including Governor Edwin W. Edwards, Mayor Moon Landrieu of New Orleans, and Speaker of the House of Representatives E. L. Henry, who also served as president of the convention.

According to Morgan, after ratification, there continued to be some grumbling that the new document eliminated the declaration that gambling is a vice. But he notes that "local law enforcement or non-enforcement of anti-gambling laws still depends on regional attitudes, and the constitutional omission can hardly be deemed to change these factors.[6] Overall, in Morgan's view, the final document is a monumental improvement over that which it displaced.

In the last few decades, a new device, limited constitutional conventions, has been used with some frequency. In such cases, the legislative act submitting to the voters the question of calling a convention has either limited the authority of the delegates to specific matters or has denied authority to the delegates in specific areas. For example, limited conventions were held in the 1940s in Rhode Island to propose, and in Virginia to make, constitutional changes to facilitate voting by members of the armed forces. Or, again, the convention which framed New Jersey's otherwise progressive convention of 1947 was prohibited from changing legislative representation. The result was the creation of a revitalized judicial system, an improved executive system, but the retention of a legislature tilted toward overrepresentation of the smaller counties. (Because of the subsequent United States Supreme Court decisions in the *Reapportionment Cases*, New Jersey had to reorganize its legislature on the basis of "one man, one vote." But it did so only because it was required to.)

Revisory Commissions. There is an interesting, and increasingly used, alternative to the revision of state constitutions by conventions. It employs what is called a revisory commission, and it works in this fashion. Ordinarily under this plan, a special commission is established by the legislature to prepare a revision of the constitution and report its recommendations to the legislature. The legislature may then submit the proposed revision to the voters, with any changes it sees fit to make. It is important to realize that, under this plan, the legislature surrenders none of its authority. It may make changes in the proposal, or it may veto the proposal in entirety.

According to Albert L. Strum, the leading authority on state constitution making, during the seven-year period 1966–1972 at least two-thirds of the states took official steps to modernize their constitutions in addition to the usual piecemeal amendments.[7] And at least ten of the remaining states held constitutional conventions or established constitutional commissions between 1950 and 1966. Since mid-century, therefore, four-fifths of the states have taken official action to revise or rewrite their constitutions. We have been in a period of constitutional revision somewhat similar to that of the 1820s.

What is different from earlier periods is the increased use of constitutional commissions in an effort to help streamline the often cumbersome process of revision by convention, in which the results may be totally unpredictable. The mounting popularity of constitutional commissions is illustrated by data gathered by Sturm for the years 1938–1972, shown in Table 3.2. As the table shows, the use of constitutional commissions as an auxiliary device to effect changes in state constitutions has been one of the most significant developments in constitutional procedure. In his masterful summarization of these developments, Sturm makes the following principal points:

1. Until the new Florida constitution which became operative in January 1969, commissions were not expressly recognized in any state constitution. Florida provides for the establishment of a 37-member revision commission ten years after the adoption of the new constitution and each twentieth year thereafter.

2. Constitutional commissions are created by statute, executive order, or legislative resolution. They may be either study or preparatory. Study commissions compose by far the larger group. Typically, study commissions are mandated to study the constitution, determine needed changes, and submit recommendations to the legislature. A preparatory commission is expected to take care of the logistics, assemble information, prepare special studies, prepare agenda, propose rules, recruit per-

Table 3.2

Uses of Constitutional Conventions and Constitutional Commissions 1938—1972 (By Date Created)

	Constitutional Conventions			Constitutional Commissions		
Period	Unlimited	Limited	Total	Study	Preparatory	Total
1938—1950	5	3	8	8	0	8
1951—1955	2	3	5	3	0	3
1956—1960	1	3	4	11	2	13
1961—1965	4	1	5	17	6	23
1966—1972	9	3	12	23*	4	27
Totals	21	13	34	62	12	74

* Two of these bodies had both study and preparatory responsibilities.
Source: Albert L. Sturm, *Trends in State Constitution-Making: 1966-1972* (Lexington, Ky.: Council of State Governments, 1973), Table 4, p. 30.

sonnel, and perform other duties necessary to set a convention in motion.

3. All legislatures that proposed new or revised constitutions during 1966—1972 were assisted at some stage of preparation by a constitutional commission. They were used because the legislators had little time to study matters of constitutional revision, and admitted so. Some states, such as California, have chosen to modernize their constitutions by a series of steps, each covering a substantial segment of the constitutional system. In order to obtain continuity and adequate analysis of the issues, California wisely relied on the constitution revision commission established in 1963 to prepare draft proposals for submission to the legislature for action before presentation to the electorate in a series of three phases during 1966—1972.

Sturm adds that other states are following the California pattern, and he concludes that revision commissions are playing an essential role in the current drive to modernize state constitutions.

A CRITIQUE OF STATE CONSTITUTIONS

Writing in 1963, Duane Lockard listed several principal criticisms of state constitutions as a whole.[8] He found that, in general, they were much too long and too profusely detailed. His basic objection was that constitutions of this type play into the hands of special interests and favor the status quo. There can be little quibbling with this contention, for most observers would agree with Lockard.

Yet, on the whole, the situation has improved since 1963. As Sturm has shown, change is possible, even if it is difficult to come by. And there is no reason why general purpose interests—consumers' groups, women's groups, environmentalist groups—cannot organize and have some impact on the revising process, as they did in Louisiana in 1973–1974.

It would be hard to prove, but it seems likely that improved television news coverage of state conventions has helped to create greater public awareness of the importance of constitutional revisions. It is also possible that the new-found popularity of so-called investigative reporting by the press has contributed to an increased public consciousness. At a time when all institutions of government are under very careful public scrutiny, there is every reason to expect that processes such as the revision of state constitutions will also acquire attention. The reason is simple: what state governments do is singularly important to the lives of the American people.

Items for Discussion

1. What would you describe as the elements of a "good" state constitution?

2. Review the recent history of amendments proposed to your state's constitution. Who has initiated the action? How successful have they been? What matters have been dealt with in the proposed amendments?

3. Why do state constitutions have so many more amendments than does the United States Constitution?

4. Describe some of the ways in which state constitutions have frustrated government action in the twentieth century.

5. In New York, Ohio, Maryland, and Oklahoma the state constitutions require that the question of calling a constitutional convention be submitted to the voters every twenty years. In spite of this, none of these states has adopted a new constitution since 1907. What reasons can be given for states' continuing to operate under constitutions adopted in the nineteenth century?

Chapter Notes

1. James Kent, in Alpheus Thomas Mason (ed.), *Free Government in the Making* (New York: Oxford University Press, 1965), p. 417.

2. *Ibid.*, p. 418.

3. Duane Lockard, *The Politics of State and Local Government*, 2nd ed. (New York: Macmillan, 1969), p. 86.

4. Cecil Morgan, "A New Constitution for Louisiana," Vol. 63, No. 7, *National Civic Review* (July 1974), pp. 343–356.

5. *Ibid.*, p. 343.

6. *Ibid.*, p. 356.

7. Albert L. Sturm, "State Constitutional Modernization by Commission: 1966–1972," Vol. 62, No. 7, *National Civic Review* (July 1973), pp. 353–357.

8. Lockard, *op. cit.*, pp. 84–90.

4

State Parties
and Interest Groups

Key Terms

Blanket primary: Election in which the voter can vote for both Republican and Democratic candidates running for various offices.

Central committee: Executive policy-making board of a party; found mainly at the state and county levels.

Closed primary: Election in which registered voters can vote only for the candidates of their party.

Cross-filing: Used in California until 1959, it allowed a candidate to be listed in both the Republican and Democratic primaries.

Democratic Reform Clubs: Groups of Democrats in New York city who break away from the official party organization to nominate candidates and support public policy.

Direct primary: Election in which the voters select the candidates who will run on a party's ticket in the subsequent general election.

Interest group: Organized group whose members share common views and actively carry on programs to influence government decision making.

Lobbying: Activities of interest group representatives aimed at influencing government decision making; includes private meetings, campaign contributions, and testifying before legislative committees.

Long ballot: Common in state and local elections in which the people elect all or nearly all the individuals who govern them; began with the administration of President Andrew Jackson.

Minor parties: Movements often based on a single idea; they have had little effect on elections, but have given publicity to economic, political, and social reform. (Also called third parties.)

Open primary: Election in which voters do not register by party and thus are free to vote for either Democratic or Republican primary candidates.

Party caucus: A meeting of legislators to make decisions on the selection of party leaders or to reach agreement regarding legislative action.

Party responsibility: Concept of political parties taking definite stands on issues, disciplining their members, and then being held accountable to the public for accomplishing their goals.

Political party: Group of individuals with some ideological agreement who organize to win elections, operate government, and make public policy.

Political socialization: Process by which individuals become educated regarding the operation of their government and their relationship to it.

Reform movement: Early twentieth-century "good government" movement to clean up politics; supported the direct primary, city managers, and referenda.

Run-off primaries: A second primary election, often held in the South, to choose a candidate when no one has received a majority of the total primary votes.

Most of the direct political input into a state's political process comes from the activities of political parties and interest groups. For this reason an examination of state party systems, including the very important role of interest groups, is in order.

The term *party* is tricky; there are clearly sharp differences between the Democratic party of Connecticut and the Communist party of the Ukraine. This is merely another way of pointing out that the roles and functions of parties differ immensely in different political cultures. Yet it is possible, using the outline developed by Frank J. Sorauf, to make some meaningful and helpful distinctions.[1]

In all the democracies of the world, a universal function of parties is the mobilization of voters behind candidates for election. In performing this function, the parties also distinguish themselves from other types of political organizations. Election to public office is the key function of American major parties. On the other hand, for minor parties, an election is a convenient occasion to obtain publicity for their favorite ideas and an opportunity to gain new adherents.

A second function of parties is to act as a teacher. The parties propagandize for their own political attitudes, ideas, and programs. In contrast to European parties, which often take a world view of problems (for example, the French Socialists), American major parties are much more likely to align themselves with a particular interest, such as labor or business. Or their statements may be so vague as to be meaningless, as when they claim their goals to be peace and prosperity. But however it is done, the American parties and their European counterparts both engage in the very broad educational task which comes under the technical term of *political socialization*.

What this means is that the party both introduces children into the basics of particular political cultures and, for adults, arranges and reorganizes what would otherwise be total confusion in the political universe. In short, parties serve as "reference groups," to employ a useful sociological expression. They bring order out of chaos; they give interpretations in a world of competing opinions. In the United States, the function of organizing and directing political perceptions is shared, as Sorauf notes, with the interest groups and the mass media. But the parties are nonetheless potent in the carrying out of this function.

In the democracies all parties perform, in various ways, the function of organizing the policy-making machinery of government. In the American states, as at the national level, it is the party caucus which decides on house leadership and on committee memberships. Of course, this function is performed by the major parties. A party that wins only an occasional seat need not be consulted by the majority party or by the out-party, which may obtain a majority at the next election.

The area in which the American parties, state as well as national, come in for criticism is not, therefore, in their ability to organize legislatures. Rather it comes directly from the failure of the winning party, once having organized, to seize and use the policy-making powers it said during the election that it so earnestly needed. The failure of parties to assume a genuine policy-making role is at the heart of the "party responsibility" debate which political scientists (but few politicians) have carried on for the last two decades. Basically, the party responsibility group would like to see parties win elections and then govern. The contrary argument rests on the belief that such an arrangement is inherently unworkable in the American political milieu as it now exists. For example, almost surely the separation of powers would have to be abandoned in favor of a fusion of executive and legislative powers, as in the European democracies or the Canadian provinces. This could happen, but it appears unlikely, given the relative conservatism of the American people when it comes to "tinkering" with basic constitutional structures.

Finally, there is a fourth, not directly "political," type of function which parties perform. These functions are social or civic in character, but the purpose in performing them is always to relate such functions to the party. For example, a hundred years ago the classic American urban "machines" performed many of the services now undertaken by social workers, legal aid counsellors, and employment advising agencies. In Europe the process is carried a good deal further. A party often sponsors a life assurance society, or a summer camp, or it may publish a daily newspaper. This last group of activities is rather alien to the various American party systems.

Now, what is the practical importance to these distinctions? According to Sorauf, "the emphasis a party places on one or two of these functions, and the style with which it carries them out, distinguishes it from its competitors and from the parties of other political systems."[2] In the United States, where the emphasis is on the electoral function, the major parties have long argued that for them to place an emphasis on developing program and ideology would penalize them at election time. This electoral preoccupation of the major American parties distinguishes them, therefore, both from minor or third American parties and from the competitive parties in the other democracies.

LEADING CHARACTERISTICS OF AMERICAN PARTY SYSTEMS

In addition to an unrivaled devotion to the electoral function, the various American party systems, national and state, possess certain characteristics which are noteworthy. These have been dealt with at length by E. E. Schattschneider in his *Party Government* and require only summarization here.[3]

In the first place, it is commonly said that the United States is characterized by the presence—and often blessing—of a two-party system. This is, of course, roughly true at the national level, where alternations in partisan control of the presidency occur at periodic intervals. It is less true, at least in recent decades, of the Congress, which has tended to be overwhelmingly Democratic since the advent of the New Deal. But the emphasis, of course, has been on control of the presidency.

At the state level the presence of a two-party system is much more difficult to find. It depends upon the definition of *two-party system*, and the time span one is talking about, as to which states are two party and which are not. In his examination of the 1930—1960 period, V. O. Key, the pioneer of modern studies of parties, found that only about a third of the states enjoyed serious two-party competition.[4] Other scholars, using a different base, have indicated that as many as half the states may have an effective two-party competition. When it comes to the cities, there is much less of a problem. Most cities, large and small, are for all practical purposes one-party operations. In Philadelphia, for example, the Republican organization was predominant for about a century: its hegemony ended in 1950—1951. This is not what is ordinarily meant by "competitiveness."

A second leading feature of American parties is that they are semipublic associations. This is truer of the national parties than of those in the states; all parties lie somewhere within the range of private clubs at one end and of public agencies at the other. All the states take the position that the parties perform certain essential public functions; the states pass laws setting party membership requirements, determining internal organizational structure, controlling the nominating process, and regulating party finance. On the other hand, the states do not regulate the party programs. Money must be raised through private subscription. Party officers are not public officers. In short, the system is a hybrid.

Thirdly, as Schattschneider emphasizes, American parties are decentralized. Decentralization, he often observed, is their outstanding single characteristic. At the national level, control rests with the state units. At the state level, control rests with the local units, usually the county organizations. The proof of the proposition is seen in the central unit's lack of control over the lesser units. In actuality, power usually resides at the base of the pyramid, not at its top.

Fourthly and lastly, American parties are multigroup associations. The parties do not constitute a homogeneous bloc of like-minded voters, united on basic principles. Though this was the ideal sought by Edmund Burke, it has never been the case in the United States, nor has it been in Burke's Britain. In fact, the parties consist of wide coalitions of voters who are apt to disagree on basic principles more then they agree. This is summed up in the familiar expression that "politics is the art of the possible," i.e., that the idea is to build a sufficiently broad electoral coalition so that one group of managers receives more votes than its chief rival. For a voter who strongly believes in issue orientation, the only sensible approach to elections is ticket splitting. And ticket splitting has been on the increase in recent elections, state as well as national.

APPEARANCES AND REALITIES OF CONTEMPORARY STATE PARTY SYSTEMS

Until the Civil War, American state parties were largely unregulated by law. However, the large number of scandals which took place in the postwar period aroused the famous American conscience. As a consequence, the states began to write statutes to regulate the activities of the parties. The rules which govern state political battles are now very elaborate, and only a few officials of the parties and of the state governments can claim any in-depth understanding of them. Nonetheless, it is easy to point out the principal matters which are regulated:

1. *Access to the ballot.* Each of the states specifies which conditions must be met for an organization to qualify as a political party and thereby have the names of its candidates printed on election ballots. The laws are usually written in such a way as to make it very difficult to organize, or if organized to maintain, third or minor parties. The same situation applies to independent candidates.

2. *Membership.* Each state spells out what is required for a person to have membership in a party, i.e., what is required in order to vote in the primary of the party.

3. *Organization.* State laws prescribe the number, composition, selection, and functions of the various officials, committees, conventions, and other bodies that make up the legal organizations of the parties.

4. *Nominating procedures.* It is the state, not the party, which prescribes the procedures for the formal selection of official candidates for public office. The usual practice today is to require that nominations be made by direct primary, rather than by party caucus or convention.

5. *Party finance.* Most of the states regulate at least some aspects of party finance. These may include how much a party may spend in election campaigns, who may or may not make contributions to party funds, and what public reports should be filed concerning receipts and expenditures.

The parties, in short, are both highly regulated and extremely visible. Yet it would be an error to infer from this that the party systems in the different states are in any sense peas out of the same pod. On the contrary, the variety in party systems is staggering. The Democratic party in Connecticut is usually highly disciplined, and as a potential Democratic candidate one has to wait in line until his or her time has arrived. As in the case of Governor Ella Grasso, this may entail service to the party in several posts over a very long period of time. On the other hand, in some states the Democratic party is nothing more than a neutral legal structure within which roam various factions, cliques, and individuals. Georgia's Democratic party is a good example.

INTERPARTY COMPETITION

For many years the degree of interparty competition was considered by political scientists to be the most important variable in state politics. As was noted earlier, this assumption has come under some attack. At first, students of the subject took it for granted that a high degree of party competition would lead to cohesive parties in the legislature. Hence, it was assumed that such parties could be the key factor in determining legislative or policy output.

However, later studies correlating a state's ranking in interparty competition with its ranking on per capita expenditures on education, old-age assistance, and unemployment compensation failed to support this thesis. The level of a state's welfare expenditures is more related to the level of wealth and resources of the state than it is—in any statistical sense—to the degree of interparty competition.

More recent studies using different techniques and measurements, especially the work of Ira Sharkansky and Richard I. Hofferbert, have found that high levels of competition are significantly related to high levels of social welfare expenditures. However, they are far from being the only factor in stimulating social welfare programs.[5]

Despite disagreement as to the relationship between interparty competition and policy output, most political scientists who study party systems remain convinced that interparty competition strongly affects the organization and activities of the parties. For that reason, a good starting point for the analysis of state parties is to group them according to their degrees of competition.

Dimensions and Measurement of Interparty Competition

There are many methods of measuring interparty competition, but the experts who engage in this exercise are in agreement with Richard Dawson and James Robinson that at least three basic dimensions must be taken into account. They are as follows:

1. *Proportion of success:* This refers to the percentage of votes won by each party for state-wide offices, and the percentage of seats in the legislature held by each.
2. *Duration of success:* This refers to the length of time each party has controlled the state-wide offices and the legislature.
3. *Frequency of divided control:* This refers to the proportion of time in which control of the governor's office and the legislature has been divided between the parties.

Building on this base, Austin Ranney, a leading student of state politics, has compiled a table which classifies the states according to the degree of interparty competition in state elections for the period 1956–1970. Ranney's classification is reprinted in

Table 4.1. Though the table itself is clear, some background may be useful in explaining how Ranney constructed it.[6]

The four basic figures used by Ranney were these: (1) the average percentage of the popular vote won by Democratic gubernatorial candidates; (2) the average percentage of seats in the state senate held by the Democrats; (3) the average percentage of seats in the state house of representatives held by the Democrats; and (4) the percentage of all terms for governor, senate, and house in which the Democrats had control.

Then, for each state, Ranney averaged together all four percentages to produce an "index of competitiveness" carried to four decimal places. This produces a possible range of .0000 (total Republican success) to 1.0000 (total Democratic success), with .5000 representing absolutely even two-party competition. After that, Ranney simply listed the states in descending order of index numbers and clustered the resulting figures into the following categories and definitions:

.9000 or higher: one-party Democratic
.8999 to .7000: modified one-party Democratic
.6999 to .3000: two-party
.2999 to .1000: modified one-party Republican
.0999 or lower: one-party Republican

By these criteria, as the table shows, no state qualified as one-party Republican.

How is one to account for one-party or modified one-party states in a country where the outcome of presidential elections alternates frequently between the two major parties?

In most cases, the condition can be traced back to the Civil War. Of the eight Democratic one-party states, all were members of the Confederacy. Of the nine modified Democratic one-party states, North Carolina, Tennessee, and Virginia were Confederate; West Virginia was the Unionist part of Virginia; and Arizona, New Mexico, and Oklahoma were settled mainly by immigrants from the South. Six of the eight Republican one-party states—Iowa, Kansas, Maine, New Hampshire, Vermont, and Wisconsin—sided with the Union, and the other two, the Dakotas, were settled principally by migrants from Union states.

Another view of the data behind the table reveals additional factors correlated with the degree of party competition among the states. For example, the two-party states are substantially more urbanized than the others. These states also have a

Table 4.1

The Fifty States Classified According to Degree of Interparty Competition, 1956–1970

One-Party Democratic	Modified One-Party Democratic	Two-Party		Modified One-Party Republican
Louisiana (.9877)	North Carolina (.8332)	Hawaii (.6870)	New Jersey (.5122)	North Dakota (.3305)
Alabama (.9685)	Virginia (.8235)	Rhode Island (.6590)	Pennsylvania (.4800)	Kansas (.3297)
Mississippi (.9407)	Florida (.8052)	Massachusetts (.6430)	Colorado (.4725)	New Hampshire (.3282)
South Carolina (.9292)	Tennessee (.7942)	Alaska (.6383)	Michigan (.4622)	South Dakota (.3142)
Texas (.9132)	Maryland (.7905)	California (.6150)	Utah (.4565)	Vermont (.2822)
Georgia (.9080)	Oklahoma (.7792)	Nebraska (.6065)	Indiana (.4450)	
Arkansas (.8850)	Missouri (.7415)	Washington (.6047)	Illinois (.4235)	
	Kentucky (.7170)	Minnesota (.5910)	Wisconsin (.4102)	
	West Virginia (.7152)	Nevada (.5742)	Idaho (.4077)	
	New Mexico (.7150)	Connecticut (.5732)	Iowa (.3965)	
		Delaware (.5687)	Ohio (.3837)	
		Arizona (.5663)	New York (.3835)	
		Montana (.5480)	Maine (.3820)	
		Oregon (.5387)	Wyoming (.3537)	

Source: Austin Ranney in Herbert Jacob and Kenneth Vines, *Politics in the American States*, 2d ed. Boston: Little, Brown, 1971.

smaller proportion of blacks than do the two groups of Democratically dominated states. They also have a larger proportion of "foreign stock" and of Roman Catholics. The two-party states are the least agricultural, while the Republican states are the most agricultural.

Outside the South, Democratic support tends to be concentrated in the big cities and is based there on ethnic groups and on trade unions. Republican voting strength tends to be concentrated in the smaller towns and cities, where the populations are predominantly WASPs (white, Anglo-Saxon Protestants). The most likely major shifts are to be found in the northern farm states, which react quickly to prosperous or depressed economic conditions.

ELECTORAL SHIFTS

Even though there is a basic stability to American state politics, enormous shifts in electoral preference occasionally take place. The state elections of 5 November 1974 offer an excellent illustration. The background was as follows.

Following the resignation of President Richard M. Nixon in the summer of 1974 as a result of the Watergate revelations of criminality on the part of certain White House and Republican officials, public disillusionment with the political process in general and the Republican party in particular mushroomed. In spite of pressing national problems—depression, inflation, and the energy crisis—Gerald R. Ford, chosen president by Congress under the Twenty-fifth Amendment, decided to spend the five weeks preceding the November elections in a frantic tour of the country. His intention was to bolster support for Republican candidates everywhere. His problem was that many Republican candidates, at all levels, wanted to stay as clear as possible of the Nixon Republican party, with which Mr. Ford was, indirectly, associated. The almost immediate pardon given by President Ford for all crimes committed or which might have been committed by Richard Nixon was felt by many voters to constitute some kind of special relationship with the former president. Some even called it a "deal."

As it turned out, President Ford's efforts were largely in vain. At the national level, the Democrats increased their majorities in both the Senate and the House. At the state level, the Democratic victories were spectacular. The Democrats won twenty-seven of the thirty-five governorships up for election. The Republicans captured six and an independent, one (in Maine).

This meant that Democratic gubernatorial control nationwide was increased from thirty-two to thirty-six, including previously Republican-held governorships in Arizona, California, Colorado, Connecticut, Massachusetts, New York, Oregon, and Wyoming. The victory of an independent in Maine came at the expense of the Democrats. Nationwide, Republican gubernatorial control slipped from eighteen to thirteen. In all, nineteen new governors were elected (in six states incumbents were prohibited by law from seeking reelection). Among the nineteen was Ella Grasso, who as governor of Connecticut is the first woman ever to be elected to such a post in her own right. At the time of her election, she was a representative in Congress.

Governor Ella T. Grasso of Connecticut. (Wide World Photos.)

Women scored some other important firsts. In New York, State Senator Mary Anne Krupsak was elected lieutenant governor on a team ticket with Democrat Hugh Carey. North Carolina Supreme Court Justice Susie Sharp became the first woman elected chief justice of a state supreme court. And Alabama elected its first woman to the supreme court, Janie Shores.

It was reported that women increased their numbers in state legislatures from 466 to 595, or 8 percent of the nation's 7,600 state legislators. New Hampshire led the list of women legislators with a total of 104.[7]

During the same elections, minorities also made important

gains. For example, in Hawaii, Democratic Acting Governor George Ariyoshi became the first American of Japanese ancestry to win a governorship. His running mate, Nelson Doi, elected lieutenant governor, is also of Japanese-American ancestry. Democrat Raul Castro became the first Mexican-American to be elected governor of Arizona. In New Mexico, Democrat Jerry Apodaca, a state senator, became the first Spanish-American governor to be elected since 1918.

Blacks won lieutenant governorships in California and in Colorado. According to the reliable Voter Education Project, blacks made significant gains in Southern legislatures. They won thirty new seats in state houses of representatives in eleven southern states, increasing their total to eighty-five. Blacks were also elected to the Alabama and North Carolina senates, increasing the total number of blacks in state senates in the South to ten.

Of course, the lion's share of public interest went to the gubernatorial races. The political map of the states in terms of governorships by party is shown in Figure 4.1.

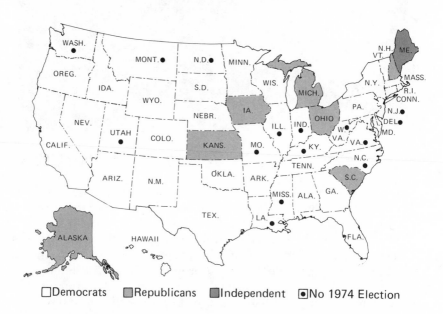

☐Democrats ▨Republicans ▉Independent ◉No 1974 Election

Figure 4.1
Governorships by party following 5 November 1974 elections.
Source: *State Government News,* December 1974, p. 10.

PARTY ORGANIZATION

Formal Structure

In most of the states the party structure is rather rigidly regulated by law. The most loosely regulated states are Alabama, Arkansas, Georgia, North Carolina, South Carolina, and Virginia.

The statutes in the vast majority of the states are very detailed. They prescribe the number, composition, powers, and duties of the committees, conventions, and caucuses that make up the formal structure of the parties. As has been noted earlier, American parties mostly nominate and elect. It is not surprising, therefore, that state laws apply to each level of party organization, which corresponds in turn with each level of election. In every state there are precinct or ward "committees," county "central committees," a state "central committee," and a state chairman or chairwoman.

How are these party officials selected? The answer is, in various ways, but most commonly they are (1) chosen by the activists in local caucuses; (2) elected by party registrants in direct primaries or by delegates to party conventions; or (3) achieve ex officio committee membership by virtue of holding positions on lower party committees.

As might be suspected, there is in no state a true hierarchy of committees in the sense that the top committee can remove members of lower committees. The reason for this is that members of the lower committees were chosen by their own local constituencies. As a consequence, authority is not legally concentrated in the state central committee. On the contrary, the law divides authority into small bundles and scatters it among precinct, county, and district committee members. It is another illustration of party decentralization, so typical of American political organizations.

Informal Structure

In some organizations "informal" authority is much more centralized than the "formal" structure would suggest. But, for the most part, in the American states the informal authority is just as decentralized as the formal or legal authority. Of course, there have been exceptions. For example, the Huey Long organization in Louisiana during the 1920s and 1930s was in firm control of that one-party state. Again, the Harry Byrd organization firmly controlled Virginia state politics from the 1930s into the 1960s. Sometimes the phenomenon can be observed in two-party states, for example, the Thomas Dewey organization in New York in the 1940s and the organization put together by Hubert Humphrey in Minnesota during the 1950s and 1960s. Yet these are exceptions. The organizations with real discipline and hierarchy have normally been found at the municipal, not at the state, level. Illustrations are the Tammany Hall organization in New York city of a hundred years ago and the Daley machine in contemporary Chicago.

It would be reasonable to assume that state party organizations tend to be more centralized where two-party competition is sharpest. But the evidence indicates that if there is such a tendency, it is not very pronounced. Rather, what gives unity to a party is a sense of common cause, not a unity of command.[8]

Because of the feebleness of state party organizations, or because of their concentration on patronage at the expense of policy, there have arisen in a few states extraparty organizations set up to bypass the regular organizations. An example is the California Republican Assembly, established by a progressive faction of California Republicans in 1934. In the same state, the California Democratic Council, founded in 1953, has played a key role in Democratic affairs. Both groups monitor the regular organizations and bring into the party elements that normally would not play a part in the activities of the regular party organizations. At a different, local level, the Democratic reform clubs in New York city, founded after 1952 by such distinguished party activists as Eleanor Roosevelt and Herbert Lehman, have attempted to contest the official Democratic party's domination of organization and nominations.

NOMINATIONS

Legal Procedures

Except for Connecticut, all states now require that party candidates for some or all public offices be nominated by direct primaries. Under the unique "challenge primary" law of Connecticut, adopted in 1956, all party candidates are to be nominated at the appropriate party conventions. However, anyone who receives at least 20 percent of a convention's votes but loses the nomination may petition the authorities to hold a primary election in which he or she challenges the convention-nominated candidate. A regular closed primary is then held. It says much for Connecticut's disciplined party system that for many years there were no challenge primaries for state-wide contests.

All direct primaries have several features in common. Nominations are made directly by voters in a primary election. Primaries are governed by state law, not by party rules. The elections are administered by state-appointed officials and, as is the case with general elections, the ballots are secret.

To be sure, there are variations in primaries as in other aspects of American elections. In the closed primary, only persons registered as members of a particular party may participate in the process for choosing that party's candidates. This is the commonest form of primary, and is used in forty-two states.

But in some states a so-called open primary is held. The basic feature of this plan is that a person may vote in whatever primary he or she chooses without having to give any disclosure of the choice made. This plan is used in Alaska, Michigan, Minnesota, Montana, North Dakota, Utah, and Wisconsin.

A third variation comes from Washington, which employs the so-called blanket primary. Here a voter may indicate preferences for candidates from any parties on the general list, but not more than one preference for each office may be indicated. This might seem like inviting total chaos. But because voters are mostly creatures of habit, they tend to vote fairly consistently for candidates from a single party slate rather than scattering their choices among a plethora of major and minor party candidates. As a result, Washington is, in fact, governable.

Besides all this, it is well to note the existence in eight southern one-party states and three modified one-party Democratic states of second, or run-off, primaries. If no candidate receives more than 50 percent of the votes in the first primary, a second primary is held between the top two candidates. This device, of course, ensures majority support for the successful party candidate and establishes the legitimacy of the candidature.

Direct Primaries

The movement to substitute direct primary elections for nomination by convention was an outgrowth of the reform movement of the early years of this country. Of course, the general objective was to give "power to the people," that is, to remove the nominating authority from the boss-controlled conventions and thus facilitate popular control over the party itself. How successful has this movement been?

In formulating a response to this important question, several considerations must be kept in mind. For example, studies have shown that there are fewer contestants in those primaries in which incumbents are running for renomination than in those for which no incumbents are running. In the second place, the same studies have revealed that the primaries are more likely to be contested if the party's chances for winning are good, especially if the incumbent is not seeking reelection. Thirdly, outside the South (because of the normal one-party status of most of that region) the voter turnout is substantially lower in the primaries than in the general elections. Ordinarily, in regions other than the South, only about a third of the registrants (i.e., those eligible to vote) actually participate in primary elections.

What difference does this make? To summarize the conclusions of the experts on state party systems, a good deal. State parties, which in many cases were rather centralized before the introduction of the direct primary, have tended toward fragmentation since that time. In short, if you are in favor of party responsibility at the state level you may have difficulty in finding a rationale for the direct primary. At least, this is the dilemma which has confounded the experts.

ELECTIONS

Campaigns

In the American states, campaigning remains a highly individual undertaking. As Daniel Ogden, Jr., and Hugh Bone have put it: "Rarely will a popular candidate permit his name to appear on an ad or a billboard with that of a much less known figure."[9] In other words, normally it is a case of each candidate for himself. Of course, party backing is welcome, but usually the candidate is expected to bring private and personal support to his or her candidacy.

Because of the long ballot common in many states, i.e., the independent *election* of a long series of state officers (in contrast to the United States system, in which the president *ap-*

points his departmental officers), the process further emphasizes individualism at the expense of policy solidarity. An incumbent may easily win reelection while his or her fellow partisans are roundly defeated.

Since 1945, several tendencies have been apparent. As everyone who watches television realizes, there has been an increasing use of professional public relations firms to plan and conduct campaigns. This has undercut the traditional role of the regular party organizations. Secondly, actual or potential candidates have made increasing use of public opinion surveys, both to determine the popularity of candidates and to weigh the possible impact of particular issues. Thirdly, it is universally acknowledged that the newly placed emphasis on public relations firms and on the use of television has tremendously increased the costs of campaigning.

Campaign Financing

It was estimated that in the 1950s it cost about $600 thousand to wage a serious gubernatorial campaign in Illinois. By the late 1960s, this figure had risen to $1 million. In other states, the trend has been similar. Even allowing for inflation and for the increase in population, this is a great deal of money. Where does it come from?

Candidates like to pretend that the funds come from small contributions of thousands of interested citizens. Students of the subject know better: most of the contributions come from very large gifts from a small number of donors. In the two-party states, the bulk of Republican funds comes from business people and the bulk of Democratic funds come from labor.

Yet despite popular belief, the side with more money does not automatically win the election. In 1974, the Republicans probably had a great deal more money at their disposal in the state elections than did their Democratic rivals. Yet, as we have seen, the result was a Democratic avalanche at the polls. In short, money, while an important factor, is still only one factor among many.

In all but a handful of states, there are laws regulating various aspects of party finance. As a result of the abuses exposed at the national level in the 1972 machinations of the Committee to Re-elect the President (CREEP), many states strengthened their laws in this area, as did the national government. Nonetheless, loopholes in the laws appear to be plentiful.

Political scientists continue to believe, for the most part, that publicizing the source of contributions *prior* to an election and encouraging small contributors to increase their donations are superior to enacting prohibitive legislation. So far as practical and detailed suggestions are concerned, the National Municipal League deals with this question in a pamphlet entitled *The Costs of Administering American Elections.*[10]

Election Administration

In a companion volume entitled *A Model Election System,* the National Municipal League has outlined the general characteristics of a "model" election system.[11] Though it is difficult to summarize a summary, the main recommendations of the league are that a model election administration system should contain these following elements:

1. A state should establish a centralized authority over elections in an administrative office headed by a single officer of state government.
2. A state should finance voter registration, training of election workers, and state-mandated meetings for election personnel.
3. The state's chief electoral officer should be given real regulatory authority.
4. Each state should establish an election council to provide partisan balance in the administration of elections.
5. A single officer at the county level should be answerable to the chief electoral officer for the local administration of registration and voting.
6. A single official should be responsible for the conduct of elections within each precinct or voting district.

The league also makes recommendations regarding the improvement of the present chaotic registration system found in most states. Essentially, the proposal is to adopt the system used almost everywhere except in the United States. This would make the public authorities responsible for election registration, instead of placing the burden upon the individual citizen. In France, for example, officials in the city hall or in the subcity hall of an arrondissement (ward) are responsible for maintaining the voting list and for keeping it up to date. The only serious arguments advanced in the United States in modern times against the adoption of this ordinarily used system are that (1) more of the poor would vote; so that (2) the Democratic percentage of the total vote would rise. These are not very persuasive reasons in the latter part of the twentieth century.

INTEREST GROUPS

Interest groups play an important role in state politics. Sometimes called, in a pejorative sense, "pressure groups," they seek to influence both the contents of legislation and, subsequently, the fashion in which the legislation is administered. Some interest groups are also active in the judicial arena, for example, the American Civil Liberties Union and, in civil rights cases, the National Association for the Advancement of Colored People.

It is useful to distinguish between permanent, continuing interest groups, such as labor or business organizations, and ad hoc, one-time groups, such as one formed to support or defeat a particular bond issue. Among the more important permanent groups are those related to business, labor, agriculture, law, medicine, and education. In addition, veterans', patriotic, and church groups are usually active in state politics.

Characteristics

At several points, interest groups contrast fairly sharply with political parties. The single most important distinction is that an interest group tries to influence the course of government without assuming responsibility for the conduct of government affairs. In short, it does not run candidates for office, though it may throw its support toward particular candidates of the parties.

In addition, an interest group consists of persons who share certain attitudes and values. In this respect, the group is homogeneous. An interest group is a private association; it is self-governing, sets its own membership criteria, and raises its own funds. It also handles its own internal problems of discipline, and may penalize or expel members who do not agree with the general positions taken by the majority of the membership.

Tactics

The principal requirement for a successful interest group is access to power holders. Access means at least three things: (1) the group must be able to approach a legislator or administrator in such a way that the power holders will listen to what is being said, even if they do not accept the proffered advice; (2) the group must be in possession of up-to-date information, with regard to both their own objectives and those of the power holders; (3) the group must try to use one power holder to affect the actions of other power holders.

But access goes beyond this. It implies a two-way street. In return for favors granted, the power holders will often want the interest group to support the position of the power holders on other matters. It is this point which some interest groups fail to grasp. The process is very much a quid pro quo arrangement, and the interest group itself must be able to deliver support, often in the form of campaign funds or votes. Labor organizations and business groups understand this condition very well. It is less well understood by church groups.

Whether an interest group is multipurpose, as is the case with the AFL-CIO, or single-purpose, as is the case with the Women's Christian Temperance Union, obviously affects both its structure and its activities. Indeed, the range of concerns of many of the larger multipurpose groups is staggering. For example, an objective of the clothing workers is to make it more difficult or expensive to import clothing manufactured in Taiwan and South Korea. One indirect way of working toward this goal is to denounce the governments of these countries as "undemocratic" and hence undeserving of the support of the American taxpayer. Other examples will come readily to the mind of any reader of the daily press.

Whatever objectives an interest group may have, its road to success depends on its ability to influence public opinion. But since "public opinion" is almost always in reality the opinion of a concerned minority, the strategy is to define and then attempt to influence that specific minority, or "target." The means of doing this will ordinarily include the use of pamphlets, letters, advertisements, news releases, motion pictures, and representatives available to give speeches on behalf of the group. Euphemistically, this is called "educating" the public.

Naturally, most active members of interest groups are affiliated with one of the major political parties. It is therefore easy for a group's opinion to be presented before the councils of the major parties. In fact, participation may even extend to the selection of candidates and the drafting of platforms. On the other hand, the group as a whole will normally follow a nonpartisan line, since it has much to lose and little to gain from outright partisan affiliation.

Lobbying

One of the most, perhaps the most, conspicuous activity of the major interest groups is lobbying. For this purpose the major groups maintain paid lobbyists at the state capitals. This is not as pernicious as it sounds. Most state legislatures are very poorly staffed and operate under great time constraints. Under these circumstances, the beleaguered legislators are likely to accept all the expert help they can get. It is at this point that the major interest groups play an important role. After all, the legislators are amateurs in most fields, while the lobbyists are experts in their own fields. It is completely natural for the amateur legislators to turn to the lobbyists for expert advice.

No skilled lobbyist expects to win his or her point all the time. After all, any lobbyist may be opposed by equally skilled lobbyists who take a contrary position, or by representatives from the governor's office, who may in their own right constitute a formidable lobby. All that a lobbyist can expect, and usually wants, is a chance to make a fair presentation of his or her views.

A TYPOLOGY OF STATE INTEREST GROUP PATTERNS

There is no single pattern of interest group activity that applies to all the fifty state political systems. Rather, there are several patterns, and they are closely related to the socioeconomic environment of the individual states. L. Harmon Zeigler and Hendrik van Dalen have identified four principal patterns, which are summarized here:[12]

Alliance of Dominant Groups. This pattern is descriptive of the southern states and of other states with similar socioeconomic settings, such as Maine. In Maine, for example, state government has historically been dominated for many years by the "big three"—a reference to the leaders in electric power, timber, and manufacturing. The key position of these interests in Maine's economy establishes their crucial position in state decision making. Though the situation may be changing (for example, Maine passed tough antipollution legislation in 1969–1970), the position of the big three remains decisive in many areas of state policy formulation.

Single Dominant Interest. A second pattern finds a nondiversified economy with two-party politics and moderate legislative cohesion. Given this situation, a single dominant interest strengthens the pressure system. The classic example is Montana, whose politics was dominated for decades by the Anaconda Company. Though well-known for its copper operations, the company also owns aluminum companies, railroads, fabricating plants, and forests. Until 1959, Anaconda controlled a chain of newspapers which had a combined circulation greater than that of all other dailies in the state.

Conflict Between Two Dominant Groups. The best illustration of this type of conflict comes from highly industrialized Michigan which is, of course, dominated by the automobile industry. Since industrialization, Michigan's politics have been bipolarized. The conflict has been between the automobile union and automobile management. In partisan terms, the union is deeply involved with the affairs of the Democratic party. Conversely, automobile management is heavily committed to the Republican party. This polarization is reflected rather brilliantly in the Michigan legislature on issues relating to such matters as labor legislation. Unlike the national parties, which mediate conflict, the parties in Michigan, which communicate interest group values, actually intensify group conflict.

However disenchanted the national leadership of the AFL-CIO may become with the national Democratic party, it is almost impossible to envision the defection of the United Automobile Workers from the Democratic party of Michigan.

The Triumph of Many Interests. The last type of group conflict occurs when there is a free play of interest groups in a legislature not usually subjected to demands originating from the political parties. California illustrates the triumph of many interests. In its economic structure, California is today highly diversified. This was not always so, for at one time in the state's history the railroads, especially the Southern Pacific, dominated both parties and the legislature.

In many respects, California was a victim of the reform legislation in which it pioneered early in the present century. One important measure was that which permitted cross-filing by candidates for office. This meant that a person could contest for both Democratic and Republican nominations without his or her party affiliation appearing on either ballot. It was not until 1959 that cross-filing was abolished, but by that time California's parties were parties in name only. Not only did cross-filing diminish the importance of the party to the legislator, it also made it impossible to build an effective party organization across the state.

Under these circumstances, interest groups moved in to fill the vacuum. They supplied funds for candidates, and they were willing and prepared to make legislative drafts. In some respects the major interest groups resembled political parties in their organization.

In the interest-group-dominated politics of California, it therefore came as a surprise to no one when newly elected Governor Ronald Reagan deserted the governor's mansion in favor of a brand new edifice constructed by his personal friends at their own expense. Indeed, to use Shana Alexander's apposite phrase expressed in 1973 in her *Newsweek* column, both Governor Reagan, during his term, and the California legislature specialized in "the art of negative politics."[13] The essence of negative politics as applied to Governor Reagan, she said, consisted in "not spending money and vetoing bills."

Contrasting Patterns: States Without a Dominant Pressure System

Zeigler and van Dalen conclude their analysis by noting that a few states possess very strong party systems which in fact dominate the interest groups. In Connecticut, for instance, parties are said to be able to take punitive action against an interest group whose demands have become intolerable. Under these conditions, the interest groups have no choice except to operate through the parties, not in competition with them. Each party in Connecticut tends to develop its own constellation of interests from which support can normally be expected.

A Note in Praise of Interest Groups

For ordinary citizens, preoccupied as they are with affairs of job and family and everyday problems, activities centering on a relevant interest group may be much more rewarding than partisan activities. There is usually a direct connection between one's job and one's interest group, while the connection between voting and the public welfare is nebulous at best. There are so many interest groups that a person may concentrate on one or two which are closest to his or her major concerns: labor unions, business organizations, church societies, tenants' associations, and so on ad infinitum.

In addition to providing participation and the possibility of affecting public policy, interest groups, knowingly or not, perform an outstanding public service: they serve as a supplementary form of representation in a society whose legislatures are built on the basis of numerical representation. Especially in the economic sphere, such additional representation seems absolutely necessary to the operations of American governments.

Items for Discussion

1. What effects have groups such as Common Cause and the Ralph Nader organization had on the operation of government in your state?

2. Why have minor parties fared so poorly in state and local elections?

3. Does the election of Ella Grasso as governor of Connecticut really offer hope to other women gubernatorial candidates? How soon will a black person be elected governor of a state? What factors explain the election of substantial numbers of women to political office in some northern states, while in others few women are elected?

4. Why do so many Rocky Mountain states (Nevada, Colorado, Montana, Utah, Idaho, and Arizona) have a high degree of two-party competition?

5. Why are people willing to work without pay in local party organizations?

Chapter Notes

1. Frank J. Sorauf, *Political Parties in the American System* (Boston: Little, Brown, 1964), chap. 1.

2. *Ibid.*, p. 5.

3. E. E. Schattschneider, *Party Government* (New York: Rinehart, 1942).

4. V. O. Key, Jr., *Politics, Parties, and Pressure Groups*, 5th ed. (New York: Crowell, 1964), chap. 11.

5. See Ira Sharkansky and Richard I. Hofferbert, "Dimensions of State Politics, Economics, and Public Policy," Vol. 63, No. 3, *American Political Science Review* (Sept. 1969), pp. 876–879.

6. See Austin Ranney, "Parties in State Politics," in Herbert Jacob and Kenneth N. Vines (eds.), *Politics in the American States* (Boston: Little, Brown, 1971), pp. 82–121.

7. This summary is taken from *State Government News*, Dec. 1974. The journal is published by the Council of State Governments.

8. This point was stressed by Key, *op. cit.*, p. 316.

9. Daniel M. Ogden, Jr., and Hugh A. Bone, *Washington Politics* (New York: New York University Press, 1960), p. 47.

10. Richard G. Smolka, *The Costs of Administering American Elections* (New York: National Municipal League, 1973). This is required reading for all serious students of campaign financing reform.

11. See *A Model Election System* (New York: National Municipal League, 1973).

12. L. Harmon Zeigler and Hendrik van Dalen, "Interest Groups in the States," in Jacob and Vines, *op. cit.*, chap. 4, pp. 122–160.

13. Shana Alexander, "The Art of Negative Politics," *Newsweek* (15 October 1973), p. 37.

5

State Legislatures

Key Terms

Advertisers: State legislators who go into politics with the intention of receiving public recognition or business contacts; they seek the limelight and often create controversy.

Bicameralism: The principle of the two-house legislature.

Conference committee: A special joint committee of members from both houses of a state legislature selected to reconcile differences when a bill passes the two houses in different forms.

Lawmakers: State legislators who devote an unusual amount of time and energy to making legislation; often show a willingness to run for future terms.

Reapportionment: The redrawing of legislative boundaries in order to maintain essentially equal population in each legislative district.

Reluctants: State legislators who did not want to run and are serving under protest; do not play an active role.

Single-member district: An electoral district from which a single legislator is chosen by a plurality vote; contrasted with *multimember districts*, from which several legislators are chosen on a proportional vote.

Speaker: Presiding officer in the lower house of a state legislature; controls legislative debate and functions as his or her party's leader.

Spectators: State legislators who sit by as passive bystanders watching the legislative show.

Unicameralism: The principle of the one-house legislature; found only in Nebraska.

Veto: Legislative power given the governor to return a bill unapproved to the legislature; in many states, governors, unlike the president, may exercise an *item veto* of sections or items of an appropriations bill while signing the remainder of the bill into law.

State legislatures all have certain features in common, and in this sense it is possible to make generalizations about them. This we shall do. But each legislature operates within a socioeconomic environment and a political culture which is unique. In this respect, it is necessary to treat each legislature as an illustration only of itself.

Part of this ambiguity in perspective can be seen in the varying treatments given legislatures when they are considered as a category when contrasted with the treatment accorded individual legislatures by particular observers. From the point of view of *The American Legislator,* which is the official organ of the National Legislative Conference and is published by the Council of State Governments, the picture which emerges is of steady if uneven progress across the state capitals of the realm.

At the same time, the great daily newspapers in Boston, New York, Philadelphia, and San Francisco maintain a running and spirited criticism of the legislative processes which they have observed in Boston, Albany, Harrisburg, and Sacramento. To the newspapers (and, to a much lesser extent, television), the legislatures and their legislators are fair game. Reporters stationed at state capitols profess to be amazed constantly at the antics of the legislators, their parochialism, and their short-sightedness.

There is an additional difficulty apparent to all citizens who make any effort at all to keep up with affairs in their own states. Though much of legislative activity is pure trivia, much of it on the other hand has an enormous effect on the lives of the citizens. One thinks of types and rates of taxation, educational policy, highways and vehicles, welfare, and all the areas in which the state dictates what its subdivisions may or may not do. Then, there is the whole field of criminal and civil law. But when changes are made in, for example, the death penalty, the treatment of drug peddlers, or the regulation of automotive traffic, the effects are of immediate and widespread concern.

As Hugh Bone has noted, state bodies are often thought of in the public mind as little congresses.[1] But, he goes on to observe, the comparison is not especially helpful. Since they do not have to deal with foreign policy, state assemblies can concentrate exclusively on domestic affairs. In addition, from a constitutional point of view the relationship between the United States Congress and the states is vastly different from the relationship between the states and local government bodies.

Continuing his comparison, Bone notes that being a member of Congress is a full-time job, with commensurate financial and fringe benefits. But in only a few of the states does the position of representative approximate a full-time position. Though most state legislatures are now in session more days per year than they used to be, the great majority of legislators still consider themselves to be amateurs. They have other occupations, such as business, law, or farming.

Addressing himself to the same comparison, another writer, Kenneth T. Palmer, offers some additional interesting contrasts between Congress and state legislatures.[2] His first point is that Congress is more institutionalized than are most state legislatures. The evidence for this statement comes from the relatively more stable nature of Congressional personnel: they stay in office much longer than their state counterparts. Congressional committees also have a far greater degree of internal complexity than do state committees. In retrospect, Palmer says, state legislatures seem to reflect about the same degree of institutionalization today as did the United States House of Representatives in the early nineteenth century.

Besides the different degrees of institutionalization, Palmer found a great contrast in the nature of legislative personnel in Congress and in the state legislatures. The principal indicator is the very high turnover of state legislators as compared with members of Congress.

There appear to be at least three identifiable reasons for this. The first is personal finance. With some notable exceptions, most states pay their legislators very little. For many legislators service to their state and district constitutes a severe financial burden. A second cause may be termed psychological. For a variety of reasons, many persons elected to state legislatures turn out to be poorly adapted to legislative life. Hence, they retire early from the legislatures. Palmer identifies the third cause as strictly political. By this he means that many of the most able legislators tend to regard their work in the legislature as an apprenticeship, or steppingstone, toward higher office. This upward mobility of many of the ablest legislators also increases the rapidity of the general turnover of personnel. In short, Congress is able to attract and to maintain a substantial corps of career members. But state legislatures ordinarily cannot.

For all these reasons, comparisons between Congress and state legislative bodies may be, and often are, misleading. However, there are certain *functions* which they all have in common, and there are certain *structural* similarities which they share. We shall now give attention to these questions. The focus is, of course, upon the states.

LEGISLATIVE STRUCTURE AND PERSONNEL

Bicameralism

Following British and colonial precedent, most of the newly formed states adopted a bicameral legislature. The federal Constitution established a bicameral system with a house of representatives and a senate. This action probably influenced the remaining unicameral states to join the others in accepting bicameralism. Georgia did so in 1788, Pennsylvania in 1790, and Vermont, the longest holdout, in 1836. As was noted earlier, in some of the states a fairly broad electorate chose the members of the lower house, while voting for members of the upper house was restricted to those who owned property. Eventually, although the bases for representation changed, uniform qualifications for the electors of both houses generally were established.

In arguing for bicameralism, the argument most often advanced is that one house will be in a position to check the supposed excesses of the other. But in actual practice, there is as likely as not to be a deadlock between the two houses. What this amounts to is a kind of veto power which almost always favors the retention of the status quo and makes change difficult. The system also allows individual members numerous opportunities to evade what outsiders might consider to be their legislative responsibilities.

**The New Hampshire House of Representatives in session.
(State of New Hampshire Photo.)**

Unicameralism

For at least the last half century, the idea of adopting
unicameralism has appealed to many experts on state government. Some ten states have explored the idea in some systematic fashion. Yet, strangely, only Nebraska has accepted the proposal. It did so largely because of the herculean efforts of then
Senator George W. Norris in the period 1933–1934. Even though
nearly every newspaper in the state opposed the plan as "un-
American," the so-called Unicam Amendment to the state's constitution was adopted by the voters in November 1934. It
provided that there be nonpartisan election of a chamber consisting of between thirty and fifty members. The legislature
itself fixed the number at forty-three. In actual operation since
1937—there was a transition period—the plan apparently has
met with the overwhelming approval of the people of Nebraska.
There has been an end to the buckpassing between the
chambers which was characteristic of bicameralism. At the same
time, the normal end-of-the-session rush to pass compromise
legislation—so notable in Harrisburg and in Albany, for in-

stance—has been eliminated because conference committees of two houses no longer exist in Nebraska. Also, the unicameral system appears to reflect the generally conservative economic and social views of the state's electorate.

Why have other states not followed suit, especially in view of the decision of the United States Supreme Court in *Reynolds v. Sims* (1964), which established the one man, one vote principle? This question has puzzled many unicameralists, for the Court decision seemed to remove the intellectual underpinning of a two-house assembly.

In his analysis of this problem, Lloyd B. Omdahl comes to some interesting findings.[3] As a starter, he reexamines the proposition that unicameralism is wanting in some rational or logical sense. But this, he finds, is simply not so. The intellectual rationale for unicameralism is impeccable. Then he looks at the alternative explanation for the failure of other states to follow Nebraska's lead, i.e., that a "politics of controversy" has frustrated adoption. This explanation he finds to be persuasive. "The only logical conclusion is that failure emanated from the politics that governs the decision makers who must act to implement unicameralism. We can no longer maintain the pretense that politics is a minor element in securing this reform for state assemblies, and until we come to grips with this fact, no ground will be gained in the next decade either."[4]

What are some of the factors that constitute a political challenge to the adoption of unicameralism? Most notably, state legislators would lose power; in some cases, their jobs would be abolished. In addition, some groups which now hold veto power under bicameralism would lose all or much of their current power. Interest groups stand to lose much by the adoption of unicameralism. Finally, unicameralism might mean a reduction in the size of the one chamber which survived; that is, the districts might be larger. What this means in practice is that substantial minority groups which are now concentrated in some small districts might be overwhelmed and outvoted in newer, larger districts. For example, in most states, the larger the legislative districts in terms of population, the less the black or other minority representation in the legislature itself.

Apportionment and Reapportionment of Legislatures

In the American colonies, representation was based on local communities, with little attention paid to population. However, what finally emerged was the practice of choosing legislators from districts. The most common practice is to employ single-member districts, but there are many more multimember districts than is usually supposed. Illinois, for example, has multimember districts.

Until the reapportionment cases of the 1960s, it was common to employ population alone as the basis of representation or, alternatively, some combination of population and area. What this meant in practice was that some voters had more weight than others in elections both of upper and of lower legislative houses. In some cases, the discrepancies were scandalous. Until 1962, it was understood that legislative districting and apportionments were "political" matters which lay outside the jurisdiction of the courts. Only the governor and the legislature could act in these areas. If they failed to act, the status quo was frozen, presumably forever. It was the United States Supreme Court which finally broke up the logjam.

In Colegrove v. Green (328 U.S. 549; 1946), judicial relief was sought from unjust congressional apportionment in Illinois. The Illinois constitution of 1870 provided that the state should be divided into fifty-one state senatorial districts, from each of which one state senator and three state representatives should be chosen. The legislature was charged with the task, after each census, of redrawing the lines of these districts to bring them into accord with population changes. Though it was obvious by the end of the century that about half the population of Illinois lived in metropolitan Chicago, downstate legislators showed no rush to reapportion in accord with population shifts.

As a result of this political bitterness, Illinois was unable to reapportion its legislative districts after 1901. All this bears on the problem of congressional reapportionment posed in Colegrove v. Green, for in that case the United States Supreme Court refused to grant relief to the inequities among congressional districts or to consider the validity of the Illinois apportionment on its merits. As Justice Frankfurter put it, the matter was "of a peculiarly political nature and therefore not [suitable] for judicial determination." This seemed to mean that the courts would not intervene even in cases of admitted inequality in apportionments.

But the same Court changed its views in the landmark case of Baker v. Carr (369 U.S. 186; 1962). The case arose from legislative apportionment in Tennessee. Yet the Court did not itself pass on the validity of the Tennessee apportionment.

Rather it announced, for the first time, that such issues were justiciable, and left for the lower courts the problem of deciding the actual cases. As these cases came in turn to the Supreme Court on appeal, that Court spelled out the specific requirements to be met.

In *Wesberry v. Sanders* (376 U.S. 1; 1964), the Court held that Article I required that each individual's vote weighs the same within a congressional district. In *Reynolds v. Sims* (377 U.S. 533; 1964), it held that the equal protection clause of the Fourteenth Amendment required this of both houses of the state legislature. Finally, in *Lucas v. Colorado* (377 U.S. 713; 1964), the Court held that even if the voters by referendum had opted for one house to be based on population and the other on counties with unequal populations, the arrangement was unconstitutional because of the equal protection clause. In other words, the Constitution takes precedence over a popular vote on the question.

From these cases there of course followed efforts in every state to bring the state legislatures in line with the Court's rulings. As a result of more than a decade of litigation—and strenuous efforts by federal district courts—the goal of one man, one vote has now largely been achieved in both the bicameral legislatures of the forty-nine states and the unicameral legislature of Nebraska. The current situation is shown in Tables 5.1 and 5.2.

Members of the Legislature

The state constitutions set qualifications for state senators and representatives. These concern citizenship, age, and residence. In addition, it is unusual for a candidate to be elected unless he or she holds membership in a major party. Occasionally, someone unqualified in a constitutional sense runs for office, but this must be considered merely a form of attracting public attention to an individual or a maverick party.

There is a good deal of disparity among the states in compensation for services rendered. The theory that higher pay attracts a higher caliber of personnel to the public service is generally accepted in America, and undoubtedly this belief is accurate as applied to career civil servants. There is no objective evidence, however, that the theory holds true of state legislators.

Table 5.1

Apportionment of Legislatures: Senate

(As of late 1973)

State	Initial reapportioning agency	Present apportionment by	Year of most recent apportionment	Number of seats	Number of districts	Number of multi-member districts	Largest number of seats in district	Percent deviation in actual v. average population per seat — Greatest +	Greatest −	Average population each seat(a)
Ala.	L	FC	1972(b)	35	35	0	1	0.67	0.72	98,406
Alaska	GB	SC	1972	20	11	2	8	4.3	22.5	15,118
Ariz.	L	L	1971	30	30	0	1	0.4	0.4	59,083
Ark.	B	B	1971	35	35	0	1	2.0	1.49	54,923
Cal.	L	SC	1973	40	40	0	1	1.92	1.02	499,322
Colo.	L	L	1972	35	35	0	1	2.48	0.67	63,129
Conn.	L(c)	B	1971	36	36	0	1	3.9	3.9	84,228
Del.	L	L	1971	21	21	0	1	1.4	0.9	26,100
Fla.	L(c)	L	1972	40	19	14	3	0.62	0.53	169,773
Ga.	L	L	1972	56	56	0	1	2.3	2.0	81,955
Hawaii	B	Con	1968	25	8	7	4	23.5	6.1	9,514(d)
Idaho	L	L	1971(e)	35	35	0	1	8.8	10.6	20,371
Ill.	L(c)	L	1973	59	59	0	1	0.8	0.6	188,372
Ind.	L	L	1972	50	50	0	1	1.7	1.6	103,872
Iowa	L(c)	SC	1972	50	50	0	1	0.0	0.0	56,507
Kan.	L	FC	1972	40	40	0	1	2.56	2.02	56,231
Ky	L	L	1972	38	38	0	1	3.07	3.02	84,791
La.	L	L	1972	39	39	0	1	5.6	8.8	93,415
Me.	L(c)	SC	1972	33	33	0	1	1.52	1.5	30,111
Md.	G	GL	1973	47	47	0	1	5.3	4.7	83,455
Mass.	L	L	1973	40	40	0	1	3.53	3.67	138,493(f)
Mich.	B	SC	1972	38	38	0	1	0.0	0.0	233,753
Minn.	L	FC	1972	67	67	0	1	1.88	1.83	56,870
Miss.	L	L	1973	52	33	10	5	9.6	9.3	41,887
Mo.	B	B	1971	34	34	0	1	4.9	4.9	137,571
Mont.	L	L	1971(e)	50	23	13	6	5.66	5.29	13,888

Nebr.	L	L	1971	49	49	0	1	1.4	1.1	30,280
Nev.	L	L	1973	20	10	3	7	7.7	9.6	24,437
N.H.	L	L	1972	24	24	0	1	3.25	4.0	30,154[g]
N.J.	B	B,SC	1973[h]	40	40	0	1	2.85	1.39	179,278
N.M.	L	L,SC	1972	42	42	0	1	4.85	4.48	24,190
N.Y.	L	L	1971	60	60	0	1	0.9	0.9	304,021
N.C.	L	L	1971	50	27	18	4	6.30	6.89	101,641
N.D.	L	FC	1972(e)	51	38	5	5	8.8	13.1	12,113
Ohio	B	B	1971	33	33	0	1	1.05	0.95	322,788
Okla.	L(c)	L	1971	48	48	0	1	0.5	0.5	53,317
Oregon	L	S,SC	1971	30	30	0	1	1.2	0.7	69,713
Pa.	B	B	1971(e)	50	50	0	1	2.29	2.02	235,949
R.I.	L	L	1966	50	50	0	1	18.6	12.2	17,190
S.C.	L	L	1972	46	16	13	5	3.18	6.75	56,316
S.D.	L(c)	L	1971	35	28	3	5	2.4	3.3	19,035
Tenn.	L	L	1973	33	33	0	1	7.1	7.4	118,914
Texas	L(c)	B	1971	31	31	0	1	2.3	2.2	361,185
Utah	L	L	1972	29	29	0	1	4.64	6.38	36,527
Vt.	L(c)	L	1973(e)	30	13	11	6	8.17	8.48	14,824
Va.	L	FC	1971	40	38	1	3	5.2	4.5	116,212[g]
Wash.	L	FC	1972	49	49	0	1	0.91	0.7	68,428
W. Va.	L	L	1964(e)	34	17	17	2	34.5	31.0	54,718
Wis.	L	L	1972	33	33	0	1	0.71	0.55	133,877
Wyoming	L	L	1971	30	16	9	5	27.9	21.6	11,080

Abbreviations: B—Board of Commission; FC—Federal Court; SC—State Court; G—Governor; Con—Constitution; L—Legislature; S—Secretary of State.

(a) Population figures given are those that were valid at the time of the last legislative apportionment and do not in all cases reflect 1970 census data.

(b) Effective 1974 election.

(c) Constitution or statutes provide for another agent or agency to reapportion if the Legislature is unable to do so.

(d) Average number of registered voters per seat.

(e) Further consideration anticipated in 1974. Idaho by court decree by February 1974.

(f) Based on 1971 special State Decennial Census of state citizens.

(g) Based on civilian or nonstudent population.

(h) Plan enacted in 1973 declared unconstitutional by state appellate court. An appeal is now pending in the State Supreme Court.

Source: The Book of the States, 1974–75.

Table 5.2

Apportionment of Legislatures: House

(As of late 1973)

State	Initial reapportioning agency	Present apportionment by	Year of most recent apportionment	Number of seats	Number of districts	Number of multi-member districts	Largest number of seats in district	Percent deviation in actual v. average population per seat Greatest +	Percent deviation in actual v. average population per seat Greatest −	Average population each seat(a)
Ala.	L	FC	1972(b)	105	105	0	1	1.08	1.15	32,802
Alaska	GB	SC	1972	40	20	8	6	4.3	22.5	7,559
Ariz.	L	L	1971	60	30	30	2	0.4	0.4	29,541
Ark.	B	B	1971	100	84	10	3	6.3	3.1	19,233
Cal.	L	SC	1973	80	80	0	1	1.94	1.90	249,661
Colo.	L	L	1972	65	65	0	1	0.97	1.09	33,993
Conn.	L(c)	B	1971	151	151	0	1	1.0	1.0	20,081
Del.	L	L	1971	41	41	0	1	2.6	2.3	13,368
Fla.	L(c)	L	1972	120	45	24	6	0.2	0.1	56,591
Ga.	L	L	1972(d)	180	128	32	6	4.26	4.79	25,502
Hawaii	B	Con	1968	51	25	19	3	15.3	16.0	4,966(e)
Idaho	L	L	1971(d)	70	35	35	2	8.8	10.6	10,186
Ill.	L(c)	L	1973	177	59	59	3	0.8	0.6	62,791
Ind.	L	L	1972	100	73	20	3	1.0	1.0	51,936
Iowa	L(c)	SC	1972	100	100	0	1	0.0	0.0	28,253
Kan.	L	L	1973	125	125	0	1	6.5	4.8	18,223
Ky.	L	L	1972	100	100	0	1	3.1	3.9	32,193
La.	L	L	1972	105	105	0	1	4.6	4.6	34,697
Me.	L	L	1964(d)	151	114	15	11	68.8	38.6	6,229
Md.	G	GL	1973	141	57	46	3	5.3	4.7	27,818
Mass.	L	L	1973	240	240	0	1	9.94	9.06(f)	23,232(g)
Mich.	B	SC	1972	110	110	0	1	0.0	0.0	80,751
Minn.	L	FC	1972	134	134	0	1	1.99	1.97	28,404
Miss.	L	L	1973	122	46	34	12	9.9	9.8	17,854
Mo.	B	SC	1971	163	163	0	1	1.2	1.3	28,696
Mont.	L	L	1971(d)	100	23	23	12	8.63	5.28	6,943

State			Year							Population[a]
Nebr.	U	U								
Nev.	L	L	1973	40	40	0	1	10.9	12.1	12,218
Nev.	L	L	1971	400	159	109	11	25.3	19.3	1,813(h)
N.H.	L	L	1971	400	159	109	11	25.3	19.3	1,813(h)
N.J.	B	B, SC	1973(i)	80	40	40	2	2.85	1.39	89,639
N.M.	L	L, SC	1972	70	70	0	1	4.92	4.95	14,514
N.Y.	L	L	1971	150	150	0	1	1.8	1.6	121,608
N.C.	L	L	1971	120	45	35	8	8.2	10.2	42,350
N.D.	L	FC	1972(d)		38	38	10	8.8	13.1	6,056
Ohio	B	B	1971	99	99	0	1	1.05	0.95	107,596
Okla.	L(c)	L	1971	101	101	0	1	1.0	1.2	25,338
Ore.	L	S, SC	1971	60	60	0	1	1.33	0.88	34,856
Pa.	B	B	1971	203	203	0	1	2.98	2.48	58,115
R.I.	L	L	1966(d)	100	100	0	1	18.6	9.7	8,595
S.C.	L	L	1973	124	28	26	12	7.26	5.93	20,891
S.D.	L(c)	L	1971	70	28	28	10	2.4	3.3	9,516
Tenn.	L	L	1973	99	99	0	1	2.0	1.6	39,638
Texas	L	B, FC	1971	150	128	9	9	5.8	4.1	74,645
Utah	L	L	1972	75	75	0	1	6.72	5.95	14,124
Vt.	L(c)	L	1965(d)	150	52	36	15	11.5	14.3	1,395
Va.	L	L	1972	100	49	28	7	9.6	6.8	46,485
Wash.	L	FC	1972	98	36	49	2	0.91	0.7	34,214(h)
W. Va.	L	L	1973	100		25	13	8.17	8.01	17,442
Wis.	L	L	1972	99	99	0	1	0.96	0.93	44,626
Wyo.	L	L	1971	62	23	12	11	41.16	45.47	5,362

Abbreviations: B—Board or Commission; FC—Federal Court; SC—State Court; G—Governor; Con—Constitution; L—Legislature; S—Secretary of State, U—Unicameral Legislature.

(a) Population figures given are those that were valid at the time of the last legislative apportionment and do not in all cases reflect 1970 census data.

(b) Effective 1974 election.

(c) Constitution or statutes provide for another agent or agency to reapportion if the Legislature is unable to do so.

(d) Further consideration anticipated in 1974. Idaho by court decree by February 1974.

(e) Average number of registered voters per seat.

(f) This figure excludes two geographical island districts whose deviations are −73.5 and −81.77.

(g) Based on 1971 special State Decennial Census of state citizens.

(h) Based on civilian or nonstudent population.

(i) Plan enacted in 1973 declared unconstitutional by state appellate court. An appeal is now pending in the State Supreme Court.

Source: The Book of the States, 1974–75.

In any event, as Table 5.3 shows, some legislators are well paid by anybody's standards. As of January 1975, New York's legislators saw fit to give themselves the highest biennial salaries in the nation—$47,000. California awarded its law-makers with biennial salaries of $42,400, and was followed in descending order by Illinois, Michigan, and Pennsylvania. At the bottom end of the scale stood New Hampshire, where the biennial salary of a legislator was $200. It is probably true that New York's legislators, collectively, carry more responsibility in absolute terms than those of New Hampshire. But surely no one would seriously contend that New York's legislators, as individuals, were twenty-five times more effective than those of New Hampshire. In addition, Table 5.3 is worthy of examination in terms of comparative retirement payments.

State senators and representatives, like members of Congress, enjoy immunity from arrest while in attendance at sessions and while going to and from sessions, except in cases of treason, felony, or breach of the peace. They are accorded freedom of speech and debate in their own respective chambers.

As would be expected, the terms and tenure of legislators vary according to the chamber and the particular state legislature. Most states set the term of senator at four years and representative at two years. In unicameral Nebraska, which terms its chamber the senate, the term is fixed at two years.

It was noted earlier in this chapter that legislative turnover is substantial, and also that it varies considerably from state to state. The authoritative figures on this subject are compiled by the Council of State Governments. Table 5.4 shows the results of a study based on the returns for 1971—1972.

Background of the Legislators

From time to time, studies have been made of the occupational backgrounds of the nearly eight thousand state legislators in the nation. The results are not unexpected. Lawyers, farmers, and business owners are heavily represented in state legislatures, presumably because they have a good deal of control over their working hours. Women are represented much more heavily in the New England and western states than in the rest of the country. It is extremely important, it appears, to have been born in the district one represents or to have lived there for very many years. More than three-quarters of the legislators

Table 5.3
Legislative Salaries and Retirement Systems
(As of late 1973)

State or other jurisdiction	Compensation set by	Regular sessions			Other income			Retirement	
		Per diem		Salary (biennial total)	Special sessions		Committee business, amount per day	Retirement system—type	Membership—type
		Amount per day	Limit on days		Amount per day	Limit on days			
Ala.	C	$10	36L	......	$10	36L	$25	None	
Alaska	L			$18,000				PE	Op
Ariz.	C;CC	20		12,000	6	None(b)		PE	Cm
Ark.	C		60C(a)	2,400			25	PE(c)	Cm
Cal.	L			38,400(d)				SL	Op
Colo.	L			15,200	30	20C	35(e)	PE	Op
Conn.	C			13,000	25(f)	None		SL	Op
Del.	C			12,000				PE	Cm
Fla.	L			24,000	25	None	25	(g)	(g)
Ga.	L			14,400				PE	Cm
Hawaii	L;CC			24,000				PE	Op
Idaho	L;CC	10	60C		10	20C	25	PE	Cm
Ill.	L			35,000				SL	Op
Ind.	L			12,000	25	30L		None	
Iowa	L		None(i)	11,000(h)	40	None	40	None	
Kan.	L	10			10	None	10	PE	Op
Ky.	L	25	60L(j)		25	None	25	PE	Cm
La.	L	50	60C(i)		50	30C	50	PE	Op
Me.	L			3,500	25	None	25	PE	Op
Md.	CC			22,000			25	SL	Op
Mass.	L			25,376				PE	Op
Mich.	CC			34,000				SL	Op
Minn.	L			16,800				SL	Op
Miss.	L			10,000	22.50(k)	None	22.50	PE	Cm(l)

Table 5.3—*Continued*

State or other jurisdiction	Compensation set by	Regular sessions			Other income			Retirement	
		Per diem		Salary (biennial total)	Special sessions		Committee business, amount per day	Retirement system—type	Membership—type
		Amount per day	Limit on days		Amount per day	Limit on days			
Mo.	L	…	…	16,800	…	…	…	PE	Cm
Mont.	L;CC	20	60L	…	20	None	20	PE	Op
Nebr.	C;L	…	…	9,600	…	…	…	None	Cm
Nev.	L	60	60L	…	60	20L	25(m)	SL	Cm
N.H.	C	…	…	200	3	15L	…	None	…
N.J.	C;L	…	…	20,000	…	…	…	PE;SL	Cm
N.M.	C;L	36	60C(i)	…	36	30C	36	PE(c)	Op
N.Y.	C;L	…	…	30,000(h)	…	…	…	PE(n)	Op
N.C.	L	…	…	4,800	…	…	…	SL	Cm
N.D.	C	5	…	…	5	None	30	None	…
Ohio	L	…	60L	28,000(h)	…	…	…	None	…
Okla.	CB	…	…	18,960	…	…	25(o)	PE	Cm
Ore.	L	…	…	9,600	…	…	…	None	…
Pa.	L	…	…	31,200	…	…	…	PE	Op
R.I.	C	5	60L	…	…	…	…	PE(c)	Op
S.C.	L	100	40L	…	100	40L	25	SL	Cm
S.D.	L	…	…	5,000	67.67	None	25	None	…
Tenn.	L	…	…	11,030(p)	…	…	…	PE	Op
Texas	C	…	…	9,600	…	…	…	SL	Op
Utah	C;L	25	60C(i)	…	25	30C	25	SL	Op
Vt.	L	30	(q)	…	…	…	30	None	…
Va.	L	…	…	10,950	…	…	…	PE	Cm
Wash.	L	…	…	7,200(h)	…	…	…	SL	Op

State	Authority			Salary					
W. Va.	CC;L	..		6,000	35	None	35(m)	SL	Op
Wis.	(r)	15		19,800(h)	..	..	..	PE	Op
Wyo.	L	..	(s)	....	15	None	15	None	..
Am. Samoa	C;L	..		12,000	..	..	..	PE	Op
Guam	L	..		24,128	..	..	..	PE	Op
P.R.	L	..		19,200	..	..	..	PE	Cm
Virgin Is.	L	..		18,000	..	..	..	PE	Op

Abbreviations: C—Constitution; L—Legislation; CC—Compensation Commission; CB—Constitutional Board; SL—Special Legislative; Op—Optional; Cm—Compulsory.

(a) Daily pay continues if session extended by 2/3 vote in both houses.
(b) Legislature may not remain in session more than 15 days after disposing of matters in governor's call.
(c) Special provisions for legislators.
(d) Effective 2 December 1974; $42,400.
(e) $35 per day for committee attendance up to $1,050 maximum. Joint Budget Committee members have a $3,500 maximum for budget committee attendance in addition to $1,050 maximum.
(f) For each day beyond the ninth day.
(g) Legislators may choose to join the compulsory statewide public employee pension system or the optional statewide public employee pension system or the optional (elected officers class) special legislative retirement system.
(h) Effective January 1975. Iowa: $1600; New York: $47,000; Ohio: $35,000; Washington: $7,600 for members elected in 1974. Wisconsin: $31,362.
(i) Limit on first session; second session limitation: Kansas 60C days unless extended by 2/3 vote of all members; Louisiana 30C; New Mexico 30C; Utah 20C.
(j) Legislators are paid for Sundays and holidays during sessions. Thus compensation period usually is 72 to 74 days.
(k) Paid for seven days per week while in session.
(l) Unless over age 65.
(m) Applicable to members of certain committees only. West Virginia: payable only to members of Joint Committee on Government and Finance and Commission on Interstate Cooperation to a limit of $1,050 per year.
(n) Repealed for all legislators elected after 1 July 1973.
(o) For 20 days.
(p) Income will be adjusted annually on July 1 to correspond to the percentage of change in the per capita personal income in the State for the preceding fiscal year.
(q) Paid at $150 per week during session to a maximum of $4,500 for biennium.
(r) Beginning with the 1975 session, legislative salaries will be set according to salary ranges determined by the Bureau of Personnel.
(s) The Legislature is limited to meeting no more than 40L days in the odd year out of 60L days during the biennium. The legislators are paid on a calendar day basis.
Source: The Book of the States, 1974–75.

Table 5.4

Membership Turnover in the Legislatures: Number of New Members in the Legislature as a Percentage of Total Number of Seats up for Election, 1971 and 1972

	Senate			House		
	Number of seats up for election	Number of membership changes	Percent	Number of seats up for election	Number of membership changes	Percent
U.S. Total	1,370	587	43	5,334	2,042	38
Ala.	No Election			No Election		
Alaska	10*	8	80	40	19	48
Ariz.	30	11	37	60	18	30
Ark.	35	7	20	100	32	32
Cal.	20*	3	15	80	17	21
Colo.	18*	6	33	65	27	42
Conn.	36	15	42	151	61	40
Del.	11*	9	82	41	20	49
Fla.	40	17	43	120	52	43
Ga.	56	13	23	180	42	23
Hawaii	No Election			51	8	16
Idaho	35	12	34	70	27	39
Ill.	59	23	39	177	57	32
Ind.	25*	15	60	100	48	48
Iowa	50	30	60	100	63	63
Kan.	40	17	43	125	48	38
Ky.	19*	13	68	100	42	42
La.	39	20	51	105	71	68
Me.	33	16	49	151	64	42
Md.	No Election			No Election		
Mass.	40	13	33	240	67	28
Mich.	No Election			110	28	25
Minn.	No Election			135	54	40
Miss.	52	24	46	122	47	30
Mo.	17*	7	41	163	70	43
Mont.	34*	11	32	100	39	39
Nebr.	25*	12	48	Unicameral Legislature		
Nev.	10*	6	60	40	21	53
N.H.	24	11	46	400	172	43
N.J.	40	21	53	80	47	59
N.M.	34*	17	50	70	15	21
N.Y.	60	19	32	150	46	31
N.C.	50	26	52	120	50	42
N.D.	25*	16	64	98	36	37
Ohio	17*	10	59	99	39	39
Okla.	24*	9	38	101	31	31
Ore.	15*	8	53	60	28	47
Pa.	25*	10	40	203	45	22
R.I.	50	12	24	100	38	38
S.C.	46	16	35	124	51	41
S.D.	35	10	28	70	22	31
Tenn.	17*	4	24	99	39	39
Texas	31	15	48	150	79	53
Utah	29	12	41	75	39	57

Table 5.4—*Continued*

	Senate			House		
	Number of seats up for election	*Number of membership changes*	*Percent*	*Number of seats up for election*	*Number of membership changes*	*Percent*
Vt.	30	8	17	150	55	30
Va.	40	17	43	100	41	41
Wash.	25*	10	40	98	32	33
W. Va.	17*	14	82	100	39	39
Wis.	17*	7	41	99	31	31
Wyo.	15*	7	47	62	25	40

* Entire Senate not up for election.

Source: The Council of State Governments, *State Elective Officials and the Legislatures*, 1971 and 1973.

have had some college education, a figure far above the national average. Legislatures tend to reflect the religious makeup of the general population: the Georgia legislature is dominated by Baptists and Methodists, while the legislatures of Connecticut, Rhode Island, and New Jersey contain substantial Catholic representation.

In his superb study of the recruitment of freshmen legislators in Connecticut, James David Barber throws additional light on the characteristics of legislators.[5] For the sake of convenience, he divides the legislators whom he interviewed into these categories: the Spectators (who simply watch what goes on), the Advertisers (who are in the legislature for public relations purposes, and of whom many are young attorneys), the Reluctants (who really do not wish to be there in the first place, but who have been drafted by the party officials), and the Lawmakers (who have a genuine interest in passing laws and in mastering the legislative process). What is of outstanding interest in Barber's study is the difficulty in recruiting candidates encountered by parties in such a strongly party-oriented state as Connecticut. The percentage of Reluctants, or draftees, turned out to be amazingly high, and they gave every indication of intending to retire after one term of office.

Duration of Legislative Sessions

Over the years, the general public has shown its relative distrust of state legislatures by enacting constitutional limitations on their sessions and the duration of such sessions. Early in the life of the nation, the annual session was normal.

But by the beginning of the present century most states had adopted a biennial plan. In recent years, there has been some trend toward returning to annual sessions. In addition, most states limit the duration of each session in order to prevent the legislators from engaging in mischief.

But those limitations are often self-defeating, with the result that it is usually provided that special sessions may be called, usually by the governor, in case of an emergency. By use of this device, many more annual sessions of state legislatures are in fact held than would appear to be the case from the constitutional provisions alone. Even so, in most states a legislature called in special session may consider only such subjects as are presented to it by the governor.

LEGISLATIVE ORGANIZATION

Any legislative body requires a formal structure, including officers, committees, and various kinds of service personnel. The task of organizing the legislature is usually left to the majority party. In some states, the party leaders are in charge of the essentials of the legislative process.

Officers

In all states except Nebraska, the presiding officer of the lower house is the Speaker. (In unicameral Nebraska, the sole chamber is called the senate and is presided over by the lieutenant governor). The Speaker is chosen by vote of the total membership, but ordinarily this merely means ratification of a decision already taken by a caucus of the majority party.

But it is not always so cut and dried, for forces inside the majority party may operate at cross purposes. An illustration comes from the selection of a speaker in the Pennsylvania House of Representatives in January 1975. But the story begins earlier.

In the Democratic primary in the spring of 1974, a Philadelphia Democrat, Representative Martin P. Mullen, ran for governor against incumbent Democratic Governor Milton J. Shapp. He did so on an antiabortion platform, and he was strongly endorsed by John Cardinal Krol of Philadelphia, then presiding officer of the United States Conference of Catholic Bishops. Mullen had, in addition to official Catholic support, assistance from Philadelphia's Democratic Mayor Frank L. Rizzo (who had supported the reelection of Richard Nixon in 1972). In the House itself, Mullen held one of the key positions, for he was chairman of the powerful Appropriations Committee. From this vantage point, he was able to sponsor financial aid to parochial schools and to offer legislation aimed at circumventing the decisions on abortion rendered by the United States Supreme Court in *Roe* v. *Wade* (410 U.S. 113; 1974), and *Doe* v. *Bolton* (410 U.S. 179; 1973).

Governor Shapp won the nomination of his party and was reelected to the governorship in November 1974. The arena of intra-Democratic party battles then shifted to the floor of the House of Representatives. Because of his defection in the primary, Mullen had been removed by his party's leadership as chairman of the Appropriations Committee. Yet he still had powerful allies, and used them to support his candidacy for House Speaker. In this battle, he was opposed by another Philadelphia Democrat, Representative Herbert Fineman, a pro-Shapp, anti-Rizzo Democrat who enjoyed the backing of Philadelphia's Democratic City Committee Chairman Peter J. Camiel.

Under the rules, 102 votes were required to elect a Speaker. Fineman managed to muster 109 votes to 93 for Mullen. Glad to help the Democrats ruin themselves, the Republican leaders enthusiastically urged their followers to support Mullen. There were 89 Republicans in the House, but 9 of them refused to follow the leadership and voted for Fineman. For this reason, Fineman was able to achieve the necessary total for victory.

The results were generally regarded as a win for Camiel and a defeat for Rizzo. Fineman's election was also a victory, of course, for Governor Shapp. For his defection, Mullen paid a substantial price. Upon his removal from his chairmanship, Mullen lost his staff of eight members, who were fired by Philadelphia Representative Stephen Wojdak, the man named by Fineman to replace Mullen as head of the House Appropriations Committee. Mullen was removed from his spacious, mahogany-paneled fifth-floor capitol office to a tiny cubicle on the first floor that he had to share with another legislator. They also shared the services of a solitary secretary.

For all practical purposes, Mullen had been thrown out of the Philadelphia Democratic party by City Committee Chairman Camiel. Mullen took his misfortunes philosophically. He declared: "When you lose at this game, you really come all the way down. You really pay the penalty when you lose, but that's the way the game is played."[6] As an aside, it may be noted most of the antiabortion and proparochial school legislation sponsored by Mullen was eventually either vetoed by the governor, declared unconstitutional in the courts, or both.

In Pennsylvania, as in most other states, the official presiding officer of the senate is the lieutenant governor. But the real power ordinarily resides in the office of the president pro tempore, who is chosen by the majority caucus and then elected by vote of the entire chamber. In contrast to the 1975 election of the Speaker of the House in Pennyslvania, the election of the president pro tempore was conventional. Senator Martin L. Murray, from Luzerne County, was unanimously reelected.

Committees

All legislative bodies in America—at national, state, and local levels—work through a system of standing committees. The objective, of course, is to achieve a degree of specialization in the handling of bills and statutes. In practically every state legislature, there is some kind of a "leadership committee," which assumes the general responsibility for organizing the chamber and for guiding its procedure. The average legislator serves as a rule on three or more committees, which could mean that his or her efforts are spread rather thinly.

When the regular committees of the two chambers are not in agreement regarding the details of a proposed statute, it is provided that a conference committee be appointed by the leadership of each house. It is here that final concurrence is sought. Ordinarily, the recommendations of conference committees are accepted by the respective chambers without extended debate. On the other hand, a conference committee also may serve as a useful way of killing a proposal that nobody really liked in the first place but had to support publicly for party or public relations purposes.

Facilities for Legislators

Legislators need all the technical and professional help they can get. Recognizing this, many states have adopted substantial facilities to aid in the legislative process. Unfortunately, many states have not.

Wisconsin pioneered in 1901 when it established the first

legislative reference library. Nearly all the other states have followed suit.

To draft a bill properly is a highly technical endeavor. Anyone can be in favor of "welfare reform," for example, but very few people in the United States can draft bills on the subject that will, if passed, be amenable to successful administration and stand up in the courts. Because of this situation, most of the states now provide assistance to legislators in bill drafting, usually through the legislative reference service or the attorney general's office.

In this respect, California has set standards which other states could emulate with profit. The legislature maintains a sizable staff of lawyers and clerks who are available day and night (including weekends) to draft bills and to offer informed estimates as to their constitutionality. There is a legislative analyst with forty or so assistants who work with the joint budget committee in an effort to bring the governor's budget in line with the legislative program. There is also a legislative bill room, which provides each member with a copy of every bill, including the latest amendments and the history to date of the bill's progress. In California, a legislator does not have a very good excuse for not knowing what he or she is voting on.

It is the same with staff and facilities for individual members. In California, each legislator has a modern office suite and a full-time secretary. But in most states, legislators' "offices" are likely to be their hotel rooms, and their secretaries are probably stenographers on temporary loan from stenographic pools. On the other hand, the party leadership in nearly all states makes sure that it enjoys both offices and secretarial services. It is the individual legislator who is at a disadvantage.

Bills Before the Legislature

The handling of bills in state legislatures is roughly parallel to the procedure used in Congress. There is therefore no need to go into the subject in great detail. For persons who wish, on the other hand, to learn the precise methods used in their own states, there is available a legislative manual which explains the procedures. For persons who only wish a general review of the process, a useful source of information is the legislative guide published in most states by the League of Women Voters.

When a bill has cleared both chambers, it is subject to action by the governor. In all states except North Carolina, a bill is subject to the governor's veto. Though essentially a negative power, the veto is nonetheless a very potent legislative weapon. In all states, some method is provided by which the legislature may override the governor's veto. In some cases, a two-thirds vote of the total membership of each house is required. In other cases, a two-thirds vote of members present is all that is required. Except for Connecticut, all states require a vote larger than a simple majority to override a veto.

In contrast to the situation in which the president of the United States finds himself, governors in the vast majority of the states possess what is called an item veto. This means that the governor may veto a specific item in an appropriations bill. In some states, the governor has the authority to reduce an item. The item veto is exercised widely and vigorously by those governors whose states confer on them this power. Viewed within the framework of checks and balances, it is obvious that a governor is often in a better position to resist interest groups by using the item veto than is the legislature. The reason for this is that legislators, responding to the demands of powerful interest groups, may vote appropriations with the almost certain knowledge that these appropriations will be vetoed. In this way a legislator's relations with an interest group are protected, and the general interest of the state may also be served.

The Initiative and the Referendum

As part of the progressive movement of the last decade of the nineteenth century and the first two decades of the present one, there developed in a number of states devices intended to "give government to the people." Under the initiative, the voters may take the leadership in drafting bills. With the so-called direct initiative, the proposal, if it has the required number of signatures, will be put directly before the electorate in the next general election. Under the indirect initiative, the proposal goes to the legislature. If passed, that is the end of the matter. If the legislature balks, there is usually a mechanism whereby the question can be voted on by the entire electorate.

The term referendum refers to the practice authorized in some states whereby a proposed statute is submitted by the legislature to the electorate for approval or disapproval. As one would expect, there is a good deal of variety in the actual mechanics in the different states.

In essence, a referendum gives a legislature a chance to avoid action on a highly emotional issue—such as the use of contraceptive devices in Massachusetts—by referring the question to a popular vote. In this fashion, the legislature is taken off the hook. From the point of view of traditional democratic theory, the legislature is also abrogating its responsibility when it does this. It is a kind of plebiscitary democracy that is the opposite of representative government. Yet the constitutions of some twenty-two states authorize the use of referenda with regard to ordinary statutes.

LEGISLATIVE IMPROVEMENT

Some of the methods by which legislative performance could be improved have been implied in the foregoing analysis. They would include efforts to avoid the rush and confusion that usually occurs at the end of a session, improvement in the structure of committees, and an expansion in supporting staffs. Some political scientists would add to this list an increased degree of party responsibility, although the proposition is open to debate. Nearly everyone would agree that a greater degree of public interest in the legislature is desirable.

One expert on state legislatures, Karl T. Kurtz, has listed seven themes in the movement for legislative improvement in recent years.[7] In capsule form, they are as follows:

1. The reapportionment revolution has resulted in a new generation of legislators whose characteristics more accurately reflect the urban population.

2. Lengthened sessions of legislatures are tending to increase legislative power in relation to the executive branch.

3. Sustained efforts have been made to streamline legislative rules and procedures.

4. Legislators have received substantial pay increases during the last decade, although much remains to be done.

5. The addition of fiscal staff has improved the ability of legislatures to make independent judgments of the taxing and spending by state governments.

6. A major emerging trend has been the expansion of professional staff to the standing committees.

7. Legislatures appear to be placing more emphasis on overseeing the performance of the executive branch. In this

respect, the state legislatures are taking their lead from Congress, which for decades has considered legislative oversight of administration one of its most important obligations.

Dr. Kurtz spells out the evidence for each of these propositions, and the evidence is convincing. What these trends amount to is a regeneration of state legislatures.

From a historical perspective, the basic factors which have led to renewed vigor of state governments in the last several years have also had their impact on the state legislatures. These factors are the greater financial security of the states, revenue sharing by the federal government, and the general conviction that too much power has gravitated toward Washington so that a reverse flow is desirable.

Items for Discussion

1. Is unicameralism one of those proposals that interests only academics? What does this tell us about its chances for adoption? What are some other governmental reforms strongly supported by the academic community but receiving little support from those in political office?

2. Can you make a case for legislative apportionment in which the districts vary by as much as 10 percent from the population norm?

3. Compile a profile of your state legislator in which you attempt to fit him or her into one of the categories suggested by James David Barber.

4. Discuss the major issues currently being debated by your state legislature. What is the general level of public awareness concerning state government?

5. Plan, in detail, how you might proceed to "initiate" action at the state level.

Chapter Notes

At the outset, attention is drawn to three standard books dealing with the legislative process in the United States. They are as follows: George S. Blair, *American Legislatures: Structure and Process* (New York: Harper & Row, 1967); Malcolm E. Jewell and Samuel C. Patterson, *The Legislative Process in the United States* (New York: Random House, 1966); and William J. Keefe and Morris S. Ogul, *The American Legislative Process: Congress and the States* (Englewood Cliffs, N.J.: Prentice-Hall, 1968).

1. Hugh A. Bone, "Notes on Legislative Improvement," *Washington Policy Notes*, Vol. 1, No. 4 (Oct. 1973).

2. See Kenneth T. Palmer, *State Politics in the United States* (New York: St. Martin's Press, 1972), pp. 64–67.

3. Lloyd B. Omdahl, "Drive for Unicameralism Needs National Support," Vol. 63, No. 10 *National Civic Review* (Nov. 1974), pp. 526–530.

4. *Ibid.*, p. 526.

5. James David Barber, *The Lawmakers* (New Haven: Yale University Press, 1965).

6. *Philadelphia Inquirer*, 9 Jan. 1975.

7. Karl T. Kurtz, "The State Legislatures," in *The Book of the States, 1974–1975* (Lexington, Ky.: The Council of State Governments, 1974), pp. 53–65.

6

Governors and State Administrative Systems

Key Terms

Commutation: Gubernatorial power to reduce a criminal punishment, making it less severe.

Hoover Commission: Appointed first in 1947 to study the organization of the national executive branch. Proposed greater consolidation of agencies and greater executive authority. Inspired the creation of similar "little Hoover commissions" in about twenty-five states.

Impeachment: A formal accusation by a lower house of a legislature that commits an individual (e.g., the governor) for trial in the upper house. Articles of impeachment are drawn up, setting the basis for removal from office.

Jacksonian Democracy: Political and social changes in the American system which resulted from the presidency of Andrew Jackson; included expanded suffrage, spoils system, and long ballot.

National Guard: Volunteer armed forces of the states, formerly called the *militia*. Each governor is commander in chief of his or her state's National Guard; the guard may be called into federal service.

Pardon: Gubernatorial grant of a release from punishment before or after conviction on criminal charges.

Popular recall: Procedure enabling voters to remove an elected official from office; used in twelve states.

Reprieve: Gubernatorial power to postpone the execution of a sentence for humanitarian reasons or to await new evidence.

Short ballot: Provides for the popular election of only a few government officials, while allowing the governor broad appointive power.

"In the past several decades governors have moved from low visibility and low activity to positions of more positive executive leadership within the states and the nation."[1] So observes J. Oliver Williams in an essay on changing perspectives on the American governor. It is Williams's thesis that "...the governor is the prime mover of significant politics and administration at the state level and that much of intergovernmental politics can be interpreted through the gubernatorial role."[2] This is to say not only that the governor plays a pivotal role in state politics, but that the governor also increasingly operates as the federal systems officer at the subnational level.

Since such a portrait is a far cry from the traditional picture of the role of the American governor, it is perhaps well to begin with a brief historic summary of the governorship in this country. In the end, Williams's thesis will be sustained. But it comes more sharply into focus when put in some perspective. The following historical summary, which is intended to achieve this objective, is drawn from the definitive study of the states' chief executives published in 1960 by Byron R. Abernethy.[3]

HISTORICAL EVOLUTION OF THE STATE EXECUTIVE

The Colonial Executive

Except for Rhode Island and Connecticut, the executive in the colonies was the local representative of an "absentee government." He was responsible to the British Crown, and his powers were extensive. They included the appointment of civil officers, the enforcement of laws, the granting of pardons and reprieves, serving as head of the highest court in the colony, and the power to adjourn legislative assemblies and to recommend and veto colonial legislation. In short, the principal characteristic of colonial government was executive supremacy. So far as the colonists were concerned, their only check upon the executive lay in the legislature's control over appropriations. In most cases this control included the determination of the governor's salary.

The Original or Revolutionary State Governments, 1776-1789

After the Declaration of Independence, the former colonies began at once to establish the first American state governments. In doing so, they reflected and reacted against the colonial experience. The new governments replaced executive supremacy with legislative supremacy.

In the newly created states, the governor was only a figurehead. Usually he was elected by the legislature, and his power was subject to the legislature. For example, he had little executive or political power. He had practically no veto power. Important appointments were made by the legislature. It was common practice for the legislature to establish executive councils for the purpose of keeping the governor under firm control. The general rule called for a one-year term of office, without eligibility for reelection.

Growing Power of the Executive, 1789-1850

As Abernethy notes, the adoption of the Constitution of the United States in 1789 marked the start of a new trend in the position of the state executive. Under the new Constitution, the executive branch was relatively strong, and it was made stronger by the influence of the federalist leaders. This example of balanced government had a spin-off effect on the states. This, plus the declining public confidence in state legislatures, further influenced the position of the state executive.

As a consequence, the governor, during the early part of the nineteenth century, was liberated from legislative domination. By about 1850, he had come to represent a coordinate, as opposed to subordinate, branch of the state government. In all but a few states, the governor was now elected by popular vote, instead of being chosen by the legislature. Furthermore, the term of office was extended, and executive councils were abandoned. In most states, the governor's position was additionally enhanced by a qualified power of veto. Some state consitutions specified the governor's salary, to remove temptation from the legislative branch to tamper with it.

But this is not the whole story. Even though the executive department gained its freedom from legislative domination, it was at the same time weakened through internal divisions. The culprit was Jacksonian Democracy. Although this doctrine led to the popular election of the governor, it also eventually decreed the popular election of the governor's subordinates. In short, the power to appoint administrative officials, which had been taken from the legislature, was transferred not to the governor but to the electorate.

With the popular election of such officials as lieutenant governor, secretary of state, state treasurer, state auditor, the superintendent of public instruction, and judicial officials, state administration tended to become a virtual fourth branch of government. Largely independent of executive or legislative control, state administration developed a momentum of its own, although it was supposed to be directly responsible to the people.

Growing Power of Governor, Enhancement and Diffusion of Administration, 1850-1917

After 1850, the power of the governor was increased in various ways. He became the leader of the majority party in the state, which tended to increase his authority in the legislature. He gained, in many states, the item veto, which enhanced his power over finances. He was accorded the power to call state legislatures into special session and to deliver special messages. Often, the principal leadership in the formulation of public policy came from the governor's mansion.

But other forces were also at work. The trend toward more independent administrators elected directly by the people continued. Another influence on the state executive was the creation of numerous regulatory agencies, for example, public utilities commissions. Whether created by legislative action or through state constitutions, what these agencies had in common was their independence from the governor. In fact, the agencies were normally independent of the legislature as well. Some states went so far as to provide for popular election of members of boards, commissions, or agencies, thus making them totally independent from both the executive and the legislature.

As Abernethy puts it, "The end result of all this evolution

by the early twentieth century was the typical state executive department, provided for in state constitutions and statutory law. It was multiheaded, with no unity of command or centralized control over the state's administrative structure."[4] In brief, there was a good deal of government, but little governing. Authority was distributed in such a way as to be largely ineffectual. And, as Woodrow Wilson repeatedly pointed out, the result was to create an atmosphere of irresponsibility which worked against the general public interest and for various private interests.

To create some order out of chaos, Wilson and others advocated plans whereby only the very highest officials would be elected. Lesser officials would be appointed by the chief officials. Apparently, the movement for administrative reorganization got into high gear in Oregon in 1909 or 1910 with a proposal of the People's Power League to concentrate executive power in the hands of the governor. Between 1911 and 1919, some twenty-seven states instituted studies aimed at suggesting ways and means for promoting efficiency and economy in state administration.

But only one study produced concrete and positive results. This was the report of the Illinois Efficiency and Economy Committee, whose recommendations for consolidation were embodied in the Illinois Civil Administrative Code of 1917. This code, which served as a model, was the first comprehensive plan of state administrative reorganization to be placed in effect. Though strictly a legislative reorganization—it did not affect those constitutional officers who shared power with the governor—it did manage to abolish more than a hundred statutory offices, boards, and commissions. The functions of these agencies were consolidated into nine major departments, which in turn were brought clearly under the control of the governor. Each department was headed by a single director, appointed by and directly responsible to the governor. In addition, the executive budget was improved, and a uniform accounting system and centralized purchasing were provided for.

In time, other states followed the example of Illinois. Acting under constitutional authority given it a year earlier, the legislature of New York in 1926 consolidated 180 existing administrative agencies into 18 departments. Most of them were brought directly under the control of the governor. Massachusetts and Virginia also shortly thereafter joined the increasing ranks of state governments which reorganized their administrative operations through centralization under gubernatorial control.

Current Trends

Though it required several decades for fulfillment, Wilson's recommendations for centralized state administration, which he first called for in 1887 and reiterated in 1910, have been accepted in a large number of states. Of more immediate application has been the *Model State Constitution* of the National Municipal League, which spells out in some detail how to achieve these objectives. In particular, the constitutions of the most recently created states, of Hawaii and Alaska, reflect the kind of thinking embodied in the *Model State Constitution.* The main point is to vest the executive power of the state in the governor, and at the same time to limit the total number of executive departments to a manageable number. There is every reason to believe that these trends will continue.

THE GOVERNOR

As we have seen, the position of governor has been immensely strengthened in the last century and a half. The pivotal consideration, of course, is the governor's control over the apparatus of state administration. But certain other qualifications for and attributes of the governorship, though varying from state to state, need amplification. In the following paragraphs, the emphasis is placed upon the gubernatorial powers and obligations from a contemporary point of view.

Qualifications, Term, and Compensation

The constitutions of most states prescribe certain qualifications for a governor. Usually, these relate to age, citizenship, and length of residence in the state. Ordinarily, the minimum-age requirement is thirty years. United States citizenship is universally required. In most states, there is a prescribed period of residence in the state, varying from one to ten years.

Most of these requirements are either obvious or superfluous. No one seriously expects that a native of Vermont, newly

Governor Edmund G. Brown of California. (Wide World Photos.)

resident in Alabama, could be elected governor in the latter state. On occasion, however, the courts have intervened and have upheld rigorously the residential requirement. Practically speaking, the principal qualification is the potential vote-gathering ability of a potential candidate. Very long residence in a state and—as V.O. Key put it in another connection—a great many friends and neighbors are indispensable.

Though the figures change from time to time, the term of office of the governor stood in a recent count at four years in thirty-five states and two years in the remaining fifteen. The trend has been toward the longer term. In about half the states with a four-year term, the incumbent governor is ineligible for a second consecutive term. What this probably reflects is the historic, if ambivalent, distrust of executive power, a carry-over from Jacksonian Democracy, which is also embedded at the federal level in the Twenty-second Amendment of the United States Constitution.

In terms of monetary compensation for services rendered, the states vary a good deal in their treatment of governors. As of late 1973, according to *The Book of the States, 1974–1975*, the lowest annual gubernatorial salary was that in Arkansas, where the salary was $10,000. The highest salary for a governor was paid by New York, where the figure was $85,000. Next in line came Texas, at $63,000, and Pennsylvania, at $60,000 (as of 1 January 1975). The average compensation hovered around $35,000. Of course, many states provide the governor with an official residence, and there are often generous allowances for entertainment and related expenses. Nonetheless, by the standards of American corporation executives, the chief executives of the states are clearly underpaid.

Nomination, Election, and Removal

In all states (except where the challenge primary is in effect), gubernatorial candidates are now by law nominated by primaries. Election is by direct popular vote.

With the exception of Oregon, a governor may be removed from office by impeachment. Though this has not often happened, it should be noted that political considerations have ordinarily been paramount when impeachment proceedings have been undertaken. In some twelve states the governor may be removed by popular recall. Yet only one governor—Lynn J. Frazier of North Dakota in 1921—has ever been removed from office by this device.

Powers of the Governor: Appointment and Removal

Even though most state constitutions declare that it is the duty of the governor to see to it that the laws are faithfully executed, the application of this dictum depends upon the degree of control which the governor exercises over his or her subordinates. In turn, this reflects the governor's ability to appoint and to remove lesser officials. In practice, this authority varies widely from state to state, with the strongest gubernatorial position found in those states that have undergone administrative reorganization.

But few states give their governors appointment and removal powers comparable to those given the president. Even in Illinois, for example, the secretary of state, the auditor, and treasurer, the superintendent of public instruction, and the attorney general, along with the governor, are elected. Despite this sharing of powers, the governor of Illinois possesses a tremendous amount of authority. For example, he appoints, with the consent of the senate, the heads of the various statutory departments. Members of various state boards and commission are also in most states appointed by the governor. In most states the governor may fill vacancies in administrative positions, or may make interim appointments which in effect become permanent, as in Pennsylvania.

The variation among state governors in the removal power is likewise extensive. At one extreme, removal may be made only with the consent of the legislature. At the other extreme, as in Illinois, the governor's determination is exclusive and final.

As was noted earlier, the trend is toward increasing the governor's powers in general, and this includes the power of appointment and of removal.

Supervision of Administration

The governor is charged, at least nominally, with the supervision of administration. But here, as elsewhere, there tends to be a large gap between theory and practice. Very few governors have anything resembling the authority given the president of the United States, or his immediate appointees, when it comes to oversight of administrative activities.

On the other hand, in many states the governor's position has been strengthened by the establishment of managerial agencies, especially those associated with finance. For instance, finance departments, budget commissions, and departments of administration—the names vary from state to state—are in reality control mechanisms which the governor may use to bring about some measure of coordination. As state governments become increasingly important in the financial lives of their citizens, the tendency has been to centralize financial control under the governor. In this, of course, the states are merely following the federal pattern established in the second decade of this century.

Military Powers

Like the president, the governor is commander in chief of the armed forces at his or her disposal. Formerly termed the *militia*, the National Guard is headed by the governor, except when it is called into federal service. The powers accorded governors authorize them to call out the guard to execute the laws, to suppress insurrection, and to repel invasion. Ordinarily, these actions will be undertaken only at the request of local law enforcement authorities. But at times the governor may proclaim a state of martial law and use the guard to take over some of the functions usually performed by civil authorities.

In the past, a very common use of the National Guard was to employ it in labor disputes, usually on the side of management. But in recent years, it has been customary for the guard to be mobilized to protect life and property when disasters such as floods or earthquakes strike. In addition to providing protection against looting, the guard now performs a positive role in rescue and relief operations. The role of the guard, in short, has undergone a distinct change in the last two or three decades.

On occasion, the governors have mobilized the guard for purely political, or even trivial, purposes. Are there any limits on a governor's capacity to declare martial rule? The answer is yes. The leading case is *Sterling v. Constantin* (287 U.S. 378; 1932), which arose when Governor Sterling of Texas sought to limit the output of oil wells in certain parts of his state. To do this, he proclaimed that a state of emergency existed in certain oil-producing counties. He then declared martial law, issued orders limiting oil production, and instructed the military authorities to enforce his orders. On appeal, the United States Supreme Court held that the governor had overreached his authority. Since in reality there was no insurrection or violence, there was no military necessity for the governor to use troops to regulate oil production. It was held that the governor's actions constituted an unjustifiable interference with liberty and property in violation of the Fourteenth Amendment of the United States Constitution.

Civil Defense

It is the responsibility of the governor to take the leadership in organizing civil defense, which is usually defined to mean protection of the civil population in case of an armed attack. The basic legislation is the Federal Civil Defense Act, which views civil defense as a joint responsiblity of national, state, and local governments.

During the early 1960s, as various war scares swept the country, some governors became involved in massive fallout shelter programs. The idea was to provide some measure of protection against radioactive fallout and biological warfare. Humorous though the idea now seems, it was taken very seriously in some quarters. Probably the leader in urging each family to dig a shelter and provision it was Nelson Rockefeller, then governor of New York. It was never clear whether he was genuinely afraid of a Soviet attack, or whether he wished to encourage the construction industry. In turn, this obsession with shelters led to some interesting moral speculations. For example, in the manner of medieval theologians, it was passionately debated whether a family did or did not have a moral right to bar persons with no shelters from using the family shelter. Then there was the question of the food supply: who first should be thrown out into the radioactive world and permitted to die either through radioactivity or starvation, whichever came first.

With the ending of the cold war and the beginning of détente with the Soviet Union, the rationale for maintaining substantial civil defense organizations tended to evaporate. For the most part, they have become either paper organizations or have been put to work to deal with floods and other emergencies. In this capacity they have frequently served as a kind of auxiliary to the National Guard and other security forces. The basic distinction is that the civil defense personnel are civilians, even though their leadership may not be.

The Governor and the Legislature

In the preceding chapter, we looked at governors from the perspective of the legislatures. In this chapter we will look briefly at legislatures from the perspective of the governor.

The governor possesses very real legislative powers, which is all for the good since the separation of powers doctrine virtually guarantees a more or less constant state of tension between the governor and the legislature. Some powers and duties are conferred on the governor by constitutional provisions; others are thrust upon the governor's shoulders by the legislature; and certain authority often accrues through personal and political leadership. In a psychological sense, the electorate tends to look upon the governor for leadership in legislative matters. Indeed, in those states with a tradition of strong gubernatorial leadership, such as New York, a very large percentage of new legislation originates from the governor's office.

How is this accomplished? Personal considerations aside, the governor has at his or her disposal certain very powerful instruments. First, in the manner of the president's annual State of the Union message, the chief executive of the states customarily delivers a "state of the state" message at the beginning of the regular legislative session. In these pronouncements, the governor usually comments on the social and economic conditions of the state, offers at least some observations on the state's financial situation, and makes those legislative recommendations that, in his or her judgment, should be dealt with by the session just beginning.

Following the national pattern, in the vast majority of states the governor also delivers, early in the session, a budget message. This is devoted exclusively to financial matters. Its overall importance, however, is that it reveals the general "game plan" of the governor. It is a planning document which sets out the governor's priorities.

Secondly, as well as delivering state messages, the governor in most states is empowered to call the legislature into special session. This is done by the issuance of a proclamation which states the business which the governor wishes the legislature to consider. Of course, the scope of the matters actually dealt with depends on a state's constitution, and practices differ widely. For example, much to their surprise, at least three governors have been impeached and removed from office at special sessions.

Thirdly, in every state except North Carolina the governor possesses the power of veto. While the state constitution always provides a mechanism whereby a state legislative majority may override a governor's veto, this action is very difficult to achieve in practice. For example, a governor who is certain that a bill of which he or she disapproves would survive a veto in any case may choose simply to let the bill become law without the governor's signature. Additionally, as we have noted, in many states a governor has an item veto with regard to appropriation bills. This is a formidable power indeed.

The Power to Pardon

President Ford's unconditional pardon to former President Richard M. Nixon for all crimes the former president had committed or might have committed drew attention to the existence of this device to every American. The pardoning power is really a judicial power, and the possession of this power by both the president and the governors serves as a splendid example of the overlapping of powers in our constitutional systems.

Underpinning the pardoning power is the theory that the chief executive should be able to correct injustices from judicial action, or to mete out mercy in deserving cases. A pardon may be either conditional or absolute.

Although in about half of the states the pardoning power is placed solely in the hands of the governor, in the remaining states there has been created an instrumentality to aid the governor. Usually called an advisory pardon board, this agency is empowered to hold hearings on applications and to make recommendations to the governor. It should be borne in mind, of course, that the governor's power of pardon extends only to violations of state law and is customarily permitted only *after* conviction.

From the governor's point of view, the power of pardon may often appear to be a mixed blessing. Not only is the governor constantly besieged by friends and neighbors and politicians who urge pardon, he or she is also inundated with requests originating from a wide variety of civic, church, and other groups. The record for granting pardons is apparently held by Miriam Ferguson who, as governor of Texas from 1933 to 1935, pardoned thirty-five hundred people in two years. Her predecessor had given out only seventeen pardons in four years. It is small wonder that the system, at least to outside observers, often seems arbitrary and even capricious.

Besides the power to pardon, the governor normally may grant reprieves and commutations. A commutation is a substitution of a lesser for a greater penalty. A reprieve is a stay or postponement of execution of a sentence, and was formerly widely employed to delay for a designated number of days the execution of the death penalty. The adverb *formerly* is used because there has not been any carrying out of the death sentence in the United States for many years. This is because the United States Supreme Court found in a number of state cases that the actual sentencing of persons to death occurred under such widely diverging circumstances as to be an unconstitutional deprivation of freedom and due process. In an effort to comply with the Supreme Court, many states have redrafted their death sentence statutes. But the constitutionality of such statutes continues to be contested, so far successfully, in the courts.

THE JOB OF GOVERNOR

It is now recognized that it is much more difficult to be a "successful" governor than it is to be a "successful" senator or representative in Washington. In the nation's capital the emphasis, from the perspective of the Congress, is to command attention by delay, by excessive rhetoric, and by promises that usually cannot possibly be fulfilled. The congressional focus in recent decades has been on negativism, with the responsibility for leadership increasingly residing in the White House. But for a governor there is no possible avenue of escape. He or she is constantly in public view and is held responsible, even if it is not entirely fair, for the legislative as well as the administrative performance of the administration of the state. In fact, the governor is held responsible by the public for activities in state administration over which the governor in reality has little command control. But neither the public nor the paid commentators in the press will accept this as an excuse.

To meet in part this reality of life, all governors have greatly expanded their public relations staffs. As in other areas of American life, the way in which a person is perceived to perform may be even more important than the performance itself. Today, what a network's state correspondent may report on evening television about the governor's activities may be worth a good deal more than the observations offered by a local ward leader in a neighborhood bar. The point is that, like the president, the governor makes news and can usually determine the timing of such news. In a contest with a divided and parochial legislature, the governor should command the major share of type.

J. Oliver Williams makes several interesting assertions about the changing perspectives on the American governor.[5] According to his views, at the center of the reverberations of the federal system is the governor. But the governor is the victim of an unbalanced system and is caught in a cross fire between growing demands for services and protests against rising taxes. On the other hand, it is at the executive level and only there that a link may be provided between people and their problems and the resources that government can mobilize. In fact, the governor has become the coordinator and administrator of federal grants-in-aid for state and local services.

As such, the governor has become the prime mover of politics and administration at the state level. What this implies is that much of intergovernmental politics can be interpreted only through an appreciation of the gubernatorial role. In the essays in the collection edited by Beyle and Williams, this interpretation is stressed.

Even so, differences of opinion remain among various experts. In one camp are those scholars who attempt to explain the significant variations among state political systems in terms of social and economic differences. But, as Williams has stated, "an equally strong and perhaps countervailing view is that elite influence is also an important dimension."[6] With that in mind, the various contributors to Beyle's and Williams's volume explore this thesis. The underlying theme, of course, is that governors are the "prime movers" of state politics. What has been presented in this chapter supports that perspective.

Yet, governors have their frustrations, as do other people. In an interesting interview conducted as he was leaving office in early 1975 after serving four years as governor of Connecticut, Thomas J. Meskill listed some of his problems.[7] His main complaint was that it was difficult to do what he had the legal and political authority to do. "The bureaucracy gets rather deep," he said. "Memos get lost or not filed. It's hard to bring about change in government."

A fiscal conservative, Meskill wanted to be remembered for the positive accomplishments of his administration: a balanced budget (he said), as against a deficit inherited from the Democrats of $244 million; penal reforms; and the shifting of retarded people from big institutions into smaller ones in order to bring them into closer touch with their communities. On the other hand, the ex-governor admitted that his position in favor of reinstitution of the death penalty had hurt him politically, as had his strong and unsuccessful stand on abortion. He had also been damaged by a long bus strike that was difficult to settle. In summary, Meskill declared: "People don't care whether you're right or wrong. They just want the problem solved."

The Relative Positions of Governors

Through the use of aggregate data analysis, it is possible to arrive at some findings regarding the relative position of the governors of the various states. A pioneer and leader in this type of analysis is Joseph A. Schlesinger, and the material cited here is taken from one of his recent studies of gubernatorial powers.[8]

Clearly, one element that defines the influence of any administrator is status. But this is difficult to pin down. Organization charts are often misleading. Yet, as has been noted, one identifiable element is salary, and the governor always outranks other political executives in this comparison.

In order to be more precise, Schlesinger developed a series of tables in which, through an ingenious system of weighting factors, he was able to rank the governors according to various important aspects of their jobs. One measure of influence is tenure. Typically, the governors have short terms of office which may reduce their influence. As of 1969, some seventeen states provided for a four-year term for their governors, with no restraint on reelection. At the very bottom of the scale stood New Mexico and South Dakota, which permitted a two-year term with one reelection only. The balance of the states, of course, fell between these extremes. In the last decade, there has been considerable improvement in the "tenure potential" of governors, but there does not appear to have been an actual trend toward increased tenure. This holds true despite such notable exceptions as Mennen Williams in Michigan and Nelson Rockefeller in New York, each of whom served for twelve or more years.

Another method by which a governor may control officials arises from the power to appoint them. In developing his index on this power, Schlesinger isolated sixteen major functions of governors and arrived at scores for each function. Though this method has its inherent problems, it still gives a rough indication of the differences among the various governors. The scores were ranked, with 5 points assigned to the states where the governor had the greatest appointive powers and 1 point assigned to the lowest category. The results are interesting and somewhat unexpected. In category 5—the highest ranking—the number one position is held by Tennessee, with 73 points. It is followed in descending order by Pennsylvania, Hawaii, New Jersey, Indiana, Massachusetts, New York, Maryland, Virginia, and Illinois. Category 4 is headed by Arkansas, with 50 points. Category 3 is headed by Alabama, with 44 points. Category 2 is headed by Maine, with 37 points. The lowest category, 1, consists, in descending order, of Texas, Colorado, Georgia, Mississippi, North Dakota, New Mexico, South Carolina, Oklahoma, and Arizona.[9]

Using a similar approach, Schlesinger also rates the governors according to their budget powers. Here, the overwhelming majority of the states entrust full responsibility to the governor. In this respect, the weakest governors are those of Florida, Indiana, Mississippi, South Carolina, Texas, and West Virginia. They must share the budget responsibility with several other independent sources of strength.

As has been noted earlier, some governors have a strong position in vetoing legislation, while others find themselves in a relatively weak position. The crucial point is the presence or absence of an item veto. Schlesinger found that twenty-five states give the governor an item veto and also require at least a three-fifths majority in the legislature to override a veto. At the very bottom of the scale stand Indiana, North Carolina, and West Virginia. In Indiana and West Virginia, there is no item veto; a simple legislative majority is all that is required to override an ordinary veto. In North Carolina, there is no gubernatorial veto at all.

Finally, Schlesinger arrived at a general rating of the governors' formal powers by combining the four measures of each governor's strength: tenure potential and appointive, budgetary, and veto powers.[10] The maximum possible rating was 20, and it was found only in the states of New York, Illinois, and Hawaii. The lowest rating was found in Texas, which scored 7 points. The median score was 15. Scoring 19 points each were California, Michigan, Minnesota, New Jersey, Pennsylvania, and Maryland. Next to Texas at the bottom of the list, with 8 points each, were South Carolina and West Virginia.

Are there any obvious correlations between the ranking of the states in terms of the formal powers of their governors and general socioeconomic conditions? Here one must proceed with caution. Except for Texas, the governors of the other populous states have strong formal strength. The urban giants all have high ratings, which means that the higher the proportion of urban population in a state, the higher the formal power index.

But there may be, and sometimes is, a distinction drawn between real and formal power. For instance, the governors of Mississippi and North Dakota may have as much *actual* influence, or perhaps more, within their states as the governors of New York and Illinois in theirs. Many explanations, most of them political, can be offered for this kind of contrast. For example, the critical factor in explaining the fact that Texas has a weak governor while Utah, Montana, and Wyoming have strong governors may be the absence in Texas state politics of a two-party competitive system and the presence of such a system in the three sparsely populated mountain states. The hypothesis seems at least a reasonable one.

Returning to a theme dealt with earlier in this chapter, Schlesinger is in full agreement with the thesis of J. Oliver

Williams that politics *does* make a difference. (Interestingly enough, Schlesinger contributed a chapter to the Beyle and Williams volume cited earlier.) His conclusion, stated in 1971, merits repeating here:

> Again, the most significant improvement in the governor's power in the last ten years, according to our index, has been in tenure potential. His budget and veto powers were already strong in most states. His appointive powers have not increased much, and in some instances they have declined. Thus, the principal structural response to the ever increasing demands on state government has been to strengthen the governor in what our theory and evidence indicate to be the most effective way. If tenure potential is turned into the reality of governors with long terms, the gubernatorial office could become a true position of political leadership in the states.[11]

ADMINISTRATIVE ORGANIZATION AND REORGANIZATION

Earlier in this chapter, a review of administrative developments was presented in historical perspective. It is now appropriate to examine somewhat more specifically what the means and methods are for making administrative reorganization possible.

Instruments of Effective and Responsible Administration

To be blunt, very little that is new has been offered in recent years with the objective of making state administration more effective. There has been some progress, of course. The new constitutional systems of New Jersey, Alaska, Hawaii, and Michigan embody many of the proposals that have been advanced for years by reform-minded experts. In other states, such as California and New Hampshire, many of the same objectives have been achieved through administrative reorganization. But in most states much remains to be done.

A commonly advanced goal of the administrative reorganization movement has been the so-called short ballot. With this system, the number of state-wide elective officers is reduced, ideally to one: the governor (with the lieutenant governor of the gubernatorial candidate's choice as a running mate). Of course, the analogy is the federal executive branch, in which the voters choose a president, who in turn appoints (with the consent of the Senate) the heads of his departments. This electoral method greatly enhances the power of the governor. Alaska is an excellent example of a state which successfully employs the short ballot.

Another objective of the movement is the elimination of boards and commissions that are purely administrative in character. No one objects to the use of independent boards and commissions in rule making and in rendering legal judgments. But there is no logical reason they should be given purely administrative assignments which could just as well be handled by regular line departments directly under the control of the governor.

As a further objective, the administrative reorganization movement seeks to simplify a state's departmental structure through consolidation of existing agencies. Again, the impetus for change in recent decades has come from the federal example. The original Hoover Commission proposed consolidation of numerous national agencies with the existing departments. The post—World War II "little Hoover commissions" made similar proposals regarding the states. As a result, New Jersey in 1948 regrouped its ninety-six administrative agencies into fourteen major departments.

In the interests of improving administration, experts have also urged that the states provide adequate management tools. These have included such factors as adequate staff assistance for the governor and an adequate personnel system. In the latter category the most frequently made suggestions include not only expansion of the merit system, but also the adoption of a personnel management department headed by a director directly responsible to the governor. Such a plan would include the retention of a civil service commission to act as a watchdog on executive personnel practices.

Besides these devices, the administrative reform movement has also urged the centralization of "housekeeping services," such as budget making, internal control of expenditures, accounting, purchasing, planning, printing, and property management, in addition to personnel. Under one rubric or another, about two-thirds of the states have established integrated management departments. In the Alaska model, the agency is called the Department of Administration, and it is headed by a commissioner directly responsible to the governor.

The Limits of Administrative Reorganization

About two centuries ago, it was observed that "the men of Massachusetts" could make any constitution operate successfully. This kind of observation should be kept in mind when considering the possibilities as well as the limitations of administrative reorganization. It is a truism that persons of good will can probably devise ways and means so that even a fairly archaic state administrative apparatus can deliver tolerable results.

But personnel considerations aside, there exist other and very real obstacles in the way of administrative reorganization as diagramed in the manuals of public administration. Some illustrations will have to suffice, for one could draw up a very lengthy list indeed. Teachers' unions, for example, believe that they know more about education than politicians appointed by the governor. They are likely to take a dim view of an educational system completely controlled by an appointee of the governor. In short, all professional groups tend to resist political control. This principle would apply to social workers, engineers, lawyers, doctors, and various others.

In addition, the clientele of an agency may support the agency in an effort to maintain the status quo. For example, the farmers' organizations want the Extension Service to be under their control, just as, in Washington, the farmers' organizations want to—and usually do—control the Department of Agriculture.

Then, too, there is the parochialism characteristic of American state legislators. It is natural for the legislators to view the governor as an enemy and therefore to resist efforts to strengthen the governor's administrative authority.

For all these and related reasons, there are very real political limits to administrative reorganization. This is perhaps another way of saying that not everyone, including specialists in public administration, believes that the principal goal of state government is operational efficiency. If this were not so, the reorganization movement would have won hands down several decades ago. The fact that the movement has been only partially successful tells us a great deal about what Americans expect from and value in their state governments.

Items for Discussion

1. Compare the historical development of executive powers for the president, governors, and mayors.

2. Why do states continue to elect such officials as auditors and secretaries of state when virtually no one even knows their names?

3. Historically, governors often have been presidential candidates, and with considerable success. What factors help explain why Franklin D. Roosevelt was the last governor to become president? Is there any possibility that this situation may be changing?

4. Under what conditions might a governor legitimately pardon convicted felons?

5. At present, who are the most effective governors? What factors help explain their success?

Chapter Notes

1. J. Oliver Williams, "Changing Perspectives on the American Governor," in Thad Beyle and J. Oliver Williams (eds.), The American Governor in Behavioral Perspective (New York: Harper & Row, 1972), pp. 1–5, citation at p. 1.

2. Ibid., p. 2.

3. Byron R. Abernethy, Some Persisting Questions Concerning the Constitutional State Executive (Lawrence, Kansas: Governmental Research Center, The University of Kansas, 1960).

4. Ibid., p. 5.

5. Williams, op. cit., pp. 1–5.

6. Ibid., p. 5.

7. Lawrence Fellows, "Meskill Terms Bureaucracy Baffling." New York Times, 8 Jan. 1975.

8. Joseph A. Schlesinger, "The Politics of the Executive," in Herbert

Jacob and Kenneth N. Vines (eds.), *Politics in the American States* (Boston: Little, Brown, 1971), pp. 210–237.

9. *Ibid.*, p. 227.

10. *Ibid.*, p. 232.

11. *Ibid.*, pp. 236-237. See also Schlesinger's article in Beyle and Williams, *op. cit.*, pp. 141–150.

7

State Courts

Key Terms

Advisory opinions: Decisions given by some state courts at the request of the legislative or executive branches; in contrast, federal courts only give opinions *after* someone has been injured and there is an adversary proceeding.

California plan: Method for selecting judges in which the governor makes appointments and the voters decide to retain or remove the judge. In the *Missouri plan* the procedure is similar, except the governor is required to select one of three persons nominated by a nonpartisan judicial commission.

Civil law: Law regulating the conduct between private persons; distinguished from *criminal law* which regulates individual conduct and is enforced by the government. In a civil suit the government may be the *plaintiff* (the initiator of the legal action) or the *defendant*. In criminal cases the government is always the *prosecutor*.

Civil rights: Positive acts of government designed to protect persons against discriminatory treatment by government or individuals, as in housing or education; *civil liberties* refers to restraints on government which protect individual rights, such as freedom from illegal search and seizure.

Common law: Judge-made law which originated in England from decisions shaped according to custom; decisions were reapplied to similar cases and slowly became common to the entire nation.

Equity: Branch of law to provide a remedy in cases in which the common law does not apply; a few states have separate courts for equity proceedings, sometimes called *chancery courts.*

Garnishment: In law, a notice ordering a person not to dispose of a defendant's property or money in his possession pending settlement of the lawsuit.

Grand jury: Body of from twelve to twenty-three members that hears evidence presented by the prosecuting attorney against persons accused of serious crime; if the grand jury believes the evidence warrants bringing the accused to trial, it will present a "true bill" that "indicts" the accused.

Judicial review: The ability of the courts to declare legislative and executive acts null and void because they are contrary to constitutional provisions.

Levy of execution: The taking of property to satisfy judgments or warrants for the collection of taxes.

Petit jury: Trial jury, typically of twelve persons, that determines guilt or innocence.

Plea bargaining: Arrangement among the prosecutor, defense attorney, and judge in which the court accepts a plea of guilty to a lesser offense than the original charge against the defendant.

Primogeniture: In law, the right of the oldest son to inherit all his father's estate.

Privy council: Group of confidential counselors appointed by the British king.

Stare decisis: Legal term meaning to let established court decisions stand.

Torts: In law, a wrongful act, injury, or damage (not involving a breach of contract) for which a civil action may be brought, e.g., personal injury in an automobile accident.

The pursuit of "justice" has long been an objective of civilized men and women. In order to further this undertaking, vast legal systems have been devised. They were not devised at one time, nor in a vacuum. In the Western world, the two principal systems are those based on English common law and on Roman law. Except for certain vestiges of Roman (in this case, Spanish) law found in some civil proceedings in states which were at one time part of Spain, the system in the United States is founded on English common law.

The most striking characteristic of the court system in the United States is its duality. Side by side, there exist federal and state courts. But for the usual and ordinary human affairs, it is to the state courts that one normally refers. It is the purpose of this chapter to look into such questions relating to state courts as the following: What is the background of the laws of the states? How are courts organized? How do we select judges for state courts? How effectively do the courts perform their functions, and what recommendations have been made for improvements in operations of the courts?

THE LAW IN THE AMERICAN STATES

The law applied by the courts consists of the state constitution and the statutes enacted by the legislature. Yet overriding all of this is an obligation to support the federal Constitution, treaties made under it, and statutes. The so-called supremacy clause of Article VI reads as follows:

> This Constitution, and the laws of the United States which shall be made in pursuance thereof; and all treaties made, or which shall be made, under the authority of the United States, shall be the supreme law of the land; and the judges in every State shall be bound thereby, anything in the Constitution or laws of any State to the contrary notwithstanding.

The succeeding section of the article continues:

> The senators and representatives before mentioned, and the members of the several State legislatures, and all executive and judicial officers, both of the United States and of the several States, shall be bound by oath or affirmation to support this Constitution; but no religious test shall ever be required as a qualification to any office or public trust under the United States.

For most laymen, this would appear on its face to be simple enough. Unfortunately, it is much more complicated than it seems. There was, after all, a Civil War, which while it lasted tore the supremacy clause into shreds. There was also deliberate sabotage of the same section of the Constitution when several southern states in the midst of the civil rights "revolution" of the 1960s decided that the clause did not apply to them. And there is also the very real possibility of overlapping jurisdiction between federal and state courts over a particular offense, for example, an infringement of civil rights, or cases involving labor disputes.

Common Law and Equity

Common law is judge-made law. It developed in this fashion: From Norman times, several varieties of law competed with each other. There was, of course, local law, administered more or less at the discretion of the feudal barons in charge of particular areas. Also, there existed a very complex system of church courts, which had jurisdiction over a wide variety of matters. But both of these systems found themselves in competition with the law as administered by justices responsible to the king. The advantage of the king's law, as against feudal or church law, was that it tended, over time, to develop a high degree of uniformity. For example, a decision made by a traveling justice responsible to the king would be reported to London and could serve in time as the precedent for handling similar situations in other parts of England. It is for this reason that the term *common law* developed, for it became *common*, or uniform, for all parts of the country. Common law was judge-made law; it was not the product of any legislative body.

Over several centuries, however, the common law tended to develop certain rigidities. In the interests of justice, it was provided that a litigant who felt he or she did not receive justice under the common law could appeal directly to the king for redress. What came out of this practice was the institutionalization of the procedure by the establishment of equity. Acting as the representative of the king, the lord chancellor was empowered under certain circumstances to grant relief from the judgment of common law courts. In the fourteenth century, a special court of chancery or equity was set up to deal on a regular basis with cases of this sort.

In time, equity itself became overburdened with procedures which worked against the interests of litigants, and special equity courts were abolished. In any case, the complexities of the industrial civilization forced the British, particularly after 1830, to modify both common law and equity by the passage of parliamentary statutes. Most law enforced today in Britain has its contemporary origins in acts of Parliament. Even so, Parliament is much more reluctant to rush into new areas of law than are the American states. For instance, Parliament appears to be perfectly willing to let the judges develop a "law of shock" on the basis of individual decisions. Such a law would deal with damages resulting from an emotional shock, for example, to a woman who faints when it appears her child may be struck by a vehicle. In the process, she may suffer physical injury. Who pays whom is the legal question. This may take a hundred years. In contrast, any American state legislature would at the drop of a hat be inclined to write voluminous statutes on the subject. There is something to be said for each approach.

Though it is self-evident, it is worth emphasizing that the English colonists who settled in North America brought with them the English system of common law. Of course, the colonial legislatures passed statutes (which were subject to judicial review by the Privy Council in London), and the cities and towns passed local ordinances. But the basic legal system was that of common law. The Revolution changed very little of this. For example, a deed to property which was valid on 3 July 1776 was equally valid on 5 July 1776. So was a marriage contract.

In time, the American states developed a law-making style of their own. In some instances, English law was simply inappropriate; for example, Governor Thomas Jefferson led and won the fight to abolish primogeniture in Virginia. In other areas, common law principles were felt to give one side an advantage over another in a manner that was palpably unfair. An illustration comes from trade unions. Under the common law, the formation of a trade union was considered a "conspiracy" and contrary to law. Eventually, all the states (and the federal government) passed specific statutes to make trade unions legal. The gradual emancipation of women furnishes another example. Under the common law, women were almost entirely dependent upon the whims of men. Under statutory law as written by the individual states, women have achieved a substantial measure of equality with men. The movement in this direction, of course, continues with the nation-wide drive to place the proposed Equal Rights Amendment in the federal Constitution.

Even though the substance of law has been dramatically changed by legislative action and judicial interpretation, the forms and procedures of the common law lie at the basis of the American legal system.

Civil Cases

Under ordinary circumstances, a civil case is concerned with a dispute between private parties. The party instituting the suit is the plaintiff, and the party being sued is the defendant. The suits involve such matters as property rights, contracts, torts (civil wrongs), and domestic relations—in other words, they relate to civil law. Examples would include efforts to recover damages from a breach of contract, or from slanderous statements, or from an automobile accident. Even though the plaintiff may win the case, there is no certainty that he or she will actually obtain the money from the defendant. However, some law enforcement officers attached to the courts —constables, sheriffs, and marshals—will attempt to help the successful plaintiff through garnishment of wages or levy of execution on the defendant's property.

As noted, the government itself in civil cases normally provides merely the judicial machinery for the resolution of a conflict. But under certain conditions the governmental units may be parties to civil suits. States themselves may not be made defendants in their own courts without their own consent. Yet they may, as plaintiffs, institute civil actions. Counties, considered to be administrative units of the state, usually share the state's immunity from suits. But cities, as municipal corporations, may sue and be sued in the same manner as natural persons and private corporations.

Criminal Cases

Criminal cases arise over infractions of the criminal law, that is, the body of the law that defines crimes and penalizes their commission. A crime is any act which a legislative body has deemed sufficiently dangerous to the public peace and safety to justify its prohibition and subsequent punishment. Crimes run the gamut from light to serious, from minor misdemeanors such as violations of traffic ordinances to serious felonies such as robbery, homicide, and treason. In a criminal case, it is the function of the court to determine whether the accused person actually committed the crime with which he or she is charged. If guilt is established, it is the duty of the court to impose an appropriate penalty as provided by law. In other words, in criminal cases, in contrast to civil cases, the government not only provides the judicial tribunals but also is itself the prosecuting party corresponding to the plaintiff in civil suits.

For this reason, the action brought against an alleged offender as defendant is brought in the name of the state or of the "people." The actions are usually initiated by the local prosecuting attorney or, in the case of municipal ordinances, by the city attorney.

Judicial Review of Legislation

A noteworthy power of American courts is their ability to exercise "judicial review." This means that a court may declare a statute to be unenforceable because it is in conflict with a section of a constitution. The result is that the law, though it remains on the statute books, in practice is dead because other courts would again refuse to recognize the statute as law.

In principle, a justice of the peace could declare an act to be unconstitutional. In practice, the definitive determination is made by the highest court in the state or, in the case of federal statutes, by the United States Supreme Court.

Research has revealed that judicial review was well known to the men who wrote the federal Constitution. They were all familiar with the occasional holding by the Privy Council in London that certain acts passed by the colonial legislatures were contrary "to the laws of England" and therefore invalid. Also, despite Jefferson's life-long opinion to the contrary, it seems clear that Hamilton and his numerous supporters believed that the Constitution empowered the federal judiciary to pass on the constitutionality of congressional legislation. In any event, the doctrine was enshrined in history in the famous case of *Marbury* v. *Madison* (1 Cranch 137; 1803). In this case Chief Justice John Marshall, speaking for the Court, enunciated the principle that henceforth the Supreme Court, and no one else, would decide the question of constitutionality of legislation. The state courts found it easy to endorse the same principle on the state level, which then became universally accepted.

In applying judicial review, the courts of most states, like the federal courts, will pass upon the constitutionality of an act only when necessary in deciding an actual controversy. That is, they will not render an advance hypothetical opinion to the legislature as to whether they would or would not hold a particular bill to be valid if it were enacted into statute.

Advisory Opinions

There are some exceptions to the general practice we have just discussed. The constitutions of Massachusetts, Maine, New Hampshire, Rhode Island, Michigan, and Colorado provide that the justices of the highest court shall or may give opinions on questions of law when asked to do so by the governor or either branch of the legislature. The exact procedures vary among the states. In summary, advisory opinions are available in eleven states to the governor, and in eight of those same states to either legislative chamber.

It must be stressed that these opinions are purely advisory. In an actual case, the court is free to construe a statute quite differently from the manner in which it was interpreted by the justices in an advisory opinion. But the objective is, of course, laudatory: to reduce the number of statutes declared to be unconstitutional.

THE ORGANIZATION OF STATE COURTS

The structure and jurisdiction of the courts which make up a state's judicial system are determined both by the constitution and by statute. As a general rule, the constitution deals with such questions as the different levels or grades of courts, the number of judges, and their method of selection. In questions of jurisdiction the legislature normally has a somewhat freer hand. Allowing for differences among the states, it is customary to place the state courts into five classes or grades: (1) justice of the peace and other petty courts; (2) courts of intermediate grade; (3) courts of general trial jurisdiction; (4) appellate courts; and (5) the state supreme court. A brief description of each of these types of courts follows.

Justices of the Peace

At the bottom of the judicial ladder is the court presided over by the justice of the peace. In most cases the justices are elected by popular vote, and the election district is the township or some other subdivision of the county. The term of office varies from two to four years. Justices are not required to have any legal training, and most do not.

The justice's duties fall into three main categories. Firstly, a justice tries civil cases in which the amount of money involved does not exceed a particular sum. Secondly, a justice tries minor criminal cases. But the fines and jail sentences which may be imposed are strictly curtailed, and a justice may not impose a penitentiary sentence. Examples of cases under this category would be traffic violations or infractions of health regulations. Lastly, a justice may, as a "committing magistrate," hold preliminary hearings in cases involving more serious crimes. It is important to note that in these situations the justice does not determine the guilt or innocence of a suspected person. What the justice does is decide whether there is sufficient evidence against the person to justify holding him or her for further action. If the justice believes that the evidence is sufficient, the next step is action by a grand jury or a prosecuting attorney. Justices of the peace in many states are also given the power to perform marriage ceremonies. In Connecticut, they are also empowered to put down riots, but how this is to be managed is not clear from the statutes.

To explain why Americans still retain the office of justice of the peace it is necessary to review a bit of history. The office began in rural England and flourished in the rural society of the American colonies and the early states. As the country developed, the office was incorporated into the judicial systems written into state constitutions, and there it remains.

What are the objections to the office in the twentieth century? In the first place, it is clear that a layman with no legal training is hardly the ideal person to administer any court. Then there is the question of payment. A justice in most states receives no salary; his or her income comes from a fee system of compensation. The more fees levied, the higher the level of compensation. Until the development of the Federal Interstate Highway System, many a justice of the peace prospered through the operation of automobile "speed traps." In this operation, there was frequently a division of the spoils between the justice and the arresting officer.

It can thus be argued that most of the justices are not qualified, the system of compensation is patently unfair, and the office should be abolished.

Courts of Intermediate Grade

In some states there exist courts which fall in level of jurisdiction between the justice of the peace courts and those of general trial jurisdiction. If organized on a county basis, these intermediate courts are considered county courts. If organized within certain cities, they may be termed municipal courts. Though the intermediate courts have powers in excess of those of justices of the peace, there may be concurrent jurisdiction. In such a situation, a plaintiff in a minor case may choose to sue before either a justice of the peace or the intermediate court. It is the usual practice to elect judges of intermediate courts on a county-wide or city-wide basis.

General Trial Courts

In contrast to the courts already discussed, general trial courts are authorized to try civil cases without limitation as to the amount involved, and all criminal cases regardless of the seriousness of the offense. These are the courts where major civil actions and criminal prosecutions for felony are usually instituted. In addition to very broad original jurisdiction, these courts often have some appellate powers. While it is sometimes possible to try cases without juries, the general trial courts make the most extensive use of petit (trial) juries in both civil and criminal cases.

The judges of these courts are chosen in most states by popular election. Depending on the history of the particular state, the general trial courts may be known by different titles, the most common being county, district, or circuit courts. When several counties are grouped together in a judicial circuit, it is customary for a judge to hold court in each county in turn. In former times, this was termed, rather aptly, "riding the circuit."

Appellate Courts

In about twelve states, one or more appellate courts have been created to reduce the volume of appeals from the general trial courts to the state's highest court. Usually the judges of such courts are elected, but in a few states they are appointed by the governor. In many cases their decision is final,

A general trial courtroom during a first-degree murder trial in Sumner, Mississippi. The circuit court judge presides on ᵥthe bench. (Wide World Photos.)

but in others they may still be appealed to the supreme court of the state. An appellate court, like a supreme court, consists not of one judge but of a bench of three or more judges. In their ordinary business, these appellate courts deal only with matters of law, not questions of fact, and therefore normally do not require the use of juries. In 1974–1975 Chief Justice Burger of the United States Supreme Court suggested that at least one appellate court should be created to review cases from the federal courts of appeal before permitting them to go on to the Supreme Court for final determination. In other words, the Chief Justice was endorsing the screening practice currently followed in about a quarter of the states. The objective in both situations is to decrease the caseload on the highest courts, federal or state.

State Supreme Courts

In all the states the judicial system is charted in hierarchical fashion, and at the top is one supreme court. Usually the highest court is called the "supreme court," although confusion arises when the practice differs. For instance, the highest court in New York state is the court of appeals.

In all of the states' highest courts, one member is designated as "chief justice" and other members are known as "associate justices." This, once again, parallels federal practice. The method of selection of the chief justice varies. In some states, he or she is appointed or elected to serve in that capacity. In other states, a person holding seniority may automatically become the chief justice.

As one would expect, a state supreme court, for the most part, fulfills an appellate function. The objective is both to correct errors from lower courts and to create a state-wide uniformity in the interpretation of the law. The use of a jury is rare.

To arrive at a decision, a supreme court uses the simple mechanism of a majority vote. In this process, the chief justice has no greater vote than any other member. On the other hand, one of the justices who voted with the majority is designated by the chief justice to write the "opinion" of the court. In this sense, not all equals are in fact equal. If a judge or judges find themselves in the minority, they may write a minority opinon. All of these decisions are published in the National Reporter System issued for many years by the West Publishing Company. Majority decisions, of course, become precedents, and under the principle of *stare decisis* become controlling in cases of a similar nature coming before inferior courts in the same state.

An appeal from the highest court of a state goes directly to the United States Supreme Court, not to one of the lesser federal courts. If one state sues another state, the United States Supreme Court has original jurisdiction.

The Number of Courts

The complexity of the state court systems varies enormously. In a compilation made in 1971, Kenneth N. Vines and Herbert Jacob give the following illustration:[1]

Hawaii Courts	*New York Courts*
Supreme court	Court of appeals
Circuit courts	Appellate division of supreme court
District courts	Appellate terms of supreme court
	Supreme court
	Court of claims

Surrogates' courts
Family courts
County courts
City courts
Civil courts
Municipal courts
Criminal courts
District courts
Justice courts
Police justice courts
Traffic courts
Recorders' courts
Police courts
Courts of special session

Is it little wonder that skilled court reporters, as well as ordinary newspaper readers, are often confused by the sheer complexity and diffuseness of the state judicial systems?

THE SELECTION OF JUDGES

In about three-quarters of the American states, judges are chosen by popular election. In some ten eastern and southern states, the judges are appointed by the governor (usually with the consent of the state senate) or are chosen by the legislature. The practice of electing judges is presumably a throwback to Jacksonian Democracy, the idea being that judges ought to be in some way responsible to the people. What this results in is the clash of two principles—one of justice, the other of egalitarianism. To the dismay and bewilderment of professional radicals, there is no reason whatsoever to believe that popular election increases the possibility that the courts will render justice. There is little merit to the old frontier adage "Give the man a fair trial, and then hang him!" For the methods used to select judges, see Table 7.1.

When it comes to actual debate, the proponents of appointment cite the federal judicial system. Here, proposed judges are nominated by the president, and the approval of the Senate is required. Once in office, judges hold their posts for life, provided their behavior meets acceptable standards. It would be encouraging to report that the federal practice has succeeded in eliminating political considerations from the process of appointment to federal courts. Unhappily, this is not the case. Beginning

Table 7.1
Methods of Judicial Selection in the States
(Appellate and Major Trial Courts)

Much party influence and little bar influence			Little party influence and much bar influence	
Partisan election	Election by legislature	Appointment	Missouri plan	Nonpartisan election
Alabama	Connecticut(b)	Delaware	Arizona	Alaska
Arkansas	Rhode Island	Hawaii	California(a)	California
Florida	South Carolina	Maine	Idaho	Colorado
Georgia	Vermont	Maryland	Michigan	Illinois
Indiana	Virginia	Massachusetts	Minnesota	Iowa
Kansas(a)		New Hampshire	Montana	Kansas
Kentucky		New Jersey	Nevada	Missouri
Louisiana			North Dakota	Nebraska
Mississippi			Ohio	Oklahoma
Missouri(a)			Oregon	Utah
New Mexico			South Dakota	
New York			Tennessee	
North Carolina			Washington	
Oklahoma(a)			Wisconsin	
Pennsylvania			Wyoming	
Texas				
West Virginia				

(a) States listed under more than one heading select judges for different courts by different methods.
(b) Formally legislature, actually by nomination of governor.
Source: *State Court Systems* (Lexington, Ky.: Council of State Governments, 1970); *The Extent of Adoption of the Non-Partisan Appointive Elective Plan for the Selection of Judges* (Chicago: American Judiciary Society, 1969).

with Washington, and continuing with Adams and his successors, the presidents have always sought to appoint judges who would share the current presidential points of view on sensitive questions.

To be sure, this has often backfired. Justices do change their minds, and often become surprisingly free spirits once on the bench. On the other hand, President Nixon constantly stated that his objective was to obtain a Supreme Court dedicated to what he termed a "strict construction" of the Constitution. As has since become evident, President Nixon and some of his associates were engaged simultaneously in large-scale sabotage of the Constitution itself. Even in presidential nomination of judges to federal district courts the element of political payoff plays a large role. A losing candidate of the president's party, for example, who runs for governor and loses, is likely to be nominated for a federal judgeship. Former Governor Meskill of Connecticut is a case in point, and there are dozens of others.

In contrast to the life tenure enjoyed by federal judges,

state judges must periodically be reappointed or reelected. As an abstract principle, this should interfere with their independence of judgment. But there is little concrete evidence that reappointment or reelection actually affects the judges' independence.

Some states have recognized that the prevailing system for the selection of state judges has its weaknesses. To improve the situation, they have decided to elect judges on a nonpartisan ballot, even though nonpartisan elections have a long history of being extremely partisan in practice. Yet several states have made serious efforts to avoid the choice between popular election and appointment. In particular, California and Missouri have adopted innovative plans aimed at avoiding this dilemma.

The California Plan

In 1934 California adopted a constitutional amendment which provided that any judge of the highest courts who decided to be a candidate for an additional term could, shortly before the expiration of his or her term of judgeship, declare a desire to remain in office. In such an event, the name of the judge was to be placed on the ballot without the name of any opposing candidate. In such a situation, the sole question before the electorate is whether the judge should be retained in office for another term. If a majority votes for retention, that is the end of the matter. If a majority votes in opposition, a vacancy occurs, which may be filled by the governor with the assent of a special commission. The name of the person appointed to fill the vacancy is placed on the ballot at the next election, and the voters then decide whether the judge should or should not serve the full term. Obviously, the plan has its attractions, for an incumbent judge may stand entirely on his or her own record, not on relative personal popularity.

The Missouri Plan

Missouri went one step further. Under a constitutional amendment adopted in 1940 and continued in the new constitution of 1945, a judge of the supreme court or of a court of appeals can, near the end of his or her term, file with the secretary of state a declaration of intention to stand for reelection. After the declaration has been filed, the voters are asked in the next general election on a separate judicial ballot whether the sitting judge should be retained in office. Again, if a majority vote for retention, the judge is returned to office.

However, if a majority votes in the negative, or if the sitting judge fails to file a declaration of candidacy, a vacancy is created. Here is where the Missouri plan is unique: All vacancies are filled by gubernatorial appointment. But in making the appointment, the governor is required to select one of three persons nominated by a nonpartisan judicial commission.

This commission consists of seven members, as follows: the chief justice of the state supreme court (who serves as chair), three lawyers chosen by the bar association, and three laymen appointed by the governor. After the new judge has been in office twelve months, he or she must stand for election in the next general balloting. But if the popular vote favors the retention of the incumbent, he or she is then entitled to serve a full twelve-year term.

While the adoption of this plan in Missouri and various other states has not proved to be a panacea for judicial problems, the general view is that it represents a considerable improvement over the earlier system of choosing judges and retaining them on purely partisan grounds.

Judicial Tenure

In contrast to federal judges, who serve for life (or good behavior), state judges are appointed or elected for fixed terms. Usually these terms are longer than those provided for governors or legislators. Also, in contrast to federal judges, state judges are usually faced with compulsory retirement when they reach a particular age—often, seventy. The actual number of state judges is shown in Table 7.2.

Removal of Judges

All the states provide one or more methods for removing judges from office. The methods are (1) by impeachment, (2) by concurrent resolution of the legislature, (3) by popular recall, and (4) by action of higher courts. In practice, very few judges are ever removed from office by any of these methods. When removal occurs, it is normally for the commission of a criminal offense or related serious misconduct. It is extremely rare for a judge to be removed on the grounds of incompetency, neglect of judicial duty, or unethical conduct.

Table 7.2
Number of Judges

State or other jurisdiction	Appellate courts		Major trial courts					
	Court of last resort	Inter-mediate appellate court	Chancery court	Circuit court	District court	Superior court	Other trial courts	
Alabama	9	8	...	98	...	...	...	
Alaska	5	...	...	...	...	16	...	
Arizona	5	12	...	...	...	60	...	
Arkansas	7	...	25	28	...	...	...	
California	7	48	...	...	...	477	...	
Colorado	7	6	...	...	81	...	...	
Connecticut	6	...	...	...	...	40	...	
Delaware	3	...	3	...	...	11	...	
Florida	7	20	...	263	...	...	...	
Georgia	7	9	...	...	...	52	...	
Hawaii	5	...	...	13	...	...	...	
Idaho	5	...	...	...	24	...	...	
Illinois	7	34	...	610	...	...	...	
Indiana	5	9	...	87	83(a)	63	4	
Iowa	9	...	...	...	63	...	...	
Kansas	7	...	...	...	63	...	...	
Kentucky	7	...	...	83	...	...	...	
Louisiana	7	26	...	...	118	...	...	
Maine	6	...	...	...	...	14	...	
Maryland	7	10	...	57	...	...	21	
Massachusetts	7	6	...	...	...	46	...	
Michigan	7	12	...	126	...	...	20	
Minnesota	9	...	...	...	72	...	...	
Mississippi	9	...	25	24	...	...	...	

Missouri	7	18	107	.	.	.
Montana	5	.	.	28	.	.
Nebraska	7	.	.	45	.	.
Nevada	5	.	.	23	.	.
New Hampshire	5	.	.	.	12	.
New Jersey	7	18	.	.	120	103
New Mexico	5	5	.	29	.	257
New York	7	31(b)	.	.	49	.
North Carolina	7	9	.	19	.	.
North Dakota	5	.	.	.	.	.
Ohio	7	38	.	138	.	291
Oklahoma	9	9(c)	66	.	.	.
Oregon	7	6	.	.	.	285
Pennsylvania	7	14	.	.	13	.
Rhode Island	5	.	16	.	.	.
South Carolina	5	.	37	.	.	.
South Dakota	5	.	50	.	.	29
Tennessee	5	16(c)	23	.	.	.
Texas	9	47(c)	.	219	.	21
Utah	5	.	.	22	.	6
Vermont	5	.	.	.	.	.
Virginia	7	.	99	.	.	.
Washington	9	12	.	.	98	.
West Virginia	5	.	34	.	.	.
Wisconsin	7	.	52	13	.	126
Wyoming	5	.	.	13	.	.
District of Columbia	9	.	.	.	44	.

(a) Unified court system with an additional 24 District Associate Judges, 6 Judicial Magistrates, and 191 part-time Judicial Magistrates.

(b) Does not include temporary designations.

(c) In Oklahoma, there are 3 judges on the Court of Criminal Appeals and 6 on the Court of Appeals. In Tennessee there are 9 judges on the Court of Appeals and 7 members on the Court of Criminal Appeals. In Texas there are 5 judges on the Court of Criminal Appeals and 42 on the Court of Civil Appeals.

Source: Book of the States, 1974-75, p. 121.

Compensation of Judges

Compared with other state officials, judges are fairly well compensated. In 1974, the salaries paid to justices of the highest courts in Pennsylvania, New York, and New Jersey were, respectively, $50,000; $49,665; and $45,000. Nonetheless, these are low salaries in comparison to the incomes earned by the most successful attorneys. It is not uncommon for a judge, even of a very high state court, to resign on financial grounds and join a private law firm.

THE QUEST FOR EQUAL JUSTICE

Efforts to improve the court systems of the states have never ceased, but the momentum has been uneven. In the last decade in particular the courts have been subjected to an increasing crescendo of criticism. There has been, at the same time, some positive response. In the next sections some of the criticisms and responses will be summarized.

Justice and the Poor

It is evident that a rich person stands a better chance of being able to defend himself or herself successfully in court than a poor person. Indeed, even for the citizen of moderate means, a legal battle may be a financial disaster. The modern drive to help poor people in need of legal aid dates from the publication in 1919 of a remarkable book by Reginald Heber Smith, entitled *Justice and the Poor*.[2] In this seminal work, Smith demonstrated beyond any doubt that the rich and the poor encounter different standards of justice—in terms of the competence and availability of counsel, in terms of consideration by the courts, and in terms of conviction and sentencing.

Even before the publication of Smith's book, there had appeared in some cities legal aid societies which enlisted the voluntary support of attorneys and of bar associations to provide legal services for the poor. But Smith's efforts resulted in a mushrooming of such societies. Since the middle of the 1960s, federally funded legal assistance offices have taken on a major role in providing legal services for the poor. Originally funded by the Office of Economic Opportunity, the legal service offices have been located in many of the poorest urban neighborhoods as well as in centers of rural poverty.

The majority of states, as a voluntary act of grace, long ago provided that indigent defendants in criminal cases should be represented by counsel appointed by the court and paid for by the state. However, as late as 1960 four states supplied such counsel only in capital cases. In 1963, in *Gideon v. Wainwright* (372 U.S. 335), the United States Supreme Court held that all states must provide counsel for indigents in all criminal cases.

There are other variations in the way indigents may be helped. One is the voluntary-defender system, under which there is a special law office to which the courts may assign indigent defendants. The system is often affiliated with the local bar association. This plan is in operation in New York city, Boston, Philadelphia, Pittsburgh, New Orleans, and a few other cities.

In other jurisdictions there is a public-defender system. In this case, the defender, like the prosecuting attorney, is a public official. This approach has been adopted in Los Angeles and Alameda counties in California; in Cook county, Illinois; and in

Charles Manson, leader of the California group linked to the Sharon Tate murders, sits with a state public defender during his preliminary hearing on charges of possessing stolen property in Independence, California. (Wide World Photos.)

many other places, including Connecticut, Massachusetts, and Rhode Island.

Finally, a combination private and public defense system for protection of the indigent has been established in certain inferior criminal courts, as in Rochester and Buffalo, New York; and Columbus and Toledo, Ohio.

Justice for Minorities

Since minority-group members are frequently poor, their plight is similar in certain respects to that of the indigent. But insofar as judges and juries may be biased on grounds of minority race or ethnic background, the problems are somewhat different. It is difficult, for example, for a person accused of radical political beliefs to obtain a fair trial in some jurisdictions. The same may be said with regard to persons holding extreme religious convictions.

A new element has entered the scene in recent years. That is the emergence into the open of members of the so-called gay liberation movement. Sexual orientation which deviates from the norms of a particular community may work hardship in court against known homosexuals and bisexuals. It is difficult to prescribe any formula for dealing with prejudice in this area. Even so, municipal ordinances to grant equal rights regardless of sexual orientation have been passed in a handful of cities. And such equal rights would presumably, at least ideally, include the judicial area.

Reorganization

Individual jurists, such as the late state Chief Justice Arthur T. Vanderbilt of New Jersey; leading law school professors; and chancellors of bar associations propose from time to time plans to improve the administration of justice. At the base of this proposed improvement is the creation of an integrated court system, which was suggested as early as 1906 by then law professor Roscoe Pound in an address before the American Bar Association. As the decades passed, some states adopted the earlier recommendations of Pound, among them New Jersey in 1947. The essence of the plan is to place the judicial system of the state in a single court of justice, which is then divided into a supreme court and various lesser courts. The chief justice is the head of the system and possesses extensive powers to reassign judges. In addition, the supreme court is given wide authority to draft rules and procedures for all of the state's courts. Under the New Jersey plan, the chief justice was named the administrative head of the courts—but was specifically given the authority to appoint an administrative (or business) director whose job was to keep the chief justice informed and to recommend changes.

In making this provision for an administrator, New Jersey was, in fact, adopting a practice begun by the United States courts in 1939. In that year, Congress established the Administrative Office of the United States Courts, which rapidly became a valuable administrative adjunct to those courts. About a third of the states, at last count, had a similar office.

Some Problems in Legal Reform

It was the custom of Justice Vanderbilt to blame the slowness in judicial reform largely on lawyers and judges. The recent spate of criticism of state courts would seem to support the position of the former chief justice of New Jersey.

For the average citizen involved in a court case, there is a period of seemingly endless delay. Court dockets may run years behind the calendar year. In the meantime, witnesses die or disappear, records are destroyed, and new officials are chosen as judges or as prosecutors. The style of justice may change before the case comes to trial. For a witness of a violent crime, there are serious risks which are likely to be involved in offering testimony. In 1870, how long would a white witness have survived in Mississippi if he had testified against the Ku Klux Klan? In some jurisdictions today, how long would a witness survive who testified in court against a crime syndicate—related defendant?

Then there is the question of who should or should not serve on either a grand jury or a trial jury. In general, the most available candidates are women whose children are grown up, and the retired. Whatever the specifics in any particular locality, computer studies have revealed that neither type of jury is usually even remotely a cross-section of the community in which the inquiry or trial is held.

To complicate the situation, there is the almost universal exclusion of persons from particular occupations: doctors, engineers, teachers, and so on. In fact, all one need to do, if actually impaneled, is to say that he or she has made up his or her mind on the situation in advance. This will bring an automatic release from jury duty. For example, in a case involving the

Long Island Railroad, simply declare when the prospective jurors are being selected: "I hate the Long Island Railroad." That will do the trick.

It was formerly common in many states to exclude women from jury service. But on 21 January 1975, in the case of *Taylor* v. *Louisiana*, the United States Supreme Court, overruling a 1961 decision, held that women could not be denied equal opportunity to serve on juries. On 1 January 1975, Louisiana itself had become the last state to destroy this barrier toward female jury duty. The importance of the case is that in Louisiana and some other states several thousand prison inmates had been convicted under a jury system now found to be invalid. In a clarification issued a week later, the Court ruled out the possibility that its decision would automatically free or result in new trials for persons convicted prior to 21 January 1975. But the Court left unanswered some important questions with which it will some day have to deal. For example, under New York state law, as it existed in 1975, women were called by lot for jury service. But they were able to keep their names off the panel simply by claiming statutory exemption. As a result, for example, the New York county (Manhattan) trial jury consisted early in 1975 of 89 thousand men and 18 thousand women. No one seriously contended that this resulted in a representative system.

Another problem, highlighted by the Watergate cases but also from time to time by events in various metropolitan areas, is the freedom enjoyed by prosecutors in plea bargaining. In a trade-off arrangement, a defendant will plead guilty if the prosecutor will accept a reduced charge. A study made for the *New York Times* found that almost eight of every ten defendants who were accused of homicide in New York and who pleaded guilty to a reduced charge were freed on probation or received a prison term of less than ten years. Of those who did receive a maximum ten-year term, most were eligible for parole in three years.[3] Published in January 1975, the study itself included all homicide indictments in 1973 that had to publication date been resolved in the city's courts.

Yet plans for general and specific reform continue to be generated, apparently in response to fairly strong public calls for change. And it is not all rhetoric from bar associations or individual reformers, whose list of complaints would require many pages to fill. A significant and extensive judicial reform took effect in January 1975 in Alabama. Edward B. McConnell, director of the National Center for State Courts, had earlier declared that Alabama was about to become "the most dramatic illustration in the country of what can be done without undue delay, to improve the quality of justice in state courts."[4] Of the three new justices who joined the Alabama Supreme Court at the time of its reorganization, one was Janie L. Shores, a law professor and the first woman to be so seated. This meant that Ms. Shores had become one of three women in the nation to hold membership at that time on top state appellate courts.

Despite various success stories which could be added, much remains to be done in the eternal quest for justice. A very competent and distinguished student of the judicial process, Herbert Jacob, summarized the results of his ten-year assessment somberly:

> The administration of justice in America is pockmarked by systematic discrimination against blacks, the poor, women, juveniles, and consumers. Although special rules attempt to place litigants on a more equal footing than they may claim in other portions of the political process, the administration of justice still reflects the inequalities of American society.[5]

Yet not all is gloom, for there are some indications of progress. Jacob concludes on a note of moderate optimism:

> Although much remains to be done, a beginning is being made by political scientists, sociologists, and legal researchers. None of the studies can be immediately translated into reform that will quickly change the inequitable administration of justice. The legal system is too intricate to obtain quick results, but small steps can be taken.[6]

Items for Discussion

1. If possible, visit a big-city municipal court (traffic, domestic, juvenile) and report on the experience.

2. As a means of lessening the burden of the courts, what kinds of presently criminal behavior might be decriminalized?

3. Argue the pros and cons regarding the popular election of judges.

4. Should there be a set age (e.g., seventy) when judges should retire? What about mandatory retirement for other state officials?

5. With reference to such things as landlord-tenant relations, consumer protection, and criminal acts, discuss how the poor are treated unjustly in our state legal systems.

Chapter Notes

1. Kenneth N. Vines and Herbert Jacob, "State Courts," in Herbert Jacob and Kenneth N. Vines (eds.) *Politics in the American States* (Boston: Little, Brown, 1971), p. 295.

2. Reginald Heber Smith, *Justice and the Poor* (New York: Carnegie Foundation for the Advancement of Teaching, 1919).

3. Selwyn Raab, "Plea-Bargains Settling 8 of 10 Homicide Cases." *New York Times*, 27 Jan. 1975. What has been happening in plea bargaining in New York appears to be typical in other metropolitan centers, for example, Philadelphia. The result is to lessen the number of cases actually brought to trial, to reduce the backlog of cases, and to make the district attorney look better. Of course, more admitted criminals are on the streets.

4. "Alabama Praised on Court Reform." *New York Times*, 19 Jan. 1975. The reformist literature is impressive. It includes a magnificent interview with Lord Widgery, Lord Chief Justice of England, in *U.S. News & World Report*, 27 Jan. 1975, pp. 45−49. In England, for example, a trial jury is completed in a few minutes; in the United States, the process may take weeks. Another item in the same journal deals with malpractice suits against doctors, with the villain being considered the attorney representing the "victim" on a fee basis. See *U.S. News & World Report*, 20 Jan. 1975, pp. 53−54. Finally, a researcher should examine the article by Laurie Overby Robinson, "Moving the Criminal Justice Machine," *State Government*, Vol. 46, No. 4 (Autumn, 1973), pp. 222−226.

5. Herbert Jacob, *Justice in America*, 2nd ed. (Boston: Little, Brown, 1972), p. 225.

6. *Ibid.*, p. 230. It is difficult to overemphasize the importance of this particular study. As Jacob demonstrates, modern social science, by feeding aggregate data into computers, is producing findings of tremendous significance for judicial reorganization and reform.

8

Community Political Systems: Forms and Institutions

Key Terms

Annexation: The extension of city boundaries to include territory previously adjacent to the city limits.

Board of commissioners: Governing body for counties. Typically there are three to seven commissioners elected at large. In a few areas a much larger *board of supervisors*, in which one supervisor is elected from each township, governs the county.

City charter: Basic law of a local governmental body that defines its powers, responsibilities, and organization.

Commission plan: Form of city government in which elected commissioners exercise both legislative and executive power; typically, each member is responsible for a particular area, such as parks.

Consolidation: Combining two or more existing municipal corporations into one governmental unit.

Council-manager plan: Form of city government in which the council selects a professional manager to act as the city's chief administrative officer.

Dillon's Rule: States that municipal governments possess only those powers granted them by the states and that the courts are to interpret such grants of power very narrowly.

Hare plan: An electoral plan which utilizes proportional voting.

Home rule: Charter drafted originally by the municipality, which gives it a high degree of independence. The city may change its own charter as it wishes, and legislative interference in local affairs is limited.

Incorporation: Creates a legal entity (a municipal corporation) at the request of the inhabitants of an area. Incorporated areas have charters and usually a large measure of self-government.

Managing director: An administrator in city government who is directly responsible to the mayor and who exercises broad power over the city administration.

Mayor-council plan: Basic form of city government with an elected council and an elected mayor; *weak* and *strong* designations refer to the strength of the mayor as an administrator in charge of the apparatus of city government.

Nonpartisan elections: Elections in which candidates do not run with party labels and political parties are prohibited from running candidates.

Proprietary functions: City activities which are similar to those performed by private business people.

Special districts: Units of local government established to provide a single service, such as fire protection; often cut across existing boundaries of local government.

Town: Major unit of local government in the New England states. Includes both rural and urban portions. In the past, governed by all the inhabitants through the town meeting.

As we have seen, community political systems operate as subsystems of the state systems. However, they vary remarkably—in size, in population, and in authority. It is a good idea to have some command of the legal relationships among the subsystems, for the rules of politics are rarely if ever neutral. Whoever masters the rules holds a decided advantage over the amateurs. We start with the overall legal framework.

THE LEGAL FRAMEWORK

In Chapter 3, dealing with state constitutions, it was pointed out that the basic distribution of governmental powers in the United States is set forth in the United States Constitution. The Tenth Amendment states specifically that all powers not conferred on the federal government are "reserved" to the states. Since cities and other local governments are not even mentioned in the Constitution, the plain assumption is that they fall under the jurisdiction of the states. This is another way of saying that there is no inherent right of a subdivision of the state—whether it be a county, a city, a borough, or a township—to exercise local governmental powers. Such powers must be conferred on the local unit by the state, either through the state's constitution or by statute.

The legal position of municipal corporations—and other subdivisions as well—was given its classic formulation in a remarkable statement by Judge John F. Dillon (1831–1914), a famous jurist and legal commentator, in a work first published in 1872. "Dillon's Rule" reads as follows:

> It is a general and undisputed proposition of law that a municipal corporation possesses and can exercise the following powers, and no others: First, those granted in express words; second, those necessarily or fairly implied in or incident to the power expressly granted; third, those essential to the accomplishment of the declared objects and purposes of the corporation,—not simply convenient, but indispensable. Any fair, reasonable substantial doubt concerning the existence of power is resolved by the courts against the corporation, and the power is denied.[1]

In this formulation, Judge Dillon went far beyond asserting that municipal corporations possess only those powers which have been delegated by the state. He is also saying that such powers as have been granted must be very strictly construed by the courts. When it is recalled that the very existence of a municipal corporation is determined by an action of the state, it is clear that, under American law, such a corporation is legally dependent upon the state.

It is true that there have been occasional challenges to Dillon's Rule, but most of them have not been successful. However, the present constitutions of New Jersey and of

Michigan are explicit in declaring that constitutional and statutory provisions concerning local government should be liberally construed. But on balance it appears that the rule of strict construction will remain the general practice for many years to come.

Municipal Liability

A city or any other municipal corporation has a particular legal status. Like a private corporation it can sue or be sued. Of greatest interest to most citizens is the liability of municipal corporations for the acts of their employees. If a city through its agents has made a valid contract, it must live up to the stipulated obligations. But if the agent acted improperly, the city escapes liability.

To what extent are municipal corporations liable for the torts (civil wrongs other than failure to live up to the terms of a contract) of their employees? As a common illustration, consider an injury to a person or property as the result of negligence of a city employee. Under the old common-law rules, the general formula is this: in the performance of so-called governmental functions, the city is not responsible for the negligent acts of its employees. But in the performance of so-called proprietary functions, the city must assume the same liability as that assumed by private corporations. Governmental functions are those commonly assumed to be of a public character, such as police, fire, health, and education. On the other hand, proprietary functions are those which are deemed to be essentially private in character, such as supplying gas or water or running a public transit system. In a period of ever-expanding governmental services, this distinction has become increasingly unsatisfactory. In some states the courts have taken steps to broaden the liability of municipal corporations.

How Are Cities Incorporated?

Legal theory holds that the power to grant incorporation to the inhabitants of any urban area is legislative in nature and may not be delegated. Yet the practice today is considerably different.

Formerly, any community wishing to incorporate itself would petition the colonial assembly, or later the state, which could if it wished pass a specific statute of incorporation. But as the country expanded and the number of such requests reached a total which made legislative action inconvenient, other devices were invented. Today state legislatures assign the task of incorporation to other agencies, usually to the chief legislative and administrative agency of the county. If and when certain statutory requirements are met, the agency is empowered to proceed with the act of incorporation. The fiction of legislative action was maintained by assuming that the county was merely performing an administrative, not a legislative, act.

So the present-day procedure is basically this: a stated but significant percentage of the residents of an area, through petition or referendum, must indicate that they favor incorporation. The petition must state the precise area of the proposed corporation. In some states a particular level of population density must exist for further consideration of the petition. If the county agency accepts the petition, the agency then appoints a set of interim officials or provides for the immediate election of permanent officials. The incorporation is then made a matter of public record. This is evidenced by the granting of a charter, which becomes, in a sense, the constitution of the municipality.

CITY CHARTERS

Today there are several forms of city charters, all of which are drafted by the state legislatures, except in the case of home rule cities. Until about 1850, the normal practice was for a legislature to incorporate a city by passing a special act. But, as we have noted, the process became cumbersome and other methods were adopted. The objective was not only to obtain a more efficient process, but also to obtain a higher degree of uniformity among the charters. So, as an improvement over the passage of specific charters, the states began to adopt general charters of incorporation. While this dealt with the efficiency problem, it failed to come to grips with the requirements of uniformity.

As a result, the states today for the most part grant *classified* charters. The idea, clearly, is to make meaningful distinctions among cities which may differ vastly in socioeconomic aspects. Commonly, the basis for classification is population, although the assessed value of taxable property is sometimes used as well. If a city's population changes rather dramatically, does it automatically move from one category to another? The general answer is no. The change from one classification to another is not automatic, but depends on some prescribed formal procedure.

Some states give their cities a choice in which they may opt for one or another plan of city charters. The most common plans are the mayor-council form, the commission form, and the council-manager form. These will be dealt with as part of the ensuing discussion of forms of city government. In the meantime, certain other aspects of city government warrant, as background, some brief analysis.

Home Rule

In the discussion of charters, the subject of home rule was avoided, because it is a subject which requires particular attention. Though the term *home rule* is open to a variety of interpretations, the basic difference between the charters analyzed so far and a home rule charter is this: an ordinary charter may be changed by the state legislature at any time, but a home rule charter may not. A home rule charter, drafted originally by the municipality, grants the municipal corporation a high degree of independence with regard to charter changes and revisions.

Broadly considered, there are two general types of home rule charters. When the state legislature permits a city to draft its own charter, the consequent action is termed "legislative" home rule. Under this procedure, the legislature, of course, retains the power to cancel or revise the existing home rule charters. But in practice, cities with this type of home rule have enjoyed a rather lasting and effective independence.

Because the second type of home rule charter comes from authority granted in the state constitution, it is called "constitutional" home rule. What this means is that the legislature has been prohibited by the constitution from prescribing the form of government which those cities shall have. As a consequence, a city may adopt whatever form of charter it believes best meets its needs, regardless of the sentiments of the legislature. The first use of constitutional home rule occurred in Missouri in 1875, when the constitution was amended to make home rule available for the two largest cities of the state.

While it is easy to understand that the concept of home rule is appealing, its practical effectiveness should not be overestimated. Constitutional home rule does not free a city from the state government. Much state action, in scores of ways, continues directly to affect the city, and general acts of the legislature remain applicable. Furthermore, the lines of demarcation of the powers of the two units of government are usually unclear, and are eventually reconciled, if at all, either in the courts or through political compromises.

Annexation and Consolidation

Though not automatic, it is relatively simple for a municipal corporation to change from one type of charter to another. For cities with classified charters, all that is normally necessary, once the stated preconditions for possible change have been met, is a favorable vote on the part of the city's voters.

But to change existing boundaries of incorporation is often difficult. The two basic methods have been annexation and consolidation. As the expression implies, *annexation* means the extension of existing municipal boundaries in order to bring contiguous unincorporated areas within the municipal limits. *Consolidation* means the combining of two or more existing municipal corporations into a single one. Here, again, state law is supreme, for annexation and consolidation must proceed in accordance with such law.

FORMS OF CITY GOVERNMENT

In the United States, there are three principal forms of city government. They are the mayor-council plan, the commission plan, and the council-manager plan. Adapted from the earlier English model, the mayor-council plan is the most traditional and common of the forms now in use. Of those cities with a population of more than five thousand, more than half are reported to operate under the mayor-council system.

But the commission and council-manager plans are of much more recent origin, having been developed in this century. Commission government probably began in the Galveston charter of 1901, under interesting circumstances. In September 1900, a disastrous flood and tidal wave inundated the city. Operating under a mayor-council system, the city government proved itself totally incapable of coping with the emergency conditions created by the flood. At the request of a group of imaginative residents of Galveston, the legislature of Texas passed a special act granting the city the commission form of charter. The plan was successful and was almost instantly accepted by other cities. For example, in 1905 Houston adopted the plan. It is said that the peak in popularity of the plan was probably reached around 1917, at which time some five hundred cities had adopted the commission form. However, though it has gradually lost favor, it retained a strong hold on local government in New Jersey until very recent times. Its popularity has always been greatest in cities with a population of fewer than fifty thousand persons.

There is disagreement as to the exact moment of birth of the council-manager plan. The prevailing view is that the honor belongs to Staunton, Virginia, which established a post of city manager in 1908. On the other hand, the first city to operate under a council-manager charter was Sumter, South Carolina, in 1912. The plan was favored from a very early period by the National Municipal League, and undoubtedly much of the success of the plan has been due to the league's continuing efforts on its behalf. The largest city ever to adopt and then abandon the plan has been Cleveland. Of all cities in the country with a population of more than five thousand persons, the council-manager plan is now used in about 40 percent. In recent years the largest cities to use the plan have been Cincinnati, Dallas, San Antonio, and San Diego.

Mayor-Council Government

Under the mayor-council plan, the main agencies of government are an elected council and an elected mayor. In theory, the council is the policy-determining body and the mayor is the chief executive. In actual practice, a strong mayor may ride herd over a weak council. The plan is characteristically American in that it retains the much-cherished separation of powers, pitting one branch against another. It should be emphasized, in this connection, that the council members are elected on one section of a ballot and the mayor is elected on another. In short, the mayor represents a city-wide constituency, while the council represents, as a rule, individual districts.

At present, nearly all city councils are unicameral, or one-chamber. But up until recent decades it was common for the councils to be bicameral. And it can be argued that New York city today, with a city council along with a board of estimate, still represents a version of the earlier system of municipal government.

Called councilmen or aldermen, council members are chosen by popular vote, usually for a term of two or four years. Nomination is ordinarily by primary election. In some cities, both the primary elections and the general elections are nonpartisan, although often this is an extremely thinly disguised fiction.

As mentioned above, the most common practice calls for the election of council members by wards or districts. But in some cities, for example, in Philadelphia, some council members are chosen from councilmanic districts and some from the city at large.

In any election based on the winner-take-all principle, i.e., that the person who gets the most votes carries the district, there is bound to be a distortion between the percentage of seats held on the council by the majority party and the percentage of all popular votes for candidates for that party. In order to overcome this obvious problem, some cities have adopted proportional representation (P.R.) in council elections. The system used in America is called the Hare plan, named after its inventor, an English barrister.

Under this plan, a voter ranks the candidates numerically in order of preferences. Once a candidate achieves the "quota" necessary for election to the council, his or her "surplus" votes are transferred and added to those of the next-ranked candidate on each ballot who has not to that point achieved the quota needed for election. Because of this characteristic, the plan is also referred to as the "single transferrable vote" system. As the transferring of votes continues; nearly every voter helps elect some persons to the council, even though the council members elected may not have been those of the voter's first choice. Inaugurated in Ashtabula, Ohio, in 1915, the plan continues to operate successfully in a number of cities, including Cambridge, Massachusetts. From 1938 to 1949, a form of P.R. was used in New York city. The individual boroughs served as the election districts, and party designations appeared on the ballot. The abandonment of P.R. in New York city apparently came about because under the system an occasional Communist was elected from Brooklyn. This was more than the civic conscience of the majority of New York city's voters could bear, and the retention of P.R. was defeated in a popular referendum.[2]

Councils meet regularly on a weekly or monthly basis. As

with most legislative bodies, a good deal of the real work is done in the standing committees. In some cities, the mayor is the presiding officer; in others, it is the council president. In the latter case, there is apt to be continual and often acrimonious rivalry between the two officials.

In their legislative capacity, councils give most of their attention to financial and regulatory matters. They regulate such fields as health, traffic, building standards, and zoning. They may let contracts and authorize public improvements. In its legislative functioning, a council can pass an ordinance, which is local law, or a resolution, which is usually an action on an administrative matter.

As state government tends to parallel the federal, the powers of the mayor tend to parallel those of the governor. He or she appoints and removes (often with the consent of council) and has the power to veto and to make recommendations. A very strong mayor may get a good deal of authority not specifically spelled out in the charter by his or her adroit use of public relations techniques, approbation by the mass media, and support from powerful interest groups and alliances. In addition, in most of the larger cities there has been created in recent years a position of managing director (the titles vary), an official directly responsible to the mayor for the day-to-day management of affairs. This position is not to be confused with that of a city manager who, as we shall see, is responsible to the council. If there is a managing director, the mayor is thereby freed to give his or her attention to activities other than administration. And many a mayor is more skilled in public relations or politics than in administration.

It is important to distinguish between two types of mayor-council governments: the weak-mayor type and the strong-mayor type. As the term indicates, the weak-mayor type gives the mayor relatively unimportant administrative powers when compared to those of the council. Under the strong-mayor plan, in contrast, the mayor has formidable administrative powers and the powers of the council are correspondingly diminished. In most of the larger cities the trend, in recent years, has been to increase the administrative powers of the mayor and to decrease those of the council. From the point of view of public administration, this makes good sense, for its lets the public know where responsibility should be placed for good or bad civic performance.

Yet the overwhelming superiority of the strong-mayor—

Mayor Richard J. Daley of Chicago. (Wide World Photos.)

council form over its rivals comes not so much from administrative as from political considerations. Cities, especially
big cities, want their mayors to be public figures of considerable
visibility. The attraction of a Richard J. Daley or of a Frank Rizzo stems mainly from his innate ability to attract public attention. Psychologically, the mayor is viewed as the local counter-
part of the governor or the president. Who handles the park
system is not very important as long as the parks are reasonably
well run. Because the commission and council-manager plans
have failed to meet these leadership standards, they have

generally not been successful in the very largest American cities.

Commission Government

Allowing for some variation in detail, the essential features of commission government are the same everywhere. Usually the plan provides for a commission of from five to seven commissioners, who are the only elected officials of the city. Normally, they are chosen at large and most frequently on a nonpartisan ballot in both primary and general elections. As a group, they form the commission and are responsible both for policy formulation and for legislation in the municipality.

The key feature of the plan is that each commissioner serves as head of one of the administrative departments. This means that the separation of powers doctrine is abandoned, since obviously both administrative and legislative powers rest in the same hands. In some cities the commissioners are elected to head specific departments; in others actual assignment is determined by majority vote of the commissioners themselves. One of the commissioners will be given the title of mayor, through one of several possible routes. But however the mayor is selected, he or she is merely the titular head of the city. Aside from presiding over meetings and greeting visiting dignitaries, the mayor has the same authority as any other commissioner.

Why did the commission form enjoy an era of popularity? Basically, the attractiveness of the plan lay in its very short ballot, for only a handful of officials are elected. The framework of the government is simple, and it is understandable. But the objections are very serious. Firstly, city administration tends to be under the control of professional politicians who are, unfortunately, likely to be amateurs in matters of public administration. Secondly, administrative responsibility is both decentralized and fragmented. As these deficiences became more apparent, the earlier popularity of the commission plan fell into decline.

Council-Manager Government

The council-manager plan was intended to overcome the deficiencies of the commission plan by providing for a professional city (or county or town or borough) manager who operates directly under the supervision of the council. Normally, the council itself is not very large. It is common to elect council members at large, but some plans employ election by wards or districts. In a great many of the council-manager cities, election is nonpartisan.

As in the commission plan, the separation of powers is discarded in favor of a fusion of executive and legislative powers. But there is, in fact, a very effective separation of *functions*. The council, of course, performs the legislative function, but the council members themselves do not carry on the administrative work of the municipality. For this purpose the council appoints a manager who is directly in charge of the department heads and supervises their performance. The council, in brief, performs two main functions: it legislates, and it appoints a manager.

Again, as with the commission plan, the council-manager plan provides for a mayor. But the office is purely titular and ceremonial and the mayor possesses no appointive or veto power. Usually, the mayor is chosen by the council from among its own membership.

The essential relationship in the council-manager plan is that between the council and the manager. This is a difficult relationship to describe, for it varies from city to city and from personality to personality. It might appear that the line between policy formulation by the council and policy execution by the manager is a clear and obvious one, but this is not the case. The most successful managers have always been initiators of policy, even if only in subtle ways. And most council members look to the manager for leadership. Yet this leadership cannot be exercised in a way that is offensive to the council, for the manager serves at the pleasure of the council. The manager may be discharged by the council at any time—that is a basic part of the arrangement.

What are the advantages of the council-manager plan? In the first place, it has great administrative strength. Administrative responsibility is centralized in the hands of one official. There is also a great emphasis on professionalism, and the managers have themselves developed a national association and supportive publications. The practice has been for successful managers to begin in small or medium-sized municipalities and move from them to larger cities. Though the risks are obviously high, the salaries are usually generous. Many a person has made a lifetime career as a manager.

But there have also been criticisms of the council-manager plan, chiefly on two grounds. It is sometimes claimed that the plan is undemocratic in that the manager is appointed and not elected. What is wrong with this charge is that democratic theory emphasizes the point that power must be exercised responsibly. Whether a person is appointed or elected is entirely secondary. The second common objection to the plan is that it often fails to provide for adequate political leadership. There is probably some validity to this argument as applied to the largest cities. As we noted in discussing the strong-mayor–council plan, the largest cities appear to want as their chief executives persons who are vigorous, effective, and visible leaders. Under these conditions, the day-to-day supervision given by a manager under the council-manager system can be entrusted to a city director appointed by the mayor and responsible only to the mayor.

Nonetheless, the council-manager plan continues to increase its popularity in the smaller cities; it has been adopted by numerous boroughs and townships, and by a few counties. It also has the great advantage of being easy to understand, at least in principle. Anyone who understands the relationship of a superintendent of education to an elected board of education automatically understands the basis of the council-manager plan. For the relationship in the two cases is identical.

OTHER SUBSTATE GOVERNMENTAL FORMS

Smaller Municipalities

The fact that most Americans now live in metropolitan areas does not mean that they reside in the central cities. On the contrary, the 1970 census revealed that a majority of persons residing in metropolitan areas live in the suburban fringes.

There are two readily distinguishable types of smaller municipalities. One type is really a suburb and stands in a socioeconomic relationship to the central city. The other is the small city, village, borough, or town—depending on the terminology of a particular state—which is outside any metropolitan area.

Even within a single county, the proliferation of local municipalities is staggering. For example, consider the case of Delaware County, Pennsylvania, which is adjacent to Philadelphia and is included within that city's metropolitan area. In addition to the county government, there are these subdivisions: third class city—one (Chester); boroughs—twenty-seven; townships—twenty-one. Nor can one judge much about the size of a community by its classification alone. For example, the population of Chester stood at about 56 thousand in 1970, while that of Upper Darby, a township, was about 95 thousand.

Counties

Except for persons who live in unincorporated rural areas, most people come under the jurisdiction of both a municipal and a county government. One exception would occur in those few areas where city-county consolidation has resulted in one combined governmental unit. Other exceptions come from New England, where the basic units of government are the town (which when populous enough may by electoral action become a city, state requirements having been met) and the state itself. For example, in Connecticut, the county is basically a judicial unit. Another exception is Washington, D.C. As a federal district, it is not part of any county. In 1973 its voters approved a home rule charter sponsored by Congressman John R. Conyers, a distinguished Democrat from Detroit.

In the United States in 1972 there were 3,044 counties, a large percentage of which were classified as rural. But a 1966 study by the Committee for Economic Development determined that as of that year 102 metropolitan areas possessed a single county government, that is, one governmental authority which embraced the entire metropolitan area. In addition, of course, many metropolitan areas include two or more counties. As of 5 April 1974 there were 269 such metropolitan areas in the country, including 4 in Puerto Rico. (The whole problem of metropolitan areas, and their governments, will be discussed in a later chapter.)

There appear to be no substantial structural differences between urban and rural counties. Though specifics differ, it may be observed that all counties have a general governing board, and all have a series of officers, boards, and commissions assigned various tasks.

Governing Boards. For the general governing board —officially called the board of commissioners, board of supervisors, or some similar name—the principal duties are to control the fiscal affairs of the county, to perform some administrative functions, and to exercise some authority over county affairs in general. Members of the county board are usually elected.

In terms of organization, two plans predominate. The first is a relatively small board of county commissioners; the second is a larger county board of supervisors. Of the two forms, the more prevalent is the board of commissioners. Used nearly everywhere in the South and West, it is commonly employed in other sections of the country as well. The membership may vary from three to seven members, and election is by the county's voters at large.

Where the alternative kind of county board—the board of supervisors—is used the membership may be quite large, as in New York, Michigan, and Wisconsin. Here the general practice is for each township to elect one supervisor, except that the more populous townships are entitled to additional representation. While the highest membership figure has never made the *Guinness Book of World Records,* the unofficial honors apparently go to Wayne County (Detroit), Michigan, whose board in 1952 had ninety-seven members.

When compared with the scope of legislative authority conferred by the states on their municipalities, the powers of the county board are not impressive. The principal legislative power relates to county finance. But the board usually possesses a good deal of executive and administrative power. Since the board ordinarily controls county property, makes contracts on behalf of the county, appoints certain county officers, and oversees elections, state courts usually regard the board as an administrative body.

Counties remain the *terra incognita* of American local government. They seem to have made very little progress toward integrating the activities for which they are responsible. Generally, county administration may best be viewed as a collection of relatively independent agencies which are rarely coordinated in their operations.

In spite of this generally bleak situation, there are a few bright spots on the horizon. For many years the National Municipal League and other civic groups have stressed the need to coordinate the activities of county government. In recent years there has been a tendency, probably in response to such pressures, to establish an overall executive power with authority over major administrative functions.

The County Executive. A county executive may be provided by election or by appointment. The practice of election goes back many years. Cook County (Chicago), Illinois, has had an "elective president of the county board" since the 1890s. Since 1900 Hudson and Essex counties in New Jersey have elected executives with the title of county supervisor. But the modern drive in this direction dates from the 1930s. During that period, both Nassau and Westchester counties in New York adopted charters which provided for an elected county executive. In practice, these executives hold and exercise powers comparable to those of a strong mayor. But one should not exaggerate the trend. A study in 1965 found that only twelve counties in the entire county did have elective executives who had the powers normally accorded a strong mayor.

There is an alternative to the election of county executives: they may be appointed by the county board itself. In 1972 more than eighty-eight counties in seventeen states operated under a county-manager plan, the county equivalent of the city council-manager plan already discussed. The results have been highly satisfactory. On the other hand, the adoption of the county-manager plan appears to be confined mainly to large urban counties.

As a variation of the county-manager system, several states have come up with a plan that has been called the quasi-manager plan. This has found favor in Tennessee, South Carolina, Ohio, and especially California. Under this approach, the manager—called the chief administrative officer—has many but not all of the powers given under the orthodox county-manager arrangement.

It is clear that there will continue to be wide variation in the kinds of county executives. Basically, the arrangement in effect in any particular county will be determined not by abstract logic but by considerations of what is politically possible, tempered by the prevailing socioeconomic situation. It is encouraging to note, however, that changes toward increasing administrative responsibility and centering it in one official are in progress in many parts of the country.

Special Districts

A very large share of governmental activity in America is carried on by special districts. The magnitude of their operations is suggested by Table 8.1. In the table, school districts and special districts are listed separately in order to show the numbers in each classification, but school districts constitute one very common form of special district. Usually, school districts are organized along the same lines as council-manager governments. There is a small elected school board, which appoints a superintendent who in fact runs the school system.

Table 8.1
Local Governments in the United
States, 1962, 1967, and 1972

Type of Government	1962	1967	1972
All local governments	91,185	81,253	78,218
Counties	3,043	3,049	3,044
Municipalities	17,997	18,051	18,517
Townships	17,144	17,107	16,991
School districts	34,678	21,782	15,781
Special districts	18,323	21,264	23,885

Source: Statistical Abstract of the United States.

Other types of special district include fire protection, transit, soil conservation, mosquito abatement, cemetery, library, irrigation, and drainage districts. Some of these districts are relatively small; others are gigantic. Consider the following four illustrations:[3]

The bi-state Port Authority of New York and New Jersey, established in 1921 under the terms of a compact between the two states, is a huge operation by anyone's standards. The governing body of the authority is a board of twelve commissioners, six of whom are appointed by the governor of each state with the consent of that state's senate. The responsibility for the administration of the authority's activities is in the hands of an executive director appointed by the board. Under the terms of the compact which created the agency, the authority has these powers: to construct, purchase, or lease, and to operate, self-supporting transportation or terminal facilities of any kind. Projects may be financed by the issuance of (tax-exempt) bonds, though the authority has no taxing power.

As of now, the authority owns port and terminal facilities valued at more than one billion dollars. Under lease, it operates additional properties. It operates the Holland and Lincoln tunnels under the Hudson River for motor traffic, the double-deck George Washington Bridge over the river, and the Staten Island bridges—Goethals Bridge, Bayonne Bridge, and Outer-bridge Crossing. In addition to dock and other port facilities, the authority operates the major New York area airports—La Guardia, Kennedy, Newark, and Teterboro. It also operates a railroad system underneath the Hudson, formerly the Hudson and Manhattan, now known as PATH. The lines run from midtown Manhattan to Hoboken, Jersey City, and Newark.

From an investor's point of view, the authority's bonds are among the securest in the world. For 1973 the authority had a gross operating revenue of $373.5 million and a net operating revenue of $137.1 million, and employed about eight thousand persons.

Or, consider the Metropolitan Sanitary District of greater Chicago. In 1973 its revenue exceeded $140 million and the system employed 2,399 employees. But the Chicago Transit Authority was even larger. For 1972 it had an income of $187.1 million and some twelve thousand six hundred employees.

A different type of special district is the Delaware Valley Regional Planning Commission (DVRPC). Created in 1965, the commission includes in its membership one representative each from the governors of Pennsylvania and New Jersey and from the Department of Transportation of each state. There is also a representative of the Pennsylvania Office of State Planning and Development and the New Jersey Department of Community Affairs. The voting membership of eighteen is completed by a representative of each of the four counties on either side of the region and each of the four cities within it.

The commission is charged with regional planning for transportation, sewer and water systems, housing, land use, and open space. Even though the commission is an advisory agency and must rely largely on federal funding for its studies and research, it carries very considerable potential clout. The goals it sets for overall regional planning in such areas as land use, open space, housing, improving the environment, and transportation are likely to receive very serious consideration. One of the outstanding successes of the DVRPC to date has been its support of the Lindenwold High Speed Line, a railway system between Philadelphia and Lindenwold, New Jersey, which transported forty-three thousand passengers on an average weekday in March 1974. The commission's present objective is to extend the line deeper into the New Jersey sections of the greater Philadelphia commuting area.

With all the governments which already exist in the United States, one may wonder why more, especially special districts, are needed. The answer is threefold. A special district, such as a school district, is in theory a way in which a governmental agency may retain or acquire some measure of independence from the "politicians"—i.e., the city or town council. A second reason is the obvious need to bring about some degree of regional cooperation and consolidation, as with planning or transportation. Finally, a special district furnishes a method for evading a limitation on taxes or debts which may be imposed by state constitutions or city charters. The Port Authority of New York and New Jersey is a splendid illustration: it is not only self-financing, it makes money for its bond holders.

INTERGOVERNMENTAL RELATIONS

In earlier chapters, we noted the web of interrelationships between the federal government and the governments of the states. In the present chapter emphasis has been placed on some of the interrelationships between the states and their leading subdivisions. But there is a further dimension which also requires identification. This is the area of interlocal relations.

Though the subject has not been the focus of extensive study in recent years, William C. Seyler has stressed its importance in a 1974 investigation. He found that the necessity for local governments to engage in interlocal cooperation, far from decreasing, is actually on the rise. He also showed that state governments are becoming increasingly aware of this situation, as shown by their willingness to permit local governments to enter into more and more agreements among themselves to improve and expand services. An example Seyler cites is a 1972 Arkansas statute that permits cities to purchase supplies at state contract prices. Other examples would include agreements to cooperate in such matters as water supply, fire protection, sewer services, tax collection, recreation, health services, and hospitals. The whole range of such services could be upgraded by more aggressive interlocal cooperative efforts.[4]

Items for Discussion

1. Within the same state, why are some cities much more successful in annexing adjacent areas than are other cities?

2. What might be some of the *negative* effects of nonpartisan elections?

3. What factors account for the growing popularity of the council-manager form of government?

4. Do county units of government continue to serve a useful function, or might it be better to abolish counties and replace them with regional units centered around metropolitan areas?

5. Since so many large metropolitan areas extend over two states (e.g., Chicago, New York, Philadelphia, Baltimore, Washington, Kansas City, St. Louis, Providence), how can intergovernmental cooperation best be accomplished?

Chapter Notes

1. John F. Dillon, *Commentaries on the Law of Municipal Corporations* 5th ed. (Boston: Little, Brown, 1911), Vol. 1, sec. 237.

2. See Belle Zeller and Hugh A. Bone, "The Repeal of P.R. in New York City—Ten Years in Retrospect," *American Political Science Review* 62 (Dec. 1948), pp. 1127—1148.

3. Sources: *Annual Reports* of the agencies.

4. William C. Seyler, "Interlocal Relations: Cooperation," *The Annals*, Vol. 416 (Nov. 1974), pp. 158—169. The entire issue is entitled *Intergovernmental Relations in America Today* and merits serious examination.

9

Community Political Systems: Conflict and Participation

Key Terms

Anglo-Saxon ethos: Citizen emphasis on goals of efficiency, honesty, and strong planning in government.

Elitism: Belief that a few select groups or persons dominate government decision making.

Federalist: Collected letters of John Jay, Alexander Hamilton, and James Madison written in support of the Constitution and, more generally, in support of a federal system of government.

Immigrant ethos: Citizens who identify with the ward or neighborhood rather than with the city as a whole.

Mass town meetings: Use of television to discuss important local issues and to allow citizens to express their policy preferences.

Model cities: Federal program begun by then-President Lyndon Johnson to direct large sums of money for projects in a few cities in order to show dramatically the effects of a large-scale, coordinated approach to renewal.

Patronage: Power to make appointments to office or confer contracts based on partisan political considerations.

Pluralism: Belief that policy-making power is shared by many competing groups within a community.

Public-regarding: Support for activities which benefit the entire community; contrasted with private-regarding or seeking only personal gain through government activities.

Ward: Division of a city for purposes of electing members to the city council; each ward is composed of smaller, neighborhood units called *precincts.*

At the community level, politics may be viewed as the management of conflict. This point seems obvious, but, as Thomas R. Dye and Brett W. Hawkins have observed, it was for many years overlooked.[1] Instead, interest tended to be focused on either immediate electoral contests or current problems of public administration.

MADISON'S CONTRIBUTIONS

In recent years the tendency has been to regard community politics with the same degree of realism that James Madison did in *The Federalist No. 10.* He, as well as the other Founding Fathers, regarded the control of "faction" as a principal task or duty of government. For Madison, the regulating of conflicts among diverse interests and groups was "the principal task of modern legislation." It is now customary to apply this insight to the politics of communities as well as to the nation.

What did Madison regard as the sources of political conflict? In his famous essay, he treats the problem in this fashion:

The latent causes of faction are thus sown in the nature of man; and we see them everywhere brought into different degrees of activity, according to the different circumstances of civil society. A zeal for different opinions concerning religion, concerning government, and many other points, as well of speculation as of practice; an attachment to different leaders ambitiously contending for preeminence and power; or to persons of other descriptions whose fortunes have been interesting to human passions, have in turn, divided mankind into parties, inflamed them to mutual animosity, and rendered them much more disposed to vex and oppress each other than to cooperate for their common good. So strong is this propensity of mankind to fall into mutual animosity, that where no substantial occasion presents itself, the most frivolous and fanciful distinctions have been sufficient to kindle their unfriendly passions and excite their most violent conflicts. But the most common and durable source of faction has been the various and unequal distribution of property. Those who hold and those who are without property have ever formed distinct interests in society. Those who are creditors, and those who are debtors, fall under a like discrimination. A landed interest, a manufacturing interest, a mercantile interest, a moneyed interest, with many lesser interests grow up of necessity in civilized nations, and divide them into different classes, actuated by different sentiments and views.

In brief, what Madison is alleging is that human diversity is a fundamental source of political conflict in urban societies. What are some of these differences?

To cite but a few illustrations, the following distinctions could be and have been the cause of conflict: (1) the numbers, density, and heterogeneity of the people living in the area; (2) the presence of a highly complex and diversified economic system; (3) differences based on income, education, and occupation; (4) differences based on race or ethnic background; and (5) differences based on family (or cultural) style of living. Obviously, the list could be refined and thereby extended indefinitely.

THE MANAGEMENT OF URBAN CONFLICT

The management of conflict in urban communities is clearly complicated by the *degree* of interdependence between a center city and its suburbs. Considering the country in regional terms, there are very great differences in the amount of dependence the suburbs may have on the central cities. Scarsdale can probably exist with or without New York city, but most of the independent municipalities in Los Angeles County could not exist without the city of Los Angeles. There is, in short, no hard and fast rule or guideline.

The reason for this is partly the high degree of decentralization which characterizes most metropolitan areas. In brief, there is not only the problem of interdependence, there is also the question of independence. In some areas, this clash brings about obvious political conflict, for instance, in the realm of regional transportation. Who is to get what services is a very serious, and highly politicized, question.

Again, in the management of conflict, the problem arises of how to maintain order. This is somewhat different from the question of why people obey the law; the usual answer to that question is because of habit. Given the existence of conflicts within a metropolitan area, or even in a smaller community, precisely how is the government to maintain order? Clearly, the answer is not the simplistic one of relying on tear gas and sidearms. Most conflicts are resolved through institutional councils, agencies, courts, and other devices. In other words, the objective is to establish rules and values and then to apply them to particular situations.

THE ROLE OF INSTITUTIONS

Of course, there have always been people who assume that the formal political institutions are little more than a façade for some ruling group. In the language of social scientists, this is the theory of "elitism." A leading proponent of this perspective is Floyd Hunter, whose study of Atlanta, *Community Power Structure*, became the standard reference work of the elitists.[2]

In contrast, the leader of the opposition forces found in his study of New Haven that actual governing power was divided not along class lines but along functional lines. In *Who Governs?* Robert A. Dahl, the distinguished Yale political scientist, concludes that the leaders in one area of political interest are unlikely to be the leaders in other areas. In short, he concluded that pluralism, not elitism, was dominant in the civic affairs of New Haven during the ten-year period during which he and his associates carried out their intensive investigation.[3] Though efforts have been made to reconcile the divergent theories, or at least to explain why able investigators arrive at differing conclusions, the debate continues. As a rule, where sociologists see elitism, political scientists see pluralism.[4]

As we shall see later, there has also been a powerful movement to remove "politics" from municipal government. Because the classic political machine served mostly the rich and the poor, it was understandable that a good deal of middle-class support would be generated for a kind of nonpartisan urban political style. In some cases, the emphasis may have arisen merely from a desire to apply businesslike methods to the management of government. In other cases, the reform movements no doubt sprang from moral convictions of good and evil.

Finally, a general cause of conflict within metropolitan areas has been whether structural reform is either feasible or desirable. Because of the importance of this question, an entire chapter is devoted to it later in this book. Here it need only be noted that efforts at reorganization in recent years have met with tremendous opposition from many quarters. The proponents of integrated metropolitan government usually stress efficiency, which is a goal that is obviously not important to a majority of the voters in most metropolitan regions. The point is that different voters have different values, and it is very difficult to arrive at a consensus on what political acts of reorganization or integration should be undertaken.

CLEAVAGES IN URBAN POLITICS

In some small communities, there are few lines of cleavage—that is, issues that arise from the more lasting divisions of society. But, as Edward C. Banfield and James Q. Wilson pointed out in their 1963 publication, *City Politics*, this is not the case in urban politics generally.[5] In urban politics the cleavages tend to be long lived, and, therefore, the sources of continuing political division. Though the specific case studies of the Banfield and Wilson work are now out of date, the general analysis of conflict by these authors remains valid. The following paragraphs represent a summary of their conclusions as to the sources of urban political conflict. It is for the reader to decide which sources should be given greater or lesser weight in particular communities.

The Urban-Rural Cleavage

From a historical perspective, the basic division affecting city politics has been not within the city but between the city and the countryside. Beginning in colonial times, city dwellers have been distrusted during most of our history. Even though the country achieved an urban majority in 1920, that distrust has continued to manifest itself in many ways.

In our literary tradition, the city dweller has been portrayed as sophisticated and knowledgeable, in contrast to the supposed backwardness and selfishness of rural people. This has been held to be the case although the most successful radical movements in American history—the Greenback and Granger movements—were agrarian in origin.

But the legend has remained and has, in fact, been reshaped. The cleavage today tends to be "upstate" or "downstate," and it can be very real indeed. Whether one lives in a rural area is no longer of much political importance in the politics of New York state. Whether one lives in or outside of New York city is, on the other hand, a factor of tremendous importance. Or again, despite some farm lands, Pennsylvania is predominantly urban today. Yet the politics of the state tends to be divided on a tripartite basis: eastern Pennsylvania (Philadelphia and its allies) versus central Pennsylvania versus western Pennsylvania (Pittsburgh and its allies).

It matters, too, whether the urban area is a fully developed large city or simply a city which meets the minimum census definition of four thousand persons. Clearly, the interests of each group may and probably will differ, for example, on matters of taxation. In New York state, for instance, the voters over the years have rather consistently refused to let New York city increase its very sizeable debt and expand its school and other facilities. Or, to take a further example, why should the citizens of New York state, through the legislature, permit the state to underwrite the free tuition policy of the City University of New York to the extent of meeting at least 50 percent of the operating budget? At the same time, the State University of New York, with branches all over the state, charges a reasonable but still substantial tuition.

As Banfield and Wilson have also noted, the cleavage between city and hinterland proably tends to prevent mayors of the largest cities from being elected to higher office. Very few mayors have ever been elected to the governorship or to the United States Senate, and even fewer have been considered seriously as presidential contenders.

Both within cities themselves and inside the great metropolitan areas, there are certain cleavages which are virtually permanent. As identified in *City Politics*, they are as follows: (1) the haves and have-nots, (2) suburbanites and the central city, (3) ethnic and racial groups, and (4) political parties. In turn, these cleavages are said to cut across each other and to become a "fundamental cleavage" separating two opposing conceptions of the public interest. Each of these cleavages will be considered, following which some observations will be made concerning the "fundamental" cleavage noted by Banfield and Wilson.

Haves and Have-Nots

As was noted earlier, Madison believed that the most fundamental cause of political conflict was the disparity in the distribution of property. In a city population, the tendency is for there to exist three large, but not sharply defined, income groups: the low, the middle, and the high. Contrary to the suppositions of doctrinaire economic determinists, the alliance is usually between the lower- and higher-income groups, which are in conflict with the middle-income group.

It is easy to see why this is the case. The rich can afford good services, public or private, and are prepared to pay for them. On the other hand, the poor are usually in favor of a high level of expenditure for any purpose. But it is the middle group, generally, that favors keeping a tight lid on local expenditures. Again, the reasons are economic. The middle class consists of people who usually own their homes and are particularly hard hit by property taxes. They are also worried about mortgage payments and installment payments on their cars.

An example cited by Banfield and Wilson is the Detroit of a decade ago (it has seriously deteriorated in the last ten years). Detroit was then a predominantly lower-middle-class home-owning town. It had one industry and one dominant union—the United Auto Workers. In state politics, the UAW was extremely successful and contributed enormously to the election of its ally, G. Mennen Williams, to the office of governor of Michigan for five terms. Yet in city politics, the UAW voters voted their pocketbooks. For four straight terms UAW members and their families were instrumental in electing conservative businessman Albert E. Cobo, a former official of the Burroughs Corporation, to the office of mayor. In local elections, white middle-class voters usually vote as property owners and taxpayers. They are not especially interested in projects aimed at the betterment of the poor, particularly if the latter group is largely black. Another way of putting the matter is that many middle-class voters will often support a "progressive" state administration while sup-

A policeman guards a fire truck during the Detroit riots in the summer of 1967. (Wide World Photos.)

porting a fairly negative city administration at the same time. The phenomenon may partly be explained by psychological considerations, but it also may be explained in terms of the incidence of taxation: who pays the bills for the services delivered by the municipality?

Suburbanites and the Central City

Though the cleavage between the central cities and their suburbs has been of long standing, it appears to have deepened in the post–World War II period. For example, especially since legislative reapportionment, a combination of the suburbs plus the hinterland may overpower the big city representation in many state assemblies.

Obviously, not all suburbs are alike, and their economic interests may be in conflict. Upper-income suburbanites insist on the basic amenities of civic life, and they get them. Above all else, such persons fear annexation by the central city, since they believe that such an action would result in a lower level of services. On the other hand, there are communities (sometimes unincorporated) that would just as soon not have such conveniences as sidewalks, community sewage disposal, and police protection. They therefore also fear being brought within the jurisdiction of the central city, but for a different reason. Annexation would result in the providing of services—through higher taxes—that this kind of suburbanite would just as soon do without.

Of course, there are other bases for the cleavage between the suburbs and the central city. An obvious one is taxation. Anyone who works in Philadelphia must pay a flat wage tax. It is not graduated, there are no exemptions, and it is deducted from one's pay in advance. To a commuting suburbanite, this may seem blatantly unfair. In reply, the city says that it provides certain services to the commuter during working hours, such as police and fire protection, and that the commuter should bear a fair share of the expenses for these services. To this, commuters reply that they pay for the city dwellers every time the urbanites get in a car and shop at a suburban shopping mall. And so the argument continues endlessly. What most suburbanites are convinced of is this: annexation by the central city would inevitably result in an increase in taxation, as the newly annexed areas would be forced to support the nonproductive areas, that is, the slums and ghettos, of the central city. For this reason, among others, annexation is usually vigorously and successfully resisted.

Ethnic and Racial Groups

A third general cause of cleavage in urban politics stems from conflicts among ethnic and racial groups. Though varying typologies could be used, that developed by Banfield and Wilson is still useful and will be used here. Their plan is to speak of three types of cleavage: that between native-born Protestants and all others; that among the various nationality groups of foreign stock; and that between the Negro and all others.

Until the last decades of the nineteenth century, both business and politics were dominated by native-born Protestants in most American cities. Under the impact of substantial non-English immigration, political control shifted toward control by the immigrants of "foreign stock." Some cities have been studied quite extensively in this respect, especially Boston and New York. In Boston, for example, by about 1890 the Irish were numerically strong enough to take charge of municipal politics—and did so. The native Protestants responded by running the city from their command post in the state house, also located in Boston. In time, the native Protestants also lost control of state politics.

What happened in Boston happened in varying degrees across the country. When the old native elite lost political control of the big cities, it tended to shift its interests to control by other means. Dominant in the higher reaches of industry, commerce, and banking, but outnumbered at the polls, this elite took over control of the community service institutions. Formerly, this meant hospitals, civic associations, and private welfare organizations. Today it also includes the great tax-exempt foundations.

It is interesting to speculate as to why the native Protestants did not do what the Irish did with such success, namely, operate as a neutral force in which all of the newer ethnic elements might play differing but important roles. According to a widely accepted interpretation, the old elite decided that local politics had become some kind of "dirty business" and therefore abandoned it on moral grounds.

But Banfield and Wilson, relying in part on their own studies and in part on Richard Hofstadter's thesis in his well-known book *The Age of Reform* (1955), offer a different and more convincing hypothesis. Basically, their argument is that the Anglo-Saxon Protestant middle-class style of politics, with its emphasis on the obligation of the individual to participate in public affairs for the communal good, was incompatible with the immigrants' style of politics, which took no account of the total community.

On this basis, one would expect that the newer groups, once assimilated—a relative term—would more and more accept the Anglo-Saxon Protestant political ethos. This seems to be happening, but at varying rates. For example, as a group, Jews have been assimilated almost completely into this ethos. They do not seem to feel, as do some other groups, that they need "ethnic recognition." On the other hand, middle-class Catholics, who have long since shed personal loyalty to a ward leader as the basis for their vote, are rarely found in the ranks of the civic reformers. "Apparently, nowadays," say Banfield and Wilson,

> the nationality-minded voter prefers candidates who represent the ethnic group but at the same time display the attributes of the generally admired Anglo-Saxon model. The

perfect candidate, then, is of Jewish, Polish, Italian or Irish extraction and has the speech, dress, manner, and the public virtues—honesty, impartiality, and devotion to the public interest—of the upper-class Anglo-Saxon.[6]

At present the most visible, and in many ways the most difficult, of the cleavages we have to deal with is that based on race. Until World War II, few northern cities had many blacks, and the "problem" of blacks was considered to be mostly a southern concern. But the immense migration of rural southern blacks to the northern, midwestern, and western cities has vastly complicated the political scene. In addition, the tremendous migration of hundreds of thousands of Puerto Ricans to northern cities, and the arrival of scores of thousands of Cubans in Florida, has altered the overall picture. Besides legal immigration from Hispanic America, there is the question of massive, illegal but de facto settlement in California, Arizona, New Mexico, and Texas of thousands of Mexicans. Inevitably, there will be a resurgence of political cleavage, of potential political conflict, based on these population shifts.

Yet the weight of the evidence shows that most people, regardless of ethnic or racial background, react to politics in terms of their own position in the socioeconomic pecking order. In the long run, class and economic considerations are more important, politically, than those based purely on race or ethnicity. The key caveat is in the long run.

Political Parties

Almost all the important central cities are Democratic, and the suburbs are usually Republican. But there are many exceptions. The elections of 1974 demonstrated, if any one needed demonstration, the fragility of Republicanism. The Democratic party has a much more stable and enduring base than the Republican party.

So great is the Democratic supremacy in most central cities that the local elections are really decided in the Democratic primaries, not in the general elections. In this sense, whether a city uses a partisan or a nonpartisan ballot is not of any great consequence. Many cities that are nominally partisan are in fact nonpartisan. When, on rare occasions, a Seth Low or a Fiorello La Guardia or a John Lindsay wins the mayoralty of New York city, it occurs because the winning candidate is considered by a majority or plurality of the voters to be nonpartisan. Otherwise, the Democratic primary in New York city is the decisive factor. The victory of a "fusion" candidate merely means that the Democrats have been feuding among themselves.

In terms of the Banfield and Wilson approach, the most significant aspect of party is that the cleavage which is created is artificial. As we have seen earlier, the task of the primaries and of the party machinery generally is to narrow down the choices available to the voter. By definition, candidates are elected on the basis of mathematics. This is not to say that the different parties in the cities, and especially the different factions of the Democratic party, do not have special interests which support them. On the contrary, the interest-group support is all important. But the result of a winner-takes-all system, which on its face stresses legitimacy and implies a regularized, agreed-upon procedure, tends to make one forget that the basic urban cleavages are far deeper than those created by elections. This may, of course, have great virtues, because some of the cleavages are probably best left in a moribund or at least unresolved state.

To conclude the Banfield and Wilson analysis, we return to their idea of the "fundamental cleavage." Though the idea is overly simplistic, and though we cannot give justice to it in a few words, it is worth summarizing here. The distinction they make is between two kinds of citizens. First, there are those who favor the middle-class ethos, which can be identified more or less with the goals of efficiency, impartiality, honesty, strong planning, model legal codes, and so on. In contrast, there is a second type, those who derive their conception of the public good, in the words of Banfield and Wilson, from the "immigrant ethos." While the term may well be unfortunate, what the conception implies is a citizen or group of citizens who identify the ward or the neighborhood rather than the city as the political universe. These people are alleged to look to politicians for favors, to regard gambling and vice as necessary if regrettable evils, and to be more interested in the favors government can confer on them than in the achievement of such objectives as efficiency, impartiality, and honesty.

Because of this type of analysis, Banfield and Wilson have been accused of all sorts of moral and intellectual crimes. But what they are actually saying is that attitudes toward politics are culturally determined, and that socioeconomic status is a determinant of cultural conditioning. Their own preference is for an urban culture based upon middle-class values, or at least upon the Anglo-Saxon Protestant ethos, which they consider about the same thing. In this respect, they are more Madisonians than reactionaries, racists, or enemies of the Republic.

CITIZENSHIP PARTICIPATION

If all the principal forces in operation in a community were divisive, the community would undoubtedly fly apart. Clearly, there exist centripetal as well as centrifugal forces. Or, to put the matter differently, citizens may resolve or at least reduce the effects of political cleavage by various kinds of group participation. The effect is the resolution, or at least the lessening, of the kind of built-in conflicts we have already analyzed.

In the next few pages, we shall briefly identify some of the ways in which citizenship participation may help to mitigate the effects of conflict. These include the following: (1) the voters, (2) the political parties, (3) interest groups, (4) neighborhood and related organizations, and (5) the new device of mass media town meetings.

The Voters

Several summary observations can be made about voters in the context of urban communities. Voter turnout in local elections is almost always less than it is in state and national elections. This is true even though only about 45 percent of eligible voters took the trouble to vote in the 1974 congressional elections, which is perhaps an all-time low, at least for modern elections. Even in the largest cities the voter turnout rarely exceeds 30 to 50 percent of eligible voters. What this means in practice is the higher socioeconomic groups are overrepresented in local elections, since they are much more likely to vote than are the poorer groups. It is this situation which helps to explain the generally conservative stance of local governments, since what is important is to cater to the middle-income groups.

In addition, the figures over the years in the *Municipal Yearbook* demonstrate quite conclusively that nonpartisanship in local elections depresses the turnout. In any series of elections, the likelihood is that about 50 percent of the voters will participate in partisan cities as against roughly 30 percent in nonpartisan cities.

Another characteristic of local elections which also probably helps to hold down the rate of participation is the widespread custom of holding them in years when there are no national or state elections. The net effect is believed to be twofold: to increase the influence of the dominant organization and to further the interests of the middle class. If nothing very exciting is going on, why should a person vote at all except (1) for loyalty to the organization or (2) because voting is regarded as a civic duty.

Everyone who has ever read a textbook on American national government knows that voting patterns are closely related to socioeconomic status. This concept is more complex than it seems at first glance, because it is possible to correlate voting preferences not only with income but with occupational, religious, ethnic, and racial status. Yet when a composite index is developed, such an instrument is remarkably useful in helping to study voting behavior. Generally, the poorer people are, the more likely they are to vote Democratic. Conversely, Republicanism is positively correlated with higher income groups. But, as in any complicated situation, there are exceptions. For example, at all income levels, Jews are more likely to be "liberal" in their political outlook than are other religious groups.

Voters also influence the course of government through participation in referenda. We have previously looked at this at the state level. But the practice of holding referenda on local issues, especially on bond issues and capital improvements, is widespread. The basic distinction in voting patterns appears to depend on home-owning versus non-home-owning voters. A person who owns real property is, on the evidence to date, far less likely to support increased municipal expenditures than is a person who owns no property. This seems rational enough as an exercise in conventional wisdom. But Wilson and Banfield have found some significant exceptions. The very rich are more likely to support increased taxes for municipal services than are the home-owning middle classes. Wilson and Banfield attribute this to the "public-regarding" ethic or the Anglo-Saxon Protestant ethos which such groups are likely to share. But it is a question of values and income, not of religion.[7] Upper-class Jews were also found to support municipal expenditures from which they personally would derive few if any real benefits.

Political Parties

Paradoxically, political parties simultaneously divide the electorate and bring large segments of the electorate together. As has been noted, the cleavage created by elections in many respects is artificial. But at the same time the alliances needed to put together a winning coalition may be very important.

Even in cities where local elections are held on a nonpartisan basis, political parties exist; their main function in such cases is to contest state and national offices. In cities where the elections are conducted on a partisan basis, there is likely to be a near monopoly of power in the hands of one party. The two-party system, so praised at the national level, is a rarity in America's cities.

As subsystems of state party systems, the parties in the cities are very highly regulated. Their committees and other structures are really the creations of state law. What complicates the system is that it is often the custom for an official—of government or of party—to wear several hats at the same time. For example, a congressman may be the dominant figure in several wards of a large city, despite the presence of ward leaders. Or, conversely, a ward leader may also serve as an elected official on the city council or even in the state legislature. There is, in short, a very highly developed system of overlapping membership. If this were not the case, the system would probably break down. It does not break down because various persons go from committee to committee and level to level, thus assuring continuity, at least on a personal basis. And local politics in the United States is mostly a politics of personality, not of issues.

The specifics of party organization in any city can only be determined by a detailed examination of the practices of that city and the laws of the particular state. Yet some generalizations may be made. Usually, party organization follows that of the existing political units. But the smallest unit of party organization—the precinct—is not governmental. It is, in fact, merely a registration and polling area. After the precinct (or in some places, the division), the next largest unit is the ward. Commonly, committeemen and committeewomen are chosen by primary or caucus in each precinct to form the ward committee. City organization is based on ward organization.

The system works in pyramid fashion, building upward on the basis of committees chosen by the party faithful. At the very top level of organization is the city committee, whose chairman or chairwoman is the official leader of the party.

In practice, the system is far less democratic than it appears to be. Some ward leaders are obviously more important than others, and influence is not distributed equally. Furthermore, the implied analogy with an administrative or military hierarchy is misleading. Studies have repeatedly shown that sizable vacancies almost always exist at the bottom levels of party organization. For example, for many years it has been possible in Minneapolis for anyone with a handful of friends to be chosen precinct committee member in certain precincts by simply registering a few favorable votes at an open meeting. In other words, in many cities the party organizations seem much more formidable in their tables of organization than they are in reality.

Party committee members are provided by state law and they are assigned some official duties. Yet the bulk of their work consists of efforts on behalf of the party: such functions as maintaining the party's local organization, raising money, and campaigning. The private nature of most of their work is demonstrated by the fact that they receive no public salaries for their services.

The position of a ward leader or other local party official is a good deal more tenuous today than it was a hundred years ago. Patronage appointments have been curtailed by the success of the civil service movement, which has resulted in selection for government service by competitive examination. In addition, what the leader had to offer in the form of private welfare services is insignificant in relation to what is available from various government-sponsored welfare and health programs.

Old-time machine leaders could hold their organizations together because they could offer something tangible in exchange for the efforts of ward and precinct leaders. Today the problem has completely shifted. The question has become: What does a city organization have to offer in return for the support it needs to function effectively? It is not an easy question to answer.

Interest Groups

If factionalism within the dominant political party (or organization, in the case of nonpartisan cities) is more important than competition between the parties, what is there that gives momentum to factionalism? In addition to the very general political cleavages referred to earlier, the specific impetuses for change are most likely to originate in the demands of powerful interest groups. In some of the technical literature of political science, political parties (or organizations) are said to perform the function of "aggregating" interests, that is, of pulling different interests together. At the same time, interest groups are said to perform the function of "articulating" interests, that is, of making it possible for group values to be formulated and expressed. The distinction is useful, because it permits a functional contrast between the two types of political institutions.

In urban America, as in the rest of America, the role of the party is to choose candidates and try to elect them to office. Interest (or pressure) groups rarely engage directly in the electoral function. Their concern, rather, is to influence public policy through contact with lawmakers, executives, and even judges. Interest groups therefore tend to be based on particular aspects of public policy.

American urban politics evinces a very wide spectrum of interest groups. These range from single-purpose groups—for example, those working for the passage or defeat of a particular bond issue—to permanent, multipurpose groups such as trade union councils.

Even though there is no generally accepted typology of interest groups, a rough classification would obviously include several categories. Normally, the most highly organized groups are those which are related to business. Labor organizations, too, may achieve a high degree of effectiveness. Professional groups wield a good deal of influence although, as in the case of the medical associations and the bar, this influence may be largely shielded from public view. In all large urban areas there are so-called good government groups. Among the most successful of these are the League of Women Voters and the National Municipal League, which have been in the forefront of civic reform for many decades. There is a vast number of groups based on race, ethnicity, or religion. Veterans' organizations also often play an important role in local politics, for example, when they urge that preference in municipal hiring be given to veterans.

One should be wary of judging an organization merely by its title, for some titles are extremely misleading. An organization devoted to "economy" in government, for example, may simply be a front operation for certain businesses wishing lower taxes. Some "patriotic" organizations have turned out to be nothing more than lobbies for various companies which supply materiel for the military establishment. Then, again, not all interests are represented in proportion to their potential strength in the community. The interests of consumers are rarely represented adequately, although there is some evidence that Ralph Nader and his associates are making consumers more aware of what they have in common.

From whatever angle one views interest groups, it is clear that they serve as the major impetus in local politics. The objective of a political organization is, mostly, to survive. But the objective of an active interest group is to influence the course of public policy. In contrast to the views of the late Professor E. E. Schattschneider, it is quite possible that a citizen may exert much more influence through an interest group than through the more conventional apparatus of the political party.

Neighborhood Organizations

An additional way in which citizens may participate actively in civic affairs is through neighborhood organizations. Such organizations should be distinguished from the ordinary interest groups, for their focus tends to be more local than that of most interest groups, and residentiality is more important than other criteria in determining membership.

Howard W. Hallman, president of the Center for Governmental Studies since its founding in 1969, has given us a summary of this relatively new and potentially very powerful movement. The following remarks are taken from his study of the subject.[8]

Before 1964, Hallman reports, public programs dealing with neighborhoods fell into fairly rigid categories. Under the Urban Renewal Program established by the Housing Act of 1954, each municipality desiring federal assistance was required to provide for citizen participation. Principally, this took the form of advisory committees, which drew mainly from the real estate and construction industries for their membership. Local groups were conspicuous by their absence.

The same pattern was followed in two new efforts of social reform initiated in 1961. In the programs of the President's Committee on Juvenile Delinquency, the basic idea was to fund sixteen planning grants for the development of community-based prevention programs. In the second program, the Gray Area

Program of the Ford Foundation, the idea was to award major grants to five communities and to one state. These programs provided the background for the Community Action Program, which was established by the Economic Opportunity Act of 1964. Under both programs, most board members came from reform-minded upper-income groups; very few board members came from the neighborhoods which were served.

But the 1964 act, which required "maximum feasible participation of residents of the areas and members of the groups served," changed the situation. Under this plan, the emphasis was placed on locally elected boards. Their responsibilities included the administration of an imaginative neighborhood-by-neighborhood attack on poverty and problems associated with poverty. In particular, the idea was to involve the poor in the solution of their own problems.

Then another new and somewhat competitive federal program came into being under the name of Model Cities. According to Hallman, its genesis was a task force on urban problems, appointed by then-President Johnson in anticipation of the new Department of Housing and Urban Development. Among other objectives, the task force proposed a program to pour large sums into a few cities to demonstrate the impact of a massive, coordinated approach. But Congress changed the proposal of the task force by requiring that smaller sums of money be distributed to a very large number of communities. In addition, it was provided that the new program would be controlled by city government, not by independent agencies like the community action agencies. However, "widespread citizen participation" was mandated. In the end, although the Model Cities Program was under municipal control, it did in fact develop widespread citizen participation in planning and program implementation.

All the plans to renew the cities came under some sort of restraint under the Nixon Administration. Either the plans were scuttled by reassignment to agencies that did not believe in them, or funds were "impounded," or both. In any event, while the form of the programs survived, their financial apportionments tended to disappear.

As would be expected, the municipalities themselves took some initiative in the development of urban neighborhoods. In New York city, then-Mayor John V. Lindsay in 1966 announced a plan to open thirty-five neighborhood city halls. Though the city council blocked the plan, Lindsay was eventually able to open six storefront operations and three mobile units through the use of private funds. Again, under the leadership of Mayor Louie Welch, Houston in December 1966 opened a neighborhood city hall in one of the city's poorest neighborhoods; and two years later Mayor Kevin H. White opened fifteen little city halls to serve all sections of Boston. In the late 1960s, Baltimore experimented with decentralization by setting up three mayor's "stations" to hear citizen complaints and to initiate remedial action when possible.

Other related developments include the use of community corporations (as in Columbus, Ohio, and Washington, D.C.) and of community development corporations. An example of the former is the United Planning Organization, established in Washington with Ford Foundation support in 1962. An example of the latter is the Watts Labor Community Action Committee, which was founded in 1965 with the support of the United Auto Workers. Eventually, the WLCAC received federal funds, stressed economic development, and established several subsidiary corporations, of which at least three were profit-making.

Whether the approach is through neighborhood governments or through neighborhood corporations, the movement toward neighborhood power appears to have become a permanent part of the urban political scene. It is surely a method by which citizens may exercise some very real measure of control over their political environment. We may conclude with Hallman's summary of a movement still in action: "Locally most of the efforts of community control commenced in the sixties have continued into the seventies. Through the years, the abrasive edges have worn off the most militant operations."[9] In other words, the story is still being written, and the script is much more promising than early critics such as Daniel P. Moynihan had prophesied a decade ago.

Mass Media Town Meetings

Except for some journalists, and handful of diehard social scientists, most experts in public opinion today are prepared to recognize the preeminent role that television plays in the formulating and the reporting of public opinion.

One such expert is John P. Keith, president of the Regional Plan Association (of greater New York). In a series of television town meetings in the spring of 1973, some 10 percent of the 20 million people in the New York urban region were confronted with fifty-one critical issues concerning the region's living conditions. Then they had a chance to choose, in Keith's words, among the hard trade-offs, using ballots available in newspapers, banks, and libraries. Ballots were also distributed by several large employers. The television town meetings were known as "Choices for '76."

The basic plan was to use local television to discuss important issues, to set up discussion groups, and to report on an individual basis the responses of people to the issues which were discussed. Those who read the book of the Regional Plan Association, watched television, discussed the issues, and voted arrived at the following general conclusions. On a majority basis, these conclusions included the following: (1) stop growth in the general New York region; (2) build communities, not just facilities; (3) build and save more housing; (4) shift school taxes in the interests of equity; (5) spend more for public transit as well as for expressways; (6) attack, in a variety of ways, the problems associated with poverty; (7) buy all parkland desired by the ultimate population of the region; and (8) improve the environment. "In summary, the New York Region envisioned by the full participants in CHOICES (distinguished from those who only voted and had no television, reading or discussion in-put) would be a more compact Region than it is now becoming, but with more public space in and around the urban areas."[10]

What was most impressive about the project, the questions and sponsors aside, was the regional aspect of it. It included participation in twenty-eight counties in New York and New Jersey and six in Connecticut. As a result of the participation of the thousands of viewers and voters who took part in the series of projects, a kind of coalition of persons concerned with regional issues began to form.

It is also interesting to note how the idea of "mass town meetings" has spread. Drawing directly on the lessons learned from the experience of the Regional Plan Association, similar meetings, using the television and small-group discussion format, were planned for Dallas, St. Louis, Detroit, Minneapolis, Jacksonville, and Washington, D.C. Other meetings were scheduled or had been held in numerous other cities, including Roanoke, Chicago, Milwaukee, Hartford, Corpus Christi, New Orleans, Philadelphia, Kansas City (Missouri), and North Adams (Massachusetts). In other words, by an adroit combination of citizen participation and television, the Regional Plan Association has succeeded in creating, in a sense, a twentieth-century "town meeting."[11]

All of this is encouraging, for it presents a new and feasible way in which citizens can help to formulate the public policies according to which they live most of their lives. No one believes that this is a panacea for all civic and urban problems, but certainly the Regional Plan Association has shown the rest of us how to increase citizen participation in public affairs. For further details, one should contact the Regional Plan Association. Or one could devise one's own format to increase citizen participation in the definition and then the solution of local and regional problems.

The concerned citizen has many avenues of approach in addition to the traditional means of political parties and interest groups. One has only oneself to blame if an adequate vehicle of approach cannot be found.

Items for Discussion

1. Would you classify the community power structure of your city as "elitism" or "pluralism"?

2. Discuss the principles of democracy. Then compare the extent to which democratic politics exists in small towns and in medium-sized cities.

3. Considering your own state, how has legislative reapportionment affected urban-rural cleavage?

4. Should an enthic group (e.g., the Irish in South Boston) be allowed, or even encouraged, to maintain their distinct culture through such means as the continuation of neighborhood schools?

5. Using a city of about 200 thousand population, evaluate the advantages and disadvantages of election by wards (as opposed to at-large city election) to the city council.

Chapter Notes

1. See Thomas R. Dye and Brett W. Hawkins, *Politics in the Metropolis*, 2nd ed. (Columbus, Ohio: Charles E. Merrill, 1971).

2. Floyd Hunter, *Community Power Structure* (Garden City, N.Y.: Anchor Books, 1963). The study was originally published in 1953.

3. Robert A. Dahl, *Who Governs?* (New Haven: Yale University Press, 1961).

4. On this general question, see Murray S. Stedman, Jr., *Urban Politics*, 2nd ed. (Cambridge, Mass.: Winthrop, 1975), chap. 9.

5. Edward C. Banfield and James Q. Wilson, *City Politics* (Cambridge, Mass.: Harvard University Press, 1963).

6. Cited in Dye and Hawkins, *op. cit.*, p. 52.

7. See James Q. Wilson and Edward C. Banfield, "Public Regardingness as a Value Premise in Voting Behavior," *American Political Science Review*, Vol. 58 (Dec. 1964); especially the figure and table on pp. 884 and 885.

8. Howard W. Hallman, "Neighborhood Power: A Ten Year Perspective," the entire issue of *Neighborhood Decentralization* (Nov.–Dec. 1974).

9. *Ibid.*, p. 9.

10. "The Metropolis Speaks," (New York: Regional Plan Association, August, 1974), p. 2.

11. On this point, see Michael J. McManus, "Creating 20th Century Town Meetings," *National Civic Review*, Vol. 64, No. 1 (Jan. 1975), pp. 9–13.

10

Community Political Systems: Styles

Key Terms

Blue ribbon leadership: Elite group of business people and professionals who often emerge as political leaders in a reform movement.

Brokerage system: Style of politics that stresses bargaining, trading, negotiating, and a leader (broker) who brings people together.

"Iron law of oligarchy": Theory of Robert Michels and Vilfredo Pareto that attacks the possibility of democracy by saying that small groups will dominate and control the majority in any organization.

Liberal democracy: Political system in which citizens are directly involved in making some political decisions, all citizens are legally equal, and all citizens enjoy widespread freedom.

Machine politics: An inner core of individuals, often associated with a particular leader (boss), which dominates city elections and policy making.

Petty bourgeois: *Bourgeoisie* was Marx's term for the ruling class; petty bourgeois indicates an inherent, narrow-minded conservatism.

Reform politics: "Good government" response to corruption which stresses that the best-informed citizens should establish policy and neutral technicians (bureaucrats) should carry it out.

Socialism: Doctrine advocating collective ownership and control of the means of economic production and an equitable distribution of goods among the members of the community.

Tammany Society: A political organization that for over a century (1786–1901) dominated New York city politics; the model of the corrupt urban machine.

Nearly all American political theorists would classify the United States as a liberal democracy. For the most part, they mean by this that the governmental process operates under certain fairly specific constitutional restraints and that decisions are generally arrived at after the type of group conflict described in the preceding chapter. Broadly speaking, the term *pluralistic democracy* is equated with liberal democracy, and the pluralistic model has normally been used to analyze the workings of American government at all levels. The most useful application of this concept has undoubtedly occurred in the area of urban politics.

THE BROKERAGE STYLE

The traditional urban political system (and it is undergoing changes, as we shall note) is characterized by a brokerage system of politics. In a manner somewhat similar to a commodities exchange, sales and purchases are handled by specialists operating under carefully specified procedures. No one is required to engage in the acquisition, trading, or selling of the commodities. But a person choosing to do so is thereby agreeing to accept the rules and regulations of the exchange.

As is true in other aspects of life, the so-called traders are also not equal in the resources at their disposal; some are far more powerful than others. In fact, the ownership of the commodities tends to be highly concentrated. A few people own a great deal, and many individuals possess only a fraction of the total. As applied to politics, the principle was expressed by the great German sociologist Robert Michels. In 1911, in his work entitled *Political Parties,* he formulated his "iron law of oligarchy": "Who says organization says oligarchy." The proposition can be restated in this way:

1. Organization necessarily produces oligarchy.

2. A political party is a form of organization.
3. Therefore, a political party results in oligarchy.

In the brokerage system, the broker is always a key figure. As a person who brings buyers and sellers together—for a fee, of course—the broker is in a position to affect the play of the game in numerous ways. Without the broker's presence, in fact, the game could not take place at all. There would be chaos, followed, no doubt, by some sort of dictatorial arrangement to counteract anarchy. So the broker is necessary. Above all else, the broker endlessly supervises bargaining, trading, and negotiating, with the result that all parties may at least have the illusion that the best arrangement possible under the given circumstances was consummated. The deals which are made—the decisions—come about not as the result of abstract appeals to justice or freedom but in response to the realities of the marketplace.

In its political manifestation, the brokerage system is built around a leader and the leader's organization. Persons or interests desiring to arrange a political accommodation must do so through the cooperation, intervention, and assistance of the dominant political group. In working out a solution to a problem—for example, whether a community group, a factory, or a school gets the use of a particular parcel of land—the political organization provides the means and the milieu for the bargaining of the different interests to take place. There is a quid pro quo, a trade-off, as in the commodities exchange system.

Naturally, brokerage politics places a high premium on organization, a fact well known in America ever since Aaron Burr used Tammany Hall to support the expanding Jeffersonian movement. Only in very recent times has the position of the political organization seemed ambiguous. Skepticism about the utility of political organizations did not become widespread, even among upper-class reformers, until around the time of World War II. In short, until recently almost everyone agreed with Michels.

The Two Subdivisions of Brokerage Politics

Brokerage politics comes in two forms, and it is probably sensible to state at this point the position taken in this chapter. The two forms are usually referred to as the "machine" type and the "reform" type. The types have different bases, as we shall see, and they stress differing objectives. But both types may be considered subdivisions of the generally accepted system of brokerage politics. In other words, in terms of policy output, it does not seem to make much difference which of the two styles a city favors. The actors may change to some extent, and the class orientation may vary, but so far as results are concerned, the differences in public policy are almost invisible.

The Machine. It is the machine subdivision which has historically attracted the greater amount of public attention. From the founding of the first New York Society of Tammany in 1785 until the present, the tactics, antics, and personalities of the democracy of New York have delighted journalists, scholars, and presumably the voting public. Even the Indian symbolism of the society—a grand sachem, twelve lesser sachems, the use of an Indian calendar in correspondence—pleased an electorate in search of political trimmings to a drab republican country.

The golden age of Tammany occurred following the Civil War, when the organization was under the leadership of William M. Tweed. The son of a prosperous chairmaker, Tweed received a fairly good education for the times. He entered politics as a volunteer fireman, became better known, and then joined in ward politics. Working his way up in the Democratic organization, Tweed became a sachem of the Tammany Society in 1857 and was elected to the New York County Board of Supervisors. He then sold his chairmaking business and devoted all his time to politics.

In 1859 the Tweed Ring, based on the Board of Supervisors, was founded for the purpose of controlling for the Democrats the appointment of inspectors of elections. Subsequently, the Tweed Ring enlarged its sphere of operations. In 1861 Tweed was elected chairman of the Tammany General Committee. Shortly thereafter, he was chosen grand sachem and earned the title of "the boss." In 1863 he became deputy street commissioner, a post which permitted him to recruit thousands of followers. In 1868 he became a state senator, a position which made it possible for him to give personal attention to the operations of the state legislature in Albany. Tweed's real estate holdings by 1869 had risen from nothing to a total value of $12 million. The next year Tweed secured from the state legislature a new charter for New York city. Reputed to have cost about $1 million in bribes, the new charter was worth every penny. In effect, the charter relieved the Tweed Ring of accountability to any state governmental authority.

By 1870 the fortunes of the Tweed Ring were on the decline. The exposure of the operations of the ring was purely accidental. In December 1870 a man named Watson, one of the chiefs of the Finance Department, was fatally injured in a sleigh-riding accident. He was of course succeeded by a new appointee, and in the course of subsequent job turnovers Matthew J. O'Rourke became county bookkeeper. Contrary to all expectations, O'Rourke collected considerable evidence of fraud and presented his evidence in the summer of 1871 to the *New York Times*. The charges were published in full, and the collapse of the ring was under way.

Tweed himself was arrested, and his bail was set at $1 million. From here on, the story becomes involved. In November 1873 he was found guilty on three-fourths of 120 counts and was sentenced to Blackwell's Island. After a year's imprisonment, he was released because of a legal technicality. He was promptly tried again and found guilty and returned to prison. But on leave from the penitentiary he managed to escape, hid out in New Jersey, reached Florida, went to Cuba in a fishing smack, and finally arrived in Spain.

However, justice, in a sense, eventually triumphed. Tweed was extradited from Spain and returned on a United States warship to this country. He was sentenced to Ludlow Street jail, where he died. The remaining members of the ring either fled the country or were imprisoned. It is estimated that the total plunderings of the ring amounted to about $200 million.

As the archetype of the political machine, the Tammany Society was imitated in large cities throughout the country. But toward the end of the nineteenth century, the concept of machine came under increasing attack from two separate but related forces. The first was a concerted effort by the reformers to take "politics" out of municipal government, which in effect meant to kill the machine. The second was a drive to make city government more efficient through the use of such devices as a merit civil service system, professionalization of services, and the impartial administration of the law. The reformers supported all these recommendations, so the movement for change had considerable support.

The classic machine of the nineteenth century is now dead. But it should be understood that machine-type politics is still very much alive. The reformers and their business allies killed the machine, but the reformers failed in their dream to take politics out of city government. Machine-type politics functions successfully in, for example, Chicago and Philadelphia, and no doubt there is still some "corruption" in both cities. But, as will be explained later in this chapter, the old-type machine could not last in the face of governmental and social changes which occurred across America in the twentieth century.

The Reform Movement. The second subdivision of brokerage politics we have classified as the reform type. It is classified as a subdivision because the operational focus remains on the brokerage function of a city's political leades, but the institutional emphasis historically has been different from that of the machine.

The reform movement coincided with and grew out of the loss of political power by the old elite which had controlled northern cities prior to the Civil War. Outgunned by the new dominant class of business people and entrepreneurs who wanted special favors from local government, outvoted by the new immigrant groups, and outraged by the excesses of the newly formed political machines, the old elite retreated—as we have seen—to community service organizations. From these vantage points, the reformers launched their appeals for municipal change and reorganization. They insisted on a political style that served the public or general interest rather than the various private interests.

In calling for a politics based on the public interest, the reformers assumed that the task of local government was basically a technical matter. The best-informed citizens would establish policy, and qualified but politically neutral technicians would execute it. Because the reformers concentrated on fundamentals, they tended to feel that political parties, at least at the local level, were superfluous, if not completely functionless. For analogous reasons, it was believed that competition among interest groups should be held to an absolute minimum, since interest groups were deemed to be inimical to the reformers' concept of the public interest. The principal strategy of the reformers was to put into office "those best qualified to serve."

To the reformers, the various programs of the National Municipal League served as models. As we have seen, this program included a professional civil service selected on the basis of merit, the city-manager plan, the short ballot, and nonpartisan elections. It is almost impossible to exaggerate the impact of the league upon the thinking of the reformers. But the results are something else. The reformers were very successful in the smaller and medium-sized cities. But while the larger cities did in fact adopt many features from the municipal program of the league, these same cities never accepted the total package.

In their evaluation of the reform movement, Banfield and Wilson—who were quoted earlier regarding the causes of urban conflict—were struck by several anomalies:

1. "Although reformers have lost most of their battles for power, they have in the main won their war for the adoption of particular measures of structural and other change."[1] *All* cities have adopted a good deal of the reform program.

2. "Although reform has won its war, victory has not yielded the fruits for which the reformers fought."[2] The reformers expected to gain efficiency and to eliminate corruption. In general, modern city governments *are* a good deal more efficient than they used to be. At the same time, they continue to be plagued by repeated scandals concerning housing contracts, welfare, gambling operations, and antipoverty programs. It is ironic that the elimination of patronage, when tried, has had unanticipated results. In Philadelphia, as a case in point, the reform Democratic officials—Joseph Clark and Richardson Dilworth—soon after their triumphs discovered that they needed patronage in order to keep their reform organization together. In this respect they were not much different from the Republicans whom they ousted in 1951.

3. "Although reform measures have not produced the effects that the reformers have anticipated (and have indeed often produced opposite ones), those desired effects are being produced by other causes."[3] That city government is much more honest than it was a generation ago is not an achievement which can solely be credited to the reformers. As Banfield and Wilson see it, the measures and improvements which have occurred "are both effects of a common cause: The steady diffusion in our culture of the political ideal of the Anglo-Saxon Protestant middle-class political ethos."[4] For those who might disagree with this formulation, the matter may be stated differently: Changes in municipal government have come about because of changes in our political culture. From any perspective, the value system has changed, and much more is expected of municipal government in the form of services than used to be the case.

THE MACHINE TYPE: NATURE, FUNCTIONS, SOCIAL BASE

The traditional urban political organization has been studied in depth, and from the wealth of studies some general observations as to its nature have emerged. Of all of the investigations undertaken during the last three decades, one of the very best remains Dayton D. McKean's 1940 appraisal of the Hague organization in Jersey City.[5]

The Hague Organization

For the Hague organization, the cardinal tenet was self-interest. What was good for the organization was assumed to be good for Jersey City, Hudson County, New Jersey, and, ultimately, the nation. It was taken for granted that whatever actions benefited the organization were morally correct, since it was assumed that the organization operated for the general improvement of the citizenry.

In line with this conviction, decision making in the Hague organization was confined to the uppermost echelon. The concept of grassroots democracy in the sense of ideas flowing upward for study, implementation, and execution was contrary to the mayor's thinking. It was the function of the leader to decide what was good for the people. On the other hand, it was the duty of the party workers to keep the citizens in line, by a wide variety of means, including tax assessments.

Mayor Hague believed in unity of command, to borrow a term from public and military administration. He also subscribed to the doctrine that patronage and spoils were facts of life and should be regarded as such. On taxes, the position of Hague was quite consistent: he favored a continually increasing public revenue. Yet, he was something of a puritan, gambling aside. He rid Jersey City of brothels, forcing them to relocate in, for example, nearby Newark or Hoboken.

Though other studies on political organizations might be noted, a reader is well advised to begin with McKean, whose study of the Hague organization remains one of the classics of American political science

Functions of Machines

Yet, it is true that any successful political organization must perform some functions that most citizens cherish, or it

Mayor Frank Hague of Jersey City, New Jersey, marches in his "Americanism" parade in 1938. (Wide World Photos.)

would be booted out of office. This is an interesting item for speculation and has been approached from two points of view, both of which are accurate and both of which deserve summarization.

From the point of view of public administration, a strongly centralized political organization is seen as fulfilling the function of bringing together what is usually a highly decentralized system of municipal administration. Given the customary formal dispersion of power among the mayor, council, and scores of boards and agencies, someone, it is argued, has to serve as a unifying, decision-making force. In the nineteenth century, this was the function of the boss. Today, it is the function of the strong mayor who heads a successful organization, for example, Mayor Richard J. Daley of Chicago. His power rests not only upon his authority as mayor, but even more importantly on his authority as the undisputed head of the major party.

But there is also an interesting sociological approach to the question of why strong political organizations (the term *machine* is now in some disrepute) continue to exist. The answer given by Robert K. Merton, in his famous essay on the subject, is that such organizations fulfill social functions that other agencies in society tend to neglect (or ignore, or be embarrassed by).[6] The article deserves to be read in its entirety; however, Merton makes these main points:

1. Even when the services provided by the political organization and by other agencies are identical—as in certain types of welfare referral—the organization often provides its services in a more satisfactory manner. For the subgroup receiving these services, this difference in style may be all important. For instance, a politician may be more understanding of the needs of a person on relief than a professionalized, socially distant, and legally constrained welfare worker.

2. Another subgroup served by the political organization, according to Merton, is "business." Here, the function of the organization is to provide political privileges leading to immediate economic gains. Big business seeks rather special protections. Historically, for example, public utilities have sought—and for understandable reasons—monopolistic charters from public authorities. Or, more currently, a department store might wish to have its taxes lowered. On the other hand, the organization also serves the needs of so-called illegitimate businesses, such as gambling and prostitution, which also seek to use the organization to secure monopolies and thereby to maximize profits. Viewed this way, the demands of legitimate and illegitimate business are basically similar. For both groups, the function of the organization is to *prevent* undue interference from the government.

3. There is a third subgroup which the political organization serves. This group consists of persons whose social mobility

has been blocked. For such persons the organization provides a means of getting "ahead" which would not otherwise exist. One thinks immediately of Irish immigrants of a century or so ago, whose social mobility was greatly enhanced by the organization. On the other hand, there are many other disadvantaged groups which the organization may help when formal governmental agencies fail to act. In this respect, the dominant organization may be viewed as a "service institution."

Social Base of Machines

Despite such services which are still rendered by the organization, the traditional machine, as we have noted, has become a rarity. The reason is very simple: It was based on an immigrant population, and large-scale European immigration was stopped by Congressional action in the 1920s. As Elmer C. Cornwell has put it, "it was the succeeding waves of immigrants that gave the urban political organizations the manipulable mass bases without which they could not have functioned as they did."[7] But since the twenties there have been two additional forms of immigration: blacks from the rural south and Puerto Ricans have moved in a steady stream to northern and western population centers. To this extent the immigrant base for urban organization continues to renew itself.

When viewed through a socioeconomic lens, the traditional big-city political organization appears as a lower-class-based organization. It is from this class that its principal support has always come. This is the case today in cities such as Philadelphia and Chicago, where machine-type politics remains the norm. On the other hand, reform-type politics, which we shall next consider, appears to thrive in a middle-class environment. Given this condition, one would expect changes in the type of politics as the socioeconomic culture undergoes change.

THE REFORM TYPE: NATURE, FUNCTIONS, SOCIAL BASE

To realize their ideals of good government, the civic reformers supported certain concrete measures. These included the initiative, referendum, and recall; the direct primary and proportional representation; nonpartisan municipal elections held in odd-numbered years; the council-manager form of government; and at-large elections. The objective of these proposals was to destroy the political machines and return governing power more directly to the people. As we have observed, the intellectual center of the movement was the National Municipal League, founded in 1894. Its *Model City Charter* continues to stress the council-manager form of municipal government, nonpartisanship, and election by proportional representation.

Nature of the Reform Type

Even though reformers agreed on certain objectives, the movement itself has appeared in several different forms. James Q. Wilson has identified five types of reform movement: citizens' associations, candidate screening committees, independent local parties, blue ribbon leadership factions, and intraparty clubs.[8] As the different titles suggest, the operations of such groups differ according to the categories Wilson has listed.

Usually, a citizens' association operates outside the party structure. It performs such functions as reviewing the record of elected officials and making recommendations regarding expenditures and taxes. The League of Women Voters is a good example.

Candidate screening committees tend most often to be found in nonpartisan cities. They examine prospective candidates, make recommendations, and may raise funds to support the slate they have recommended.

On occasion, reform movements assume the form of an independent local party. One such type of party is the Fusion party, which helped elect mayors of New York city in 1901, 1913, and 1933. In reality, this was a combination of reform-minded voters in temporary alliance with the normally minority Republican party. A more continuing type of organization is the independent City Charter Committee in Cincinnati. In every sense, this is a permanent, local party.

A blue ribbon leadership faction sometimes emerges when a reform movement occurs within the ranks of a major party. Here the emphasis is on purging the current leadership. If ousted, the machine-oriented leaders are then replaced by a reform-oriented elite. As one would expect, there is often a pronounced class difference between the leaders of the two contending factions. The Clark-Dilworth seizure of power in the Democratic party in Philadelphia during the early 1950s illustrates the blue ribbon type of reform.

Finally, there is the intraparty reform club. Members of these clubs consider themselves amateurs when compared with the professional politicians. Reform clubs tend to be issue oriented and, relative to the "regular" organizations, somewhat ideological. Reform Democratic clubs are scattered throughout the Upper West Side of Manhattan and in Greenwich Village in New York city. They also play an active role in the Democratic politics of Philadelphia's Northeast, and in other big northern and midwestern cities as well.

Contributions of the Reform Movement

Of the various contributions that the reform movement has made to American politics, one that is lasting and influential is nonpartisanship. Nearly two-thirds of America's cities use the nonpartisan ballot to elect *local* officials. Nonpartisan elections are held in large as well as smaller cities. In the former category are found Boston, Chicago, Cincinnati, Cleveland, Detroit, Los Angeles, Milwaukee, San Francisco, and Seattle.

There appear to be several distinct types of political systems in the various nonpartisan cities. In one type, for example, the parties operate quite openly but party designations do not appear on the ballot. Chicago is an illustration. In another type of local political system, the parties disguise themselves behind other formal organizations. Where this occurs—as in Detroit or Dallas—no one is deluded by the transparent deception. In the smaller cities, there tends to be a third form of nonpartisanship: the parties play no role at all in local contests.

What have been the effects of nonpartisanship on the vitality of the political parties? While some consequences have been found, it is difficult to establish firm general relationships. In some cities, nonpartisanship does not seem to have affected the vitality of party politics. Boston, Chicago, and Detroit are examples. In other cities, such as Toledo, there does seem to have been a negative effect. Given the present state of information on the subject, it is necessary to examine a particular city over time in any effort to judge the relationship.

Social Base of the Reform Movement

There is a good deal of very hard evidence, and therefore more agreement, as to the social base of the reform movement as a whole. One careful student of municipal politics.

Duane Lockard, has concluded: "Efforts to initiate or to maintain 'nonpolitical' operations in municipal government tend to divide communities along class-status lines with upper-class elements favoring and lower-class elements opposing these procedures."[9] If this is so, as it seems to be, the question is, why? Lockard would reply that a larger percentage of upper-class voters turn out at the polls than do lower-class voters, so that the importance of the former is magnified. For Banfield and Wilson, the answer would be that the higher up one is on the socioeconomic ladder, the greater are the chances that a person will be public-regarding—that is, will take into account the needs of the entire municipality, not just one section of it.

Another interesting question is whether any appreciable differences have been found in spending and taxing between reformed and unreformed cities. In a very careful study of two hundred American cities, Robert L. Lineberry and Edmund P. Fowler found that reformed cities do, in fact, tend to spend less and to tax less than unreformed cities.[10] Of special importance was the finding in the same study that reformed cities were less responsive in their decision making to socioeconomic cleavages. To put the matter differently, reformed cities are relatively unresponsive in their taxing and spending policies to distinctions related to income, education, and ethnic characteristics of their populations. Another way of looking at the same phenomenon is to note that reformism tends to diminish the impact of ethnicity, home ownership, education, and religion in city politics.

SOME ASPECTS OF BROKERAGE POLITICAL ORGANIZATIONS

Operations

In the course of their continuing operations, political organizations—whether of the machine or of the reform type—have three guiding principles. The principles are more or less beyond debate, because they are an essential part of the rules of the system in which the organization functions.

The first principle is that the organization responds to demands made on it in proportion to the relative strength of force of these demands. Since the resources available to a municipal government are almost always less than the demands presented to it, some method must be devised for choosing one option over another. Besides the problem of supply versus demand, there is the added factor that rival groups often claim exclusive rights—monetary and otherwise—in the same area. For example, several community groups may be in contention for recognition as the exclusive bargaining agent in a given neighborhood of the city. In such cases, the municipal authorities must decide not only whether the function itself deserves public support, but also which group should receive the funds and authority if they are in fact granted.

As a system, this mode of decision making is apparently quite prevalent. Even the most casual watcher of evening local television newscasts can hardly fail to be impressed by the clamor with which claims are put forward by the leading organized interests in the community. The presentation of demands and the mustering of support for them make up the active side of the picture. On inspection, there is also a decidedly passive side. This becomes clear when the organization decides that it will adopt the stance of referee or mediator of the dispute. If the interests themselves can work out an acceptable compromise, the organization can then announce that a "consensus" has been reached.

In the absence of this form of resolution, the organization has certain options. In the unlikely event that there is a perfect stalemate, the authorities can presumably elect to do nothing. But since in the real world such a perfect balancing of forces would be unusual, the organization more probably would decide to go along with the interest with the broadest and most intensive support. Thus, in brokerage politics, demands work their way up the ladder of political attention, and only those that survive in the elimination contest are recognized as entitled to support. In the process, the organization does not really lead; it acts as a moderator, or broker.

A second leading principle of brokerage political organizations is that they tend to concentrate on the solution of problems that, in the narrow sense, are essentially administrative. Political organizations do, of course, give attention from time to time to great questions of public policy. But these are issues which, on the whole, they prefer to avoid. The reason is that such decision making is apt to be divisive and, hence, costly to the organization in terms of electoral support. But organizations are usually quick to react to problems involving matters of personnel and of patronage. What is at stake here is the party apparatus itself. Because of this important consideration, personnel management is therefore a top priority of the organization. This concern is aided and abetted by the mass media, whose chiefs love nothing better than to publish or to telecast a lead story in which, for instance, the city solicitor suggests that the sheriff be arrested. This is much more titillating, and less controversial, than, say, the extent of busing necessary to achieve a racial balance in the public schools.

The third guiding principle of brokerage politics is that the sphere of governmental activity should be limited. Within the sphere itself, there may be and often is a high level of action. But this action is confined to the very narrowly defined area of what is considered proper for municipal governments to do. As a consequence, brokerage political organizations place great importance on the private sector of the community.

At first glance it may seem strange that a political organization would voluntarily agree that the area reserved to the public sector should be restricted, for the self-interest of the dominant organization would appear to lie in the direction of increasing the governmental sphere. Socialism—or government ownership—would then appear to be a logical demand of the local organization. The legendary if middle-level Tammany leader George Washington Plunkitt made it quite clear that he was for municipal ownership of most of the public utilities. But he had a condition attached to this: the civil service laws should first be repealed. As it turned out, the voters of New York city were not disposed to pursue their love affair with Tammany Hall to the point at which that organization took over the entire regional economy.

But there developed in New York city another form of party patronage which was available even after the election to the mayoralty of reform candidate Seth Low in 1901, and after the civil service ordinances passed during his term in office. This was private patronage, by which Plunkitt meant that through alliances between the organization and private contractors, hundreds of party workers could be shifted from public to private employment. So the net effect of civil service reform on Tammany was less serious than Plunkitt had originally evisaged.

Though less open today than in the earlier years of the century, the practice of awarding jobs to party workers through the use of private employers holding contracts from the city obviously continues. This was the sort of alliance between government and business which Lincoln Steffens so vigorously exposed. Today, the arena is much broader, for it also includes alliances with particular unions as well as the contractors. It is not at all a question of graft, as it would have been during the Tammany period of the late 1800s. It is rather a question of knowing on which side the bread is buttered and acting accordingly. No one had to order construction workers to vote time after time for the reelection of Nelson Rockefeller to the governorship of New York state. It was obvious that he was the most dedicated sponsor of large-scale construction projects since the pharaohs of ancient Egypt.

Psychological Perspectives

The psychological outlook of brokerage organizations is another factor which both defines and limits their role. Though at times the traditional organization might seem to reflect a petty bourgeois bias, this is not really a very accurate description. *Petty bourgeois* is more than a term of stratification in the social system. It also connotes an inherent and petty conservatism which does an injustice to the more flamboyant and successful political organizations. In any event the term is of Marxist origin, it is French, and it is therefore generally considered "un-American."

It is more accurate, under American conditions, to regard the city political organizations as possessing a trade-union mentality. Both political organizations and the labor union tend to have a cadre of permanent careerists. Both are dependent for success on the occasional support—at election times—of a much larger group of followers. Both solicit sympathy and support from the general public.

Yet the most notable similarity lies in their approach to proclaimed goals. Just as labor unions stress short-range objectives, so do political organizations emphasize the here and now. Trade unionism in the United States means a bread-and-butter approach. In itself, this is not much different from the concept of awarding a share of the benefits to an important interest. What the unions and the political organizations have in common are strictly limited objectives. Because of this situation, both the union and the organization are as nearly shorn of ideology as it is possible to be, despite occasional flights of great, impassioned, and utterly unbelievable rhetoric.

Though the political organizations adopt a trade-union outlook in opting for limited objectives, they entertain a capitalistic perspective when it comes to economic matters. But it is a particular kind of capitalism which is involved. The organizations do not especially favor the psychology of large-scale industry, though they may both grant favors to and fear such businesses. Nor do the political organizations share in any sense the point of view of the cooperative movement. What they do subscribe to is the individualistic economic outlook of middle-scale competitive enterprises, including both individual businesses and the professionals who work for them. The ideal is a small-sized company, or the lawyer who works in a small law firm. It is the kind of marketplace capitalism that the political organization understands and finds congenial. Under these circumstances the "deal-me-in-too" philosophy so evident in the actions and words of urban political leaders appears as natural as the city debt.

The political organization inevitably tends to accept middle-class values which other large social organizations also share. Though these values may be becoming more difficult to realize, they are and will no doubt remain part of the "American way of life." For example, one such value is held to be home ownership for the average family. Public housing may be a necessity to keep the poor from rioting, but the ideal is private home ownership (including cooperatives and condominiums). This idea is as firmly held by the lower-paid working classes as it is by the very wealthy.

Social Responses

The response which a political organization gives to a particular demand will depend largely on its assessment of the intensity, imminence, and depth of the demand. In this respect a political organization follows the bureaucratic formulas of all large organizations. What distinguishes the political from other organizations, however, is not only the exercise of public power—there is also the element of continuous publicity. It is often possible for a corporation, as it used to be possible for a university, to keep its deliberations secret. But a reigning political organization finds itself constantly in the public spotlight. Because of this, it tends to develop an awareness of public opinion not characteristic of other types of organizations. The ability to gauge public reactions is among the most highly prized of the political arts.

It is evident that neither brokerage politics nor some new development or style growing out of it can deal conclusively with the ills of urban America. As has often been observed, the national government has the money, the state governments have the authority, and the municipal governments have the urban problems. Most of the great urban crises of our time—race relations, education, housing, and crime—are very complex issues that can only be handled through cooperative efforts at all levels of government. By themselves, the cities, and the political organizations which operate their governmental agencies, simply cannot handle matters of this magnitude and interdependence. It is a fact that urban political organizations have shown little ability to cope with the results of large-scale social change. Partly, of course, this is because the resources needed to solve the problems exceed the capacity of any one urban complex. But it may also be due in part to the political system itself.[11]

Brokerage politics at best provides only a limited-response mechanism. It may be that the brokerage, trade-off system will in time give way to a somewhat more authoritative approach to urban politics—at least, this is the prediction of Philadelphia's former Mayor Joseph Clark. Clark, a noted reformer, was dismayed that the system of urban politics now in operation—what we have called brokerage politics—could not set priorities and then enforce them. If it could not do this, he wondered, how is it possible in any rational way to govern the cities at all. He added that he was not able to present a position paper which would offer an instant solution to so difficult a political, social, and economic problem.

From all of this, we may tentatively conclude that brokerage politics, while not satisfactory, is likely to be around for some time to come.

Items for Discussion

1. What were the *positive* contributions of machine-type politics?

2. How can Richard Daley continue as a "boss" in Chicago long after most other political machines have lost their control?

3. Considering the evidence presented on reform politics, might it not be well to reform the reformers?

4. Is it fair to contend that organized crime cannot exist within a city unless it has the protection of government officials? How great an influence do you believe organized crime has on the operation of city government?

5. Discuss the "iron law of oligarchy." How might this law be applied to organizations such as universities and state legislatures?

Chapter Notes

1. Edward C. Banfield and James Q. Wilson, *City Politics* (New York: Vintage, 1963), p. 148.

2. *Ibid.*, p. 148.

3. *Ibid.*, p. 149.

4. *Ibid.*, p. 150.

5. See Dayton David McKean, *The Boss: The Hague Machine in Action* (Boston: Houghton Mifflin, 1940).

6. Robert K. Merton, "Some Functions of the Political Machine," pp. 72–82 of a longer article, "Social Theory and Social Structure," in *American Journal of Sociology* (1945). The section of the article referred to in this text is reprinted in Garold W. Thumm and Edward G. Janosik (eds.), *Parties and the Governmental System* (Englewood Cliffs, N.J.: Prentice-Hall, 1967), pp. 25–32.

7. Elmer C. Cornwell, Jr., "Bosses, Machines and Ethnic Groups," *The Annals*, Vol. 353 (May 1964), pp. 27–39.

8. James Q. Wilson, "Politics and Reform in American Cities," in *American Government Annual, 1962–63* (New York: Holt, Rinehart & Winston, 1962), pp. 37–52.

9. Duane Lockard, *The Politics of State and Local Government* (New York: Macmillan, 1963), p. 247.

10. Robert L. Lineberry and Edmund P. Fowler, "Reformism and Public Policies in American Cities," *American Political Science Review* Vol. 61, No. 3 (Sept. 1967), pp. 701–716.

11. For a critique of brokerage politics, see Murray S. Stedman, Jr., *Urban Politics*, 2nd ed. (Cambridge, Mass.: Winthrop, 1975), chap. 7.

11

Metropolitan Areas: Cities and Suburbs

Key Terms

Emerging model: Stresses the independence of suburbs from central cities; this is the *actual model* for many metropolitan areas.

Historic model: View of metropolitan areas which suggests that suburbs are economically, politically, and socially dependent upon central cities.

Metropolitan area: Concept of the Standard Metropolitan Statistical Area (SMSA); refers to the existence of a city of 50,000 or more population (or a city of at least 25,000 and an additional 25,000 population in adjacent areas) which is the economic and social center for a basically urban county.

Metropolitics: The political problems which exist in metropolitan areas.

No-party politics: Typically found in suburbs, this pattern deplores partisan political activity and seeks broad agreement; contrasted with *one-party localism* of small towns in which there is considerable fighting within the dominant political party.

Politics of accommodation: In city government (typically suburbs), the strong desire to avoid conflict situations through compromise.

Silk-stocking wards: Wealthy wards within a city.

Suburbs of consumption: A residential, or dependent suburb; contrasted with *suburbs of production* which are industrial and essentially self-sustaining communities which could exist without the central city.

Zoning ordinances: Acts of local legislatures which control the uses of land, e.g., establishing residential and industrial areas within a city and protecting park areas.

A chief—probably the chief—characteristic of modern urban America is its very high degree of metropolitanization: the centering of the urban population in metropolitan areas. The term *metropolitan area* is a loose one which is used to refer to any large concentration of urban dwellers who evidence a high degree of economic interdependence and social interaction. This particular use of the expression disregards government boundaries and emphasizes instead the common social and economic interests of the population.

But a more precise definition has been devised by the federal government, a definition which makes it possible to contrast one metropolitan area with another in a meaningful way. The definition also reminds one that government in metropolitan areas is highly fragmented. Too often, studies of urban politics tend to concentrate on the central cities, leaving out in large measure the politics of suburbia. In this chapter, we first take a look at metropolitan areas and then give some specific attention to the problems of suburbia. In Chapter 12, we examine some of the plans which have been suggested to bring about greater political integration within the great metropolitan areas.

STANDARD METROPOLITAN STATISTICAL AREAS (SMSAs)

The concept of the SMSA was developed to give government and industry a basis for comparative research. A definition has been created by the United States Bureau of the Budget and has been used extensively by the Census Bureau. The present term—*standard metropolitan statistical area*—was adopted for use in the 1960 census. Based on certain criteria (which we shall look at in a moment) the Bureau of the Budget (now the Office of Management and Budget) has been able to establish precise geographical boundaries with the advice of an interagency federal Committee on Standard Metropolitan Areas.

The principal objective in setting up standard definitions was to "make it possible for all Federal statistical agencies to utilize the same boundaries in publishing statistical data useful for analyzing metropolitan problems."[1] In clarifying this, the bureau added: "The general concept of a metropolitan area is one of an integrated economic and social unit with a recognized large population nucleus."[2]

How does one go about determining whether or not a particular area qualifies as an SMSA? The bureau's definition of the term is all-important:

> The definition of an individual standard metropolitan statistical area involves two considerations; first, a city or cities of specified population to constitute the central city and to identify the county in which it is located as the central county, and, second, economic and social relationships with contiguous counties which are metropolitan in character, so that the periphery of the specific metropolitan area may be determined. Standard metropolitan areas may cross State lines, if this is necessary in order to include qualified contiguous counties.[3]

To determine whether a specific area should be included within the meaning of the definition, it is necessary to apply specific criteria relating to population, metropolitan character, and integration. These criteria change from time to time. The current criteria were adopted in November 1971. The key consideration regarding population is a total of fifty thousand or more inhabitants. This total may come from one city, or from a city of at least twenty-five thousand persons which, with the addition of the populations of contiguous areas, reaches the fifty thousand minimum required. (In New England, the cities and towns qualifying for inclusion in an SMSA must have a total population of at least seventy-five thousand).

There are various criteria to determine metropolitan character. These are intended primarily to establish that the county is a place of work or a home for a concentration of nonagricultural workers. For example, at least 75 percent of the labor force of the county must by in the nonagricultural force.

The third set of criteria relate primarily to the extent of economic and social communication between the outlying counties and the central county. What is sought is to determine that the area is in fact an integrated unit, not an unrelated collection of communities.

Distribution of SMSAs

Because of population growth, the number of SMSAs constantly increases. The listing also changes from time to time because the definition of an SMSA may be amended. As of 5 April 1974 there existed 269 SMSAs (including four in Puerto Rico). The population included within the SMSAs amounted to 72.9 percent of the entire American population as of the same date. In terms of land area of the country, however, these same metropolitan areas accounted for only 13.9 percent of the total. Figure 11.1 gives a recent picture of the distribution of SMSAs for the entire country. Table 11.1 lists the two hundred largest such areas.

SOCIOECONOMIC COMPARISONS BETWEEN CITIES AND SUBURBS

One of the outstanding—but not surprising—findings of the 1970 census was the degree of racial polarization which it found in the largest metropolitan areas. During the 1960s, the trend accelerated. In the sixty-six largest metropolitan areas, accounting for half the population of the United States, the white population—during the decade—declined 5 percent while the black population went up 30 percent. This is another way of saying that the exodus of white residents to the suburbs, coupled with the inflow of black migrants to the central cities, drastically affected the racial composition and distribution in the largest metropolitan regions.

Of the nation's fifty largest cities, three—Washington, Newark, and Atlanta—were reported to be more than half black. Another major city—Gary, Indiana—also had a black majority. In percentages, the black population accounted in 1970 for 71.1 percent of the population of Washington; 54.2 percent of Newark; 52.8 percent of Gary; and 51.3 percent of Atlanta. Of the twelve largest cities, the only one to gain in white population was Los Angeles, where the whites increased by 5.3 percent to 2.17 million. During the 1960–1969 decade, the largest loss of white residents took place in Chicago. This came to 505 thousand persons, a drop of 18.6 percent from the total 1960 population.

The National Commission on Urban Problems gave considerable attention in its 1968 *Report* to current and projected population trends within metropolitan areas. On the basis of recent developments, the commission predicted that between 1960 and 1985 the central cities would lose 2.4 million, or 5 percent, of their whites but gain 10 million nonwhites, a 94 percent increase. This, if it happens, will mean that nonwhites will move up from 18 percent to account for 31 percent of the population of the nation's central cities.

· In its *Report* the commission examined population data for metropolitan areas as well as for central cities. After noting that the 1920 census was the first to record that a majority of Americans lived in urban areas, the commission pointed out that current growth inside the metropolitan areas is in the suburbs. If present trends continue, said the commission, by 1985 the central cities would grow by about 13 percent, but 89 percent of all metropolitan growth would be in the suburbs.[4]

What may be expected to be the impact of these vast population changes in the metropolitan areas? One obvious probability is that there will be black majorities in the big cities. The continuation of present trends will produce black majorities by 1985 in New Orleans, Richmond, Chicago, Philadelphia, St. Louis, Detroit, Cleveland, Baltimore, and Oakland. There is no reason at present to anticipate a major shift in nonwhite population from the central cities to the suburbs, although there are indications that more middle-class blacks are moving to the suburbs. The reverse flow of whites back to the central cities, a very minor one, seems mostly to consist of upper- or middle-class couples who do not produce children, or whose children have left home.

Also unequally distributed in metropolitan areas is poverty. Inside the metropolitan areas, the poor are concentrated in the central cities. The reason for this is very simple: the great majority of nonwhite poor live in the central cities. For example, in 1971, of the 14,561,000 persons living in metropolitan areas who were classified as "poor," some 4,586,000 were black. Very few of them lived in the suburban rings of the great cities.

In almost every aspect, including better housing and better schools, the suburbs have the advantage over the central cities. Yet there are many qualifications which must be made, since suburbs vary considerably. It is simply a fiction of antisuburban novelists that the suburban population of this country is almost entirely upper-class, white, and "main line" Protestant.

What seems to lead to the confusion here is, at least in part, explained by one very clear fact: In the aggregate, there are certain significant differences between central cities and

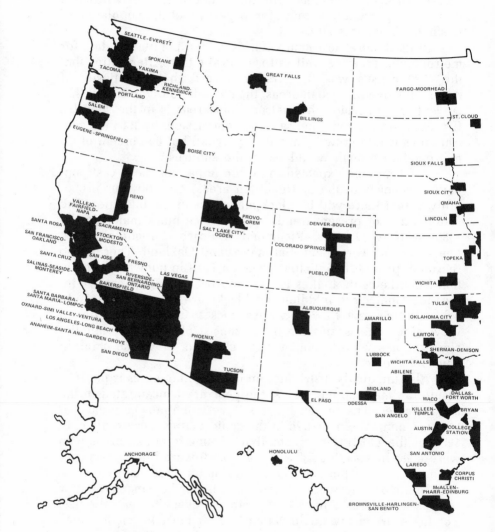

Figure 11.1
Standard Metropolitan Statistical Areas as of 1 January 1974.

Source: Bureau of the Census.

DAVENPORT-ROCK ISLAND-MOLINE
PEORIA
SPRINGFIELD
DECATUR
CHAMPAIGN-URBANA-RANTOUL

GREEN BAY
APPLETON-OSHKOSH
MILWAUKEE
MADISON
RACINE
KENOSHA
ROCKFORD
CHICAGO
GARY-HAMMOND-
EAST CHICAGO

DULUTH-
SUPERIOR

MINNEAPOLIS-
ST. PAUL

LA CROSSE

ROCHESTER

WATERLOO-
CEDAR FALLS DUBUQUE

DES MOINES

CEDAR
RAPIDS

ST. JOSEPH
KANSAS
CITY

COLUMBIA

SPRINGFIELD

ST. LOUIS

FAYETTEVILLE-
SPRINGDALE

FORT
SMITH

MEMPHIS

LITTLE ROCK-NORTH
LITTLE ROCK
PINE BLUFF

TEXARKANA-
TEXARKANA

SHREVEPORT JACKSON

MONROE
TYLER ALEXANDRIA

LAKE CHARLES

BEAUMONT-
PORT ARTHUR-
ORANGE

GALVESTON-
TEXAS CITY
HOUSTON

LAFAYETTE

MUSKEGON-MUSKEGON HEIGHTS
GRAND RAPIDS
KALAMAZOO-PORTAGE
LANSING-EAST LANSING
BAY CITY
SAGINAW
FLINT
DETROIT
BATTLE CREEK
JACKSON
ANN ARBOR
TOLEDO

SOUTH BEND
FORT WAYNE
LIMA
MANSFIELD
LAFAYETTE-WEST LAFAYETTE
ANDERSON
MUNCIE
SPRINGFIELD
COLUMBUS
INDIANAPOLIS
HAMILTON-MIDDLETOWN
DAYTON
CINCINNATI
LEXINGTON-FAYETTE

LORAIN-ELYRIA
CLEVELAND
AKRON
CANTON
YOUNGSTOWN-WARREN
STEUBENVILLE-WEIRTON
PITTSBURGH
JOHNSTOWN
ALTOONA
WHEELING
PARKERSBURG-MARIETTA

BUFFALO
ROCHESTER
SYRACUSE
UTICA-ROME
ALBANY-SCHENECTADY-TROY

ERIE

TERRE HAUTE

LOUISVILLE
EVANSVILLE OWENSBORO

NASHVILLE-
DAVIDSON

CHATTANOOGA
HUNTSVILLE

FLORENCE
GADSDEN

ANNISTON
BIRMINGHAM
COLUMBUS

TUSCALOOSA

MONTGOMERY

BILOXI-
GULFPORT

BATON ROUGE

MOBILE
NEW ORLEANS

CHARLESTON

HUNTINGTON-
ASHLAND

KINGSPORT-BRISTOL

KNOXVILLE

ASHEVILLE

ATLANTA

COLUMBIA

AUGUSTA

CHARLESTON

MACON

SAVANNAH

ALBANY

TALLAHASSEE

PENSACOLA

GAINESVILLE

JACKSONVILLE

DAYTONA BEACH

ORLANDO

MELBOURNE-TITUSVILLE-
COCOA

TAMPA-
ST. PETERSBURG

LAKELAND-
WINTER HAVEN

SARASOTA

FORT MYERS

WEST PALM BEACH-
BOCA RATON

FORT LAUDERDALE-
HOLLYWOOD

MIAMI

ROANOKE

CHARLESTON

MANCHESTER
NASHUA
LAWRENCE-HAVERHILL
LOWELL
FITCHBURG-LEOMINSTER
PITTSFIELD
BOSTON
SPRINGFIELD-CHICOPEE-HOLYOKE
WORCESTER
NEW BEDFORD
FALL RIVER
PROVIDENCE-WARWICK-PAWTUCKET
NEW LONDON-NORWICH
MERIDEN
NEW BRITAIN
HARTFORD
BRISTOL
WATERBURY

LEWISTON-
AUBURN

PORTLAND

NEW HAVEN-WEST HAVEN
DANBURY
NORWALK
BRIDGEPORT
STAMFORD
POUGHKEEPSIE
NASSAU-SUFFOLK
NEW YORK
PATTERSON-CLIFTON-PASSAIC
ALLENTOWN-BETHLEHEM-EASTON

NEWARK
JERSEY CITY
NEW BRUNSWICK-PERTH AMBOY-SAYREVILLE
LONG BRANCH-ASBURY PARK
TRENTON
PHILADELPHIA
ATLANTIC CITY
READING
VINELAND-MILLVILLE-BRIDGETON
WILMINGTON

ELMIRA
BINGHAMTON
NORTHEAST PENNSYLVANIA
WILLIAMSPORT
LANCASTER
HARRISBURG
YORK
BALTIMORE
WASHINGTON

RICHMOND
LYNCHBURG
NEWPORT NEWS-HAMPTON
NORFOLK-VIRGINIA BEACH-PORTSMOUTH
PETERSBURG-COLONIAL HEIGHTS-HOPEWELL
GREENSBORO-WINSTON-SALEM-HIGHPOINT
BURLINGTON
RALEIGH-DURHAM
ASHEVILLE
GREENVILLE-SPARTANBURG
CHARLOTTE-GASTONIA
FAYETTEVILLE
WILMINGTON

Table 11.1
Standard Metropolitan Statistical Areas as of 5 April 1974: SMSAs with 200,000 Population or More

	1970 Population[1]
Akron, Ohio	679,239
Portage County	125,868
Summit County	553,371
Albany-Schenectady-Troy, N.Y.	777,977
Albany County	286,742
Montgomery County	55,883
Rensselaer County	152,510
Saratoga County	121,764
Schenectady County	161,078
Albuquerque, N. Mex.	333,266
Bernalillo County	315,774
Sandoval County	17,492
Allentown-Bethelem-Easton, Pa.-N.J.	594,382
Carbon County, Pa.	50,573
Lehigh County, Pa.	255,304
Northampton County, Pa.	214,545
Warren County, N.J.	73,960
Anaheim-Santa Ana-Garden Grove, Calif.	1,421,233
Orange County	1,421,233
Ann Arbor, Mich.	234,103
Washtenaw County	234,103
Appleton-Oshkosh, Wis.	276,948
Calumet County	27,604
Outagamie County	119,398
Winnebago County	129,946
Atlanta, Ga.	1,595,517
Butts County	10,560
Cherokee County	31,059
Clayton County	98,126
Cobb County	196,793
De Kalb County	415,387
Douglas County	28,659
Fayette County	11,364
Forsyth County	16,928
Fulton County	605,210
Gwinnett County	72,349
Henry County	23,724
Newton County	26,282
Paulding County	17,520
Rockdale County	18,152
Walton County	23,404
Augusta, Ga.-S.C.	275,787
Columbia County, Ga.	22,327

	1970 Population[1]
Richmond County, Ga.	162,437
Aiken County, S.C.	91,023
Austin, Tex.	323,158
Hays County	27,642
Travis County	295,516
Bakersfield, Calif.	330,234
Kern County	330,234
Baltimore, Md.	2,071,016
Baltimore city	905,787
Anne Arundel County	298,042
Baltimore County	620,409
Carroll County	69,006
Harford County	115,378
Howard County	62,394
Baton Rouge, La.	375,628
Ascension Parish	37,086
East Baton Rouge Parish	285,167
Livingston Parish	36,511
West Baton Rouge Parish	16,864
Beaumont-Port Arthur-Orange, Tex.	347,568
Hardin County	29,996
Jefferson County	246,402
Orange County	71,170
Binghamton, N.Y.-Pa.	302,672
Broome County, N.Y.	221,815
Tioga County, N.Y.	46,513
Susquehanna County, Pa.	33,344
Birmingham, Ala.	767,230
Jefferson County	644,991
St. Clair County	27,956
Shelby County	38,037
Walker County	56,246
Boston, Mass.	2,899,101
Essex County (part)	347,031
Middlesex County (part)	1,083,385
Norfolk County (part)	594,606
Plymouth County (part)	138,889
Suffolk County	735,190
Bridgeport, Conn.	401,752
Fairfield County (part)	338,295

	1970 Population[1]
New Haven County (part)	63,4
Buffalo, N.Y.	1,349,
Erie County	1,113,
Niagara County	235,
Canton, Ohio	393,7
Carroll County	21,5
Stark County	372,
Charleston, S.C.	336,1
Berkeley County	56,1
Charleston County	247,6
Dorchester	32,2
Charleston, W. Va.	257,1
Kanawha County	229,5
Putnam County	27,6
Charlotte-Gastonia, N.C.	557,7
Gaston County	148,4
Mecklenburg County	354,6
Union County	54,7
Chattanooga, Tenn.-Ga.	370,8
Hamilton County, Tenn.	255,0
Marion County, Tenn.	20,5
Sequatchie County, Tenn.	6,3
Catoosa County, Ga.	28,2
Dade County, Ga.	9,9
Walker County, Ga.	50,6
Chicago, Ill.	6,977,6
Cook County	5,403,7
Du Page County	490,8
Kane County	251,0
Lake County	382,6
McHenry County	111,5
Will County	247,8
Cincinnati, Ohio-Ky.-Ind.	1,385,1
Clermont County, Ohio	95,3
Hamilton County, Ohio	923,8
Warren County, Ohio	85,5
Boone County, Ky.	32,8
Campbell County, Ky.	88,7
Kenton County, Ky.	129,4
Dearborn County, Ind.	29,4

[1] Corrected figures. See U.S. Bureau of the Census, Census of Population; 1970, vol. 1, *Characteristics of the Population.*

Table 11.1—*Continued*

1970 Population[1]	1970 Population[1]	1970 Population[1]
eland, Ohio 2,063,729	Denver County 514,678	Gary-Hammond-East
ayahoga County 1,720,835	Douglas County 8,407	Chicago, Ind. 633,367
auga County 62,977	Gilpin County 1,272	Lake County 546,253
ke County 197,200	Jefferson County 235,300	Porter County 87,114
edina County 82,717	Des Moines, Iowa 313,562	Grand Rapids, Mich. 539,225
rado Springs, Colo. . .239,288	Polk County 286,130	Kent County 411,044
Paso County 235,972	Warren County 27,432	Ottawa County 128,181
ller County 3,316	Detroit, Mich. 4,435,051	Greensboro-Winston-
mbia, S.C. 322,880	Lapeer County 52,361	Salem-High Point,
xington County 89,012	Livingston County 58,967	N.C. 724,129
chland County 233,868	Macomb County 625,309	Davidson County 95,627
mbus, Ga.-Ala. 238,584	Oakland County 907,871	Forsyth County 215,118
lumbus city, Ga. 167,377	St. Clair County 120,175	Guilford County 288,645
attahoochee	Wayne County 2,670,368	Randolph County 76,358
County, Ga. 25,813	Duluth-Superior, Minn.-	Stokes County 23,782
ssell County, Ala. 45,394	Wis. 265,350	Yadkin County 24,599
mbus, Ohio 1,017,847	St. Louis County,	Greenville-Spartan-
laware County 42,908	Minn. 220,693	burg, S.C. 473,454
irfield County 73,301	Douglas County,	Greenville County 240,774
anklin County 833,249	Wis. 44,657	Pickens County 58,956
adison County 28,318	El Paso, Tex. 359,291	Spartanburg County . . .173,724
ckaway County 40,071	El Paso County 359,291	Hamilton-Middletown,
us Christi, Tex. 284,832	Erie, Pa. 263,654	Ohio 266,207
eces County 237,544	Erie County 263,654	Butler County 226,207
n Patricio County 47,288	Eugene-Springfield,	Harrisburg, Pa. 410,505
as-Fort Worth, Tex. 2,378,353	Oreg. 215,401	Cumberland County 158,177
llin County 66,920	Lane County 215,401	Dauphin County 223,713
llas County 1,327,695	Evansville, Ind-Ky. 284,959	Perry County 28,615
nton County 75,633	Gibson County, Ind. 30,444	Hartford, Conn. 720,581
lis County 46,638	Posey County, Ind. 21,740	Hartford County
od County 6,368	Vanderburgh County,	(part) 610,608
nson County 45,769	Ind. 168,772	Litchfield County
ufman County 32,392	Warrick County, Ind. 27,972	(part) 3,970
rker County 33,888	Henderson County,	Middlesex County
ckwall County 7,046	Ky. 36,031	(part) 23,290
rrant County 716,317	Fayetteville, N.C. 212,042	New London County
se County 19,687	Cumberland County 212,042	(part) 6,603
nport-Rock Island-	Flint, Mich. 508,664	Tolland County
Moline, Iowa-Ill. 362,638	Genesco County 445,589	(part) 76,110
ott County, Iowa 142,687	Shiawassee County 63,075	Honolulu, Hawaii 630,528
nry County, Ill. 53,217	Fort Lauderdale-	Honolulu County 630,528
ck Island County,	Hollywood, Fla. 620,100	Houston, Tex. 1,999,316
Ill. 166,734	Broward County 620,100	Brazoria County 108,312
on, Ohio 852,531	Fort Wayne, Ind. 361,984	Fort Bend County 52,314
eene County 125,057	Adams County 26,871	Harris County 1,741,912
ami County 84,342	Allen County 280,455	Liberty County 33,014
ntgomery County 608,413	De Kalb County 30,837	Montgomery County 49,479
ble County 34,719	Wells County 23,821	Waller County 14,285
er-Boulder, Colo. . . 1,239,477	Fresno, Calif. 413,329	Huntington-Ashland,
ams County 185,789	Fresno County 413,329	W. Va.-Ky.-Ohio 286,935
apahoe County 162,142		Cabell County, W. Va. .106,918
ulder County 131,889		Wayne County, W. Va. . .37,581

Table 11.1—Continued

	1970 Population[1]	1970 Population[1]	197... Popul... tio...

Boyd County, Ky. 52,376	Washington County,	Jefferson County, Ky. ..695,
Greenup County, Ky. ...33,192	Va. 40,835	Oldham County, Ky. 14,
Lawrence County,	Knoxville, Tenn 409,409	Clark County, Ind. 75
Ohio 56,868	Anderson County.......60,300	Floyd County, Ind. 55,
Huntsville, Ala. 282,450	Blount County..........63,744	Lowell, Mass.-N.H. 218,
Limestone County 41,699	Knox County 276,293	Middlesex County
Madison County 186,540	Union County 9,072	(part), Mass. 212
Marshall County 54,211	Lakeland-Winter Haven,	Hillsborough County
Indianapolis, Ind. 1,111,352	Fla. 228,515	(part), N.H. 5,
Boone County 30,870	Polk County 228,515	Macon, Ga. 226,
Hamilton County 54,532	Lancaster, Pa. 320,079	Bibb County 143,
Hancock County 35,096	Lancaster County......320,079	Houston County 62,
Hendricks County 53,974	Lansing-East Lansing,	Jones County 12,
Johnson County 61,138	Mich. 424,271	Twiggs County 8,
Marion County 793,769	Clinton County 48,492	Madison, Wis. 290,
Morgan County 44,176	Eaton County 68,892	Dane County 290,
Shelby County 37,797	Ingham County 261,039	Melbourne-Titusville-
Jackson, Miss. 258,906	Ionia County 45,848	Cocoa, Fla............230,
Hinds County 214,973	Las Vegas, Nev..........273,299	Brevard County 230,
Rankin County 43,933	Clark County..........273,288	Memphis, Tenn.-Ark.-
Jacksonville, Fla. 621,827	Lawrence-Haverhill,	Miss.................834,
Baker County 9,242	Mass.-N.H. 258,564	Shelby County, Tenn. .722
Clay County 32,059	Essex County (part),	Tipton County, Tenn. ...28,
Duval County 528,865	Mass. 221,208	Crittenden County,
Nassau County 20,626	Rockingham County	Ark. 48,
St. Johns County 31,035	(part), N.H. 37,356	DeSoto County, Miss. ..35
Jersey City, N.J..........607,839	Lexington-Fayette, Ky. 266,701	Miami, Fla. 1,267,
Hudson County 607,839	Bourbon County 18,476	Dade County 1,267,
Johnstown, Pa. 262,822	Clark County...........24,090	Milwaukee, Wis. 1,403,
Cambria County.......186,785	Fayette County 174,323	Milwaukee County ...1,054,
Somerset County 76,037	Jessamine County 17,430	Ozaukee County 54,
Kalamazoo-Portage,	Scott County 17,948	Washington County 63
Mich. 257,723	Woodford County 14,434	Waukesha County 231,
Kalamazoo County 201,550	Lima, Ohio..............210,074	Minneapolis-St. Paul,
Van Buren County 56,173	Allen County..........111,144	Minn.-Wis. 1,965,
Kansas City, Mo.-Kans .1,273,926	Auglaize County 38,602	Anoka County, Minn. ..154,
Cass County, Mo. 39,448	Putnam County.........31,134	Carver County, Minn. ...28,
Clay County, Mo.......123,702	Van Wert County 29,194	Chisago County,
Jackson County, Mo. ...654,178	Little Rock-North Little	Minn.................17,
Platte County, Mo. 32,081	Rock, Ark. 323,296	Dakota County,
Ray County, Mo. 17,599	Pulaski County 287,189	Minn................139,
Johnson County,	Saline County 36,107	Hennepin County,
Kans. 220,073	Long Branch-Asbury	Minn. 960,
Wyandotte County,	Park, N.J. 461,849	Ramsey County,
Kans. 186,845	Monmouth County 461,849	Minn. 476,
Kingsport-Bristol,	Lorain-Elyria, Ohio 256,843	Scott County, Minn. 32,
Tenn.-Va. 241,154	Lorain County.........256,843	Washington County,
Hawkins County,	Los Angeles-Long Beach,	Minn................83,
Tenn. 33,757	Calif. 7,041,980	Wright County,
Sullivan County,	Los Angeles County ..7,041,980	Minn. 38,
Tenn. 127,329	Louisville, Ky.-Ind. 867,330	St. Croix County, Wis. ...34,
Bristol City, Va..........14,857	Bullitt County, Ky. 26,090	Mobile, Ala. 376,
Scott County, Va. 24,376		Baldwin County 59,

[1] Corrected figures. See U.S. Bureau of the Census, Census of Population; 1970, vol. 1, *Characteristics of the Population*

Table 11.1—_Continued_

1970 Popula-tion[1]	1970 Popula-tion[1]	1970 Popula-tion[1]

Mobile County 317,308

Montgomery, Ala. 225,911

Autauga County 24,460

Elmore County 33,661

Montgomery County 167,790

Nashville-Davidson,
Tenn. 699,271

Cheatham County 13,199

Davidson County 447,877

Dickson County 21,977

Robertson County 29,102

Rutherford County 59,428

Sumner County 56,266

Williamson County 34,423

Wilson County 36,999

Nassau-Suffolk, N.Y. ...2,555,868

Nassau County 1,428,838

Suffolk County 1,127,030

New Brunswick-Perth
Amboy-Sayreville,
N.J. 583,813

Middlesex County 583,813

New Haven-West
Haven, Conn 413,722

Middlesex County
(part) 12,702

New Haven County
(part) 401,020

New London-Norwich,
Conn.-R.I. 241,862

Middlesex County
(part), Conn. 8,468

New London County
(part), Conn. 210,754

Washington County
(part), R.I. 22,640

New Orleans, La. 1,046,470

Jefferson Parish 338,229

Orleans Parish 593,471

St. Bernard Parish 51,185

St. Tammany Parish 63,585

New York, N.Y.-N.J.....9,973,716

Bronx County, N.Y. ..1,471,701

Kings County, N.Y. ...2,602,012

New York County,
N.Y. 1,539,233

Putnam County, N.Y. 56,696

Queens County, N.Y. ..1,987,174

Richmond County,
N.Y. 295,443

Rockland County,
N.Y. 229,903

Westchester County,
N.Y. 894,406

Bergen County, N.J. 897,148

Newark, N.J. 2,057,468

Essex County 932,526

Morris County 383,454

Somerset County 198,372

Union County 543,116

Newport News-
Hampton, Va. 333,140

Hampton city 120,779

Newport News city ...138,177

Williamsburg city 9,069

Gloucester County.......14,059

James City County 17,853

York County 33,203

Norfolk-Virginia Beach-
Portsmouth, Va.-
N.C. 732,600

Chesapeake city, Va. ... 89,580

Norfolk city, Va. 307,951

Portsmouth city, Va....110,963

Suffolk city, Va. 45,024

Virginia Beach city,
Va. 172,106

Currituck County,
N.C. 6,976

Northeast Pennsylvania ...621,882

Lackawanna County ...234,131

Luzerne County 342,329

Monroe County 45,422

Oklahoma City, Okla. 699,092

Canadian County........32,245

Cleveland County 81,839

McClain County 14,157

Oklahoma County 527,717

Pottawatomie
County 43,134

Omaha, Nebr.-Iowa 542,646

Douglas County,
Nebr. 389,455

Sarpy County, Nebr. 66,200

Pottawattamie Coun-
ty, Iowa..............86,991

Orlando, Fla............453,270

Orange County 344,311

Osceola County 25,267

Seminole County 83,692

Oxnard-Simi Valley-
Ventura, Calif. 378,497

Ventura County 378,497

Paterson-Clifton-
Passaic, N.J...........460,782

Passaic County 460,782

Pensacola, Fla. 243,075

Escambia County 205,334

Santa Rosa County 37,741

Peoria, Ill 341,979

Peoria County..........195,318

Tazewell County 118,649

Woodford County 28,012

Philadelphia, Pa.-N.J....4,824,110

Bucks County, Pa......416,728

Chester County, Pa. 277,746

Delaware County, Pa. ..603,456

Montgomery County,
Pa...................624,080

Philadelphia County,
Pa. 1,949,996

Philadelphia, Pa.-N.J.-
Conn.
Burlington County,
N.J. 323,132

Camden County, N.J. ...456,291

Gloucester County,
N.J. 172,681

Phoenix, Ariz............969,425

Maricopa County 969,425

Pittsburgh, Pa. 2,401,362

Allegheny County 1,605,133

Beaver County 208,418

Washington County 210,876

Westmoreland
County 376,935

Portland, Oreg.-Wash. ...1,007,130

Clackamas County
Oreg. 166,088

Multnomah County,
Oreg. 554,668

Washington County,
Oreg. 157,920

Clark County, Wash. ...128,454

Poughkeepsie, N.Y. 222,295

Dutchess County 222,295

Providence-Warwick-
Pawtucket, R.I.-
Mass. 908,887

Bristol County, R.I.......45,937

Kent County (part),
R.I. 140,541

Newport County (part),
R.I. 2,911

Providence County
(part), R.I. 573,684

Washington County
(part), R.I. 53,844

Corrected figures. See U.S. Bureau of the Census, Census of Population; 1970, vol. 1, _Characteristics of the Population._

Table 11.1—Continued

1970 Population[1]	1970 Population[1]	19. Popul tio
Bristol County (part), Mass. ...78,687	Clinton County, Ill. ...28,315	Springfield-Chicopee-Holyoke, Mass.-Conn. ...541
Norfolk County (part), Mass. ...4,953	Madison County, Ill. ...250,911	Hampden County (part) Mass. ...450
Worcester County (part), Mass. ...8,330	Monroe County, Ill. ...18,831	Hampshire County (part), Mass. ...80
Raleigh-Durham, N.C. ...419,391	St. Clair County, Ill. ...285,199	Worcester County (part) Mass. ...3
Durham County ...132,681	Salinas-Seaside-Monterey, Calif. ...247,450	Tolland County (part), Conn. ...6
Orange County ...57,707	Monterey County ...247,450	Stamford, Conn. ...206
Wake County ...229,006	Salt Lake City-Ogden, Itah ...705,458	Fairfield County (part). 206
Reading, Pa. ...296,382	Davis County ...99,028	Stockton, Calif. ...291
Berks County ...296,382	Salt Lake County ...458,607	San Joaquin County ...291
Richmond, Va. ...542,242	Toocle County ...21,545	Syracuse, N.Y. ...636
Richmond city ...249,431	Weber County ...126,278	Madison County ...62
Charles City County ...6,158	San Antonio, Tex. ...888,179	Onondaga County ...472
Chesterfield County ...77,045	Bexar County ...830,460	Oswego County ...160
Goochland County ...10,069	Comal County ...24,165	Tacoma, Wash. ...412
Hanover County ...37,479	Guadalupe County ...33,554	Pierce County ...412
Henrico County ...154,364	San Diego, Calif. ...1,357,854	Tampa-St. Petersburg, Fla. ...1,088
Powhatan County ...7,696	San Diego County ...1,357,854	Hillsborough County ...490
Riverside-San Bernardino-Ontario, Calif. ..1,141,307	San Francisco-Oakland, Calif. ...3,108,782	Pasco County ...75
Riverside County ...459,074	Alameda County ...1,073,184	Pinellas County ...522
San Bernardino County ...682,233	Contra Costa County ...555,805	Toledo, Ohio-Mich ...762
Roanoke, Va. ...203,153	Marin County ...206,758	Fulton County, Ohio ...33
Roanoke city ...92,115	San Francisco County ...715,674	Lucas County, Ohio ...483
Salem city ...21,982	San Mateo County ...557,361	Ottawa County, Ohio ...37
Botetourt County ...18,193	San Jose, Calif. ...1,065,313	Wood County, Ohio ...89
Craig County ...3,524	Santa Clara County ..1,065,313	Monroe County, Mich. ...119
Roanoke County ...67,339	Santa Barbara-Santa Maria-Lompoc, Calif. .264,324	Trenton, N.J. ...304
Rochester, N.Y. ...961,516	Santa Barbara County ...264,324	Mercer County ...304
Livingston County ...54,041	Santa Rosa, Calif. ...204,885	Tucson, Ariz. ...354
Monroe County ...711,917	Sonoma County ...204,885	Pima County ...351
Ontario County ...78,849	Savannah, Ga. ...207,987	Tulsa, Okla. ...549
Orleans County ...37,305	Bryan County ...6,539	Creek County ...45
Wayne County ...79,404	Chatham County ...187,816	Mayes County ...23
Rockford, Ill. ...272,063	Effingham County ...13,632	Osage County ...29
Boone County ...25,440	Seattle-Everett, Wash. ..1,424,605	Rogers County ...28
Winnebago County ...246,623	King County ...1,159,369	Tulsa County ...399
Sacramento, Calif. ...803,793	Snohomish County ...265,236	Wagoner County ...22
Placer County ...77,632	Shreveport, La. ...333,826	Utica-Rome, N.Y. ...340
Sacramento County ...634,373	Bossier Parish ...63,703	Herkimer County ...67
Yolo County ...91,788	Caddo Parish ...230,184	Oneida County ...273
Saginaw, Mich. ...219,743	Webster Parish ...39,939	Vallejo-Fairfield-Napa, Calif. ...251
Saginaw County ...219,743	South Bend, Ind. ...280,081	Napa County ...79
St. Louis, Mo.-Ill. ...2,410,492	Marshall County ...34,986	Solano County ...171
St. Louis city, Mo. ...622,236	St. Joseph County ...245,045	
Franklin County, Mo. ...55,127	Spokane, Wash. ...287,487	
Jefferson County, Mo. ...105,248	Spokane County ...287,487	
St. Charles County, Mo. ...92,954		
St. Louis County, Mo. ..951,671		

[1] Corrected figures. See U.S. Bureau of the Census, Census of Population; 1970. vol. 1, *Characteristics of the Population*

Table 11.1—*Continued*

	1970 Popula- tion[1]		1970 Popula- tion[1]		1970 Popula- tion[1]
shington, D.C.-Md.-		Waterbury, Conn. 216,808		New Castle County,	
Va. 2,909,355		Litchfield County		Del. 385,856	
District of Columbia . . .756,510		(part) 30,712		Salem County, N.J. 60,346	
Charles County, Md. 47,678		New Haven County		Cecil County, Md. 53,291	
Montgomery County,		(part) 186,096		Worcester, Mass. 372,144	
Md. 522,809				Worcester County	
Prince Georges County,		West Palm Beach-Boca		(part) 372,144	
Md. 661,082		Raton, Fla. 348,993			
Alexandria city, Va. 110,927		Palm Beach County 348,993		York, Pa. 329,540	
Fairfax city, Va. 22,009				Adams County 56,937	
Falls Church city, Va. . . .10,772		Wichita, Kans 389,352		York County 272,603	
Arlington County, Va. . .174,284		Butler County 38,658			
Fairfax County, Va. 455,032		Sedgwick County 350,694		Youngstown-Warren,	
Loudoun County, Va. 37,150				Ohio 537,124	
Prince William County,		Wilmington, Del.-N.J.-		Mahoning County 304,545	
Va. 111,102		Md. 499,493		Trumbull County 232,579	

orrected figures. See U.S. Bureau of the Census, Census of Population; 1970, vol. 1, *Characteristics of the Population.*

rce: *Statistical Abstract of the U.S.,* 1974, pp. 926-929.

their urban fringes. A 1964 census study examined the socioeconomic status for urbanized areas based on measures of occupation, education, and income.[5]

Using a four-range scale, the researchers found that proportionally more persons of high status were found in the suburbs. Some 23 percent of the suburban residents were placed in the highest status category, while less than 4 percent were in the lowest. In the central cities only about 14 percent of the population achieved highest status rank and some 9 percent fell into the lowest classification.

Yet when the investigators focused their attention on the middle range of scores rather than the extremes, they found that the supposed urban-suburban wall between haves and have-nots does not really exist. There is instead a substantial overlap. One-fourth of the suburban residents were discovered to be in the lower two of the four categories, while more than one-half of the central city population was in the two highest categories.

In addition to this census study, there is abundant evidence to indicate that class composition varies from suburb to suburb. For example, it has been estimated that about half of all AFL-CIO members live in the suburbs; for those under the age of forty, the figure rises to three-quarters. In short, the suburbs are not the locale of only the rich and the well-born. They contain in fact a broad middle range of American society.

An analysis of the St. Louis metropolitan area also pointed

up the fallacies of the central city–suburban stereotype. Employing the techniques of social area analysis, the study confirmed the general impression that the central city contained more neighborhoods of low social rank, high urbanization, and high segregation than its suburbs. But it was also learned that the governmental boundary between the city and the suburbs was not a social boundary separating the poor from the rich. In short, there were prosperous and poor neighborhoods on both sides of the city line.[6]

In view of such findings, how is one to account for the readily observable suburban-urban disparities? Leo F. Schnore has come up with a reasonable explanation.[7] He concludes that the two basic determinants of differences among metropolitan areas are the size of the metropolitan area and the age of the central city. Given this information, one could account for the differentials which did in fact exist within particular metropolitan regions.

SOME PROBLEMS IN METROPOLITICS

At many points in this book, reference is made to one or another of the various problems which afflict metropolitan American. The reason is that the problems themselves and the governments which try to solve them are highly interdependent. For the sake of clarity and symmetry, it seems desirable to list four leading problems at this point, with the understanding that they will surface at various other points in different chapters.

Firstly, there is the question of metropolitan services. A common and entirely reasonable view is that local governments exist primarily to provide services which are unlikely to be obtained in any other way. From this perspective, the local governments are basically service institutions. They perform those functions which law, convention, and popular preference indicate are in their proper domain, such as education, utilities, highways, public welfare, hospitals and health, sanitation, police protection, housing and urban renewal, fire protection, and parks and recreation. In practice, of course, who should administer these functions generates continuing political conflict.

Secondly, there is the question of metropolitan finance. Not only is there conflict as to the performance and assignment of governmental services in a metropolitan area, there is also conflict over who should pay for the services. Currently, the general question of metropolitan finances has been brought into broad public view by revenue sharing. In some states, the use of the property tax to support public education has generated ferocious conflicts. The impact of taxation, the availability of funds, and the level of services remain perennial questions.

Thirdly, metropolitan politics may be regarded from the perspective of governmental structure. For many urban experts, one cure for many urban ills lies in the direction of political reorganization of the metropolis. We shall consider some of the alternatives in the next chapter.

And, finally, metropolitics may be viewed as a set of problems in decision making. Within this framework, such questions arise as these: Who makes certain types of decisions within the metropolitan area? What is the claim of the decision makers to legitimacy? Which group or groups hold power within the area and within the individual communities? How are conflicts among different power groups resolved?

Most of the political conflict that occurs within any particular metropolitan area falls within one or more of the above categories. For example, the existence or operation of an integrated public transport system raises questions which come under all four classifications. On the other hand, conflicts occur inside particular jurisdictions. With this in mind, the balance of the chapter is devoted to a look at political conflict within that often-neglected political unit: the suburb.

SUBURBIA: AN OVERVIEW

The 1970 census confirmed what experts on population had long suspected would eventually happen: it was this census that indicated for the first time that more than half of the population of metropolitan areas was located in the suburbs. This shift in the balance of metropolitan populations from the central cities to their suburbs has had obvious consequences in a large variety of fields, including marketing and distribution of goods, communication of ideas, finance and banking, and governmental services. In focusing attention on the importance of the suburbs generally, the census also suggested their importance in specific sectors, including the political.

Interest in the politics of suburbia is at an all-time high, even though as yet few college-level courses are offered specifically on that topic. But the politicians clearly know where the voters are, and they work just as hard to win votes in the suburbs as they do in the central cities.

From a political point of view, a dominant force in the electoral and governmental processes of the 1970s is suburbanization. This is true at the state level as well as inside particular metropolitan areas.

As we have observed earlier, the term suburb encompasses a wide variety of actual localities. As far back as 1925, H. Paul Douglass advised his fellow sociologists to distinguish between the "suburb of consumption"—the residential type—and the "suburb of production"—the industrial type.

More recent research has thrown a good deal of light upon the socioeconomic differences in American suburbs. These are considerable and cover a very wide range, as the study of 154 suburbs undertaken by Frederick M. Wirt has shown.[8] What emerges from his study is a continuum of suburbs, each with its own socioeconomic composition and its own life style.

Chestnut Hill Mall, a suburban shopping plaza in Chestnut Hill, Massachusetts. (Photo by Steve Scott.)

People move to the suburbs—stay there and raise their children there—for a wide variety of reasons. There is both a "push" and a "pull" effect. The push forces are such things as crime in the cities, bad schools, and deteriorating housing. The pull forces have also been important: the desire for more space, the wish "to own our own home," and the attraction of superior suburban schools.

Whether, or to what extent, people who have willingly moved from central city to suburbs have achieved their objectives is not readily determinable. What is clear is that the great social problems of education, housing, crime, health care, drug addiction, and care for the elderly are becoming increasingly more serious in metropolitan areas outside the central cities.

Politics of Accommodation

For a political scientist or sociologist, one of the characteristics of government in the noncentral city areas of the metropolis is fragmentation. Suburban governmental services are provided by a large and diverse number of governmental units: municipalities, counties, towns, and overlapping special districts. There are usually several layers of government. As a result, one is likely to receive public services from several different local governments.

Despite the differentiation among suburbs and the evident fragmentation of suburban political systems, there is one theme which pervades the politics of suburbia: a politics of accommodation. In other words, there is general opposition in the suburbs to conflict for its own sake. The objective, on the contrary, is to achieve goals through cooperation. To what end? The general objective of the politics of accommodation has been to retain suburban autonomy in the face of steadily rising pressures for more goods and services.

The desire to retain autonomy is related to the very high value placed on self-government. The solution to the general problem of reconciling autonomy and efficiency has been found in the creation of a system of accommodations based on the use of specific devices to achieve this result, such as special districts to supply such services as water supply or sewage disposal for contiguous suburban municipalities.

Intermunicipal cooperation is also a very common method for providing goods and services. This ranges from informal agreements to specific contractual arrangements. Sometimes counties are able to help suburbs adjust to new situations brought about by urban growth and social change. The greatest development along this line has taken place in California, where the urban county has played an important role in helping the suburbs to provide for increased public services. In addition, making use of their increased political clout, the suburbs are receiving more and more support from both state and federal governments.

The politics of accommodation has in fact preserved local autonomy and is therefore viewed by most suburbanites as a decided success. But a price is paid for the maintenance of this autonomy. The increasing use of special districts and other devices—a form of functional autonomy—has resulted in shifting broad areas of public policy from locally elected officials to relatively autonomous and distant functional agencies which are insulated from the local political process.

Yet the effects of functional autonomy over local control are limited by several factors. The most important local concern is land use, and functional autonomy only rarely affects this facet. In addition, most of the relationships are voluntary, and a suburb can withdraw from them if it can afford to pay the price of proceeding on its own. A community can also accommodate by refusing to act at all on particular problems. This may adversely affect the residents of the nonacting suburb (for example, a refusal to build sidewalks), but it is a legitimate instance of the politics of accommodation.

Political Characteristics of Suburbs

Congressional representation is rapidly shifting in favor of the suburbs. In 1966, 171 members of Congress came from rural areas and small towns, while the remaining 264 were from districts that were predominantly metropolitan. Of these metropolitan districts, 110 were located in central cities, 98 were dominated by the suburban areas surrounding the central cities, and 56 districts contained a mixture of central city and suburban populations along with a minority of rural residents.

By 1972, the effects of reapportionment according to the 1970 census were felt. As a result of the 1972 elections, 291 members of Congress came from metropolitan areas and 144 from rural areas. Of the metropolitan group, 100 were from districts dominated by the central cities, 129 were from predominantly suburban districts, and 62 represented districts that were mostly composed of central city and suburban voters but had a minority of rural residents.

This shift meant that the suburban portions of metropolitan

areas picked up some 31 new representatives and senators between 1966 and 1972. For the first time in American history, suburban representation in Congress was greater than that of the central cities. More members of Congress came from suburban areas than from either cities or rural districts.

Taken by itself, the logic of the shift implied that the Congress of the 1970s would be somewhat more liberal than the Congress of the 1960s. This is because the suburbs—though conservative in relation to the voting behavior of the central cities—are definitely liberal in comparison to the rural districts. On the other hand, there is no evidence at all that the members of Congress from suburban areas constitute anything approaching a "bloc," probably because they do not perceive themselves as such.

Nonpartisanship. In contrast to contests for national and state office, many elections for suburban offices are conducted on a nonpartisan basis. The use of nonpartisan elections is, of course, widespread in the smaller and medium-sized communities of the country. As we have seen earlier, nonpartisanship is accepted in theory in some of the largest cities, but in practice the partisanship is only thinly disguised. In such cities (and in many smaller ones), politics is nonpartisan in name only.

But the popularity of the genuine nonpartisan approach is especially noteworthy in the suburbs. In approximately 60 percent of the suburbs nonpartisanship is the offically recognized electoral system. Suburban nonpartisanship may take several forms. Sometimes it is simply a means to add another party to the local scene to show independence from the dominant regional party, as in the Washington, D.C., suburbs. Or it may take the form of inclusion of members of the minority party in local councils, as happens in suburbs in New York and Connecticut. But most frequently nonpartisanship takes the form of no association at all between local politics and the established parties. Public affairs are considered to be the province of various civic organizations whose goals are said to be "what is best for the community."

In this connection, it should be noted that a large percentage of suburban officials are appointed, not elected. Such people are not likely to have long-range political ambitions, since they presumably do not care whether they are gaining or losing political support. The suburban officials most likely to take a metropolitan-wide perspective are those who expect to run for higher office. The true "locals" are those most likely to resist regional perspectives.

Many communities that are not suburban also emphasize local politics, but it is important to distinguish between the no-party pattern common to suburbia and the one-party localism which occurs in many small towns. Under one-party localism, there is apt to be a good deal of intraparty fighting, as is shown in the primary battles. After the primary, it is expected that the ranks will close and that party regularity will prevail. Party per se is valued.

In the suburbs, the political ethos is considerably different from that in most small towns. For example, this ethos deplores partisan activity and strives for a politics based on consensus. The ethos also requires that a suburbanite, if qualified, agrees to participate in civic affairs. This may include unpaid part-time service, for example on a borough council. There is also the belief that the citizen knows best: men and women should make up their own minds. They do not need ward leaders and politicians to tell them what to think and how to act.

Big-city political leaders and some political scientists have attempted to ridicule the nonpartisanship orientation of suburban politics. But they are wasting their time. There is absolutely no indication that nonpartisanship is about to vanish from the suburban political systems. On the contrary, both as a practice and as an ideology, it seems here to stay.

Economic Correlates of Suburban Voting Patterns. For some years now, social scientists have noted a close relationship between economic indexes and partisan voting. For example, an association has been found between persons with high incomes and those who vote Republican. Even though psychological factors may depress any one-to-one ratio between economic factors (rent, income, occupation) and voting behavior, the association between the two remains statistically high. In other words, suburban political variety is related to variety in the suburban economic base.

To translate these general propositions into the political behavior of a particular suburb presents obvious hazards, for the propositions are derived from aggregate data. Nonetheless, suburban political leaders have usually assumed the existence of some general correlation between economic characteristics and voting behavior. Their hunches have largely been supported by scientific data.

From a partisan point of view, what does this portend for the suburbs, especially in state and national elections? It is likely that the "exploding metropolis" will to some extent duplicate the patterns in the central city, where there are working-class, mixed, and silk-stocking wards. Since the out-migration consists only in small part of upper-class Republicans and in large part of middle-class and lower-class Democrats, the expectation is that the Republican margins in suburbia in state and national elections will be progressively reduced. What we do know about political socialization implies that the new migrants to the suburbs will retain their party affiliations, which are largely Democratic. Although there may be some reverse migration of rich Republicans into fashionable city sections, on balance the continuing migration ought to help the suburban Democrats.

Political Issues of Suburbs

Observers have long noted that much of suburban politics is concerned with family-related issues. In particular, questions concerning the schools and housing attract continuing interest and attention. Of almost equal prominence is the perennial problem of taxes. Occasionally in the limelight are such additional subjects as the police, recreational facilities, and corruption in government. But corruption is much more likely to become an issue at the county level than within a particular suburb. In short, the politics of small communities tends to be focused on local issues. Local government in the suburbs usually pays very careful attention to the interests of its constituents.

Schools. Everywhere in America, education is a prominent issue in local politics. But it is especially stressed in the residential suburbs since, as we have noted, one of the reasons people historically have moved to the suburbs is the presumed superiority of suburban over central-city schools. While there is wide variety in suburban school systems, there is no doubt that those found in the more affluent suburbs are at the top of the educational pyramid. Presumably this is because of the high socioeconomic status of the residents.

In the nonpartisan atmosphere of suburban politics, a sharp line traditionally has been drawn between politics and education. The task of the citizens was to see to it that the necessary funds were raised for school operations, and to attend PTA meetings from time to time.

In recent years the schools in suburbia have increasingly

been the subject not only of public interest but of public controversy. The reasons for this development are clear in a very broad way, but the specifics are hard to deal with unless one considers a particular school system over time. In general, the reasons for discontent stem from money and from dissatisfaction with what the student gets out of attending school.

The financial problem in part comes from the fact that in most states the principal source of revenue for suburban schools has been the local property tax. Dependence on local property taxes means that rich suburbs can spend more money on school systems than the poorer suburbs. This situation has been attacked in the courts, and various moves toward equalization of funding are under way. A second reaction has come from the taxpayers themselves. During the 1960s, the percentage of school bond issues that were voted down in referenda rose dramatically. But those were comparatively good financial years for most people. The results of the very deep recession which occurred in the mid-1970s made earlier taxpayers' resistance look tame by comparison. For example, in March 1975, 60 percent of proposed local school district budgets in New Jersey were rejected by the voters. This happened even in the affluent suburbs.

There are, of course, other problems: whether or not to recognize a teachers' union, the extent of busing, racial integration, and so on. But it also seems that a large part of parental objections to the management of many suburban school districts is the alleged decline in the quality of the educational product. As a result, there has been nearly everywhere a renewed emphasis on basic skills and a reimposition of curricular sequences and requirements. In the depressed 1970s, suburban parents are concerned more over the question of whether their offspring will obtain good jobs than over how they will spend their leisure hours.

Housing and Land Use. Problems of housing and of land use generally are in the forefront of suburban political controversy. This is not unexpected, since one of the leading reasons for moving to, or living in, the suburbs is comfortable housing with adequate space. These considerations go to the very heart of the concept of suburban living.

When proposals are entertained for changes in land use—for instance, by amending the zoning ordinances to rezone an area from residential to light industrial—the disagreements tend to be very sharp. Such proposals always guarantee a full house at the hearings of the zoning board. This is understandable, because zoning changes have not only economic but also social consequences. Changes in the zoning code have an immediate impact on individual families and property owners. In short, the disruption of existing patterns is viewed in highly personal terms.

POLITICAL DIFFERENCES BETWEEN THE CENTRAL CITIES AND THE SUBURBS

The overall socioeconomic differences between central cities and suburbs have been touched on earlier in this chapter. How does all this affect voting behavior? The political importance of such distinctions is that they furnish a rationale for explaining differing political systems. As applied to voting behavior, this is fairly clear cut. The prevailing theory of voting behavior in America holds that differences in voting preference are primarily related to differences in socioeconomic status, and this status, it may be noted, includes religious affiliation as one of its elements.

The most obvious illustration of voting differences explicable on socioeconomic grounds comes from state-wide elections. Here, where the ballot is ordinarily partisan, there is the opportunity to compare the central city vote en masse with that of the surrounding suburbs. As we have seen, in the big cities outside the south this tends to establish a Democratic/Republican contrast. But this is only the aggregate picture. When voting in state-wide elections of rich city wards is compared with the voting behavior of rich suburbs, the results are comparable.

Political Systems

The political differences between central-city and suburban political systems are only partly explained on general socioeconomic grounds, for the differences are heightened by the relative autonomy of the suburban systems.

To return to a point made earlier, there is a measurable degree of economic, cultural, and social cohesiveness in any particular metropolitan area. This cohesiveness is not simply a sleight-of-hand trick of the Bureau of the Census—it exists. The precise degree of cohesiveness can be determined, of course, only by means of statistical gradation.

But even though there is ordinarily a relatively high degree of economic cohesiveness within an American metropolitan area, the outstanding *political* fact is the degree of diversity. This differentiation is due, clearly, to the large number of independent municipalities which exist within a given metropolitan area. The result, as has been underscored, is that the politics of the suburbs possesses an autonomy of its own. In any particular metropolitan area there are many different suburban political systems, and they show considerable independence from the political system of the central city.

Other Considerations

In examining the political differences between cities and suburbs, one could add a number of other considerations One of these is the shifting of the center of power in the metropolitan area, at least in terms of numbers of voters, from the central cities to the suburbs. Another factor to study would be attitudes toward questions of public policy, for example, crime control, education, and matters of social concern generally. A further approach would be to examine the attitudes toward politics and the patterns of political activity in both central city and suburban environments.

Studies have been made in all these areas, but the results have shown little consistency. A good deal more systematic research is needed on all these issues.

THE FUTURE OF THE SUBURBS

Most writers on metropolitan affairs—including this author—would like to see both the central cities and the suburbs survive. Because of this preference, people often overlook or minimize evidence that suggests that the suburbs might well survive even if the cities do not. They seek elaborate reasons for contesting the prediction that most large cities will, sooner or later, follow a downward path.

Personal preferences aside, there appear to be two reasons for the confusion which often surrounds predicting the future of suburbia. In the first place, some of the evidence is contradictory. It is often possible to cite opposing trends. And much of what passes for evidence has been carefully sifted by chambers of commerce on the one hand or by reform groups on the other in order to lead to a particular conclusion.

But there is a second—and probably more profound—reason for the difficulty. It comes from the failure to distinguish sharply between two models of the metropolis. As a result, the analysis is often less focused than it could be.

The *historic model* stresses the linkages between the city and its suburbs. The impression is given that most suburbanites are directly dependent upon the city for their economic survival. The social and cultural dependence of the suburbs on the city is also emphasized.

The basic objection to the historic model in the 1970s is that it is outmoded. While it is still applicable to certain of the small and medium-sized metropolitan areas, it is rapidly becoming obsolete in regard to the largest of such areas, especially in the East and in the Midwest.

The *emerging model* emphasizes the autonomy of the suburbs. It suggests that the suburbs of New York city, of Boston, of Philadelphia, and of St. Louis—to take a few prominent examples—will in all probability survive no matter how desperate the condition of the central cities becomes. The emerging model—which is an *actual* model for many of the largest metropolitan areas—acknowledges that the suburbs have become increasingly independent of the cities economically and socially as well as politically. More and more jobs are found in these suburbs, as is shown by almost daily announcements that firms are abandoning downtown for suburban locations. Fewer and fewer suburbanites have any reason to come into the city at all as life in the suburbs becomes increasingly self-sufficient.

At the heart of the situation is the question of function. What does the city today do better than some other place? To confirmed urbanites, the answer may well be discouraging, for the big cities have been losing many of their historic functions. They are becoming less important, for example, as manufacturing and as commercial centers. And ever since the advent of the automobile—about 1910—they have been losing out to the residential suburbs as attractive places in which to live.

The entire picture is complicated by the racial splits that seem firmly entrenched in the largest metropolitan areas. Yet it is vital to realize that the emerging or actual model of the metropolis was not created solely or even mostly by the heavy migration of blacks to the cities and the migration of whites to the suburbs. The movement of whites from the central cities began many decades ago, though black migration may have speeded it up in recent years. Yet the basic reasons for departure were and remain mostly economic. At least until the recession and inflation of the mid-1970s, one got more for one's money in the suburbs than in the cities. This was true both for home owners and for owners of industrial plants.

In speculating as to economic, social, and political trends in the suburbs, it is useful to clearly realize to which of the two metropolitan models the particular area under examination more nearly corresponds. The chances are that more and more metropolitan areas will approximate the conditions postulated by the emerging model.

Items for Discussion

1. Examine and evaluate a plan to revitalize an inner-city area, such as the "New Town In Town" in Minneapolis.

2. Is it possible that working-class suburbs soon will develop the same problems as central cities? How can suburbs learn from the sad experience of cities and avoid some of their problems?

3. Considering the out-migration of whites from central cities to suburbs, will busing simply accelerate this movement, leaving cities in worsening economic condition? Given the experience in such cities as Boston, should busing to achieve racial integration in the public schools continue?

4. Some small towns do not have zoning ordinances. If possible, visit and compare the appearance of such communities with that of towns with strictly enforced zoning ordinances.

5. How can cities such as Newark, Detroit, Cleveland, and Buffalo reverse several decades of decay?

Chapter Notes

1. Office of Statistical Standards, Executive Office of the President, Bureau of the Budget, *Standard Metropolitan Statistical Areas* (Washington, D.C.: U.S. Government Printing Office, 1967), p. vii. While this remains the basic document on the subject, occasional revisions are made to it.

2. *Ibid.*, p. vii.

3. *Ibid.*, p. 1.

4. These data are taken from the National Commission on Urban Problems, *Building the American City* (Washington, D.C.: U.S. Government Printing Office, no date). Published as House Document No. 91–34, 91st Congress, 1st Session.

5. Bureau of the Census, *Current Population Reports, Technical Studies*, Series p. 23, No. 12, 31 July 1964.

6. See John C. Bolen (ed.), *Exploring the Metropolitan Community* (Berkeley and Los Angeles: University of California Press, 1961), pp. 17–18.

7. Leo F. Schnore, "The Socio-Economic Status of Cities and Suburbs," *American Sociological Review*, Vol. 28 (Feb. 1963), pp. 76–85.

8. Frederick M. Wirt, "The Political Sociology of American Suburbia: A Reinterpretation," *The Journal of Politics*, Vol. 27 (August 1965), pp. 647–666.

12

The Politics
of Metropolitan
Reorganization

Key Terms

City-county consolidation: The merger of a county and city into a single governmental unit.

City-county separation: Process occurring when a major city leaves the county and henceforth performs all functions previously associated with the county government.

Extraterritorial powers: Ability of a city to exercise political control over adjacent, unincorporated areas.

Federation: Modeled after our national federal system, this *two-tier* system of metropolitan government divides power between an area-wide government and local governments.

Functional problems: Difficiencies in the way in which services such as education, housing, and transportation are performed.

Intergovernmental agreements: Arrangements in which smaller, local governments contract with larger governmental units for services, such as police protection.

Structural problems: Difficulties with the many units of government, often providing only limited services, which exist within metropolitan areas.

Unincorporated areas: Quasi corporations created by the state with regard for the wishes of the inhabitants of an area; include townships and counties.

Urban county plan: The county is given authority to provide the services normally provided by city governments, such as pollution control and housing.

Everyone agrees that metropolitan areas, especially the larger ones, face real and difficult social, economic, and political problems. In the light of this, it has often been proposed that the areas themselves ought to be restructured in such a way as to make possible a coordinated attack upon problems of concern to the entire metropolis.

In this chapter we examine the merits of nine proposals which have been advanced as structural reforms for metropolitan area governments. Then we take a look at the political realities of structural reform proposals. First, however, it is well to recall some of the restraints which arise purely from the political environment.

POLITICAL ENVIRONMENT

State-imposed Restrictions

The failure of local governments to respond effectively to metropolitan problems stems partly from the restrictions imposed upon these municipalities by the constitutions of the various states. State constitutions are the ultimate source of legal authority needed to attack metropolitan problems. However, since there are no formally established metropolitan-area-wide governments in the United States, the subject does not come up in the constitutions themselves. As a result, one must turn to the interpretations of state constitutional provisions concerning the powers of local jurisdictions in order to see how metropolitan problems may be approached.

In this respect, Dillon's Rule, previously discussed, asserts the general principle that local governments are derivative; their powers come, that is to say, only by an express action of the state. Even though this view has been somewhat modified in recent years with the passage of home-rule charters in various municipalities, many state governments remain reluctant to grant wide latitude to local governments in questions of structure and of powers.

This is especially true of the county. Even though a county may include an entire SMSA within its boundaries, it normally does not possess the structural and functional flexibility to cope adequately with growing metropolitan problems. Alterations of county structure (such as city-county consolidation) are prohibited by many state constitutions unless a cumbersome referendum process is followed. Though state constitutions have often been amended, it has proved difficult to alter the structure of county governments through such a method. The county unit of government is generally protected by state constitutions.

This is not true, however, of many of the other local jurisdictions, which are not mentioned in some of the constitutions at all. The major responsibility for the multiplicity of local governmental units must be borne, therefore, not by the constitutions but by the legislatures themselves. If they wished to do so, state legislatures could do a good deal more than they have done to encourage governmental reorganization in metropolitan areas.

Structural Problems

As we saw in the last chapter, one of the most serious problems affecting the structure of metropolitan area governments is the stark fact that most of the SMSAs are not confined within the boundaries of a single political unit or jurisdiction. Many of the largest SMSAs are not only multicounty, but they cross state lines. The political fragmentation is further compounded by the existence of thousands of special districts. As a result, within any given metropolitan area there are inevitably to be found serious disparities concerning services, taxes, education, and so on.

In addition, the multiplicity and fragmentation of governments within an SMSA may be advantageous to those citizens who are knowledgeable about politics. This is another way of saying that such people know how to receive the benefits available to them from their local political system. In this respect, as we have observed earlier, a middle- or upper-class suburb, with a strong tax base and limited problems, has a decided edge over the central cities, or at least the run-down sections of such cities.

Some Functional Problems

As the Committee for Economic Development (CED) has pointed out, America's metropolitan problems have produced two relatively separate movements for reform.[1] One has been concerned with substantive problems, such as education, transportation, housing, welfare, and pollution. The other analyzes the structure that governs metropolitan areas. The CED report notes that the relationship between structure and substance is seldom examined in depth. Because the present system of fragmented government divides the tax basis, an ironic consequence is that resources tend to be the most scarce in those jurisdictions that have the most difficult problems.

In such areas as education, welfare, housing, transportation, and environmental pollution, it is obvious that a high degree of coordination is needed to produce an adequate delivery of services. But the governmental structure tends to make it very difficult to deal with these functions on a regional basis. As a result, many experts have come to the conclusion that it is necessary to change the governmental structure of metropolitan areas if there is to be any chance at all of dealing with the substantive problems. We shall now turn our attention to the principal proposals which have been advanced for reorganization.

STRUCTURAL REFORM PROPOSALS FOR METROPOLITAN AREA GOVERNMENTS

There is no dearth of specific proposals for reorganizing government in metropolitan areas. In fact, the sheer flood of such proposals from politicians and pundits is somewhat staggering and often confusing. In this respect, the Advisory Commission on Intergovernmental Relations (ACIR) has rendered the cause of reform a distinct service by cataloging and analyzing the major proposals under nine headings.[2] The following discussion is based upon the ACIR's study of the subject.

Extraterritorial Powers

One method of reorganization of governments within the SMSAs involves the use of extraterritorial powers. This situation occurs when a city under a grant of authority from a state legislature exercises some authority over adjacent, unincorporated areas. For instance, a number of states have permitted their cities to go outside the municipal boundaries to ensure an adequate water supply and to provide for waste disposal. In the field of planning and zoning, it was found that only about 10 percent of the cities had zoning regulations that could be applied to the adjacent unincorporated areas.

This approach, then, has severe limitations. Many cities are prohibited outright by state law from engaging in comprehensive planning outside their own borders. However, the most serious drawback is imposed more by geographic reality than by state law: the absence of any unincorporated areas adjoining the city in question. Though the situation was different in earlier decades, practically all fringe areas surrounding urban centers today have governments of their own. These governments are not subject, of course, to extraterritorial powers exercised by a city.

Intergovernmental Agreements

Another type of arrangement among local governments that are attempting to cope with metropolis-wide problems is the intergovernmental agreement. This is a contractual agreement between local jurisdictions whereby they jointly perform—or, more commonly, one jurisdiction agrees to perform for both governments—some municipal function such as tax collection or health service. In some states, municipalities have made widespread use of intergovernmental agreements to upgrade the delivery of services to their residents.

It is said that the outstanding example of this type of cooperation is Los Angeles County. For more than half a century, through a series of contracts with municipalities, the county has provided a wide variety of services. When Lakewood was incorporated in 1954, it asked the county to provide *all* the services needed by that new municipality. This was a novel and apparently successful idea: the offering by the county of total municipal services to a city in one package.

What are the advantages of intergovernmental agreements? Three are usually cited. Firstly, they make it possible to lower the costs of administration by broadening the geographical base for planning and administering governmental services. Secondly, these devices encourage other municipalities to join in a common effort, that is, to become working partners of the original compact. And thirdly, such agreements threaten neither the existence of a governmental unit nor the positions held by civil servants in the unit. In addition, these agreements do not usually require the approval of the voters of the respective jurisdictions. Because they are politically acceptable and therefore feasible, many intergovernmental agreements have been consummated and are functioning today.

There are, however, some disadvantages to the use of the intergovernmental agreement as a mechanism for dealing with metropolitan problems. The agreement may not withstand the pressure created by a divergence between area-wide and purely local interests. Especially in functional areas like zoning and water and sewer facilities, the disparity between local and regional interests may result in the termination of an agreement between governing units. Moreover, the use of intergovernmental agreements may necessitate the formation of new municipal corporations to perform the required services or controls, thereby adding to the already large number of governmental and quasi-governmental agencies within the metropolitan areas. Finally, there is a tendency for an agreement to be signed with a particular and limited service in mind, so that the coordination that will be necessary is only dimly realized. In short, one sees the tree but tends to neglect the forest.

The Urban County

The urban county is another approach involving local governmental reorganization in an attempt to solve metropolitan problems. Urban counties are formed as a result of a county, through state or municipal action, acquiring the authority to deliver services usually associated with urban jurisdictions—for instance, housing and welfare. Though state constitutions normally limit the structure and functions of county government, in the last two decades there have been several important exceptions involving the transfer of urban functions to country government.

Probably the outstanding example of the urban county plan can be found in Dade County, Florida. In 1954, studies indicated the need for governmental reorganization in the Miami metropolitan area. In 1956, a constitutional amendment granting home rule to Dade County was adopted. The following year, an urban county charter was approved by a majority of the fewer than two thousand persons who actually voted. Many eligible voters did not vote.

As a result of this approval, Dade County was given responsibility for a number of county-wide, urban-type services. These include transportation, pollution control, housing, zoning, water and sewer facilities, and fire and police protection. The cities within Dade County retain authority over the remaining governmental functions, although they have the option of performing them jointly with the county or of requesting that the county assume total responsibility for these functions.

How well has the urban county plan worked in greater Miami? One observer, Daniel R. Grant, has said that the most notable accomplishments have been in area-wide planning, traffic regulation, and traffic courts.[3] Two other specialists on the subject, Stanley Scott and John Bollens, have this to add:

> The area-wide powers granted to the metropolitan government in Dade County to adopt and enforce comprehensive plans, zoning regulations, and uniform building and technical codes, constituted a major breakthrough at the metropolitan level in the United States .... These powers are also ... some of the most jealously guarded prerogatives of local governments in virtually all metropolitan areas.[4]

Even so, the Miami–Dade County experiment has had its share of problems. The basic conflict has been between the "consolidationists," who would like to abolish the cities entirely, and the "localists," whose aim is to erase the metropolitan powers of the county government. Another weakness has been the antiquated tax structure of the county. This problem is accented by the county's obligation to deliver many more services under the consolidation plan than it had done previously. It would appear that financial assistance from the state government or removal of certain legal restraints on the county's system of taxation are needed to ensure the viability of the urban county plan in metropolitan Miami.

Annexation and Consolidation

Annexation and consolidation are two other mechanisms for reorganizing governments within metropolitan areas. As we observed earlier, annexation refers to the action of a city when it acquires additional unincorporated territory which results in creating a larger governmental unit. Consolidation involves the merging of two or more separate local jurisdictions into one local jurisdiction.

What are the major strengths and weaknesses of annexation? Firstly, annexation, unlike the creation of special districts, enhances the status and viability of local general-purpose government. Secondly, it permits the provision of services in a larger geographic area than would be possible before the city annexed the unincorporated territory.

But there are three principal reasons annexation, popular in the nineteenth century, has lost much of its earlier appeal. In the first place, the absence of unincorporated territory around our cities precludes the widespread use of the device in the last decades of the twentieth century. Secondly, local officials of the area proposed for annexation are almost certain to campaign against annexation, due to their understandable fear that their jobs may be on the line. Thirdly, unincorporated areas may engage in the process of becoming incorporated as a way to counter the threat of annexation by their neighboring city. Though such an action undoubtedly, when taken, reflects the wishes of the residents of the territory, it very much compounds the problem of a multiplicity of fragmented local units within our SMSAs.

Consolidations usually have their origins in petitions circulated in the local areas considering such action. If the requisite procedures are followed on the petition, the consolidation is placed before the voters in the respective jurisdictions for their approval. Usually the approval of the governments involved in the proposed consolidations is also required.

On the positive side, consolidation, like annexation, allows the merging jurisdictions to cope more effectively with area-wide problems, since decisions will be made henceforth by one government only. At least in theory, therefore, it ought to be possible to make some progress toward the resolution of regional problems, and perhaps to save some money in the process.

The objections to consolidation come from local officials, some of whom are almost certain to lose their jobs, and from the residents themselves. The latter group may feel a sense of lessened involvement in and identification with government because of the new and larger regional jurisdiction. For these reasons, in addition to constitutional obstacles, consolidations have been used sparingly in recent decades. But there have been some outstanding exceptions in the case of city-county consolidation, which will be discussed next.

City-County Consolidation

In city-county consolidation, a county and the cities within it merge into a single governmental unit. The achievement of consolidation usually includes the necessary state legislative approval followed by popular approval at the ballot in both the central city and the other communities in the county.

New York, Philadelphia, Boston, and New Orleans achieved city-county consolidation in the nineteenth century. But our attention here will be focused on more recent efforts toward consolidation. In the 1950s, city-county consolidation plans were proposed for Nashville, Tennessee; Albuquerque, New Mexico; Macon, Georgia; Durham, North Carolina; and Richmond, Virginia. All were rejected by the voters in those areas.

But in the 1960s several city-county consolidations did in fact occur, the most notable being that in Nashville—Davidson County, Tennessee. In 1958, such a consolidation proposal received only 48 percent support from the electorate. Between 1958 and 1962, Nashville annexed a substantial portion (some fifty square miles) of Davidson County, which bordered the city. As a result, by 1962 a number of voters in the county believed they would fare better in a consolidated city-county government than by being annexed by the city of Nashville. Other voters wanted to strike back at Nashville's mayor, who was the leader of the annexation drive but an opponent of consolidation. He feared that his political power might be eroded under the proposed new government. In 1962, consolidation was approved by 57 percent of the total electorate in Nashville and the county.

One of the major features of the Nashville—Davidson County plan was the creation of two zones. One is the urban service district, composed at the beginning only of Nashville. The other zone is a general service district, including Nashville. Functions performed and financed on an area-wide basis through the general services district include schools, police, courts, welfare, transit, housing, urban renewal, health, refuse disposal, and the enforcement of building codes. In contrast, functions performed only in the urban service district, and also financed by it, include water supply, fire protection, intensified police protection, and street lighting and cleaning.

What is the general evaluation of the Nashville—Davidson County consolidation thus far? Throughout the metropolitan area, improvement in the quality of public education, increased racial integration in the schools, additional water and sewer facilities, and coordinated tax assessment have been noted. A number of financial inequities have been eliminated by shifting various services and placing them on a county-wide rather than a city-wide tax base. On the other hand, it has been said that rural residents have had to pay higher taxes without gaining compensating benefits.

Students of government are mostly in agreement that some form of metropolitan reorganization is necessary. But is city-county consolidation *politically* feasible? In an important study of city-county consolidation from 1949 through 1974, Vincent L. Marando concludes that it is difficult politically to achieve this goal.[5] A statistical summary of his findings is shown in Table 12.1. But it also is important to highlight his own interpretations of the study. He makes the following principal points:

1. As the table shows, in the forty-nine reorganization referenda from 1945 through 1974, all adoptions occurred in single-county metropolitan areas.

Table 12.1

City-County Consolidation: Voter Support for Local Government Reorganization 1945–1974

Year	Reorganization Referendum	Reorganization Support (%)	
		Success	Defeat
1949	Baton Rouge-East Baton Rouge Parish, La.	51.1	
1952	Hampton-Elizabeth County, Va.	88.7	
1953	Miami-Dade County, Fla.		49.2
1957	Miami-Dade County, Fla.	51.0	
	Newport News-Warwick, Va.*	66.9	
1958	Nashville-Davidson County, Tenn.		47.3
1959	Albuquerque-Bernalillo County, N.M.		30.0
	Knoxville-Knox County, Tenn.		16.7
	Cleveland-Cuyahoga County, Ohio		44.8
	St. Louis-St. Louis County, Mo.		27.5
1960	Macon-Bibb County, Ga.		35.8
1961	Durham-Durham County, N.C.		22.3
	Richmond-Henrico County, Va.		54.0**
1962	Columbus-Muscogee County, Ga.		42.1
	Memphis-Shelby County, Tenn.		36.8
	Nashville-Davidson County, Tenn.	56.8	
	South Norfolk-Norfolk County, Va.	66.0	
	Virginia Beach-Princess Anne County, Va.	81.9	
	St. Louis-St. Louis County, Mo.		40.1***
1964	Chattanooga-Hamilton County, Tenn.		19.2
1967	Jacksonville-Duval County, Fla.	64.7	
	Tampa-Hillsborough County, Fla.		28.4
1969	Athens-Clarke County, Ga.		48.0
	Brunswick-Glynn County, Ga.		29.6
	Carson City-Ormsby County, Nev.	65.1	
	Roanoke-Roanoke County, Va.		66.4**
	Winchester City-Frederick County, Va.		31.9
1970	Charlottesville-Albermarle County, Va.		28.1

Table 12.1—*Continued*

		Reorganization Support (%)	
Year	Reorganization Referendum	Success	Defeat
	Columbus-Muscogee County, Ga.	80.7	
	Chattanooga-Hamilton County, Tenn.		48.0
	Tampa-Hillsborough County, Fla.		42.0
	Pensacola-Escambia County, Fla.		42.0
1971	Augusta-Richmond County, Ga.		41.5
	Charlotte-Mecklenburg County, N.C.		30.5
	Tallahasee-Leon County, Fla.		41.0
1972	Athens-Clarke County, Ga.		48.3
	Macon-Bibb County, Ga.		39.6
	Suffolk-Nansemond County, Va.*	75.7	
	Fort Pierce-St. Lucie, Fla.		36.5
	Lexington-Fayette County, Ky.	69.4	
	Tampa-Hillsborough County, Fla.		42.0
1973	Columbia-Richland County, S.C.		45.9
	Savannah-Chatham County, Ga.		58.3**
	Tallahasee-Leon County, Fla.		45.9
1974	Augusta-Richmond County, Ga.		51.5**
	Portland-Multonomah County, Ore.		27.5
	Durham-Durham County, N.C.		32.1
	Charleston-Charleston County, S.C.		40.4
	Sacramento-Sacramento County, Calif.		24.9
	Total Outcome (#)	12	37
	Local Reorganizations Attempted	49	

* Warwick, Virginia, was a city at the time of the referendum. It had incorporated in 1952; it was Warwick County just six years prior to the referendum. A similar situation preceded the consolidation of Suffolk and Nansemond cities.
** The type of majority requirement is vital in consolidation referenda. In these four instances city-county consolidation was not possible despite the majority voting percentage in its support.
*** St. Louis-St. Louis County portions of the 1962 statewide referendum.
Source: Vincent L. Marando, *National Civic Review* (Feb. 1975), p. 77.

2. Reorganization referenda generally fail. For every acceptance, there are three rejections.

3. The twelve voter-approved reorganizations have occurred in the seven states, mostly in the South, where the most attempts have taken place. Five of the successes occurred in Virginia, where state law grants all first-class cities a status independent of counties.

4. Reorganization was not successful in metropolitan areas of more than one million population. The voters in Cleveland and in St. Louis turned down reorganization plans by rather hefty majorities.

5. The community problems which stimulated most governmental reform efforts were of a noncrisis nature. The only exception appears to be Jacksonville—Duval County, Florida. Here the severity of urban problems stimulated considerable in-

terest in reform. The reform movement was triggered by public concern over criminal indictments of certain government officials and the discreditation of the public schools. Reorganization was perceived as a means of getting rid of corrupt and incompetent officials and bringing good government to the area.

6. Voter reponse to reorganization proposals is complex. Interest normally begins with the civic associations, not the politicians. But eventually an opposition surfaces, and it has generally triumphed.

7. Movements to establish city-county consolidation tend to rest upon mass media campaigns. This has proved to be insufficient. "Political organization is necessary to gaining support for consolidation," concludes Marando.[6]

Federation, or Two-Tier Plan

The federation or two-tier government reorganization plan has been the subject of much discussion as a possible technique for solving problems of the metropolis. What is involved is the division of local government functions inside a metropolitan area between two levels. Area-wide functions are assigned to an area-wide or metropolitan government, with boundaries that take in all of the individual units. The local functions are left to the existing municipalities. In London, England, and in Toronto and Winnipeg, in Canada, the local units are called boroughs. There has been no specific adoption of this plan by any SMSA in the United States.

It is claimed that the chief advantage of this plan lies in its ability to provide one metropolitan government to deal with regional problems while allowing the diverse municipalities to cope with their own local problems. Ideally, there is a blend of the requirements of metropolitan efficiency and local political identity and participation.

Despite these theoretical advantages, it is easy to see that barriers exist which work against the adoption of the plan in the SMSAs in the United States. At the outset, there is the question of which functions will be assigned to which level of government, and the decision will affect the relative strength of each of the two tiers. Secondly, the constitutions of the states which desired to permit federated government would have to be amended, as we observed earlier. Finally, the support of local officials and of their constituents would be indispensable for the plan to win approval within any particular SMSA. In short, if either the political leadership or the electorate in these areas felt threatened by the concept of a "big" metropolitan government, the chances of adoption of the plan would be slim. In this connection, it should be noted that two-tier governments were established both in Toronto and in Winnipeg by *provincial* legislation, not by local referenda.

As a case study of the federal plan in action, it is useful to examine the scheme as it was developed and implemented in Toronto, Ontario. This metropolitan region, with more than two million inhabitants, had experienced a very rapid population growth (about 75 percent in the last fifteen years), much of which had occurred in the suburban areas around the central city. Corresponding to this rapid population increase was a rise in problems confronting local jurisdictions, including poor planning, limited sewer and water facilities, poor transportation systems, rising pollution, and inadequate resources.

Studies of the situation led to a recommendation for a federation of the thirteen municipalities that make up metropolitan Toronto. Such a measure was introduced in the Ontario provincial legislature, and it became law on 1 January 1954. A Metropolitan Toronto Corporation was established to provide for the delivery of services that could be maintained on a local basis. In many problem areas, a sharing of functions between the metropolitan and the local governments was initiated; for example, in planning, in local libraries, in grants to cultural societies, in snow removal, in street cleaning, and in traffic regulations.

During the early years of the corporation, one of the vexing problems was that of representation. Each suburban municipality had one representative in the metropolitan government, although the municipalities varied in size from 10,000 to 360,000 people. Moreover, by the 1960s the total population of the suburban areas substantially exceeded that of the city of Toronto itself. Yet the city had equal representation with all of the suburban units. Change finally came in 1967, when the thirteen municipalities were consolidated into five boroughs and one city, and representation was made more equitable, with the boroughs receiving twenty representatives and the city, twelve.

After more than two decades of effort, have there been any really major accomplishments of metropolitan Toronto? The answer is yes. The achievements include impressive strides in the public works area, with a new subway and new expressways, new water and sewage facilities, and plans for a regional park system. Efficiency of the police has been upgraded by centralization of the force. Perhaps the most significant accomplishment has been to increase the financial strength of metropolitan Toronto by broadening the tax base. This greater financial stability enabled Toronto to save an estimated $50 million on lower bond interest rates between 1954 and 1967.

Of course there have been criticisms; there are always critics. Some have charged that metropolitan Toronto has overemphasized the construction of public works projects at the expense of certain social problems. In defense, the government has argued that it had to demonstrate a high level of visibility in order to generate and maintain support for the federation idea. In any event, there is almost universal agreement that living in Toronto today is vastly more comfortable, gracious, and safe than is living in Buffalo, Cleveland, or Chicago. It is therefore no accident that United States experts on urban problems have given and will continue to give very close attention to developments both in Toronto and in Winnipeg.

Special Districts

We have previously discussed special districts in our general analysis of governmental forms. Here the emphasis is on special districts as a means of bringing about some kind of metropolitan integration. The use of such special districts, whether limited or multipurpose, has become increasingly popular as a method for local governments to attempt a resolution of their area-wide problems.

An illustration comes from the integration of public transportation in metropolitan Philadelphia through the creation of the Southeastern Pennsylvania Transportation Authority (SEPTA). Created by the state legislature in 1963, SEPTA was formed on 18 February 1964 to plan, develop, and coordinate a regional transportation system for Philadelphia, Bucks, Chester, Delaware, and Montgomery counties. It was given the right to acquire, construct, operate, lease and otherwise function in the public transportation field in the five counties.

SEPTA was also authorized ro raise money through the sale of bonds and equipment trust certificates and to receive grants from local, state, and the federal government. After public hearings, it can adjust rates and services over the property it owns in the five counties.

As a result of a complicated series of outright acquisitions and leasing, SEPTA now is responsible for the operation of the subway, bus, and trolley systems in Philadelphia, as well as the operation of suburban bus and rail systems. It is also responsible for the railroad commuting services on the Pennsylvania and Reading lines. The net result, although there are the inevitable financial problems from time to time, is that metropolitan Philadelphia has one of the best public transit systems in the United States.

Looking back into American history, it is clear that the great explosion of the special district idea took place during the administration of Franklin D. Roosevelt. State governments found the special district a useful means of implementing many of the programs designed in Washington to combat the Depression. In addition, by using the device of the special district, state governments were able to circumvent the tax and debt limitations imposed upon local governments by the various state constitutions. Another advantage of the special district is that it does not jeopardize the existing political system or its office holders.

In some cases, however, special districts may create problems that did not exist before. It is possible that a district may compete with local jurisdictions in a particular field, such as housing. The result may be duplication of services, or at least competition. Again, the very success of special districts outside the city limits, as in the areas of water supply or fire protection, may work against drives to achieve annexation or incorporation. Once an area has solved, through the use of special districts, its water, sewer, and fire protection problems, it is likely to take a somewhat jaundiced view of the presumed advantages of annexation to a nearby municipality.

Then there is the troublesome question of accountability. For example, it is possible, if one is especially diligent, to learn the names of the directors of SEPTA. But they are appointed, not elected, and it is difficult to know in what ways, if any, they are responsible to the electorate. Their primary allegiance would seem to be to the appointing authorities. In addition, since the board members are nonsalaried, it is difficult to portray them as anything other than public-regarding citizens, even if their visibility is low and their public accountability hard to trace.

Though most special districts are created to serve a particular function, it is possible to envision the creation by a state legislature of a multipurpose district. This might provide a variety of services throughout the metropolitan area. Although this is an attractive idea at first glance, it becomes clear after some reflection that a really successful multipurpose district would render much of the existing governmental apparatus redundant. It would also probably flout our most cherished democratic dogma. It would be difficult to muster political support either to create such a district or to sustain it. For these reasons, a study by the Advisory Commission on Intergovernmental Relations, in 1962, was able to find only one true multipurpose district in the whole United States. That existed in Seattle, but in fact, despite its charter, the agency was limited to water and sewer control functions. In short, it was multipurpose in name only.

State Assumption of Local Functions

Another method of governmental reorganization in metropolitan regions occurs when the performance of local services is turned over to a state agency. An illustration would be the construction and maintenance of local roads. Usually this technique of reorganization has been utilized in service areas where the state government and the local unit jointly share responsibility. Generally it occurs in a municipality that has neither the resources nor the population base to serve adequately the needs of its citizens. California provides an excellent illustration of this kind of arrangement:

> In Southern California, after the individual metropolitan areas, such as Los Angeles and San Diego, had developed all their available local water resources, the State undertook to develop a State-wide plan which would meet the growing needs of the metropolitan areas, as well as the State's needs in such other fields as flood control, agriculture, and recreation.[7]

To be sure, this approach is attractive. It broadens the geographical base for planning and control of area-wide problems. It permits taking advantage of the economy of scale and the avoidance of duplication. It has a high degree of political feasibility because it creates little disturbance of the local political power structure. Nor does it require approval by local referenda.

Yet this approach may contain a major liability. When the state assumes responsibility for the performance of previously local functions, the strength and status of local governments conceivably can be seriously weakened. This might be a higher price for potentially increased efficiency in planning and operations than many citizens are willing to pay.

City-County Separation

The last method to be considered in our analysis of structural reform proposals for metropolitan area governments is city-county separation. This is an action by which the major city of a county separates from the county. The advantage of such an arrangement is that henceforth the city may exercise both city-assigned and county-assigned functions. Usually, special constitutional provisions must be made in order to utilize this method.

The thrust behind the city-county separation movement was the concern of city dwellers that they were paying too great a share of the cost of county services without receiving commensurate benefits. It was also believed that some advantages would accrue from the elimination of duplicated efforts by two governments. Of course, the plan has its drawbacks, of which the principal one is that the plan makes it extremely difficult to achieve integrated control of area-wide problems.

For this reason, the idea of city-county separation is no longer in favor. Most of the major city-county separations occurred in the latter part of the nineteenth century, including ones in Baltimore, Denver, St. Louis, and San Francisco.

POLITICS OF STRUCTURAL REFORM PROPOSALS

Many of the arguments put forward for structural reorganization of government in our SMSAs emphasize the opportunities for improved, more efficient delivery of services. However, they frequently fail to take into account that local government must also manage conflicts inherent in our metropolitan areas. For example, the organization that is best designed for efficient administration may be ill suited for the settling of political conflicts. In short, there are real political questions which must be dealt with if any scheme of reorganization is to have a chance for approval. It is to these questions that we now turn.

Political Parties' Response

The major political parties are not particularly interested in metropolitan reorganization. In general, they prefer to maintain the status quo inside the metropolitan area. This is the case whether the object of reorganization is metropolitan integregation or merely neighborhood government.

As we have noted from time to time, the aggregate suburban population is predominately white, middle to upper income, and oriented toward voting Republican. Conversely, central-city populations have lower incomes, a very high and increasing percentage of blacks, and a tendency to vote strongly Democratic. It would therefore appear that neither suburban Republican (or even nonpartisan) governments and their constituents, nor big-city Democratic voters and their governments, are likely to show unbridled enthusiasm for any reorganization of metropolitan government. On the contrary, both groups might support weaker plans which would leave the city and the suburban political structures intact. They become allies when attempts are set in motion to create a truly metropolitan government which would create great changes in the existing political structures. The evidence is to be seen in the very limited number of major governmental reorganizations that have been approved in this country.

Interest-Group Response

Though the parties almost uniformly may be counted on to oppose restructuring, some interest groups are very strong proponents of metropolitan reorganization. A study conducted by the Advisory Commission on Intergovernmental Relations in 1965 revealed that the strongest supporters of the reorganization cause were the metropolitan newspapers, the League of Women Voters, big-city chambers of commerce, downtown business interests, radio and television stations, research organizations, and banks.[8]

Presumably the business groups hoped that reorganization would improve their general financial position. The League of Women Voters and other similar good-government groups are committed to reorganization on the basis of philosophical principle. The leadership of the opposition to reorganization proposals, it was found, usually came from suburban newspapers and county government employees, as well as from prominent individuals who feared that the suburbs would lose their identity by metropolitan reorganization.

(Photo by Linda Bartlett; courtesy Martin W. Sandler.)

There is also a racial dimension to the question. Though they do not constitute anything like a formal coalition, many urban whites have been predisposed toward consolidation with the suburbs when the black population has reached the point at which it threatens to achieve majority control of the city. For their part, the black voters, who have gained increasing influence in city politics as their numbers have increased, are more and more reluctant to opt for area-wide metropolitan government in which their influence would obviously be drastically reduced.

Voter Response

In those cases in which reorganization proposals were turned down by the voters—which was most of the time—John H. Baker, an urban specialist, found five factors to be present.[9]

These are as follows:

1. the failure of the general public to perceive any crisis at all
2. the fear of higher taxes
3. very low voter participation in the referenda
4. competition with other "reform" approaches
5. overemphasis on "efficiency" and "good government" and an underestimation of the political realities and interests of the metropolis.

In the 1965 ACIR study previously referred to, it was found that only about 25 percent of the eligible electorate participated in the eighteen referenda which were examined. The ACIR suggested that overreliance on the media and failure to reach the voters on a face-to-face basis was probably a major factor in the low voter turnout.

If we consider those who do vote, David Booth's study of voter attitudes toward the proposed Nashville–Davidson County consolidation is enlightening.[10] His examination of suburban residents in Davidson County revealed that the proconsolidation people perceived better services and more efficient government as the chief benefits of the plan. But suburbanites opposed to the plan registered a fear of higher taxes and satisfaction with the present government as justification for their outlook.

More significant, perhaps, was the fact that an antiurban bias seemed to be the primary factor in much of the suburban residents' hostility toward the concept of consolidation with the city of Nashville. At the heart of this bias, Booth found, was a desire to preserve values—or a way of life—which could not be found in the central city. In short, those who emphasized essentially "suburban values" were almost predictably disposed to vote against master plans stressing efficiency and economy—that is, consolidation.

IN SUMMARY

In light of the previous analysis, what are the necessary social and political ingredients for successful metropolitan government reorganization? Once more, we must turn to the situation in Miami–Dade County. We have noted that Democratic

dominance in the cities versus Republican control of the suburbs militates against the possibility of consolidation of city and
suburbs in any form. Metropolitan Miami, however, is predominantly a nonpartisan region, emphasizing candidates rather
than party affiliation. Therefore, political cleavages were substantially muted. In addition, blacks and other minority-group
members who might be expected to fear that consolidation with
the suburbs would threaten their political clout represented—at
the time the plan was adopted—only a minor fraction of the
total population of greater Miami. Union membership in the
area was both limited and politically inactive. The electorate
was mostly apathetic and neutral toward the proposed reorganization. As a consequence, those who supported the urban-county
concept (newspapers, Chamber of Commerce, business and professional groups, the League of Women Voters, academic
groups) did not run into insurmountable obstacles. And as a result, the urban-county plan became a reality. But the 1957 referendum, even so, was a cliff-hanger, since the proposal carried
by a vote of 51 percent in favor and 49 percent opposed.

The conditions which existed in Miami in 1957 are not likely to be duplicated in many other metropolitan areas. Large-
scale metropolitan reorganization in a structural sense, therefore, will probably be something of a rarity. At the same time,
there is every reason to expect that various kinds of functional
integration will gain ground. This is especially true of the special district device, which brings about an integration based on
functions within a region while maintaining political fragmentation. Apparently, this is what most Americans want—functional,
but not political, consolidation.

Items for Discussion

1. Compare the quality of life in Toronto,
Canada, under a federation government with the quality of life
in American Great Lakes cities such as Buffalo, Cleveland, and
Detroit. How much credit for the difference can be given to
governmental structure?

2. Is it merely a coincidence that eleven of
the twelve successful city-county consolidations have occurred
in the South?

3. Can a serious case be made for creating several "city-states" by having cities such as New York, Chicago, and Los Angeles separate from their states?

4. Of all the proposals for metropolitan reorganization presented in this chapter, which do you believe would be the most workable in your local area? How would you go about "selling" it to the local political leaders and the voters?

5. Can you present an argument aimed at blacks and other minorities to convince them that city-county consolidation would be in their best interest?

Chapter Notes

1. Committee for Economic Development, *Reshaping Government in Metropolitan Areas* (New York: Committee for Economic Development, 1970), pp. 23–24.

2. Advisory Commission on Intergovernmental Relations, *Alternative Approaches to Governmental Reorganization* (Washington, D.C.: ACIR, 1962).

3. Daniel R. Grant, "The Metropolitan Government Approach: Should, Can, and Will it Prevail?" in James E. McKeown and Fred Tietle (eds.), *The Changing Metropolis* (Boston: Houghton Mifflin, 1971), p. 174.

4. Stanley Scott and John Bollens, *Governing A Metropolitan Region* (Berkeley, California: Institute of Governmental Studies, University of California, 1968), p. 70.

5. Vincent L. Marando, "The Politics of City-County Consolidation," *National Civic Review*, Vol. 64, No. 2 (Feb. 1975), pp. 76–81.

6. *Ibid.,* p. 81.

7. *Alternative Approaches to Governmental Reorganization, op. cit.,* p. 47.

8. Advisory Commission on Intergovernmental Relations, *Factors Affecting Voter Reactions to Governmental Reorganization in Metropolitan Areas* (Washington, D.C.: ACIR, 1965).

9. See John H. Baker, *Urban Politics in America* (New York: Scribner's, 1971), p. 115.

10. David A. Booth, "Metro and the Suburbanite," in Philip Coulter (ed.), *Politics of Metropolitan Areas* (New York: Crowell, 1967), pp. 270–284.

13

Law Enforcement

Key Terms

Arraignment: Stage in criminal proceedings in which the accused is brought to court to hear the formal charges being brought by the grand jury or prosecutor; the accused is then asked to plead guilty or not guilty.

Bail: Funds provided to assure that a person will appear in court at a certain time.

Civilian review boards: Groups of private citizens who review charges of misconduct by the police.

Information: Formal accusation filed by the prosecutor; in state-level criminal proceedings this is a common alternative to grand jury indictment.

Misdemeanors: Minor crimes punishable by fine or short jail term; contrasted with *felonies*, which are more serious violations of the law punishable by longer terms in a state penitentiary.

Ombudsman: An individual who acts as an official mediator between the people and government officials.

Parole: Conditional release of a prisoner who has served part, but not all, of a prison sentence.

Peremptory challenges: Limited number of dismissals of potential jurors by the defense or prosecution without stating a *cause*, such as bias or personal acquaintance with the accused.

Preliminary hearing: Held before a judge shortly after the arrest of a suspected criminal to determine if there is sufficient evidence to hold the accused for further action by the grand jury or prosecuting attorney.

Probation: Suspension of a prison sentence

by the court with provisions limiting the activities of the defendant over a set period of time.

  Retribution: Criminal sentence aimed at
punishing the offender; contrasted with *rehabilitation*, which
seeks to change the behavior of the convicted criminal to prevent future unlawful acts.

  Warrant: In law, a court order authorizing a
law enforcement officer to make an arrest, seizure, or search.

  To this point, we have analyzed the constitutional and legal structures of state and local governments.
We have also examined the decision-making agencies of such
governments. In this and the following chapters we look at some
of the principal functions which these governments perform. In
the language of systemic theory, our attention will be directed
toward the policy outputs stemming from the actions of the
decision-making agencies.

  One of the most important functions of government is the
enforcement of criminal law. (As we have noted, in civil cases
the government merely lays down rules and provides an arena
for settlement.) The approach taken here is, firstly, to examine
the agencies and principal officials of the law enforcement process. Secondly, the focus of attention is shifted toward the activities of the police in our municipal areas.

  Even though there has developed over the years a substantial body of federal criminal law enforced by federal officers
through federal courts, the fact remains that American criminal
law is mostly state law and its enforcement is basically a state
function. Put this way, it may sound as though the law enforcement agencies of the states were rather centralized and perhaps
monolithic institutions in their relations with the local authorities. But this is not the case: the basic responsibility for law enforcement has been delegated largely to units of local government.

  Some of the officials and agencies involved in the law enforcement process have been discussed in other connections, for
example, the governor, the national guard, and the sheriff. But
here the emphasis is placed upon certain important agencies in
order to underscore their roles in enforcing the law. We begin
with the principal state law enforcement agencies.

STATE LAW ENFORCEMENT AGENCIES

The most important state agencies in the enforcement of criminal law are the governor, the attorney general, the national guard, and the state police. In principle, the governor stands at the top of a hierarchy and is universally charged with the constitutional responsibility of seeing to it that the laws are "faithfully executed." In practice, the governor in most states has little control over the activities of those officers upon whom he or she must rely for law enforcement: the attorney general and the prosecuting attorneys. Because in most instances these officials are popularly elected, they are quite independent of the governor. This is in great contrast to the federal system, where the attorney general is responsible to the president, not to the electorate, because this official is appointed, not elected. Almost every student of the subject of state law enforcement believes that efficiency would improve if the states adopted the federal model.

Under these conditions, the actual participation of the state attorneys general is not impressive and is not extensive. They do perform some functions in the prosecution of accused persons before the courts. As we have observed, governors have not hesitated to use the national guard when ordinary law enforcement agencies have not been able to deal with a situation.

The State Police

Every one of the states has a state police force, although the forces are given varying titles. In some states, the force is simply a special highway patrol, charged with enforcing motor vehicle regulations. In other states, the state police have a general jurisdiction to enforce all state laws. The police system may be a separate department of state government, or it may be merely a subdivision of a department. Whether known as commissioner or superintendent of police, the head official is normally appointed by the governor and is responsible directly or indirectly to the chief executive. In some states there is also a state bureau of criminal identification, patterned loosely after the Federal Bureau of Investigation.

In an age when the vast majority of Americans live in urban areas, it is clear that the state police force is primarily an agency for the enforcement of laws in rural areas. Whether by statute or by custom, state police forces usually operate within municipalities only at the specific request of the municipal authorities. It is now common to prohibit the use of state forces in connection with labor disputes, activities which at one time took up a good deal of their energies. This limitation is a direct result of the legitimization of and increase in power of the labor movement, especially since the passage of the Wagner Act in 1935, which established the National Labor Relations Board, and the passage of related statutes by the states.

The professionalization which has occured in police forces generally has also included state police systems. In the last two decades, as a result of the civil rights movement, there have been strenuous efforts to step up the recruiting of black and Hispanic-surnamed candidates. Yet progress has been discouragingly slow. A 1974 survey conducted by the Race Relations Information Center came up with some specific findings:[1]

1. Alabama, after three years of hiring under terms of a federal court order, had achieved the largest percentage of blacks of any state police force. What this meant in practice was that Alabama had 28 blacks on its force of 623, or 4.5 percent.

2. Maryland was next with 4 percent.

3. Nationally, blacks constitute 1.5 percent of the state police forces. Hispanics and Indians made up about an equal percentage. New York had 19 blacks on a force of 3,407. The 1970 census found that blacks constituted 11.1 percent of the national population.

4. Every southern state had some blacks on its state police force, with Mississippi's six being the lowest reported figure.

5. Of the 41,894 state enforcement officers throughout the nation, 135 were women.

LOCAL LAW ENFORCEMENT AGENCIES

The principal law enforcement officers are the sheriff in the county, the constable in the township, and the town marshal and city police within incorporated municipalities. However, usage varies throughout the country; there is no standard terminology that is employed everywhere. At the local level, there are two other law enforcement agencies which deserve special attention. These are the grand jury and the prosecuting attorney, and they are considered next.

The Grand Jury

The grand jury as an institution goes far back into English law. Its primary function is to consider cases of law violation laid before it by the prosecuting attorney. The objective is to determine whether the evidence against suspected persons is sufficient to warrant bringing them to trial. It should be emphasized that the grand jury does not determine whether a suspected person is guilty of the offense charged. Because the grand jury proceeding is not a trial, the suspected person has no right to appear before the jury, which is concerned only with the evidence against a suspect. If the jury considers that the evidence justifies a formal trial, it returns an indictment, which is a formal charge or accusation. On the other hand, should the jury deem the evidence insufficient for an indictment, the suspected person is not brought to trial.

In addition to this primary function, another power that may be given to a grand jury is to act as an investigatory body. Acting in this capacity, a grand jury may investigate matters of public concern, which may range from alleged election frauds to who murdered President John F. Kennedy to allegations that television quiz shows going out over a national network from New York city were "rigged." Though this function of a grand jury obviously has value, it is also subject to the dangers of manipulation by the prosecuting attorney. Sometimes, in fact, this use of a grand jury seems to amount to giving a disgruntled prosecuting attorney a hunting license to gun down enemies. At the end of its investigations, the grand jury may issue a special report, or it may return indictments.

How are members of a grand jury chosen? Usually this is handled by lot, often in the same manner as members of the trial jury. In most states, the names for the jury list are taken from either the local assessment rolls or voters' registration lists. The grand jury varies in size in the different states from five to twenty-three members. Under common law, the size was fixed at twenty-three members, the vote of twelve being necessary to return an indictment. This common-law rule is still followed in some states, though others have reduced the number to twelve members. Indictment, incidentally, does not require a unanimous vote in any of the states. Michigan invented an ingenious system under which a single official, a judge, in effect performed most of the functions of a grand jury. It has popularly been dubbed a "one-man grand jury."

The Prosecuting Attorney

From what has been said to this point, it is evident that the key figure in law enforcement in the states is the prosecuting attorney. Again, while the official title may vary (prosecuting attorney, state's attorney, county attorney, and so on), the chief function is to prosecute in the name of the state. An officer of the state, the prosecutor is usually chosen locally and serves a particular community. That is, the prosecutor is in reality a local official charged with the execution of state duties in law enforcement. The two principal powers of a prosecuting attorney are (1) the preferring of formal charges against persons suspected of having committed crimes; and (2) the prosecution in the courts of persons against whom charges have been filed. Though in rural counties the office of the prosecutor may consist of two or three people, in the big cities the office is a major operation, employing scores of attorneys, researchers, and secretaries.

It is difficult to exaggerate the discretionary power of a prosecuting attorney when it comes to presenting a case to a grand jury for action, for it is the prosecutor who drafts the indictment document. Normally, members of a grand jury will consider only matters brought to its attention by the prosecutor. As a result, whether an indictment is returned or not usually depends upon the ability and skill of the prosecutor (and staff) in marshalling and presenting the evidence.

Because of the obvious weaknesses of the grand jury system, a majority of states now permit at least some use of the *information* as an alternative to grand-jury indictment in the preferring of criminal charges. This is especially true in cases of lesser crimes. In a few states it has become the practice to use the device of an information almost exclusively.

Exactly what is an information? It is a formal accusation or charge of crime filed against a suspected person by the prosecuting attorney. It has exactly the same effect in bringing an accused to trial as an indictment, except that it is filed by the prosecutor on his or her own initiative. There is no grand jury action at all. To file or not to file an information in a particular case lies solely within the discretion of the prosecutor. The prosecutor therefore holds the power to determine who shall and who shall not be charged with crime.

The next step is up to the prosecutor as well. Whether the suspected person has been charged with a crime by indictment or by information, it becomes the duty of the prosecuting attorney to prepare the case against the accused. In all respects, the prosecutor is in command: he or she participates in the selection of the jury, presents evidence against the accused, examines the state's witnesses and cross-examines defense witnesses, and makes the final plea to the jury. If successful in securing a high percentage of convictions, and if acceptable to the mass media, an outstanding prosecutor may stay on the front pages of newspapers or be highlighted in television newscasts on a regular basis. His very high rate of convictions brought Thomas E. Dewey to the attention of the electorate both of New York city and of the state. And eventually he was chosen to be governor of the state and, after that, a Republican nominee for the presidency.

It is the practice of many very able young lawyers to work in the office of a prosecutor (or district attorney) at relatively modest pay in order to gain invaluable experience as to how the legal system works. Having gained such experience, these attorneys, if competent, are then likely to go into private practice at much higher salaries than those paid from the public treasury. The most successful and able of criminal lawyers in the United States are themselves celebrities. It should be noted, however, that only a tiny minority of the American bar engages in the practice of criminal law. Most lawyers are concerned with civil law only, and many of them earn their fees by keeping their clients from ever seeing the inside of a courtroom.

The Attorney General

Contrary to what a layman might expect, the role of the attorney general in all but three states is negligible in criminal prosecutions. The exceptions are Alaska, Delaware, and Rhode Island. In those states, the responsibility for conducting criminal prosecutions is imposed on the attorney general instead of on the locally elected prosecuting attorneys.

But in the overwhelming majority of the states, the attorney general is likely to take the view that prosecutions should originate with the local prosecuting attorney, even in cases of concurrent jurisdiction. The attorney general, after all, is also an elected official and has everything to lose and nothing to gain by taking a course of action contrary to that of a locally elected prosecutor.

Attorneys general do have assignments to fill, for example,

in advising the governor regarding the possible constitutionality of a bill. But in the area of law enforcement their role is minimal.

THE PROCESS OF LAW ENFORCEMENT

The process by which criminal laws are enforced is generally considered to comprise seven successive stages. We now describe these phases, with the understanding that actual practices vary a good deal from state to state.

Maintenance of the Peace

An axiom in law enforcement is that the first duty of the enforcement officers is to preserve the peace. For this purpose, the officers—state police, sheriffs, constables, city police, and town marshals—patrol highways and streets and appear at establishments and gatherings where disorder is likely to occur. The theory is that the presence of such officials will act as a deterrent to criminal violations.

Arrest of Law Violators

When the law has been violated, it is the responsibility of the police officers to locate and arrest the perpetrator of the criminal act. It is at this point that an exchange of information among police jurisdictions may be useful. For example, fingerprints and other identification aids may be employed to pinpoint a suspect.

A standard definition of arrest is "the taking of a person into custody in order that he may be forthcoming to answer for the commission of an offense."[2] Sometimes an arrest is made with a warrant; sometimes it is not. It depends on the circumstances. A warrant of arrest is in fact a court order directing the arrest of a particular person or persons. It is issued upon the complaint of a private citizen, usually the injured party, or of a law enforcement officer. However, the general rule is that a police officer may arrest without a warrant any person who commits a crime in the officer's presence. When a crime has not been committed in the presence of an officer, a warrant is usually necessary, with one general exception. In the case of felony, arrest may be made without a warrant if the officer has

reasonable cause to believe that the person arrested has committed the crime.

In law as well as in folklore, it is possible for an individual
citizen to make an arrest if a crime takes place in his or her
presence. But this may involve considerable personal risk
because of either physical danger or a subsequent civil damage
suit for false arrest.

Preliminary Hearing

Once an arrest has been made, it is followed by a
preliminary hearing. Ordinarily this hearing, held before a
judge of a minor court, occurs within a few hours after the
arrest. The point is to determine whether the evidence against
the suspected person is sufficient to hold him or her for action
by the grand jury or prosecuting attorney. In order to hold the
suspect, the court must be convinced that the evidence submitted indicates a reasonable ground to believe that the defendant is guilty. If the magistrate is so convinced, he or she "binds
over" the suspect to the grand jury or to wait for the filing of an
information by the prosecutor. Conversely, if the magistrate is
unconvinced by the evidence, the suspected person may be
freed at that point.

Bail. When a magistrate has ordered a suspected person held for further action, the same magistrate must, unless the
offense is nonbailable (as is frequently the case with capital
offenses), permit the release of the suspect on bail pending such
action. In doing so, the judge sets the amount of the bail bond
which the subject must post as security for his or her future
appearance at a set time. If the suspect is unable to supply the
required bail, or if the offense in question is nonbailable, the
person is placed in jail to await further disposition of the case.

Clearly, the whole bail bond system is open to serious objections. Especially in the big cities, professional bondsmen may
work with politically oriented magistrates and prosecuting attorneys so that a small group of favored bondsmen develops a
monopoly of the trade. Then, too, the fixing of the size of the
bond often seems capricious. In general, the system works
against the poor and favors the rich. Nor does the system actually guarantee that the suspected person will ever show up for
trial. If the stakes are high enough, many a suspect prefers to go
underground or leave the country, feeling that the forfeit of the
bail is a small price to pay for freedom.

Preferring of Charges

Following the bail procedure, the next step in the law enforcement process is the preferring of formal charges against the suspected person. As has been explained earlier, this may be done by indictment or by information, the latter method being favored by legal reformers. One of the arguments in favor of the information route concerns the responsibility of the prosecutor. While he or she may be able to control any actions of a grand jury, the same official cannot be held responsible for the grand jury's action. On the other hand, when the information device is employed, it is simply impossible for the prosecutor to shift the responsibility for the action to anyone else.

In determining whether to continue with grand juries or to adopt the information approach, the states have more freedom of choice than does the federal government. A provision in the Fifth Amendment requires that no person may be held to answer for a capital or otherwise infamous crime except on a presentment or indictment of a grand jury. As a result, all major criminal offenses against the federal government are prosecuted on grand-jury charges. But misdemeanors may be prosecuted in the federal courts on information.

Arraignment and Plea

Once the formal charges have been preferred, the next step is for the accused to be arraigned before the trial court. The indictment or information is read to the accused, who is given the opportunity to plead guilty or not guilty to the charges. If the accused declines to plead, a plea of not guilty is entered by the court. In most instances, a plea of guilty means that a trial is dispensed with and the court proceeds to pronounce its judgment and sentence. A plea of not guilty brings the case to trial.

Prosecution and Trial

As we have observed earlier, misdemeanors are often tried in the first instance in minor courts. When the charge involves felony, the prosecutions are normally begun in the general trial courts. The prosecuting attorney presents the state's case against the accused, who is represented by private counsel, counsel appointed by the court, or a public defender. Usually, the state's constitution will guarantee the right to be tried by a jury in criminal actions. It is rare to waive a jury trial in felony cases.

The Trial Jury. Even if they have never served on a petit or trial jury, most persons know someone who has. It is the trial jury which decides whether or not the accused is guilty, and returns its verdict accordingly. In common law the trial jury consisted of twelve persons, and a jury of this size is almost universally required in the trial of major crimes. On the other hand, some states provide for the trial of misdemeanors by juries of fewer than twelve persons.

Depending on the state, certain categories of persons may be automatically exempted from jury service. These may include clergy, lawyers, physicians, schoolteachers, state and local officers, police, and fire fighters. In the past, juries were composed exclusively of men. This barrier has been overcome in recent decades, and today women have the same obligations toward jury duty as men.

In selecting a jury, the first step is to prepare a list of names from which a panel may be drawn. Those responsible for preparing the list vary from state to state. The assignment may be handled by a county board, certain town officers, jury commissioners appointed by the court, or other designated officers. In compiling the list, recourse is had to local assessment rolls or voters' registration lists, though some jurisdictions make use of city directories and telephone directories as well.

When the list has been prepared, names up to the total required by law are chosen at random and placed in the jury selection box. When a new panel of jurors is required, the court clerk draws a designated number of names from the box. The persons so chosen are then summoned to appear for service. Traditionally and currently, the summoning of jurors has been a job of the sheriff. But it is, of course, possible to handle the entire matter through registered mail which, incidentally, eliminates the sheriff's fees.

The idea, then, is to place in a box the names of all jurors present and not engaged, and to draw twelve names for presentation to the parties for examination and challenge. Since each party is entitled to a specified number of *peremptory* challenges (challenges without a cause stated) and an unlimited number of challenges *for cause* (such as bias or a relationship to involved parties), a process which seems at first glance to be very simple usually becomes extremely complex. In England, a jury is selected in a matter of hours. In the United States, the process may drag on for weeks.

In criminal cases most states require a unanimous vote for conviction of the defendant. This process ought to operate to the advantage of the accused, since defense counsel need only convince one juror that there is reasonable doubt of guilt. But about half the states have abandoned the rule of unanimity in civil cases.

Punishment of Convicted Persons

If the verdict is guilty, the defendant's attorney will probably offer motions to arrest the judgment or to be granted a new trial. A convicted defendant will usually be able to find statutory grounds upon which appeal may be taken to a higher court. Should the higher court consent to review the case, the effect is to stay the imposition or execution of a sentence until the appeal is acted upon. The sentence, if upheld, may take the form of a fine, a term of imprisonment, or both.

Even though "law-and-order" police and politicians are likely to invoke the doctrine of an eye for an eye, a tooth for a tooth, the idea of retribution carries less weight today than it did in the past. At least in the textbooks on the subject, the modern ideal is said to be rehabilitation. In fact, remarkably little rehabilitation takes place in any prison. Today the principal justifications for imprisoning criminals are to protect society from persons who would be dangerous if they were set free, and to attempt some measure of reform of the criminals themselves. No one keeps exact statistics on the subject, but it appears that in many instances a prison is merely a revolving door; the percentage of repeaters for such crimes as rape, burglary, robbery, and assault and battery is remarkably high.

THE DETENTION SYSTEM

The County Jail

In rural areas it is the almost universal practice to establish a county jail, which is controlled by the county board but actually managed by the sheriff. Generally, such a jail is used to detain two classes of prisoners: (1) those held awaiting action by a grand or trial jury, and unable to provide bail; and (2) those persons serving short sentences for offenses of which they have been convicted.

County jails have been subjected to a steady and vigorous stream of criticism by persons concerned with reforming the penal system. These criticisms range from poor living conditions to charges of outright exploitation of the prisoners for private gain. An example of the latter occurs when a sheriff permits a private employer or company to use the services of the jail's inmates, for example, on an orange ranch during harvesting season. The possibilities of abuse are obvious.

To offset some of the deficiencies of county jails, state governments from time to time try to centralize control over them and to create some set of standards applicable throughout the state. Yet resistance to reform proposals often takes an unexpected turn. A quarter of a century ago, when United States Senator John O. Pastore was governor of Rhode Island, he proposed the abolition of the Washington County jail and its absorption into the state system. Much to the governor's surprise and chagrin, his suggestion provoked a wave of resistance from many residents of Washington County who themselves were not in jail. It seemed that locally minded Rhode Islanders had developed some fondness for all of their local institutions, including the jail. Governor Pastore abandoned his project in the face of such resistance.

State Penal Institutions

When conviction is for a felony, a prisoner is sent to a state penal institution. Included in this category are penitentiaries, reformatories, houses of correction, and various types of training schools for women and juvenile offenders. In contrast to county jails, the state institutions try to provide some kind of employment for the prisoners. Despite this ideal, the testimony of ex-felons is that they spent a good deal of their time in relative idleness. Where goods are manufactured, the objective has been to limit them to use by the state itself, so as to avoid competing with goods made by free labor and offered on the open market for sale. A typical example is the use of prisoners to manufacture the state's automobile license plates. Another is to produce clothing for inmates of various kinds of state institutions.

Prisoners at New York's Attica State Prison negotiate
demands in 1971. (Wide World Photos.)

Probation and Parole

For a generation which has achieved a fairly high
degree of amateur training merely by following the Watergate
trials, it may seem superfluous to define such terms as *probation*
and *parole*. Yet the purpose of such devices warrants brief comment.

Both probation and parole are intended to promote the
reformation of persons convicted of crime. Probation is defined
as the conditional suspension by a trial court of the imposition
or execution of a prison sentence. Probation is employed when,
in the opinion of the court, no useful societal purpose would be
served by incarcerating the offender. During the period of
probation, the probationer must abide by terms set by the court
and report regularly to probation officers. If the terms of the
probation are violated, the probationer may be arrested at once
and required to serve his or her sentence.

The other administrative device intended to facilitate
rehabilitation—parole—is defined as the conditional release of a

person who has served part but not all of a prison sentence. It therefore differs from probation in two important respects. Firstly, it is granted by an administrative agency, not the courts. And secondly, it is granted only after part of the sentence has been served. This method is most commonly employed in connection with the "indeterminate sentence," that is, one which specifies a minimum and a maximum number of years of imprisonment rather than a fixed term. The parolee must report to parole officers from time to time, as prescribed by law. A parolee who violates the conditions of his or her freedom may be taken into custody and returned to the penal institution for the remainder of the maximum term.

It is difficult to generalize about the degree of effectiveness of probation and parole as means of rehabilitation. All that one can say with certainty is that there is little uniformity among the states.

THE POLICE

Municipal Police Forces

As noted earlier, one of the principal characteristics of metropolitan areas is their very high degree of political fragmentation. Nowhere is this better illustrated than in the case of the police. Consider an illustration from metropolitan Philadelphia which is, unhappily, typical of a number of regions.

The four suburban counties of Philadelphia are Delaware, Montgomery, Bucks, and Chester. They contain 237 municipalities of which some are less than one-tenth of a square mile in area. The combined population of the counties is more than 1.9 million persons.

In these counties, there were in 1975 about twenty-three hundred policemen and policewomen, including the chiefs. Some small municipalities had no police departments of their own but relied on working arrangements with neighboring communities. In all, there were 194 separate police departments.

In addition to fragmentation and lack of coordination of police efforts, it was found in two studies that 80 percent of the suburban police departments offered no training programs for personnel once they had joined the force. In some 14 percent of the departments, there was not even any training for recruits. A study by the Governor's Justice Commission of police departments in the four suburban counties with fewer than twenty-five uniformed officers found that the departments generally failed to reach nationally recognized standards. A related study conducted by the Crime Commission of Philadelphia of suburban departments with twenty-five or more officers reached similar conclusions.

As the *Philadelphia Inquirer* put it: ". . . the basic problem is too many police departments, police chiefs, and police headquarters—each determined to protect and preserve its own autonomy."[3]

The Police: An Overview

The police establishment in America is immense. As Table 13.1 shows, as of 1972, 410,765 persons were employed by local police forces. Law enforcement is a growth industry: in 1970, the number of men and women in the nation's local police forces was about 394 thousand. The police were at that time organized into forty thousand seperate agencies. More than two-thirds of the police in the same year were in the 39,695 agencies serving county and smaller local units, and one-third were in the large departments of cities with a population in excess of 250 thousand. The largest force, numbering thirty-two thousand, was found in New York city.

Though the police perform many functions, their primary objectives are to maintain order and to enforce the law. To some extent, these objectives are more antithetical than complementary. While the police like to publicize their law enforcement role, it is a role which is widely shared with other agencies—the correctional, judicial, and penal systems. In addition, only a small fraction of the working time of the ordinary patrol officer is spent on law enforcement. On the other hand, maintaining order takes the lion's share of the average police officer's time and energy, and it is in this area that the police role is paramount.

The problem of standards or criteria further complicates an assessment of the importance of the two principal police objectives. Generally, police administrators are not in agreement as to what constitutes a satisfactory performance of the order maintenance function. When it comes to the other main func-

Table 13.1
State and Local Government Police and Correction Employment and Police Expenditure, 1970–1972, and by States, 1972

| | Employees | | | | | | Police Expenditures (mil. dol.) | | |
| | Police Protection | | | Correction | | | | | |
State	State and local	Total	Local Percent	State and local	Total	Local Percent	State and local	Total	Local Percent
1970	449,656	393,810	87.6	142,307	51,973	36.5	4,491	3,803	85
1971	472,066	402,691	85.3	172,821	68,776	38.6	5,361	4,488	84
1972	486,162	410,765	84.5	177,864	70,079	39.4	5,941	4,948	83
Ala.	6,238	5,124	82.1	1,590	587	36.9	57	44	77
Alaska	945	418	44.2	442	72	16.3	14	5	37
Ariz.	5,086	4,068	80.0	1,450	706	48.7	62	45	73
Ark.	3,389	2,808	82.8	761	218	28.6	29	22	78
Cal.	55,913	44,850	80.2	29,039	17,148	59.0	787	634	81
Colo.	5,010	4,185	83.5	1,778	379	21.3	51	42	82
Conn.	7,111	5,977	84.0	2,087	–	–	90	74	82
Del.	1,430	823	57.6	690	–	–	16	9	59
Dist. Col.	6,349	6,349	100.0	2,850	2,850	100.0	76	76	100
Fla.	17,998	15,531	86.3	8,472	2,641	31.2	187	157	84
Ga.	8,645	7,228	83.6	4,050	1,457	36.0	83	67	81
Hawaii	2,380	2,350	98.7	432	81	18.8	30	30	99
Idaho	1,453	1,200	82.6	458	89	19.4	15	10	71
Ill.	30,392	27,228	89.6	7,391	2,481	33.6	399	350	88
Ind.	9,000	7,533	83.7	2,828	972	34.4	95	74	78
Iowa	4,477	3,417	76.3	1,508	393	26.1	47	35	76
Kan.	4,374	3,686	84.3	2,208	297	13.4	40	32	78
Ky.	4,936	3,633	73.6	1,763	431	24.4	52	36	69
La.	8,580	7,328	85.4	2,556	814	31.8	82	67	82

Me.	1,855	1,335	72.0	751	110	14.6	18	12	65
Md.	10,945	8,818	80.6	5,323	815	15.3	132	105	79
Mass.	14,935	13,574	90.9	4,709	1,814	38.5	184	165	90
Mich.	20,174	17,325	85.9	5,782	2,650	45.8	281	239	85
Minn.	6,630	5,746	86.7	2,671	860	32.2	80	67	84
Miss.	3,891	2,930	75.3	760	182	23.9	35	23	65
Mo.	11,070	9,453	85.4	3,229	1,485	46.0	117	100	86
Mont.	1,421	1,082	76.1	556	101	18.2	13	9	73
Nebr.	2,908	2,350	80.8	870	163	18.7	30	23	78
Nev.	1,980	1,811	91.5	842	424	50.4	25	22	89
N.H.	1,523	1,261	82.8	454	177	39.0	16	12	79
N.J.	21,605	18,760	86.8	6,573	3,491	53.1	269	228	85
N.M.	2,464	1,787	72.5	802	169	21.1	26	18	72
N.Y.	67,817	62,400	92.0	20,512	9,880	48.2	1,051	980	93
N.C.	8,865	7,112	80.2	5,332	588	11.0	89	67	76
N.D.	978	834	85.3	233	41	17.6	9	8	84
Ohio	19,275	16,696	86.6	8,881	2,635	29.7	227	191	84
Okla.	5,150	3,934	76.4	1,759	324	18.4	44	31	70
Ore.	4,310	3,326	77.2	2,094	700	33.4	54	39	73
Pa.	25,448	20,115	79.0	7,855	3,909	49.8	319	245	77
R.I.	2,248	1,951	86.8	519	–	–	25	22	85
S.C.	4,555	3,500	76.8	2,267	691	30.5	44	30	69
S.D.	1,108	864	78.0	329	87	26.4	11	8	72
Tenn.	6,910	5,844	84.6	2,844	829	29.1	65	53	82
Texas	21,510	18,892	87.8	6,451	2,772	43.0	211	172	81
Utah	2,072	1,690	81.6	683	131	19.2	21	16	76
Vt.	895	540	60.3	438	–	–	9	4	50
Va.	9,448	6,683	70.7	3,732	1,010	27.1	97	67	69
Wash.	6,693	5,223	78.0	3,718	1,291	34.7	84	65	77
W.Va.	2,352	1,649	70.1	867	239	27.6	21	14	64
Wis.	10,721	8,995	83.9	3,362	836	24.9	117	100	85
Wyo.	700	549	78.4	313	59	18.8	7	5	71

[Employees, full-time equivalent, as of October. Direct expenditures for police protection are for fiscal years ending in year stated. Local government data are estimates subject to sampling variation.]

— Represents zero or rounds to zero.

Source: U.S. Law Enforcement Assistance Administration and U.S. Bureau of the Census, *Expenditure and Employment Data for the Criminal Justice System,* annual. From *Statistical Abstract of the U.S.,* 1974, p. 157.

tion—law enforcement—there is more agreement. The law is to be enforced and crime is to be eliminated. However, there is no agreement on the strategy to be employed to achieve this agreed-upon objective. Because of their inability to agree on the answers to these questions, police administrators differ markedly in their approach to and their handling of concrete situations.

Crime Rates

As crime has grown, so have public expenditures to contain it. Table 13.1 indicates that the amount of money allocated to local police forces increased by more than a billion dollars between 1970 and 1972. Usually, crime statistics have been based on offenses reported to the Federal Bureau of Investigation and published annually in a series called *Uniform Crime Reports for the United States*. On the basis of the figures given to the FBI during the 1960s, crime increased 148 percent during the decade, while the population increased only 13 percent.

For 1971–1972, the FBI figures indicate a reversal of this trend. However, there is reason to suspect that either the FBI or the reporting departments arranged the data in such a way as to force this conclusion. In any event, the FBI tables for 1973 and 1974 show a dramatic increase in the number of serious crimes reported in the United States. The conventional wisdom held that such an increase was to be expected because of the severe economic recession which occurred during the mid-1970s.

Not wishing to rely on local police departments for crime figures, the Law Enforcement Assistance Agency (LEAA) conducted a detailed crime survey in 1974 through the facilities of the Bureau of the Census. The survey was administered to about two thousand commercial establishments in thirteen selected cities. Utilizing detailed questionnaires, the survey examined whether or not the respondents had been victims of crimes, and whether or not they reported such victimization the the police.

The results were startling. It was found that twelve of the thirteen cities experienced two or three times more crime than was reported by the police. The only exception to this pattern was Philadelphia: that city experienced five times more crime than was suggested by Philadelphia crime statistics. What the study pointed out was that a very large percentage of crimes, especially those relating to robbery, burglary, and rape, are simply not reported by the victims. Therefore, they do not show up on the police statistics.

Political Action and the Police

It has been a cherished American belief that politics and the police should be insulated from each other. This belief rests on the assumption that any combination of the two factors will result in the corruption of the police by the politicians. That the police might corrupt the politicians is a sentiment that is rarely voiced, and would not be believed if it were. Like oil and water, the two elements are held to make a poor mixture.

In fact, the separation has never been as clear as idealists have hoped it would be. Studies of particular cities have shown that powerful political organizations have rarely hesitated to use the apparatus of the police department for purely personal or partisan ends. A recent illustration comes from the Chicago police force which, during the mayorship of Richard J. Daley, engaged in a type of surveillance over a wide variety of persons. This secret surveillance was eventually exposed, but during its existence, it constituted something like a secret police espionage activity. Nobody outside the inner circles of big-city police forces has any accurate idea as to how widespread this practice is.

Yet partisan activities and private espionage aside, there has in the last decade developed an entirely new kind of police activism. If the early municipal reformers were upset by what they considered laxity or corruption on the part of urban police forces, they would be totally appalled by the police activities of the last few years. This activism has involved the police in political and social areas that in the past have been considered outside the interests or even the competence of the police.

What is new is police militancy, as shown in illegal police strikes, lobbying, and political organizing. In effect, the police guild, fraternal, and social organizations have been transformed into effective interest groups which lobby and propagandize on behalf of what the police believe to be their proper concerns. One of these groups, the Fraternal Order of Police, claims a membership of 130 thousand. This means that militancy and politicization have been able to build upon an organizational framework already in existence.

Indeed, the concerns of the national Fraternal Order of Police and similar local organizations have proved to be

remarkably broad. As one would expect, there has been substantial activism on behalf of material benefits: higher wages,
shorter hours, and working conditions. In these areas, police
organizations have acted in the same manner as trade unions or
guilds.

But it is police activism in the area of social policy that has
raised the most serious questions. The famous confrontation
between the police and demonstrators at the 1968 Democratic
National Convention in Chicago was termed "police violence"
by some observers. Other examples of police involvement in
matters of broad social policy are efforts to defeat proposals for
civilian police review boards, lobbying activities to raise
salaries, and attempts to have state legislatures revise criminal
procedures and criminal statutes. Taken together, the combination of the new and the traditional interest-group activities of
police associations has produced a nationwide police militancy
that is unprecedented. "Blue power" is an established political
force in most large and many smaller cities.

Women in the Law Enforcement System

Women are playing an increasingly important part in
the law enforcement system. A study of the records of eighty-six
male and eighty-six female recruits in the Washington, D.C.,
police force carried on over a period of a year indicated that
there was no significant difference in job performance on patrol
duty. Early in 1975, the same police force reported that one of its
policewomen had been killed in the line of duty, apparently the
first instance of this kind in American police history.

Even so, the majority of police departments continue to
assign women to what have traditionally been considered
"women's jobs." Yet the evidence indicates that women can
serve effectively in such positions as patrol, investigation, civil
disturbance control, and traffic control, as well as in technical
services and administration. Indianapolis was the first city in
the United States to assign uniformed policewomen regularly to
patrol cars. Many other cities have followed this lead, and many
more will.

The role of women in policing has been widened not only
by social but also by legal pressures. It is now a violation of
federal law for a police department to discriminate solely on the
basis of sex. It is therefore almost certain that the employment
of women in various elements of the municipal law enforcement
systems will grow dramatically in the coming years.

An armed policewoman and her partner patrol the Times Square area in New York city. (Wide World Photos.)

Some Problems Concerning the Police

Like other municipal agencies, police departments in the 1970s are plagued with problems brought about both by inflation and by the economic recession. But they face two additional problems which do not affect most municipal agencies.

Civilian Review Boards. The principle that acts of an individual police officer should be subject to review by higher authority has long been accepted in the United States. But application of the principle is anything but simple and self-executing. For most police forces, an internal review board has been the device most commonly relied upon to hear citizens' complaints against individual officers. Under this procedure, the board is composed of police officials, that is, higher-ranking colleagues of the officer against whom the complaint has been lodged. The review board and the defendant officer are thus "insiders" while the complainant is an "outsider." The system is open to the obvious criticism that the interests of justice and of police morale may be in conflict—to the possible detriment of the complainant.

In reaction against this internal system, a good deal of public support developed during the 1960s for civilian review boards, that is, those composed of persons not on the police force. Many variations have been suggested, but the basic principle is that the police should be deprived of the authority to review the activities of a member of the force against whom serious complaints have been brought.

Generally, the police have opposed such a system while civil rights attorneys have favored it. In the most famous test of public reaction, the referendum of 8 November 1966 proposing the establishment of a civilian review board in New York city, the concept was rejected by a very large margin. From that time on, interest in civilian review boards has waned.

As an alternative, some civil libertarians have suggested the creation of an ombudsman. Most plans call for the ombudsman to have suggestive rather than mandatory authority, and the plan has certain attractive features if applied to all municipal agencies, not just to the police. Yet the idea has received little support from the general public, which apparently prefers that the role of ombudsman be played by members of the city council, as in the past.

Community Control. A second issue faced by police departments is that of community control over some activities of the police force. The case for some measure of community control rests in part on the assumption that the style of law enforcement varies from community to community, and also on the assumption that the leading ethnic groups of particular communities should be represented proportionately on the local district force. Often, there is also the assumption that the police are an alien force, and that a new force under the control of a locally elected police board should be created.

In rebuttal, the proponents of the centralized police model hold that it is not really feasible to break a city into a large number of local communities, each possessing its own force. The analogy with suburban police forces is, they say, not applicable. If decentralization is the goal, the proponents argue that much of this may be achieved simply by altering the existing model.

Since the 1960s, public attention to the question of community control has apparently waned. Partly this may be a result of new police recruiting policies, which have meant that fairly large numbers of minorities have been added to the police forces and are visible to the residents of the communities. Partly it may also be a result of the realization that the price required to achieve community control of police forces inside a big city may be too high. The net effect could be counterproductive, in that the total effectiveness of the forces in the maintenance of order throughout the entire city might be lessened. Though the debate between those who want to retain a centralized force and those who want some measure of community control continues, it has lost its strident tone of a decade ago.

Items for Discussion

1. Should criminal sentences stress deterrence (keeping others from committing criminal acts), or should their emphasis be on rehabilitation (considering the behavior of the particular defendant)? Depending on your answer, what would you then recommend in terms of prison reform?

2. More so than other elected state-wide officials, attorneys general use their positions as steppingstones to higher office. Through what specific actions can the attorney general use that position to *political* advantage?

3. Discuss a situation in which plea bargaining truly furthers the cause of justice.

4. Should jury selection be revamped in order to place better-educated and better-informed persons on these panels?

5. In order to prevent disturbances such as

the one at the Attica State Prison in New York, what changes should states make in their prison policy?

Chapter Notes

1. "Alabama's State Police Leads in Black Percentage With 4.5%." *New York Times*, 10 Dec. 1974.

2. American Law Institute, *Code of Criminal Procedure* (1930), sec. 18.

3. "195 (Count 'Em) Police Forces." *Philadelphia Inquirer*, 29 Nov. 1974.

14

Education

Key Terms

Collective bargaining: Negotiation between an employer and a union representing the employees.

Decentralization: To move power away from the central government to be exercised by state and local authorities.

De facto segregation: Situation in which there are separate facilities for blacks and whites based on the existence of, e.g., predominantly black or white neighborhoods; in contrast, *de jure segregation* is separation required by law.

Foundation program: The formula which describes how a state will allot money to local school districts.

Guild members: Those who belong to an association for mutual aid and the promotion of common interest; in contrast to *union members* whose organization typically is more formalized and whose main concern is bargaining with management.

Land-grant colleges: Agricultural or mechanical colleges established under provisions of the Morrill Act of 1862; they have broadened their academic interests over the years and include most of the great state universities, such as the University of Minnesota.

The United States Constitution makes no reference to education. Therefore, under the provisions of the Tenth Amendment, providing public education is left primarily to the states. As a result, the states and the localities play the major role in public elementary and secondary education, even though the federal government has become increasingly active in this area.

This education is free, in the sense that it is publicly financed. In addition, the principle of free or heavily subsidized higher education has also been widely accepted. Public education is by far the largest single enterprise engaged in by state and local governments. For the school year which ended in the summer of 1975, a total of $61.1 billion was spent on public elementary and secondary schools. Of this total, local governments contributed 49 percent, state governments 43 percent, and the federal government 8 percent.

As of 1972, the number of pupils enrolled came to 46.1 million. For the same year, enrollment in private elementary and secondary schools totaled 4.7 million. By anyone's standards, public education is big business. It is second only to national defense in terms of public expenditures.

In this chapter, we briefly trace the rise of public education in the United States. Then we deal with some aspects of educational administration, problems related to financing, the principal groups and interests involved in the system, the politicization of education in recent years, and the organization of higher education. We conclude with some recent findings which indicate that public education has probably come to the end of one era and is entering another.

THE RISE OF THE PUBLIC SCHOOL

The history of education in the colonies is intertwined with the preservation of religious orthodoxy. But the interest in education was deeply grounded. In 1642, the General Court of Massachusetts directed parents to see to it that their children received a basic education. In 1647, Massachusetts required each town to establish a school. Other colonies took similar measures, but the religious emphasis varied with the colony. In the southern colonies, for example, the Church of England was considered to be responsible for both secular and religious instruction. School systems were organized along the lines of the existing episcopal structure rather than on civil entities like the county. In contrast, there existed no centralized authority in the congregational church structure of New England. For this reason, the government authorities were expected to operate schools, but to do so in accordance with Puritan orthodoxy.

Even though the principle of state responsibility was recognized in the colonies, the actual practice was to assign control of the schools to local authorities. The result was extreme decentralization, with obvious differences in the educational product available in different localities.

Besides the origin of the educational system in a desire to preserve the faith, there came onto the educational scene a new element after the Revolution. This was the idea that a dominant social class could reinforce its position by resisting public education. Gradually, as we know, the principle of state-supported universal education came to be accepted, but not without a long struggle.

The picture was therefore a mixed one. In the Northwest Ordinance of 1787, Congress provided that throughout the Northwest Territory one-sixteenth of one section of each township be set aside for support of public schools. In other new states, similar federal grants of land were made to support public education. In the North, Massachusetts proclaimed the principle of general tax support for schools in 1789, and Connecticut did so in 1795 by establishing a money fund from proceeds of sales of public lands. In 1812, New York provided state funds to match local money. Yet in the South, until the Civil War, publicly financed education was primarily charity for the poor.

The Growth of State Control

It was not enough to establish the principle of free public education; it was also necessary to create mechanisms for providing it. This proved to be extremely difficult, given the long history of decentralization in school affairs. Public control, as it grew, tended to downplay earlier theological elements in the curriculum and also to come to terms with controversial political and social matters. In short, it was necessary to develop some ground of social consensus if the schools were to play a public rather than a private function.

New York pioneered in this development. In 1784, that state established the Board of Regents of the University of the State of New York. In 1812 New York created the first state superintendent of schools. When it came to setting effective standards of state leadership, the honors go to Horace Mann in Massachusetts and to Henry Barnard in Connecticut. Mann was appointed as the first secretary of the Massachusetts Board of Education in 1837, and Barnard was given a similar assignment in Connecticut in 1839.

As usual, the South had special problems. In the post–Civil War period, it was almost impossible to legislate in order to raise educational quality. In addition to possessing a very weak tradition in the area of public education, the southern states were faced with the problems of poverty and of race. It was not until the end of the nineteenth century that segregation in public education was firmly established, thus ending one of the fears of southern whites, who had tended to equate public education with integration.

Yet in other parts of the county the momentum toward educational inclusiveness was considerable. Compulsory school attendance laws were passed in Massachusetts in 1852, and thirty-two states had similar laws on their books by 1900. There were of course, offshoots, as there always are when new social mechanisms are devised. For example, the public school system was enlarged to include both high schools and universities. During the same era—the post–Civil War period to 1900—the parochial schools underwent a period of spectacular growth, partly in reaction against the alleged "Protestant character" of the public school systems.

A milestone in providing for state control of educational standards was the decision by the University of Michigan to admit to the university all students graduating from public schools accredited by the university. What this meant in practice was that the University of Michigan in effect set standards for teacher training and curriculum that local school authorities had to accept. This practice was widely emulated in other states with distinguished and powerful state universities.

To set standards, the final weapon is money, though its power has been challenged from time to time. In any event, educators desirous of raising educational standards have always considered money to be an important part of their arsenal of educational persuasion. Because of the significance of this question, we shall deal with it separately at a later point in this chapter.

PUBLIC SCHOOL ADMINISTRATION

When it comes to determining which governmental unit shall assume the basic responsibility for the financing and administration of the elementary and secondary schools, each state is master of its own house. In consequence, there is a wide variety among the fifty states. Yet a rather rough typology is useful.[1]

Two states have established a centralized school system in state government and may be classified as employing a state-unit system. They are Delaware and Hawaii. In the remaining forty-eight states, primary responsibility for providing schools is imposed upon local governmental units of various kinds. Fifteen states use the county as the predominant administrative organization, nine use the town or township unit, and twenty-three employ the district system. Clearly, there are overlappings in such a classification system, but it is useful to make these distinctions in order to explain and analyze how the different systems work.

The School District

Under the commonly used district system, responsibility for providing elementary and high school education rests primarily upon school districts. As recently as 1942, the situation was somewhat out of control, for at that time there were more than 100 thousand districts in the United States. Because of deliberate state efforts at consolidation, the number has, happily, decreased. In 1972 the total of such districts had reached only 15,781.

It is the custom for districts to be managed by an elective board, usually of three members. The board has custody of school property, hires teachers, and exercises general administrative control over school affairs. As to finances, the practices vary. In some states, finances are controlled by the district board, and in other states by the district's voters in annual school meetings.

In the past, the leading argument leveled against the school district as an institution was that its smallness and lack of financial resources tended to result in a very limited educational perspective. Because of these charges, most of the states have encouraged districts to consolidate, and have offered the consolidating districts certain incentives in the form of financial inducements.

The duties of the members of the school board vary widely. In the spring of 1975, when they discovered that they were personally liable for any deficit incurred by the local school system, the board in East Haven, Connecticut, voted unanimously to close down the system in order to avoid personal liabilities to the possible extent of $300 thousand. It is to be hoped that this quaint practice of personal liability will be changed so that in the years to come citizens who are not millionaires can serve on the East Haven board.

Towns and Townships

All six New England states use the town as the primary unit for school administration. In New Jersey, Pennsylvania, and Indiana, the township is used for this purpose. The New England town system is built around a central elective body called the school committee. Generally, this body manages the schools within the towns as well as in strictly rural areas. Of course, some of the larger municipalities have their own city boards of education. The point is that a New England town tends to be rather large and often includes both urban and rural areas.

In New Jersey and Pennsylvania, each township is considered a school district, with a board of education responsible for the administration of all schools except those which are separately incorporated for school purposes, such as municipalities. The Indiana plan also uses the township as the basic educational unit. An elective township trustee manages the rural schools located in the township.

Though there are merits both to the district system and to the town or township plan, it should be noted that the latter approach tends to establish a larger attendance area. This should, at least in theory, make possible the operation of larger and better-equipped and better-staffed schools than the district system.

The County

Throughout most of the South, and also in the western states of Nevada, Utah, and New Mexico, the county is the basic unit of school administration. Schools are managed and financed on a county-wide basis. Usually there is a county board of education with a county superintendent of education appointed by and responsible to the board. As the executive officer of the board, the superintendent is charged with the management of the rural schools of the county. In some cases, city schools fall under the jurisdiction of the county board. In other cases, the cities are separate units and have their own school boards and superintendents.

In general, the trend during the last three decades has been in the direction of larger school administrative units. For this reason, the county-unit plan has found increasing favor on the part of professional educators.

The State

As we have observed, only Delaware and Hawaii have centralized the administration and financing of local schools to the point at which they may be considered to have state-unit systems. But one must hasten to add that all fifty states have assumed important functions in the area of education. These may be grouped under four general categories: (1) legislation establishing and regulating a system of public schools, (2) supervision and control of local schools through state administrative agencies, (3) financial support for elementary and secondary schools, and (4) the maintenance of state colleges and universities.

The last two categories will be considered at a later point. Here, some examples will be given of the first two kinds of state activity. It is, of course, the state legislature that enacts the basic laws setting up and maintaining the public school system. Such legislation deals with a wide variety of subjects: how local units shall be organized, what their responsibilities are, how their officers are chosen, and what powers of taxation they have. The legislature may also determine what subjects are to be taught in the schools. The state certifies teachers and determines the length of the school year. School attendance is mandated by compulsory-attendance laws, and age limits are established. Most states have set minimum salary standards for public school teachers.

Each state has one or more boards concerned with supervision and control. In most states there is one agency, commonly termed the state board of education, which exercises some degree of control over elementary and secondary schools. Such a board may be established either by the state constitution or by statute. While practices vary, the most widely used method of choosing board members is appointment by the governor. Each state also has a chief state school officer, usually called superintendent of public instruction or commissioner of education. In about half the states this official is elected by popular vote; in the other half the method employed is appointment by the governor or by the state board of education. In accordance with the continuing belief that state administrative responsibility should ultimately rest on the shoulders of the governor, the trend in recent years has been to favor the appointment route.

Despite their impressive powers, it would be a mistake to picture state boards of education as monolithic agencies possesing dictatorial authority. For the most part, the boards set minimum standards and provide state funds. The boards also share some of the general educational power with other agencies, for example, in the enforcement of antitruancy laws.

MONEY AND SCHOOLS

The basic issue in public schools is money. Of course, there are other issues—an urban-rural split, consolidation, aid to religious schools, and so on. But money provides the leverage for upgrading education, for equalizing educational opportunity, and for recruiting and keeping the most competent teachers and administrators.

There was a time when American schools depended for their support almost entirely upon the proceeds from a local property tax. Taken as a whole, this remains the largest single source of educational funding. But the growth in state aid has been impressive. For example, by 1900 every state provided important aid to local schools. Yet the techniques and programs varied so widely that it was difficult to find out where a school system stood in relation to others, let alone make accurate projections for the future.

The Foundation Program

The credit for bringing some order out of chaos is generally accorded to a small but extremely able group of scholars at Columbia University's Teachers College. Building on the pioneer work of Ellwood Cubberley, *School Funds and Their Appointment* (1905), people such as George Strayer, Robert Haig, and Paul Mort labored for two decades to develop general principles to govern state aid to schools. An important product of their endeavors was the conception of the *foundation program*, which continues to be a leading factor in state aid programs.

Basically, a foundation program is a formula which sets out

the particular pattern of support that a state proposes to give to its schools. Once adopted into law, the foundation formula provides a continuing basis for allocating state money. By setting a minimum total amount and by prescribing the bases for dividing the total among local districts, the formula makes it possible for local districts to engage in some measure of rational planning.[2]

As would be expected, the formulas developed by the different states vary. Yet they all have one thing in common: they all stress equalization. As Strayer and Haig insisted, the equalization principle demands that the state assure a satisfactory minimum program in every district. A local district would be expected to raise as much of its capital and operating expenses as its resources permitted. Conceivably, a wealthy district could finance its whole program. For those districts that were below the minimum in resources, state aid would make up the difference. The overall goal of equalization is to develop a minimum educational program throughout the state.

Advantages of the Foundation Program. There are two general but very substantial advantages in having a foundation formula. First, the business of supplying state aid to local schools is based on a continuing if complex system. The relationship between state and local programs is made concrete. Educational policy, by use of the formula, can be converted into dollar values. It is therefore possible to set a figure of so many dollars per pupil in average daily attendance as the desired minimum and to compare this figure with that in other states. It is possible to estimate and evaluate the revenue requirements needed to meet the figure. In many ways, therefore, the foundation approach clarifies a whole thicket of policy questions.

The second advantage of the foundation idea is that it greatly simplifies state policy making for the public schools. It does so because, once adopted into law, the foundation plan centers discussion on whether to provide more or less state aid. In short, it avoids a new agenda every time educational policy comes up. The plan has also made more manageable the political aspects of state aid. For professional educators, this is obviously a great advantage.

Disadvantages of the Foundation Program. Despite these advantages, the foundation concept did not in fact equalize educational opportunities for children in poor districts. The reason was the continuing reliance upon the local property tax as the main basis for educational revenue. Signs of disenchantment with school financing began to be apparent in the 1960s, during which period the percentage of school bond issues approved by local voters steadily dropped. A study made of the spring 1970 school bond elections by the Investment Bankers Association of America showed that only 32.6 percent of the school bonding proposals, in dollar value, were approved at the polls.

Reform of School Financing

The movement to reform the financing of the schools began in 1971, when the California Supreme Court made the decision that the state's school-funding arrangement was unconstitutional under the state's constitution. In the landmark case of *Serrano v. Priest* (89 Cal. Rptr. 345, 1971), the court held that the level of expenditure for a child's public education must not depend on the wealth of that child's family or community.

Subsequently, at the federal level, the United States Supreme Court was asked whether the equal protection clause of the Fourteenth Amendment made it unconstitutional for a state to rely mostly on local property taxes to finance school districts. In view of the earlier decision by the California court, this was a reasonable question to ask. The United States Supreme Court, in a case coming from San Antonio, rejected the argument that the present and common funding arrangement violates the United States Constitution. The opinion by Justice Powell (in a five-to-four vote) held that Texas's system did not infringe upon a fundamental right either explicitly or implicitly guaranteed by the Constitution. (See *San Antonio Independent School District v. Rodriguez*, 411 U.S. 1, 1973).

Even though, for the time being at least, the federal question has been resolved, the role of the states has not been. On the contrary, by the mid-1970s a growing if uneven drive was under way across the county to find new ways to pay school taxes. Because of the decision in the Texas case, the arena of conflict shifted to state courts—because of the *Serrano* analogy—and to the state legislatures. By the summer of 1975 more than thirty states were testing or studying new ways of financing public schools.

The Financing Problem in New Jersey: A Case Study.

Yet the antagonists are formidable, and prediction is hazardous.

The case of New Jersey is illustrative. On 3 April 1973, the state supreme court declared that the current practice of relying on local property taxes to finance public education was in violation of the state constitution. The highest court thereby upheld unanimously a lower-court decision calling for a new method of financing education. Inevitably, this led to demands for a state income tax, not in effect in New Jersey, or a higher sales tax, or both. In the spring of 1974, Governor Brendan Byrne formally proposed a state income tax, saying that income from it would enable the state to underwrite a substantial share of local school costs and thereby make it possible for localities to reduce their local property taxes at the same time.

The magnitude of the governor's problem may be seen from certain New Jersey educational statistics. As of 1974, Englewood Cliffs had $246,000 in assessed property value for every schoolchild. As a result, with a tax rate of only ninety-nine cents per $100 of property value, the town was able to spend $2,000 per year educating each student. In Camden, New Jersey, there was only $18,000 of property value behind each child. Even with a tax rate of $1.94 and generous amounts of state aid, its schools could spend only $1,000 per pupil.

In New Jersey, the state legislature failed to meet the 31 December 1974 deadline to find a new financial structure for its schools. The legislature adjourned in deadlock, with the governor still pledged to an income tax, and the legislature, the labor unions, and persons generally skeptical of public education remaining in opposition.

Finding the money to raise additional funds for education was only one of New Jersey's problems. The other was to find a formula for distribution. One possible solution was to create a system that would minimize per-pupil grants and rely almost entirely on grants that would equalize the tax-raising power of local districts. On this basis, if at a given mill rate a wealthy district could raise $1,600 but a poorer one only $1,100, the state would subsidize the latter by $500.

The potential impact of such a plan may be seen by looking at Tenafly, New Jersey. With $103,000 in property values behind each student, Tenafly spent in 1974 $2,100 per pupil on the basis of a tax rate of $2.07. Such a level of assets is well above the cut-off point for eligibility for equalization funds. But Tenafly still received the basic state grant of $132 per pupil. With thirty-one hundred students in its schools, this aid amounted to $461,-536—6 percent of the year's budget of $7.5 million.

But if the state legislature had adopted the so-called district power equalizing plan, Tenafly stood to lose this $461,536. As a result, the owner of a $50,000 house would be forced to pay an increased tax bill of $77.50 if the school district were to maintain existing expenditure levels. To this sum would be added the portion that Tenafly residents would pay for the package of new taxes, which in many cases would amount to several hundred dollars per household.[3]

Criticism of the Tax Equalization Idea. The drive toward reforming educational finance through property tax equalization has not gone unchallenged. Minot W. Tripp, Jr., a San Francisco attorney and an authority on tax law, has questioned the entire movement. Instead of such equalization, he has proposed at least a partial substitute for the residential property taxes that are at the heart of the problem. Property taxes paid by the homeowner, he pointed out, have little relationship to the total wealth or income of the community. In fact, he said, most such taxes are considered to be regressive. He favored a program under which industry and the wealthy would bear most of the burden of tax increases, while giving relief to middle- and lower-class homeowners.

Tripp's conclusion is as follows:

> Obviously, any program to provide additional school aid and reduce residential property taxes requires a number of difficult and far-reaching decisions. If we are serious about the need for tax reform in educational finance, however, we would do well to start preparing to make them instead of allowing our eyes to be dazzled with the illusory concept of property tax equalization.[4]

To return to what was asserted at the start of this section, the role of the state is the central question in public education in the last part of this century. And at the heart of that question is money.

GROUPS AND INTERESTS

In addition to the institutions created by law to deal with the educational process, there are scores of groups and interests which play important roles. We have already referred to the special role of the early innovators during the first third of this century. This tradition has been continued in our time, frequently by persons not associated with the educational establishment itself. Such persons as James Conant, Arthur Bestor, and Hyman Rickover have contributed ideas about the teaching of mathematics and of the sciences. Some of their concepts have worked their way into school curricula.

Teachers' Associations

On the other hand, there are formal groups composed of persons who are professionally employed in public education. Of the many associations, the most prominent, historically, has been the National Education Association (NEA). It is the largest of the teachers' organizations, has affiliates in practically every state, and claims a current membership of about 1.1 million of the nation's 2 million public school teachers.

In the past, the state associations have considered themselves a voice for both classroom teachers and school administrators. In some states, the latter group has its own organizations as well. The reasoning was that both teachers and administrators believed they had more in common, especially when confronting the state legislature, than they did as potential opponents. Until the 1960s, the NEA and its state affiliates stressed professionalization with a special commitment toward educating the young. As a result, very little attention was given to seeking teacher welfare legislation to provide such things as fringe benefits, tenure protection, and pensions. The NEA opposed the organization of teachers into what amounted to trade unions and took a very strong position against teachers' strikes.

All of this has now changed. What shook the NEA out of its relative lethargy and brought about a dramatic reversal of its general outlook was the quick victory won by its chief rival in New York city in 1962. For many years labor unions had tried to unionize teachers in New York and other large cities. Generally, their successes were infrequent, and the results were meager. Of the unions, the best known was the American Federation of Teachers (AFT), an affiliate of the AFL-CIO. In New York city the local branch of the AFT is known as the United Federation of Teachers (UFT).

From its inception in 1916 until the early 1960s the AFT, like the NEA, opposed strikes by teachers. But events in 1960–1962 in New York city brought about drastic changes. In that time the UFT held two strikes, won a collective bargaining election, and secured substantial salary increases. As a result of these victories, AFT membership climbed from about 60,000 in 1960 to 112,000 in 1965.

Even so, the AFT represented in 1965 only 6.4 percent of all teachers. But the UFT victory in New York city had an electric effect on teachers throughout the country. Within a few years, the AFT was chosen as collective bargaining agent in Chicago, Detroit, Cleveland, Philadelphia, and Washington, D.C. By 1970, AFT membership had risen to 205,000, and it is reported still to be growing.

The overall effect on the huge NEA of victories in New York city and elsewhere by affiliates of the AFT has been tremendous. The larger organization has changed its attitude toward collective bargaining, which it now favors. The NEA also supports strikes initiated by its affiliates.

How is one to account for the rise of militant unionism in the teaching profession? Experts have come up with no simple, single answer, but they have made various suggestions. One factor has been found to be the percentage of male teachers in a school system. In New York city, for example, the percentage of men nearly doubled between 1924 and 1960, rising from 11 to 20 percent of the total. Another factor may well have been the massive influx of former militant anti–Vietnam War students into the ranks of the teaching profession. For them unionism represented merely another type of social activism. Finally, it has been suggested that the vast increase in the number of teachers during the 1950s may to some extent have resulted from a different class basis for the teachers themselves. In short, more teachers may have been recruited from working-class families, which are traditionally prounion to begin with.

Teacher militancy, whether expressed through the NEA, the AFT, or some other organization, tends to take the teachers from the periphery of political combat and put them in the center of the struggle. An important illustration is supplied by the confrontation of a strong teachers' organization with the or-dinary school board. The odds very often favor the teachers' un-ion in such clashes. This is because they can and do employ ex-pert negotiators to represent them in bargaining sessions. These organizations may be backed by a strong state-wide organization which can command expertise, experience, and research resources totally beyond the capacity of the local board. Furthermore, if a teachers' organization loses out at the local level, it is always in a position to renew the battle at the state level. In short, it is not a very equal contest when a strong teachers' group confronts an isolated board of willing but inexperienced amateurs.

In a way, of course, all of this may be of some long-range value to the local boards. Unionization has at least in some cases revitalized the boards, since collective bargaining involves both parties in the most minute aspects of the school day. Still, as the United Federation of Teachers has repeatedly shown in New York city, a skilled union can successfully compete with a board as powerful and as prestigious as New York's.

Both the NEA and the AFT envision an increasingly active political future. Given the apparent movement toward the convergence of goals of the two leading organizations, an observer would have expected a campaign for merger of the groups. Such a campaign did, in fact, develop during the early 1970s, and negotiations were held by representatives of each group. However, the NEA in March 1974 angrily broke off the merger negotiations, deploring the AFT's "inflexible" insistence on AFL-CIO affiliation. Were the negotiations to succeed, the new national teachers' organization would have a membership of nearly two million, second in size only to the Teamsters.

Besides the question of the merging of the two unions, another issue which commands the increasing attention of education experts is that of state-wide collective bargaining. It is quite possible that this practice may be adopted in some states.

Other Associations and Interests

Though educators try to present a united front before the state legislature, this is often difficult to achieve. As we mentioned, in some states the administrators have merged with the teachers in a single group. But in others—for example, Michigan—the administrators have acted separately. As a result, the teachers' association has made greater demands for teacher welfare.

Whether school boards form a state-wide organization or not depends on the situation in a particular state. When teachers and board members join forces to increase state aid to schools, they are obviously allies. But in some states there is considerable conflict between the two groups, and the end result is a labor-management controversy.

Another very familiar organization relating to schools is the

PTA or its equivalent. On occasion, such groups are given formal representation on state-wide coordinating committees. But their principal role has been to provide lay support for the recommendations made by the professional educators.

In the making of important decisions about public schools, many organizations that are noneducational in nature may be directly concerned. Labor, farm, business, and religious groups are continually involved in the legislative battles, especially when the question is how much money is to be raised for the schools and who is to pay it.

Some issues are felt, at the state level, to be too hot to handle. For example, most blacks and a very large percentage of Roman Catholics live in the big cities. Often the response of the state to special demands by these groups is to grant the city educational system a wide degree of local autonomy. If devisive issues can be localized, the thought is that greater unity may be achieved by educators in their approaches to the state government.

THE POLITICIZATION OF EDUCATION

It is apparent that the old theory that politics and education should be kept as far apart as possible is no longer very tenable, if it ever was. Driven by the necessity to develop additional revenues for school purposes, the educators have more and more frequently entered directly into the political arena. In the process, they have behaved much as do other groups in search of state monies. Where the educators have most nearly mastered the arts of coalition building and of lobbying, they have been the most successful in achieving their monetary objectives.

It is also evident that unionization has further politicized education. This is more apparent at the local than at the state level. Here, again, the path to success involves alliances with other labor unions as well as with the ordinary educational support groups (such as the PTAs). Where there is an active trade union council representing the interests of all or most of the trade unions within a city, support by the council for the demands of the teachers' unions may be the key to satisfactory collective bargaining agreements. Conversely, members of teachers' unions will be expected to reciprocate by backing up the demands of other trade unionists. This issue is not clear-cut, because many members of teachers' unions feel more like guild members than like unionists. But the arena of political negotiation in the largest cities has been tremendously widened by the mere existence of teachers' unions.

A third and final factor in the politicization of education has been the continuing drive for equal educational opportunity regardless of race or income. The general contour of the situation is well known, and there is no need to retrace the familiar terrain here. Instead, our focus will be placed on some developments in the largest cities.

Social Change

The massive post—World War II black and Puerto Rican migration from rural areas to metropolitan centers seriously challenged established educational patterns. So did the concomitant large-scale movement of whites from the cities to the suburbs. Some entire school systems—Washington, D.C. is an example—shifted from a majority of white students to a majority of blacks.

Social change of this magnitude is bound to have repercussions in the worlds of politics and education. Even where the changes in racial composition of school populations have been less dramatic than in Washington, the tendency for population change to affect political action has been marked. In Boston, for example, Louise Day Hicks was able to achieve prominence as a mayoralty candidate by using busing of public school students—which she opposes—as her leading issue.

In the face of serious racial problems, most local school boards are helpless. The Evanston, Illinois, and Berkeley, California, boards were able successfully—through a combination of skill and luck—to meet the issue of de facto segregation. Yet their success has proved to be atypical. The average school board may make a good whipping boy, but it is a very poor instrument of social justice. Meanwhile, in the largest cities the school systems, because of continuing population changes, are becoming increasingly segregated.

School Integration

The politics of school integration has taken some unexpected turns. Much of the controversy surrounds court-ordered busing, as in Boston. In some cities, the percentage of white students in the public schools is so small that integration in any meaningful sense is impossible. With this in mind, some educators and a handful of judges have looked into the question of school integration not on a city-wide but on an area-wide basis. This would entail massive daily transfers of students from residence to school and back. The problem is the old cost-benefit one: would the social gains be worth the costs in money and time?

Atlanta came up with a different idea, which amounted to a trade-off. Engineered in the spring of 1973 by the local NAACP, the city adopted a controversial minimum-desegregation plan. Basically, the scheme called for token busing, with the result that most of Atlanta's twenty-one thousand white students remained in predominantly white schools and most of the city's seventy-five thousand black students remained in predominantly black schools. In return for this minimum of busing, the city promised it would give blacks half the key jobs in the school administration (until then controlled by whites because of relatively higher white registration and voting). The plan received widespread endorsement in the black community, including the support of the Rev. Andrew Young, himself a progressive and a member of the United States House of Representatives.

At the overall state level, the percentages of black students in elementary and secondary schools is shown in Table 14.1.

Decentralization

A final factor in the drive for equal educational opportunity is the movement to decentralize the school systems of the largest cities. This usually takes the form of locally elected school boards, which have some measure of jurisdiction over the elementary and middle schools in a neighborhood. Control over the senior high schools is lodged in the city-wide board of education. The leading model is the system presently in effect in New York city, although other cities have experimented with varying kinds of school decentralization.

In effect, the proponents of decentralization are rejecting the old unitary community ideal. Under this approach, it was believed that a city-wide board would be most effective if it decreed and enforced city-wide educational standards. The basic idea was not only to produce graduates with a certain minimum of skills but also to reinforce a standardized value system regarding the attributes of citizenship.

Table 14.1
Black Elementary and Secondary Pupils by Geographic Area

	Total Pupils	Total Black Pupils	*Percentage of black pupils in schools that were:*						
			Majority White	50-100% Black	80-100% Black	90-100% Black	95-100% Black	99-100% Black	All Black
Continental U.S.									
1970	44,910,403	6,712,789	33.1	66.9	49.4	43.3	38.2	28.0	14.0
1972	44,646,625	6,796,238	36.3	63.7	45.2	39.2	34.8	25.1	11.2
32 Northern and Western States									
1970	30,131,132	3,188,231	27.6	72.4	56.6	49.5	43.1	29.2	11.7
1972	29,916,241	3,250,806	28.3	71.7	55.9	49.0	43.3	29.9	10.9
5 Border States and D.C.									
1970	3,724,867	640,667	28.7	71.3	61.9	58.5	54.7	45.7	24.1
1972	3,742,703	650,828	31.8	68.2	59.8	56.0	53.0	42.8	23.6
11 Southern States									
1970	11,054,403	2,883,891	40.3	59.7	38.6	33.2	29.2	22.7	14.4
1972	10,987,680	2,894,603	46.3	53.7	29.9	24.5	21.1	15.7	8.7

Source: Office for Civil Rights, Department of Health, Education & Welfare.

In 1969, students in New York city's Harlem wait for a resolution to their school's decentralization problems. When parents discovered the school was to remain segregated, a struggle ensued among parents, teachers, and the New York Board of Education. (Wide World Photos.)

In challenging this ideal, the persons in favor of school decentralization argue that the needs of students in different neighborhoods of the city are not necessarily uniform. For example, in some areas, bilingual education may be desirable; in other areas, the main emphasis might be on the mastering of certain trades. In any event, local control would mean that the principal ethnic and racial groups would be dominant on the community school boards. It was argued that such a situation would result in fairer treatment of the needs of the students.

It is not possible to keep decentralization out of politics, as the case of Ocean Hill—Brownsville, a district in New York city, illustrated in 1968. The issues included the United Federation of Teachers against nonunion members, and white teachers against black teachers, and finally required state intervention. Even the Ford Foundation got into the fight.

Though the scene of action has since shifted to other districts, the issue of school decentralization remains highly political and devisive and almost always has ethnic and racial undertones.

HIGHER EDUCATION

All the states maintain various kinds of institutions of higher education, and such public institutions enroll an increasing majority of all students enrolled in higher education. Most readers will be familiar with the patterns in their own states.

Typically, there will be a state university, or a state university system. In the former case, the university may have a very real degree of independence, as with Indiana University. In the latter, real authority may reside in a board with an executive officer. There may be a chancellor to oversee the whole system, or a board of regents.

Every state maintains one or more so-called land-grant colleges. These were institutions entitled to receive federal aid under the Morrill Act of 1862. Originally specializing in agriculture and mechanical arts, the land-grant universities have broadened their curricula and are no longer functionally distinguishable from other state universities. For example, the University of Michigan and Michigan State University, the latter of which is a land-grant university, offer virtually the same subjects and courses.

As everyone knows, higher education is in trouble these days. Part of the difficulty comes from soaring costs of operation. Even low-tuition state universities have found it difficult to persuade the legislatures to make the kinds of increases necessary to balance budgets. Instead, the legislatures have tended to demand increased faculty productivity, something which is hard to define and even harder to control.

In addition, the universities overextended themselves during the boom period of 1950–1965. Not only did they overbuild their faculties, but in many cases they overbuilt their physical facilities. On the other hand, there has been a tremendous growth in the number of community colleges. Sometimes controlled by the state, sometimes by the county, sometimes by a city, these colleges usually provide instruction for a period of two years. Their principal objectives are vocational, although most offer numerous courses in such fields as literature and social science.

Also in a growth phase is adult or continuing education. Most state universities, especially those in metropolitan centers, have expanded their offerings in these areas in the last few years. The return of middle-aged women to the marketplace after the growing up of their children has increased interest in this type of education. For such women, the objective is usually not the accumulation of degrees or accreditation of some kind in a credential-oriented society. Rather it is the opportunity to bring one's skills up to date or to develop new ones. The current enrollment of students by level of institution and the projected figures until 1983 are shown in Figure 14.1.

The politics of higher education has little relationship to elementary and secondary schools.[5] The financing is different, the governing bodies are different, and the relationship to the state is different.

But in at least one respect, unionization, higher education and education at the elementary and secondary levels may be coming together. For example, many states now permit instructors in their publicly supported colleges and universities the right to organize into unions and to engage in collective bargaining. Where this has happened, the relationships inside the institution have tended to change. Under the nonunion arrangement, bargaining on salary questions, for example, was between individual instructors and the administration, or between departments and the administration. Under a union arrangement, the union bargaining committee negotiates with the top financial authorities of the institution and a settlement is reached

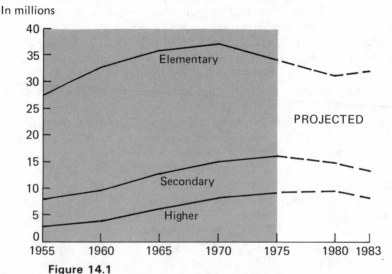

Figure 14.1
School enrollment in the United States, 1955—1983.
Source: National Center for Education Statistics.

which constitutes a formal and binding contract for the life of the agreement. Obviously, this very formal way of setting sala ries differs considerably from the individualistic and relatively informal approach which formerly prevailed.

Faculty unionization raises further and difficult questions. For example, should the contract deal in any respect with the governance of a university? Should "academic freedom" be defined in the contract? Under what conditions should outside arbitration be sought, for instance, when a department wishes to grant tenure and the administration opposes the move? These and other questions remain to be resolved in a systematic fashion.

TRENDS

"Nineteen seventy-four was the year that American education began seriously coming to terms with no-growth."[6] So begins a perceptive analysis by Edward B. Fiske, the chief expert on education of the New York Times.

The shift from growth to nongrowth involved, he said, the convergence of at least four separate factors:

1. *Economics*. Education is a $108 billion-a-year industry in this country. Like all other industries, it has been hard hit by rising costs, the falling stock market, and the energy crisis. By its nature education is poorly equipped to deal with such problems. It is difficult if not impossible to raise teacher productivity, even though 85 percent of the budget goes for personnel.

2. *Enrollment*. The number of elementary school pupils has been falling since 1970. Empty classrooms and even surplus schools have become commonplace. Secondary school population has peaked. College enrollment may suffer an absolute decline in the 1980s.

3. *New attitudes*. Most institutions in the country are going through a period of enjoying less public confidence, and schools are no exception. The employment situation has discouraged high school graduates from going to college.

4. *Psychology*. These external forces have coincided with changing attitudes among educators and the public at large toward the learning process. The experts are in disagreement as to how to deal with the situation, although they all agree that hard choices will have to be made.

Fiske and other commentators on education are quite certain that Americans will continue to support education. The problems are at what level and in what directions. And, it should be added, education does not operate in a social vacuum. Those decisions which are made, deliberately or by default, will take place within the larger spheres of politics and economics in the national community.

Items for Discussion

1. Do states have any responsibility for preserving private, church-related colleges located within their jurisdiction? Should new ways be sought to channel state funds to parochial elementary and secondary schools?

2. In spite of the recent Supreme Court decision, should states move voluntarily to provide equal financial aid based solely on the number of students enrolled to each school district in the state?

3. From the standpoint of quality education, compare the public and private colleges in your state. Also compare the quality of the major state universities in your state with other major state universities around the country.

4. Should public school teachers resort to strikes when their negotiations with school boards fail? Should state law protect them when such action is taken?

5. Relative to busing, what actions would you recommend be taken in the major metropolitan areas throughout the country?

Chapter Notes

1. This typology is taken from Clyde F. Snider, *American State and Local Government*, 2nd ed. (New York: Appleton-Century-Crofts, 1965), pp. 544–545.

2. See Robert H. Salisbury, "State Politics and Education," in Herbert Jacob and Kenneth N. Vines (eds.), *Politics in the American States,* 2nd ed. (Boston: Little, Brown, 1971), pp. 388–432.

3. From Edward B. Fiske, "N.J.'s Need Is a New Math to Pay For Schools." *New York Times,* 22 Dec. 1974.

4. Minot W. Tripp, Jr., "Reforming Educational Finance: Property Tax Equalization Is Not the Answer." *National Civic Review,* Vol. 64, No. 3 (March 1975), pp. 123–127, citation at p. 127.

5. The relationship between a state's political system and its institutions of higher learning is discussed in detail by Samuel K. Gove, Carol E. Floyd, Carroll R. McKibbin, Allan Rosenbaum, and Joseph B. Tucker in "A Special Symposium: Higher Education and the Statehouse." *AAUP Bulletin,* Vol. 59, No. 3 (Sept. 1973), pp. 286–323. The states studied are Illinois, Nebraska, Wisconsin, and Ohio.

6. Edward B. Fiske, "Education Feeling No-Growth Pains," in the *New York Times's* "Annual Education Section," 15 Jan. 1975.

15

Transportation

Key Terms

Ad valorem levy: A tax levied in proportion to the value of the property in question; in contrast to a fixed-rate levy.

Bond: A certificate of indebtedness given by a borrower to a lender; constitutes a written obligation for the borrower to repay the debt plus interest. Often issued by municipal governments to pay for needs that cannot be financed from current revenues.

Federal Highway Act of 1944: Provided funds for secondary, rural roads and also authorized the national system of interstate highways.

Modal split: State departments of transportation organized by modes of travel—air, water, highways.

No-fault insurance: Insurance system that does away with placing blame in automobile accidents and allows the victim to recover damages from his or her own insurance company.

Primary highway system: Major highways for which the state has been responsible; *secondary* systems have been financed by counties and municipalities.

Public highway policy has developed into a tripartite effort in which federal, state, and local governments all play major roles. At the beginning of the present century, most expenditures for roads were made by local governments.

But the introduction of the Model T Ford in 1908 changed both the American way of living and the methods for financing roads. Today the automotive and trucking industry ranks as the largest in the United States. Indeed, the economic health of the country, when judged in terms of conventional economic wisdom, is based on the economic conditions which prevail in Detroit. One out of every five or six Americans is said to be dependent economically on the automotive industry. When that industry is in trouble—as it has been during the 1970s—the whole country feels the effects.

In addition to creating jobs, highways, and suburbs, the automobile has had numerous sociological consequences. Because freeways have reduced travel time, they have contributed to the stagnation of small towns by making it easier to shop in giant shopping centers located in the countryside far from Main Street. They have also, usually adversely, affected the rural areas of the country.

Next to education and sometimes public welfare, highway expenditures have become the second or third most costly function of state and local governments. For example, in 1970 these governments spent $40.1 billion on education, $12.5 billion on highways, and $11.2 billion on public welfare. In 1972, the figures were $38.9 billion for education, $11.4 billion for highways, and $12.6 billion for welfare. Since 1960, the trend has been for expenditures for education to remain relatively stable, while expenditures for highways have dropped and expenses for public welfare have risen substantially.

Outside the cities, very few hard-surfaced roads existed in the country at the start of the century. But the automobile—and its allied interests—forced the states into the building of highways on a massive scale. Only the railroads have been in substantial opposition to this movement, and they have lost. Every state was forced to establish a state highway department charged with the responsibility of constructing highways in rural areas. In the process, the states tried to distinguish between a "primary" state highway system, for which they were responsible, and a "secondary" system, financed by counties and municipalities. Though logical, this plan ran into trouble as communities tried to shift the tax burden from themselves to the states by having the states classify more roads as part of the "primary" system. In all of this development, there was a strong rural bias, the remains of which are still visible today. The proportion of road mileage classified as part of the state highway system has steadily increased.

FEDERAL HIGHWAY POLICY

The federal government first provided regular funds for highway construction under the Federal Aid Road Act of 1916. This was done through its Bureau of Public Roads, which began to exercise considerable influence over state highway policy. To receive federal monies, a plan proposed by a state highway department required approval of the bureau. In 1921, federal assistance was restricted to a connected system of principal state highways called the "federal aid primary system." In addition to prescribing uniform standards, the federal authorities established the now familiar system of numbering roads—e.g., "U.S. 202." The idea was to limit federal aid to a maximum of 7 percent of the total mileage of each state and to connect the principal cities of the state. The states were required to match federal grants on a dollar-for-dollar basis, and the formula for receiving aid was clearly rural in emphasis.

Another milestone statute was the Federal Highway Act of 1944. It continued to provide aid to the primary highway system, but it also extended the program in two important ways. Firstly, it designated a federal aid secondary system of farm-to-market roads. Secondly, it provided for urban extensions of primary roads. Called "ABC funds," federal funds for primary and secondary and urban extension roads are determined by three separate formulas. Yet all take into account area, population, postal routes, and mileage. The federal ABC funds are given to the states on a matched, dollar-for-dollar basis.

Under the impetus of improving national defense, the Federal Highway Act of 1944 also authorized the national system of interstate highways. This has since become the most important feature of federal highway policy. Before 1956, only token sums were appropriated by Congress for the interstate system. But under the aegis of the Eisenhower Administration, the Federal Highway Act of 1956 authorized mammoth sums for the system. Congress provided for completion of the system by 1972—the target was not met—and, more importantly, Congress changed the matching basis to 90 percent federal and 10 percent state.

Given this irresistible inducement, the states responded promptly. The goal of the act was to establish forty-one thousand miles of highway, intended to connect principal metropolitan areas and industrial centers. This represented a shift in congressional interest from rural to urban needs. Though the completed interstate system will constitute less than 2 percent of total highway surface in the country, it is expected to carry more than 20 percent of all highway traffic.

The administration of the act is interesting. The Bureau of Public Roads was given strong supervisory powers, but administration and execution were left to state highway departments. In short, federal funds are paid to the states, not to the individual contractors. How are such huge funds handled? The answer is that the Federal Highway Trust Fund of the Bureau of Public Roads has been assigned the responsibility for the orderly scheduling of federal aid and the handling of reimbursement requests for the states. In an effort to create some measure of landscape beautification, the 1956 act also agreed to reduce by 0.5 percent the state's share of the cost of interstate highways if a state prohibited advertising on such highways. Despite this bribe, most states have given in to the billboard lobby, ignored the garden clubs, and refused the federal subsidy to limit billboards.

The results, directly and indirectly, of the federal interstate highway system have been impressive. In general, federal funds for highway construction now account for about a third of all state highway revenues. In addition, until the Nixon-Ford recession which began in 1973, the automobile and related industries flourished. For example, automobile registration climbed from 74 million in 1960 to 119 million in 1972. Passenger car factory sales jumped from 6.7 million domestically produced cars and 0.4 million foreign cars to 8.8 million and 2.5 million, respectively, in 1972.

Figure 15.1 shows how the national system of interstate and defense highways will appear when completed.

STATE HIGHWAY ADMINISTRATION

Responsibility

Although the famous Cumberland Road, or National Pike, was built by the national government during the first half of the nineteenth century, and though Congress appropriated funds for the Alaskan section of the Pan-American Highway, the construction and maintenance of highways in this country remains primarily a responsibility of the states and their local governments. How is this responsibility carried out?

— **OPEN TO TRAFFIC:** Completed to full or
acceptable standards, or improved to standards
adequate for present traffic
····· **MAJOR TOLL ROADS:** Incorporated in the Interstate System
═══ **UNDER CONSTRUCTION**
– – **ENGINEERING AND RIGHT-OF-WAY IN PROGRESS**
····· **PRELIMINARY STATUS OR NOT YET IN PROGRESS**

Under Construction 3,776 Miles
Engineering and Right-of-Way in Progress 3,778 Miles
Preliminary Status or Not Yet in Progress 1,424 Miles

Figure 15.1
National system of interstate and defense highways as of 30
June 1972.
Source: U.S. Department of Transportation, Federal Highway Administration.

Open to Traffic 33,522 Miles

Even though legal responsibility varies from state to state, some general observations may be offered. The providing for city streets is a municipal function, except in those cases in which a particular street may also constitute a segment of a state or county system. In some cases, the states assume all responsibility for rural highways. More commonly, however, there is a division of responsibility, which will include the state and county and often the township.

For tax purposes, as well as for more philosophical reasons, the trend in recent years has been to shift the responsibility for providing rural highways from smaller to larger governmental units. This shift has also been abetted by technological considerations, for example, the regulation of weights on trucks, and the enforcement of the highway codes.

Organization

As we have seen, every state has a highway department. This has come about not only by the increased recognition of the importance of the highway function, but also because of federal funding requirements. In some states, this department is headed by a commissioner; in others, by a multimembered commission. Normally, the principal highway officers are appointed by the governor, though it is not uncommon for them to be elected.

The chief functions of such bodies are as follows: selection of roads for inclusion in the state highway system; distribution of funds to local governments; supervision of and cooperation with local units in highway matters; dissemination of highway information to the public; collection of motor-vehicle license fees; and policing of the highways.[1]

Who has control of country roads varies from state to state. In some states, such roads come under direct control of the county governing board; in others, there is a county highway commissioner or superintendent. This official may be appointed or elected, depending on state law.

In a township, the principal road officer is usually a highway commissioner or supervisor, elected or appointed, as the case may be. The duties of this official are to improve and maintain all local roads which do not fall under the jurisdiction of some other authority.

In the cities, the city streets are built and maintained by a municipal street department, engineering department, or department of public works. In cities with the mayor-council plan, the head of this department is normally designated by the mayor, or by the mayor's managing director. Sometimes, the official may be elected, though this is a practice that has little to commend it.

STATE HIGHWAY FINANCE

State and local highway revenues come from five principal sources. These are (1) toll roads, (2) property taxes, (3) special assessments, (4) user taxes, and (5) federal aid.

Toll Roads

During the early years of the nineteenth century, many of the intercity roads were toll roads. Some were operated by the states, but most were managed by private companies. By 1850, most of such roads had run into insurmountable financial problems, and their control was taken over by the states with maintenance assigned to local governments.

Interestingly, the principle of toll roads was revived a hundred years later. Since current taxes proved inadequate to provide the expanding highway network required by the millions of new cars and trucks, some states reverted to the earlier toll principle of highway financing. In 1940 the pioneer project—the famous Pennsylvania Turnpike—was opened between Pittsburgh and Harrisburg. Subsequently, it was extended from Pittsburgh to the Ohio border, and from Harrisburg to the Delaware River. Other states, including New Jersey, New York, and Ohio, shortly followed suit.

In most cases, the revenues derived from toll payments have proved sufficient to meet the costs of the bonds which were floated to finance the highways. At one time, it was believed that the expanding interstate highway system, which is free, would put the toll roads out of commission. But the Pennsylvania and New Jersey turnpikes continue to be profitable enterprises and there is no indication that the states in question intend to get out of the toll highway business. Even if motorists may on occasion vent their frustration about the system, there is not much they can do to change it. Meanwhile, turnpike commissioners and bond holders are happy with the present arrangement.

Property Taxes

A property tax is defined as an ad valorem levy at a uniform rate on all taxable property, although the recent trend has been to classify property and tax each classification at a different but uniform rate. At one time the leading source of highway revenue, this method has lost ground to user levies as the primary way of raising funds. In some states, the method is still important in obtaining monies for local highway expenses.

Special Assessments

The special assessment plan rests on the theory that a property owner receives a special benefit from a new highway abutting or in proximity to his or her property. Therefore, a special charge is made against the property. Though it could also be argued the other way, that is, that a highway pollutes the air and destroys the peace and quiet of the property owner, the plan is still widely used inside municipalities. Special assessments of this type continue to be widely used in financing the construction of city streets. They have become uncommon in the financing of rural roads.

User Taxes

In recent decades, there has been a continuous shifting to those who use the highways of the costs of road construction and maintenance through the imposition of different kinds of user taxes. The most obvious of these taxes are those on motor fuel and motor-vehicle license taxes. All states now have a tax on the sale of gasoline, and most states distribute a substantial portion of the funds so collected to local governments. It is estimated that about half of all state and local highway revenue is now derived from the various user taxes. It is common practice for a state legislature to provide that the revenues raised from these taxes may be used only for highway purposes. Under the 1956 Federal Aid Highway Act, it was provided that the Federal Highway Trust would be the recipient of the lion's share of the federal gallonage tax on gasoline. From this fund, which is prospering, are made all federal-aid highway payments, including those for the interstate system. From this it is apparent that a large proportion of highway costs is borne by motorists and truckers through user taxes.

Federal Aid

We have already noted the increasing importance of federal aid in the construction and maintenance of the nation's highway system. In addition to the comments previously made, it should be noted that there are further costs which are passed on by the federal government to the motorist, for example, when the Environmental Protection Agency in effect increases the cost of automobiles by demanding new and more expensive antipollution devices on new vehicles.

Highway Bonds

No matter from what source state and local highway funds are ultimately derived, the common practice when heavy monetary outlays are needed is to borrow money through the issuance of bonds. For this reason, highway indebtedness accounts for a very large share of all state and local indebtedness. For 1974, it is estimated that the total debt outstanding amounted to $24.415 billion. Of this total, the states accounted for $18.279 billion; county and rural units for $1.828 billion; and municipalities for $4.308 billion. To put the matter differently, about two-thirds of the indebtedness is secured by limited-obligation bonds, and only one-third by the general taxing power of the state.

RECENT DEVELOPMENTS IN TRANSPORTATION

State Departments of Transportation

In the mid-1970s, many of the states turned their attention to the development of state departments of transportation. Part of an overall effort to modernize state government, "the reorganization is a response to the challenge to traditional institutions of decision-making brought about by urbanization, reapportionment, and environmental concerns."[2] The key element in the movement has been the formation of a single executive agency directly responsible to the governor.

State departments of transportation have been created to serve a variety of related functions. These include the creation of a unified state policy for transportation, promotion of public transit, enhancing the effectiveness of state work with local governments, facilitation of communication and cooperation with the United States Department of Transportation, providing a stronger state viewpoint in regional and interstate transportation matters, coordination of transportation planning with other planning, making government agencies more responsible to local control, improvement in communication between the state government and its various constituencies, and improvement of efficiency and promotion of economy in government.[3]

As of 1974, twenty-five states had established or were in the process of establishing departments of transportation. The organization of the various departments varies considerably. For example, California and Maryland have organized along the "modal split." This means that their departments are organized by transportation modes: a division of highways, a division of public transit, a division of aviation, and so on. Other states, such as New York and New Jersey, have favored a functional organization in approaching their transportation problems.

National Transportation Report

In an effort to bring about comprehensiveness in dealing with transportation questions, the United States Department of Transportation prepared in 1972 a National Transportation Report. The report, prepared with the cooperation of the states, contains the first all-inclusive tabulation of transportation needs ever made. It includes highway, rail, air, and mass transit.

As a result of this and other efforts, the states have by and large come to consider the various types of transportation to be interrelated. The objective is a well-balanced program, in contrast to the former practice whereby each type of transportation was dealt with as a separate problem.

The 1972 report also points out, if any emphasis is necessary, that the highway system has been and will continue to be the backbone of the nation's transportation system. Highway transportation dominates the country's transportation by all modes in a ratio of about 10:1. Some 93 percent of all person-miles of travel by all modes is performed by highway vehicles, both automobile and buses. Within the urban area, the ratio is even higher: 98 percent (94 percent by car and 4 percent by bus). Even in those large cities where rail and bus mass transit are available, the person-miles traveled by both of these methods amounts to only 5 percent of the daily travel. Within urban areas, the dependence on a street and highway network for freight and service vehicle movements approaches 100 percent.

No-Fault Insurance

An idea whose time has apparently come is no-fault insurance. Here, the basic idea is to provide benefits to victims of auto accidents without regard to who caused the accident; that is, there is "no fault." Congressional interest in mandatory state no-fault insurance has spurred the states into enacting their own no-fault insurance plans. This insurance system does away with establishing blame except in cases involving serious injury or death. It also allows an accident victim to recover damage from his or her own insurance company without the need to institute legal action. Popular with insurance companies, the plan has, understandably, been opposed by many lawyers whose incomes are largely derived from actions involving automobile accident claims.

Though Congress has been reluctant to pass a nation-wide no-fault system, nineteen states and Puerto Rico had set up their own systems by the end of 1974. The first state-type no-fault insurance program was approved by the Puerto Rico legislature in 1968. It is said to be very successful. Under the Puerto Rico plan, some ninety cents in benefits are returned for every dollar of premium collected. In comparison, the ordinary liability-based insurance system is estimated to return fifty cents in benefits for every dollar of premiums.

In 1970, Massachusetts became the first state to adopt a genuine no-fault system, that is, one which limits tort liability for pain and suffering cases. Again, in 1972, Massachusetts led the way when it abolished tort liability for property damages. The Massachusetts law provides no-fault benefits up to $2,000 for medical expenses, wage-loss coverage, and substitute services.

To date, *all* states have considered no-fault and other reforms of the motor vehicle insurance system. But, since restriction of tort lawsuits is a key element in the system of compensating motor vehicle accident victims on a no-fault basis, only ten states, as of the end of 1974, could be said to have genuine no-fault laws. These states are Massachusetts, New Jersey, Connecticut, Michigan, New York, Kansas, Utah, Nevada, Colorado, and Hawaii. Despite resistance from some elements of the legal fraternity, there is no question at all that the system will spread to include other states. In any prolonged battle between lawyers on the one hand and motorists and insurance companies on the other, the latter coalition is bound to win in the long run. It is merely a question of time—somewhat complicated by the fact that a very large percentage of legislators are themselves lawyers.

Urban Mass Transit

Railroad buffs will find the figures discouraging, but the fact is that during the last twenty-five years the number of persons carried by public transit has declined from 23 billion passengers annually to 6.8 billion. In short, the public clearly prefers the automobile, at the expense of buses, subways, surface rail, and trolleys.

Even so, state legislators do read the newspapers, are aware of actual and potential Arab oil boycotts, realize that the price of operating cars is going up daily, and have begun to consider problems of urban mass transit. For most states, improved mass transit means more buses, using exclusive bus lanes and enjoying other preferential facilities designed to move large numbers of people quickly and comfortably. At the end of 1974, rail rapid transit systems were in operation or under construction or being planned in fifteen American cities. But this is a mere handful. In addition, in many communities, large as well as small, there is simply no public transportation at all.

It is obviously vital, if public transportation is to be improved, that the states give the question a very high priority. Since farebox revenue is unable to support mass transit (the subway systems of New York and Philadelphia are prime examples), public subsidies are clearly necessary. It is possible that the federal government and the states will have to assume total responsibility for capital expenditures. For instance, the Maryland Department of Transportation has the sole responsibility for providing public transport—rail and bus—in the Baltimore metropolitan area, and is also contributing most of the local share for the Washington Metro Rapid Rail project.

To finance public transit the states resort to a bewildering variety of devices. Massachusetts relies on a cigarette tax; New Orleans has upped its gas and electric rates; Colorado employs a half-penny tax; Toledo, Ohio, uses a special property tax; Baton Rouge, Louisiana, depends on parking meter revenues; and Portland, Oregon, raises its subsidy through a payroll tax. There are other methods used, but this listing gives some idea of the ingenuity employed to subsidize public transit. The lesson, of course, is that urban transportation is so complex that the

Cars for the new BART (Bay Area Rapid Transit) system overlook San Francisco freeways. (Photo courtesy Bay Area Rapid Transit District.)

states must act. Otherwise, the situation would become hopeless, both in a financial and in a coordinating sense.

The Federal Aid Highway Act of 1973 authorized for the first time the use of the Highway Trust Fund for public transportation. For the urban system, the act authorized $780 million of the Highway Trust Fund for fiscal 1974 and $800 million each for the fiscal years 1975 and 1976. Under the law, these urban projects were to be selected by appropriate local officials with the concurrence of state officials.

Beginning in the fiscal year 1975, urban areas were permitted the option of using up to a total of $200 million of their allocations for the purchase of buses. Beginning with the fiscal year 1976, they could use all or any part of the allocations for buses, rail transit systems, or highways. However, federal funds could not be used for operating subsidies.

It is still too early to write a definitive scorecard, but the results of the act to the middle of 1975 were unimpressive. As of March 1975, only $34.6 million had been awarded out of the hitherto sacrosanct $2.4 billion Highway Trust Fund. Furthermore, only two cities had actually received funds: New York and East St. Louis, Illinois.[4] Only a handful of other communities had even applied for money. In one of the great understatements of the decade, Frank C. Herringer, the urban mass transit administrator, declared: "I would have to say the results have been disappointing to say the least."

How did the two successful cities use their funds? New York city was awarded $33.017 million for the purchase of 398 new buses, and East St. Louis was awarded $1.597 million toward the purchase of 40 buses.

As is customary in such situations, a survey was launched in order to affix the blame for the obvious failure of the program. In this case, the sponsor of the survey was the *New York Times*. Two principal explanations were provided. Firstly, it was found that transportation officials in many states were heavily biased in favor of building roads, not in favor of encouraging public transportation. Secondly, it was found that the matching formula—cities and towns had to underwrite 30 percent of the costs in order to qualify for the 70 percent federal matching grant—discouraged many cities from applying. One possible solution was to decrease the percentage of the local contribution.[5]

State Aviation Programs

For those who believe that state governments should increase their authority and the authority of the national government should lessen, it is axiomatic that the state should play a great role in the development of the nation's air transportation system. But how and where this is to be done remain complicated questions.

It is easy to make a case, for example, that the state of Texas should be very active in the regulation not only of airport facilities but also of intrastate airlines. But it would be ridiculous to advance the same argument as applied to Delaware or to Rhode Island.

Nonetheless, despite these and other difficulties, the Department of Transportation, under the philosophy of President Nixon's "New Federalism," made a number of serious efforts to improve federal-state cooperation in the area of aviation. There were proposals, for example, that a number of FAA functions be transferred to state aviation agencies. In addition, the National Association of State Aviation Officials (NASAO) has concerned itself with such problems as airport inspection and the certification of pilots.

In spite of such efforts, it seems clear that most citizens look to federal agencies for the regulation of the aviation industry. One indication of this comes from the area of airport development. During fiscal year 1972, $215 million in state funds was made available for airport development. Of that amount, however, only $116.2 million was actually spent. This reflects the fact that many communities, even if desirous of new or improved airport facilities, simply were unable to raise the matching funds required by the states. In addition to airport development, the states spend funds for navigation aids and for regulation, safety, and education. In fiscal year 1972 these items came to a total of about $3.956 million which, by American statdards, is not a great deal of money.

TRANSPORTATION PROBLEMS IN LARGE URBAN AREAS

How are political decisions made with respect to the transportation problems of large urban areas? This important question was asked by Frank C. Colcord, Jr., in a significant study released in 1967.[6] The study remains the best of its type, has been widely reprinted, and relevant parts of it are summarized in the following paragraphs.

After reviewing some of the history of the development of transportation policy, Colcord notes that urban transportation has become a matter of *public* policy in all large urban areas and may be regarded because of its nature as a case of *metropolitan* decision making. Though other metropolitan problems are also complicated, urban transportation represents an extreme situation because of the many political actors involved and because no one government has the sole responsibility for dealing with the problem.

According to Colcord, urban transportation problems can be divided into several subcategories, all of which must be explored to comprehend the totality. The listing is formidable, and includes decisions relating to (1) the structure of government for transportation, (2) transportation planning, and (3) the financing, construction, and operation of facilities. In all these considerations, decisions must be made as to whether the approach will be comprehensive or piecemeal. Other decisions related to transportation include those concerning the general structure of metropolitan government, metropolitan land-use planning, home rule and the relationship between local and state governments, and financing and taxes.

Colcord then defines the principal actors in the complex process of setting transportation policy. He considers them to be as follows: (1) the general policy makers (for instance, governors and mayors); (2) public officials directly or indirectly concerned with transportation policy (e.g., city, county, and state public works directors, planning heads, police chiefs, state motor vehicle and traffic safety directors, urban renewal officials, traffic management and transit chiefs); and (3) private organizations and individuals actively interested in transportation policy. This category would include newspapers, chambers of commerce, labor unions, downtown business groups, transit companies, automobile clubs, contractors, truckers, and, in recent years, certain civil rights groups. It is apparent that one could extend the list of private actors almost indefinitely.

As the locale of his study, Colcord chose the cities of Baltimore and Seattle. The basic research method was to conduct open-ended interviews with the significant "political actors," as defined above. The interviews were augmented by additional interviews with journalists and academicians, as well as by an intensive review of newspaper clippings and published documents.

It does not serve our purposes to review in any detail the specific findings which emerged from the studies of the two cities. As expected, they differed in substantial ways, but they also showed similarities in others. In any case, the specific decisions are now only of historical interest. What is important is to record Colcord's general findings regarding the politics of transportation.

"First," he noted, "federal policy has clearly been a major influence."[7] To put the matter differently, the cast of characters has changed radically since the early 1950s. In this change of cast, the increased prominence of the federal role has been marked.

"Secondly, the local stimulus for a rethinking of existing policy and for innovate action in the field of transportation has come almost entirely from central city actors."[8] This was not the case prior to the mid-1950s.

"Third, it seems clear from our own study of these two areas that the creation of new metropolitan institutions has resulted in new allies for the central city proponents of 'balanced transportation.' "[9] In other words, it is now held to be axiomatic that transportation planning ought to be comprehensive and should serve general land-use objectives.

"Fourth, there is considerable evidence in these two states that the governor's office is becoming a more important source of initiative for innovations in transportation planning and programming."[10] As we have noted, since the appearance of Colcord's article, numerous states have established departments of transportation responsible to the governor. What Colcord saw as a trend has become an actual development in many states.

In the most general terms, what does this add up to? According to Colcord, the appearance of new actors on the scene, both public and private, essentially has created an entirely new bargaining system. The basic concepts of metropolitan planning have generally been accepted in theory by all the actors, even if some of them oppose it in practice.

Though his principal emphasis is on transportation at the state level, another expert finds himself substantially in agreement with Colcord when the subject is metropolitan transportation. Summarizing his findings in a 1971 study, Robert S. Friedman remarked: "There is . . . little evidence of a relation between the wealth or industrialization level of states and their emphasis on highway expenditure. There is, however, a significant relation between highway expenditure and metropolitanism in which the states with the highest proportion of their population living in standard metropolitan statistical areas devote the smallest proportion of state and local expenditure to highways."[11] Presumably, this condition reflects not so much hostility against highway programs as such but preference for spending available public funds for the positive support of schools, hospitals, welfare programs, or public housing.

No one is prescient enough to foretell specific developments in transportation policy during the next decade or two. But it is evident to everyone that the role of governments at all levels will remain crucial in the decision-making process. Governments, in brief, will become even more important actors than they are at present.

Items for Discussion

1. Explain how the interstate highway system has been detrimental to the interests of many central cities.

2. Should states divert revenue from gasoline taxes to help subsidize mass transit systems in a few major cities?

3. How can individuals best be encouraged to use public transportation rather than traveling to work separately in automobiles?

4. Other than being harmful to the economic interest of lawyers, can an effective case, from the standpoint of the individual car owner, be made against no-fault insurance?

5. Is there any action which individual states can take to improve significantly railroad transportation?

Chapter Notes

1. See Clyde F. Snider, *American State and Local Government* (New York: Appleton-Century-Crofts, 1965), p. 566.

2. Charles G. Whitmire, "Transportation," in *The Book of the States, 1974–1975* (Lexington, Ky.: The Council of State Governments, 1974), pp. 350–355, citation at p. 350.

3. *Ibid.*, p. 350.

4. Ralph Blumenthal, "Mass Transit Use of Road Fund Lags." *New York Times*, 21 April 1975.

5. "Cities Ignore Transit Funds." Week in Review, *New York Times*, 27 April 1975.

6. Frank C. Colcord, Jr., "Decision-Making and Transportation Policy: A Comparative Analysis." *The Southwestern Social Science Quarterly*, Vol. 48 (Dec. 1967), reprinted in Thomas R. Dye and Brett W. Hawkins (eds.), *Politics in the Metropolis* (Englewood Cliffs, N.J.: Prentice-Hall, 1971), pp. 205–222.

7. Colcord, in Dye and Hawkins, *op. cit.*, p. 216.

8. *Ibid.*, p. 217.

9. *Ibid.*, p. 219.

10. *Ibid.*, p. 220.

11. Robert S. Friedman, "State Politics and Highways," in Herbert Jacob and Kenneth N. Vines (eds.), *Politics in the American States*, 2nd ed. (Boston: Little, Brown, 1971), pp. 477–519, quotation at p. 518.

16

Welfare, Health, and Housing

Key Terms

Almshouse: Historically, a home for those poor persons unable to work.

Categorical assistance programs: Grants for special welfare programs such as aid for the blind or disabled; contrasted with *general* assistance programs for those not qualifying for special programs.

Eminent domain: Power of all governments to take over private property provided it is for a public purpose and adequate compensation is paid.

Gross national product: The total value of all goods and services produced in a year.

Medicare: Health insurance for individuals sixty-five years and older; *plan A* provides for hospital care and *plan B* provides for physicians' services; *Medicaid* is health insurance for the poor of all ages funded under a cooperative state-federal program.

Poor Relief Act of 1601: Act by which, for the first time, government (in England) became responsible for the care of the poor.

Rent subsidy: Government payment of a proportion of rent for individuals who qualify under an income guideline.

Social Security Act of 1935: The basic social welfare legislation in the United States; includes social insurance, public assistance, child-health care, and welfare services.

Urban homesteading: Plan to give abandoned, inner-city homes free to those willing to restore them to good condition.

Three of the most important state and local functions are welfare, health, and housing. In each case, there has been a growing federal involvement, with the result that each function is a mosaic of intergovernmental relations. Yet the functions and their histories are sufficiently different to warrant separate, if relatively brief, treatment. We begin with the general question of welfare, and then continue with health and housing problems.

WELFARE POLICIES

Along with education and highways, public welfare is a chief recipient of state expenditures. The growth in spending has been phenomenal. In 1929 total state and local governmental outlays for public aid and other social welfare programs amounted to only $134 million. In the same program areas, federal expenditures came to $1.4 million. What this indicates is that before the 1930s state and local governments participated in a minimum number of welfare programs. There was also little uniformity among the programs. Today there are several dozen different types of welfare programs, and they do not vary much in form or organization from state to state. But they do vary in amounts of money spent.

Before the 1930s it was held to be axiomatic that the primary responsibility for welfare activities belonged to local governments. State governments did very little except to offer advice. Since then, of course, the state governments have played a very important role. Much of the overall burden has been borne by the federal government. For example, as Table 16.1 shows, social welfare programs in 1972 received a total of $106,-186 million from the federal government, while the states and local governments contributed a total of $86,563 million. But in

Table 16.1

Social Welfare Expenditures Under Public Programs, 1950–1973

Year and Source of Funds	Total social welfare[1]	Social insurance[1]	Public aid	Health and medical programs	Veterans programs	Education	Housing	Other social welfare	All health and medical care[2]	Total Social Welfare as Percent of	
										Gross National Product[1]	Total Government expenditures[1]
Total											
1950	23,508	4,947	2,496	2,064	6,866	6,674	15	448	3,065	8.9	37.6
1955	32,640	9,835	3,003	3,103	4,834	11,157	83	619	4,421	8.6	32.7
1960	52,293	19,307	4,101	4,464	5,479	17,626	177	1,139	6,395	10.6	38.0
1965	77,175	28,123	6,283	6,246	6,031	28,108	318	2,066	9,535	11.8	42.4
1968	113,840	42,740	11,092	8,459	7,247	40,590	428	3,285	20,030	13.8	43.2
1969	127,149	48,772	13,439	9,006	7,934	43,673	532	3,792	22,936	14.1	44.7
1970	145,894	54,676	16,488	9,753	9,018	50,848	701	4,408	25,232	15.3	47.8
1971	171,901	66,304	21,304	10,890	10,396	56,885	1,047	5,075	28,583	17.0	51.8
1972	192,749	74,715	26,092	12,771	11,465	60,741	1,396	5,569	33,392	17.5	53.4
1973 (prel.)	215,228	85,892	28,327	14,603	12,953	65,247	1,922	6,284	37,554	17.6	55.0
Federal											
1950	10,541	2,103	1,103	604	6,386	157	15	174	1,362	4.0	26.2
1955	14,628	6,385	1,504	1,150	4,772	485	75	252	1,948	3.9	22.3
1960	24,957	14,307	2,117	1,737	5,367	868	144	417	2,918	5.0	28.1
1965	37,712	21,807	3,594	2,781	6,011	2,470	238	812	4,625	5.8	32.6
1968	60,314	35,390	6,455	4,233	7,214	5,000	325	1,697	13,069	7.3	35.1
1969	68,355	40,847	7,829	4,543	7,883	4,923	426	1,905	15,229	7.6	37.5
1970	77,337	45,245	9,649	4,775	8,952	5,873	582	2,262	16,600	8.1	40.1
1971	92,547	53,830	13,032	5,148	10,331	6,580	872	2,749	18,766	9.1	44.9
1972	106,186	61,163	16,304	6,322	11,405	6,699	1,196	3,097	22,065	9.6	47.0
1973 (prel.)	122,331	72,204	17,847	7,194	12,899	6,947	1,697	3,544	24,620	10.0	49.6

State and Local

Year											
1950	12,967	2,844	1,393	1,460	480	6,518	(x)	274	1,704	4.9	60.1
1955	18,017	3,450	1,499	1,953	62	10,672	15	367	2,473	4.7	55.3
1960	27,337	4,999	1,984	2,797	112	16,768	33	723	3,477	5.5	58.3
1965	39,464	6,316	2,690	3,466	20	23,638	80	1,254	4,911	6.0	61.7
1968	53,526	7,350	4,630	4,226	33	35,589	103	1,589	6,970	6.5	60.0
1969	58,794	7,925	5,610	4,464	51	38,750	107	1,888	7,707	6.5	59.8
1970	68,557	9,431	6,839	4,978	67	44,975	120	2,147	8,632	7.2	62.4
1971	79,355	12,468	8,273	5,742	65	50,306	175	2,327	9,816	7.8	64.2
1972	86,563	13,552	9,788	6,449	60	54,042	200	2,472	11,327	7.9	65.4
1973 (prel.)	92,897	13,688	10,481	7,409	54	58,300	225	2,740	12,934	7.6	65.2

Percent of Total Expenditures by Type

Year											
1950	100.0	21.0	10.6	8.8	29.2	28.4	0.1	1.9	13.0	(x)	(x)
1955	100.0	30.1	9.2	9.5	14.8	34.2	0.3	1.9	13.5	(x)	(x)
1960	100.0	36.9	7.8	8.5	10.5	33.7	0.3	2.2	12.2	(x)	(x)
1965	100.0	36.4	8.1	8.1	7.8	36.4	0.4	2.7	12.4	(x)	(x)
1970	100.0	37.5	11.3	6.7	6.2	34.8	0.5	3.0	17.3	(x)	(x)
1973	100.0	39.9	13.2	6.8	6.0	30.3	0.9	2.0	17.4	(x)	(x)

Percent Federal of Total

Year											
1950	44.8	42.5	44.2	29.3	93.0	2.4	100.0	38.8	44.4	(x)	(x)
1955	44.8	64.9	50.0	37.1	98.7	4.3	84.3	40.7	44.1	(x)	(x)
1960	47.8	74.1	51.6	38.9	98.0	4.9	81.4	36.6	45.6	(x)	(x)
1965	48.9	77.5	57.2	44.5	99.7	8.8	74.8	39.3	48.5	(x)	(x)
1970	53.0	82.6	58.5	49.0	99.3	11.5	82.8	51.3	65.8	(x)	(x)
1973	56.8	84.1	63.0	49.3	99.6	10.6	88.3	56.4	65.6	(x)	(x)

(In millions of dollars, except percent. For Federal Government, most States, and some localities, years ending June 30. Represents expenditures under public law and from trust accounts. Includes administrative expenditures and capital outlay; also includes some expenditures and payments outside U.S.)

X Not applicable.

[1] Although total welfare and insurance expenditures including workmen's compensation and temporary disability insurance payments through private insurance carriers and self-insurers, such private payments have been omitted in computing percentages relating to all government expenditures.

[2] Combines "Health and medical programs" with medical services provided in connection with social insurance, public aid, veterans, and other social welfare programs.

Source: U.S. Social Security Administration, *Social Security Bulletin*, January 1974. From *Statistical Abstract*, 1974, Table No. 430.

terms of public assistance alone, the federal contribution exceeded that of the states and local governments—$16,304 million to $9,788 million. What is included under social welfare is made evident by the table headings.

The Development of Welfare Policy

Public welfare means acceptance of the principle that society at large is responsible for the basic needs of persons who are unable, for a variety of reasons, to provide for themselves. In almost all cultures, this principle has been accepted on the basis of custom or law.

In sketching the high points in the development of Anglo-American public welfare, one begins with the secular concern that developed over public care for the destitute when the feudal and religious institutions of the Middle Ages began to be unequal to this task. In the beginning, the focus was on beggars and on the moving from one place to another of working classes. By 1572 government action took definite form, for the English Parliament at that time placed the responsibility for raising funds for poor relief on local governments. But the Poor Relief Act of 1601, called the Elizabethan Poor Law, codified earlier legislation and practice and spelled out for the first time the nature of governmental responsibility for the care of the poor. For more than three hundred and fifty years this act has affected public policies for the relief of the poor both in England and in America.

The Poor Relief Act, while recognizing governmental responsibility for the care of the destitute, assigned or delegated the actual provision of aid to the smallest unit of local government: the parish. Included in the act were these by now familiar features: the provision for tax funds to support poor relief and to establish workhouses and almshouses; the recognition as a legal principle that relatives have an obligation to support impoverished members of their families; and the establishment of residence requirements to discourage indigent travelers. It was only in 1969 that the United States federal courts declared unconstitutional state laws which limited welfare eligibility to residents only.

Both in England and later in the North American colonies, the early laws reflected the belief that—with some obvious exceptions—poverty was caused by a person's individual shortcomings or weaknesses. Much of this sentiment remains in the

United States, where welfare recipients are often thought of as being too lazy to work. (On the other hand, persons who are laid off in large numbers—as during the Nixon-Ford recession of the 1970s—are considered to be in an entirely different category. They are in fact temporarily and involuntarily unemployed and are entitled to unemployment insurance as a legally guaranteed right.)

The English settlers in North America brought with them the basic principles formulated in the Elizabethan Poor Law. For example, the colony of Connecticut required that each town establish a workhouse for those able to work and also an almshouse for those who patently were incapable of work. At the same time, every effort was made to place primary responsibility upon the family, when that was possible.

By the time of the Revolution, this pattern, in one form or another, had been accepted in all the colonies, and it was continued by the states. Its leading feature was to place responsibility on local governments to establish, support, and administer welfare programs. As noted, this governmental unit in New England was the town. In the South, the responsibility was first assigned to the local parish, then to the counties. As usual, the Middle Atlantic states were somewhere in between, in some cases employing the township, in others the county government.

Except for certain specialized categories—for example, the deaf and dumb, the insane, and the blind—the state governments during the nineteenth century largely stayed out of the welfare picture. Welfare continued to be mainly a responsibility of local governments.

During the first three decades of the twentieth century, the states began to assume a more active, if limited, role. For example, Wisconsin passed a state law providing for state aid to the blind in 1907. Illinois adopted the first program for aid to dependent children in 1911. Both Montana and Nevada enacted programs to aid the aged in 1923.

To be a beneficiary of these categorical assistance programs, a person had to live in a particular state. There was, in short, no nation-wide policy in these areas. But the various categorical assistance programs were later grouped together and placed in the structure of the landmark 1935 Social Security Act. This form of assistance, under new auspices and relationships, became under that act the very heart of state welfare programs.

Even though the establishment of old-age, survivors', and disability insurance programs by the federal government were the most dramatic innovations of the 1930s, other important developments took place as well. From 1930 to 1941, a tremendous shift occurred from local to state and federal governmental units in the financing of assistance and work programs. For example, the federal percentage rose from zero to 66.5 during the twelve-year period.

For a change of this magnitude to occur very basic social problems must exist. These grew out of the Great Depression. Slowly but steadily, it became recognized that the United States in such fields as social security and unemployment relief was perhaps a half century behind the other Western industrialized countries. More important than this intellectual recognition was the fact that drastic measures were needed to deal with the severe economic and social crises of the time. The court of last resort was, in such extreme conditions, the federal government itself.

To this day, the Social Security Act, as amended many times, provides the basic framework and delivery system for public welfare policy in the United States. It was one of the very great achievements of the Roosevelt New Deal.

Welfare Policy Today

The core of state welfare efforts now consists of income maintenance programs. Programs administered exclusively by the federal government are excluded from the discussion here. These include the old-age, survivors', and health insurance programs; railroad workers' insurance; and services to veterans. Some programs are joint federal-state ones, including old-age assistance, aid to the blind, aid to dependent children, aid to the disabled, unemployment compensation, crippled children's services, and child welfare services. Various other programs have remained wholly state or local, including general assistance, workmen's compensation, and disability insurance.

It is the public assistance program which at present is at the heart of nonsocial insurance welfare programs. Included within these programs are various categorical assistance programs which have been brought under the Social Security Act, as well as traditional state and local assistance programs. The Social Security Act originally provided a system of matching grants to the states if they would set up and operate certain special assistance programs that met certain standards. At first

(Photo by Arthur Tress; courtesy Martin W. Sandler.)

confined to old-age assistance, aid to the blind, and aid to dependent children, the program has since been broadened. In 1950 it was enlarged to include aid to the disabled, and in 1960 and again in 1965 it was extended to include medical assistance. Nearly all states have accepted all phases of the enlarged program. What it amounts to is arriving at uniform national standards by having the federal government offer financial inducements that the states cannot afford to reject.

To participate in this type of federal matching program, a state must develop and administer its own programs within the framework of guidelines and regulations established by the federal government. The general procedure goes along these lines: A state must design and submit a proposed program to the federal government. It is required that the state participate in the financing and that the plan be applied to the entire state. The program must be administered by a single state agency, whose employees are appointed through civil service procedures, not patronage. Though eligibility may be determined by the state, federal law specifies that the recipient of aid must be "in need." The state must define *need* in the light of stipulated criteria.

Though this system provides a nation-wide minimum in welfare efforts, it does not bring about the degree of uniformity in financial benefits that the preceding paragraph might imply. This is because the states have some leeway in making the arrangements, and also because the formulas are changed from time to time. For example, in 1968, the federal contribution to state public assistance payments varied from a low in New Jersey of 39.1 percent to a high in Mississippi of 82.0 percent. The national average was about 60 percent.

Besides these categorical assistance programs in which the federal government plays a leading part, each state has some kind of general assistance program financed wholly by state and local funds. These programs usually are intended to service persons who do not qualify for aid under the existing federal programs. In all states, there is a central state welfare agency which oversees the administration of the varying public assistance programs.

Some Problems

In addition to the inequities in social welfare support which occur purely because of the state a person lives in, there are other problems which merit at least a listing. They tend to become especially prominent in periods of severe economic difficulty, such as the Nixon-Ford recession of the 1970s. Without going into the arguments of the economists—which tend to be contradictory at best—we can discuss the following questions:

1. Can a state unemployment fund go broke? The answer is yes. If a recession lasts long enough, and if a sufficient number of workers are unemployed, the state may exhaust its unemployment fund, which is actually an account carried in Washington, D.C., to the credit of the particular state.

2. Can a state exhaust the welfare benefits given it by the federal government? In theory, this could happen. In fact, the federal government, in conjunction with the state, would act to prevent hunger riots in the streets.

3. Do Social Security beneficiaries have protection against the type of inflation which characterized the mid-1970s? The answer is no, unless the federal government increases the

benefits in accordance with some cost of living index. Other countries have managed to do this.

4. What happens to union members, for example, members of the United Automobile Workers, whose contract guarantees them about 95 percent of their usual pay if they are seasonally laid off? If the unemployment period is short, and the number of persons laid off is small, the payments may continue for up to one year. But if there are massive layoffs, as there were in 1974–1975, the supplemental unemployment benefits stipulated in the union contract may not last a year. In such a situation, the workers involved must eventually apply for public assistance, which amounts to a fraction of their usual earnings.

5. Does the federal food stamp program help to set a minimum nutrition standard for those in the poverty classification? The answer is yes, but the stamps must still be bought. They are in reality sold at a discount, but welfare payments may be used to purchase them. One problem with the program is that it is administered by the Department of Agriculture, which does not really want to administer it because it believes the program interferes with the department's chief concern: the support of its own clientele, the farmers and the farm corporations.

Other questions could be, and inevitably will be, asked. The basic point, however, has been made. We have come a long way from the Elizabethan Poor Law, which tended to put the blame for poverty and economic misfortune on the individual, and the cost on the local parish. We now understand that social welfare policy is national in scope, that there must be national standards of administration, and that individuals are not always in control of their economic destinies. In short, whereas we once considered social welfare to be an individual and private problem, now we consider it to be a societal and governmental concern.

STATE HEALTH PROGRAMS

Health programs are closely related to social welfare programs. Despite advances in recent decades, health and the treatment of illness remain major problems. Indeed, as the average age of the population advances, these questions are assuming an ever larger importance.

It is somewhat difficult to judge the extent to which illness afflicts Americans. For example, the gross national product (GNP) figure, so revered by economists, includes in its total both the sales value of tobacco sold for cigarettes and the medical costs of treating lung cancer, largely caused by the smoking of cigarettes and other tobacco products. The real share of the GNP relating to health is obscured by this accounting practice.

Nonetheless, it is apparent in the mid-1970s that millions of Americans do not experience adequate health service. There is not only a shortage of personnel and facilities, but they are distributed unevenly across the country. Generally, those states and areas with the highest per capita incomes enjoy the best health care. Yet in all the states medical care for persons of average or below-average income fails to come up to the standards of the Western European democracies, as well as those of the Soviet Union. As a result, the American Medical Association, which currently enrolls only about 50 percent of all medical doctors in this country, finds itself not only the object of criticism but is itself divided into rival blocs. The problem is what is to be done for persons whose low incomes will not permit them to take advantage of the splendid medical services which are available on a fee basis to the well-to-do.

Health Viewed as a Public Responsibility

It is held as axiomatic that government exists to promote the general welfare. Obviously, this implies a concern for the state of physical and mental health of any group of citizens. There can hardly be any moral objection to the statement that government should try to prevent sickness and to raise the general health level of the community.

Because the United States Constitution does not mention the subject of health, the so-called police power of the states has been invoked to deal with the subject. Of course, the national government has also been involved in health matters for many years. In the first place, it has carried on a wide variety of activities through the famous United States Public Health Service and other less well known agencies. Secondly, the national government has developed a widespread program of federal grants-in-aid to state and local governments. This program has included such areas as maternal and child health, industrial hygiene, control of various diseases, and assistance to state and local units. Recent excitement over extension of the principle has centered on such questions as whether the federal government's programs should support birth control efforts undertaken by the states and whether federal funds should be made available to subsidize abortions for indigent women who desire such treatment. For many years, of course, the Veterans Administration has operated an extensive medical care program for veterans. This program includes both hospitals and rehabilitation centers.

As we observed earlier in connection with welfare, the tendency for many decades was for the states to assign health services to their units of local government. Drawn into the field first by the necessity of controlling epidemics, the states subsequently found it advisable to assume a more direct role in disease prevention and in health education. In recent years, both state and local governments have enlarged their activities in the effort to control or regulate chronic diseases. An example is the effort to eradicate sickle cell anemia in the black communities.

There are many ways in which the states have taken an increased responsibility in the public health field. The chief methods are the direct undertaking of new health activities by the state, the extension of state supervision over local health activities, and the subsidization of local health services through state grants-in-aid. Yet, despite recent developments which will be summarized later, the primary responsibility for public health programs remains in the hands of the local units of government.

Local Organization

Apparently, the first local boards of health were established in Massachusetts in 1797. During the next century, the movement to establish health boards and health officers was emulated in most of the country. In the early years, the powers of such agencies and officials were limited mostly to efforts to check the spread of communicable diseases and abate nuisances.

As both medical science and communications improved, local public health services developed along more complex lines. The powers of local authorities were expanded; part-time, nonprofessional personnel were replaced by full-time professionals, and health services were reorganized on a larger geographic basis.

The records indicate that the first local health department to provide full-time service on a county-wide basis was established in 1908 in Jefferson County, Kentucky, which contains the city of Louisville. Other counties containing sizable cities followed this pattern, but it was Robeson County, South Carolina, that was first to establish a full-time department in a predominantly rural county. The vast majority of counties now have health units under the direction of full-time health officers—a movement greatly spurred by the federal grants-in-aid provided by the Social Security Act of 1935.

State Organization

To Louisiana goes the distinction of creating, in 1855, the first state board of health. But the agency became inactive for many years. Massachusetts established in 1869 the first health board to maintain a continuous existence. Other states quickly adopted the Massachusetts model. As the process developed, state boards of health tended to be replaced by state health departments under single administrative heads. At the same time, it became customary to retain within such departments a board with certain administrative or advisory powers. Today, every state has such an agency, usually presided over by a physician. The divisions of the typical agency include those concerned with vital statistics, maternal and child health, sanitation, laboratory services, control of certain diseases, and public health nursing.

It would, however, be an error to imagine that all state activities in the public health field are administered by or centralized in the health department. On the contrary, various other agencies may perform health functions, including the departments of public works, education, welfare, agriculture, labor, mining, conservation, and public safety.

Functions

Disease Control. A large portion of public health activities deals with the control of communicable and preventable disease. As a matter of law, physicians are required to report cases of communicable disease to the local health authorities. Though isolation and quarantine are still important, emphasis has shifted toward immunization. To this end, state authorities supply physicians with various kinds of free vaccines for use in their private practices. The same authorities supply local health departments with vaccines to be administered to the indigent and in epidemic conditions to the general public.

In recent years, special control programs have been established. These include efforts to control tuberculosis, pneumonia, trachoma, malaria, and polio. Increasingly an endeavor has been undertaken to diagnose and control potential diseases of the heart. Most states also have a special program to combat venereal disease. With the widespread use by women of intrauterine devices, the diaphragm, and "the pill," the responsibility for the prevention of unwanted pregnancy has apparently fallen upon the female section of the population. One consequence of the decreased use of the traditional male contraceptive device—the condom—has been a dramatic increase in venereal diseases, especially gonorrhea, among teenagers. Gonorrhea is generally described as having reached epidemic proportions. Though the disease is easily detected among males, it is less obvious in women. Once detected, it can be cured. Even syphilis can be completely cured if treated at an early stage.

Sanitation. Local health authorities are charged with overseeing various sanitation measures that affect the health of the citizenry. Such activities include the inspection of water supplies, the disposal of wastes, and the examination of facilities at pools and trailer camps.

Another function of the local health authorities is the protection of the community's food supply. Normally, hotels, restaurants, and food markets require for their operation a license issued by sanitation officers. In some localities there is provision for the licensing of local slaughterhouses and of animals at the time of slaughter. An alternative, sometimes used in America and widely used overseas, is to provide for municipal abattoirs, which the local authorities oversee.

Besides these activities, another important health function is to safeguard the milk supply. Many of the states have milk control boards, which set the price at which milk may be sold. When it comes to sanitary conditions on dairy farms, in barns, and in milk rooms, the local authorities usually are responsible. But the licensing and inspection of pasteurization plants are customarily an assignment of the state health department.

Vital Statistics. To operate the very large public health

programs of the states, it is necessary to collect and record certain vital statistics. The most commonly maintained statistics in terms of public health include birth statistics, sickness statistics covering certain diseases, and mortality figures. Generally, physicians are required to report all three kinds of data. Births are also reported by midwives and deaths by coroners and undertakers.

When birth certificates are required of persons seeking employment in defense industries or trying to obtain a passport, problems may arise. There is considerable laxity in the reporting of births. In addition, it is said to be remarkably easy to forge birth certificates. The problem is reported to be particularly acute with regard to illegal aliens, who do not find it especially difficult to develop or have developed documents attesting to the supposed legitimacy of their presence in the country.

Related Public Health Activities. Certain other aspects of public health work warrant brief mention. Most states and many cities operate programs in the areas of industrial hygiene and maternal and child hygiene. In both cases, the programs are financed in part by the federal government. States maintain laboratories, for instance, to test the safety of water supplies. They also make examinations for local health departments, for private physicians, and for hospitals. The movement for the state to increase the availability of psychiatric services is growing. At the same time, there is a widening concern with the problems of drugs, including alcohol.

Other regular functions of state and local health departments include health education, public health nursing, and the supervision of training of nurses. In short, the state is involved, at one point or another, with practically every phase of public health activity.

Hospitals. The states and localities have been assuming a distinctly larger role in the operation of hospitals. In 1972, there were 401 federal hospitals of all types and 6,660 nonfederal hospitals. Of the hospitals not under federal ownership or control, 570 were managed by the states, while 1,730 were operated by local governments. These figures compare with a total of 3,515 nongovernmental nonprofit hospitals, and a total of 845 profit-making hospitals.

To say that the hospital enterprise is big business is an understatement. In 1972, state and local government hospitals had assets of $6.577 billion, and expenses of $5.758 billion. They employed about 477 thousand persons. Nonetheless, many governmental and a large percentage of private hospitals have found themselves increasingly beset by financial problems.

Health Insurance Programs. For many years, the country relied mainly on private organizations to provide health insurance. Blue Cross and Blue Shield are, of course, the most famous and widely used organizations of this type. Yet this type of nonprofit insurance organization has several flaws, the principal one being that it assumes that the insured is employed. For the unemployed, the disabled, or the retired, it is nearly impossible to raise the funds needed to remain in good standing in any of the voluntary insurance plans.

It was with this problem in mind that Congress in 1965 passed the Medicare amendments to the Social Security Act. The amendments established two related health insurance programs for persons sixty-five or over. The basic plan—plan A—provides protection against the costs of hospital and related care. Plan B is voluntary and supplemental and covers payments for physicians' services and other medical and health services not covered by the basic plan.

By further amendments in 1972, Medicare coverage was extended to persons who had been receiving Social Security disability benefits for twenty-four consecutive months, effective 1 July 1973. Since then further extensions of the plan have been put into effect.

Medical insurance—i.e., plan B—is voluntary, and persons who enroll pay a monthly premium which is matched by the federal government.

An example of the scope of both programs comes from Medicare payments in Pennsylvania for the period 1 July 1973 to 30 June 1974. During this period, the state paid out $460 million in part A and $168 million in part B of Medicare. The United States totals during that year were $7,805 million and $2,-865 million in parts A and B, respectively. During the same period the enrollment figures for Pennsylvania stood at 1,424,841 under part A and 1,384,004 under part B.

The federal Medicare program has had a profound impact on the public assistance administrations of the states. It has forced the states to reorganize their previously existing programs, and has encouraged administrative centralization. State programs usually are called "Medicaid." New Jersey is more or less typical. On 1 January 1970, the New Jersey Health Services Program, or "Medicaid," went into operation. It is administered by the State Division of Medical Assistance and Health Services of the Department of Institutions and Agencies. The program provides payment for the cost of health care to eligible persons, including all individuals receiving financial assistance under the categorical assistance programs (dependent children, the blind, the disabled, the working poor, the elderly).

In addition, the program provides payment for the cost of health services for persons under state programs of medical assistance for the aged and of assistance to families of the working poor. It also processes claims for a federal program of health care for Cuban refugees.

Covered items and services include hospital and nursing home care, physicians' services, drugs, home health care, and vision care. From July 1972 through June 1973, persons receiving care averaged about 224,413 monthly. Eligible persons averaged about 567,551. From this it is apparent that about 39.5 percent of those who were eligible were receiving services during any given month.

HOUSING

For many reasons, government is interested in housing. Some of these reasons may be philosophical, such as the association of the quality of living with good housing. Others are purely practical; for example, slums require higher public expenditures than other areas for police and fire protection and for public health work. In other words, good housing may be justified on economic grounds.

Though housing in the United States has been undertaken mostly by private enterprise, government is concerned with housing in several ways. Firstly, government regulates private housing through techniques we shall examine. Secondly, government promotes and encourages private housing. And thirdly, government may directly build at public expense houses or apartments which are sold or rented to the public. The situation is complex, for it involves, at various points, all levels of government: local, state, and national. In practice, federal and local governments have been more active than the states in the housing field.

We begin with a brief consideration of the leading housing activities of state and local governments. In approaching the area, it is well to bear in mind that these governments have available to them three principal powers when it comes to housing. They are: (1) the police power—that is, the power to regulate generally for the public welfare; (2) the power of taxation; and (3) the power of eminent domain. The last power refers to the right of government to take private property for public use upon payment of just compensation. An example would be the condemnation and demolition of dwellings in the slums and also the acquisition of sites for new construction.

Building Codes and Zoning Regulations

Most large cities have ordinances, known as building codes, which deal with such matters as materials of construction; fire escapes; standards of sanitation, ventilation, and lighting; and the safety of plumbing and electrical installations. Simply listing these aspects of building codes indicates the potential political conflict which they may engender. For example, a labor union may insist on retaining uneconomic features of a code because it means more of their members are employed. Or the product of one company or industry may be in conflict with that of another. An illustration is the use of copper as opposed to plastic piping. Insurance companies are obviously concerned with the safety of electrical installations, the adequacy of fire escapes, and the performances of elevators in high-rise buildings. A listing of this sort could be extended indefinitely. What is being stressed is that everyone has at least an indirect interest in the building codes, and a large number of business concerns and unions have a very direct economic interest in them. So, of course, do such public services as the fire and police departments, among others.

Distinguishable from but related to the building codes are provisions for local zoning ordinances. Some are concerned with safety, for example, the structure of buildings. Others deal with aesthetics: in downtown Philadelphia, custom and practice have decreed that no building may exceed in height the brim of the hat which adorns William Penn's statue on the top of city hall. Zoning ordinances are also intended to bar certain types of manufacturing and commercial enterprises from residential districts. In recent years, some regulations have required that new buildings provide off-street automobile parking facilities. Baltimore and Boston have set aside special districts in which burlesque shows and related enterprises are concentrated, while at the same time prohibiting such enterprises in other sections of the cities.

It requires a fairly elaborate administrative apparatus to enforce building codes and zoning regulations. Most cities have a bureau of inspection and licensing, and permits must be secured for the construction of new buildings or for extensive alterations to old ones. While most residents pay little daily attention to such inspection and licensing activities, it is clear that builders and developers must work closely with the municipal or county officials in order to create new projects.

Rent Control

Under normal conditions, the level of rents is determined by the so-called law of supply and demand and government regulation of rents is deemed unnecessary. But in emergency situations—such as overcrowding brought on by the failure to create new buildings—the national government and sometimes state and local governments have stepped in and imposed rent controls. As an illustration, during World War II, the federal government controlled rents in several hundred defense-rental areas. The scope of the control is shown by noting that about half of the nation's population came under it.

The federal government also empowered state and local governments to vote their areas in or out of the federal control program. Three decades after the end of World War II, vestiges of the wartime control still remain, notably in New York city. It is arguable whether, from the point of view of the residents of New York city, the retention of rent control in a substantial percentage of that city's apartments has been a blessing or something of a curse. Because the low maximum rents do not cover increased costs of maintenance and repair, there is a tendency for landlords to abandon buildings rather than perform necessary services. Beyond any question, rent control has discouraged the construction of new apartment buildings intended for persons of moderate or middle incomes. Under New York's provisions, new buildings do not come under rent control. One result has been a heavy concentration on the construction of "luxury" apartment buildings. This has had obvious social consequences.

Tax Concessions

On occasion, state and local governments have tried to encourage housing construction by tax concessions. In 1920, the legislature of New York authorized its local units to exempt newly constructed houses from local taxes for a period of ten years. Even though New York city was the only local government to take advantage of the law, it appears that it did accomplish what it was intended to do—stimulate residential building.

Another method of tax concession is to separate the assessment of land and of buildings. Under this plan, buildings are taxed at a lower rate than land. The objective is to encourage owners of building lots either to build on them or sell to persons who will. As early as 1914, Pittsburgh established a graded-tax plan which put these principles into effect. The experts are in agreement that the plan stimulated residential construction in Pittsburgh. Clyde F. Snider noted that between 1914 and 1938, while land-value assessments increased only about 15 percent, building-value assessments increased more than 93 percent.[1] The plan is also credited with playing an important role in Pittsburgh's extensive redevelopment program which began in the 1950s.

However, it should be noted that it would be necessary to amend constitutions in many states if they were to attempt either tax exemption or graded taxation to encourage new construction. This is because those existing constitutions require uniformity in taxation, a principle obviously in conflict with the tax concession concept.

Urban Development Corporations

In an effort to attract private capital, especially that of insurance companies and other financial institutions, some states have passed laws enabling the creation of urban redevelopment corporations. While the statutes differ in detail, they most often rely on partial tax exemption for a limited number of years and use the power of eminent domain. Approval of state or local authorities for such projects, many of which are massive, must be obtained by the corporation before undertaking any operations.

Another kind of urban development corporation is one established under the auspices of a state government. The prototype is the Urban Development Corporation created in New York in 1968 at the insistence of then Governor Nelson A. Rockefeller. It began building its first projects the next year. From 1969 to 1975, about 150 thousand housing units (apartments or single-family units) were built or started in construction in New York state under government-aid programs of all types. Of these, some 34 thousand units—more than one in every five—were in projects sponsored by the Urban Development Corporation. In New York city, where about 108 thousand government-aided apartments were built during the six-year period, some 16 thousand, or 15 percent, were projects of the U.D.C. From these figures it is obvious that the agency played a major role in the housing programs of the entire state.

It therefore came as a shock in March of 1975 when the U.D.C. announced that it could not repay some of its bond-anticipation notes. Appeals to the New York city banks were unsuccessful in solving the financial problems of the agency. The best the U.D.C. could hope for was a temporary bailing-out through appropriations by the state legislature. In the view of financial experts, the collapse of the U.D.C. meant that the agency would be unable to undertake any additional projects, no matter how far along they were on the drawing board.

But the failure of the U.D.C. extended beyond the borders of New York state. There developed something of a ripple effect which jeopardized the housing-finance agencies in other states. In particular, the Michigan and New Jersey housing agencies ran into immediate trouble in marketing their bonds. In short, although the agencies established in roughly thirty states in recent years to finance housing for the most part differ considerably from the U.D.C. model, the distinctions apparently were lost on many potential investors throughout the country.[2]

As an alternative to meeting public housing needs through private banks, it was suggested by some observers that the example of North Dakota should be followed. The Bank of North Dakota, created after World War I, is the only state-owned bank in the country. Basically, the bank serves as a central banking facility for smaller commercial and savings institutions located far from the nation's central money markets. It does not compete with commercial banks but cooperates with them in an effort to meet the needs of the people of North Dakota. Yet few persons really believed that New York state would or could establish a state-owned bank on the North Dakota model. The preference was to rely on the money market itself to allocate credit for housing.

Public Housing

In comparison with the Western European democracies, as well as with members of the Soviet bloc, the United States has made only limited use of public housing. Usually such housing has been constructed in response to an emergency.

During the 1917−1918 period the federal government, operating through the United States Housing Corporation and the United States Shipping Board, built sixty-six projects for housing workers in war industries. In World War II the activities of the national government were much more extensive. More than 850 thousand dwelling units were built by the federal Public Housing Authority and other federal agencies. The problem was that a large proportion of the buildings were thought of as being only temporary in character.

The Depression stimulated a renewed interest in federal housing. The United States Housing Act of 1937, though it made no provision for federal construction, gave financial assistance for slum-clearance and low-rent housing projects built and operated by local public housing authorities organized under state law. The basic concept was to build a new unit for each slum unit eliminated. As a result of the statute, state legislatures took speedy action to permit the organization of local housing authorities, which could qualify for financial assistance from the federal government. In this manner the basic organizational pattern was set which has prevailed ever since 1937. Nearly every city of any consequence now has its own housing authority.

But federal support, in terms of money, has fluctuated widely. For example, in 1964 the federal government subsidized 55,100 new units. As a consequence of the vigorous support given public housing by the Johnson Administration, the number rose sharply after 1966, and the momentum carried to a peak of about 400 thousand units each year in 1970 and 1971. But a Nixon Administration moratorium on most housing subsidies, announced in January 1973, cut the support level to about 122 thousand for 1974.[3]

Much more important than the decline in federally supported housing was the decline in construction undertaken by private developers. The period 1974−1975 was the worst for the private construction industry in forty years. According to a study prepared by the Library of Congress, one reason for the weakness of the housing industry was the fact that many middle-class families had been priced out of the market.

The study, released in April 1975, said that 23 percent more income was required in 1974 than in 1973 to buy the average priced house. It was found that only 15 percent of the families in the country in 1974 had the $23,330 annual income required to buy the median-priced new home, estimated to cost $41,300.[4]

What these figures imply is that public pressure will mount for a higher level of federal support for new housing, either directly or through lower interest rates on mortgages—in 1975 at an all-time high.

Urban Renewal

Though the basic laws have been amended from time to time, the Housing Acts of 1949 and 1954 remain the principal weapons in the effort for slum clearance and urban renewal. These acts authorized federal loans and grants to local government agencies for these purposes. Involved in urban renewal is input by the federal government, local governments, and private enterprise.

Slum property is acquired through the power of eminent domain or through purchase. The land may then be resold to private investors, with the aim of redevelopment for commercial or residential purposes. Or, in the case of a governmental agency, the land may be used for public housing or for some other public purpose such as parks or schools. In contrast to public housing projects, which have been largely confined to a few large cities (suburbs do not want them), urban renewal projects may be found almost anywhere.

In 1975, a new program of urban rehabilitation got under way. It resulted from the rewriting in 1974 of four decades of federal housing laws. It was designed to replace the Depression-born public housing system, and more recently the subsidy approach during President Lyndon B. Johnson's Great Society era. Most of these programs were suspended in 1973 by President Richard M. Nixon, who called them rife with waste and scandal. The new program was approved by Congress and signed into law by President Ford in August 1974.

As part of the Housing and Community Development Act of 1974, the new rent-subsidy program features an elaborate system of rent supplements rather than the usual construction subsidies. The first project under the program was scheduled to be the rehabilitation over the period of one year of eleven decayed apartment buildings in the South Bronx section of New York city. Under the program, the total rent for an apartment is to be shared by the occupant and the federal government. As usual, the program had vigorous supporters, mostly from the federal government, and numerous critics, mostly state and local officials as well as private builders.[5]

Urban Homesteading

Since the mid-1960s, housing abandonment has been ravaging the slum neighborhoods in many of the country's largest cities. It was estimated, early in 1974, that each year landlords in New York city were walking away from buildings containing a total of 10,000 apartments. This condition was found to exist in most other large cities as well. No one is quite sure who the principal culprit is, although the tendency is to blame the HUD, along with "absentee" landlords, the bankers, and private investors who shun putting their money into the central cities.

A frequently suggested partial solution to the abandonment problem has been termed *urban homesteading*. Based on the idea underlying the 1862 Homestead Act that helped start a mass movement to the frontier, the updated idea is to offer a house—free, or for a nominal fee of one dollar—if a family will restore it to decent condition and live in it for a stated period. According to the best available estimates, about nine million houses and apartments are empty, and many of them could be rehabilitated by homesteading. In theory, the homesteaders get relatively inexpensive houses, even if repairs are needed, and the formerly empty houses go back on the city tax rolls. Baltimore, Philadelphia, and Wilmington, Delaware adopted the plan in 1973. It is under study in numerous other cities.

As backers of the plan see it, urban homesteading will not cost the cities a lot of money. Some cities already own a great many houses because of nonpayment of taxes. The federal government owns many more from foreclosures in subsidized programs, and quite conceivably could make them available.

Yet there are problems. For example, Philadelphia, in 1973, had thirty-six thousand vacant houses, but held actual title to only about twelve hundred of them. Apparently because of lack of funds to oversee the program, only sixteen houses were actually rehabilitated under Philadelphia's urban homesteading program during 1974. The record was somewhat better in Wilmington and Baltimore.

Yet, even if the plan is no cure-all, it has obvious potential. Since very little else is succeeding in rundown inner-city residential areas, urban homesteading as a practice has much to gain and little to lose. As Philadelphia Councilman Joseph Coleman, one of the initiators of the plan, has expressed it: "We don't say homesteading is going to be easy. But it has the possibilities of providing homes, of removing blight from the inner city. We think it is worth a try."[6]

Items for Discussion

1. How can health-care services be upgraded in rural and small-town areas?

2. Should women on welfare be able to have abortions at state expense?

3. In a period of depression for the construction industry, can individual states take any meaningful action to stimulate building?

4. On a metropolitan basis, what action can be taken to disperse public housing throughout suburban communities? Should such an activity be undertaken?

5. Is the ranch house in the suburbs on a half-acre of land still a central part of the "American dream"? As a young person moving to take a job in, for example, downtown Chicago, in what type of area would you choose to live?

Chapter Notes

1. Clyde F. Snider, *American State and Local Government* (New York: Appleton-Century-Crofts, 1965), p. 535.

2. Joseph P. Fried, "U.D.C.'s Ripple Effect." *New York Times*, 3 March 1975. Also Maurice Carroll, "U.D.C. 'Fear' Stops a Billion in Work." *New York Times*, 15 April 1975.

3. *U.S. News & World Report*, 17 March 1975, p. 40. Figures from United States Department of Housing and Urban Development.

4. "Housing Costs Found Hurting Middle Class." *New York Times*, 29 April 1975.

5. Joseph P. Fried, "U.S. Hopes Rent Subsidies Spur Construction Area." *New York Times*, 27 April 1975.

6. As quoted in *U.S. News & World Report*, 5 Nov. 1973, p. 43.

17

State and Local Finance

Key Terms

Allotment system: Budgetary device by which each government department divides its budget into quarterly or monthly allotments and expenditures are not permitted to exceed the allotment.

Auditor: State official who checks on the expenditures of appropriated funds to determine if they have been spent as the legislature intended.

Capital budgeting: Budget appropriations for long-term projects, such as building a dam; contrasted with *operating budgeting* for day-to-day expenditures.

Comptroller: Main accounting officer in a government agency who is responsible for seeing to it that funds are spent as the legislature intended.

Equalization agency: Government office established to make sure that similar properties will receive similar tax treatment.

Executive budget: State budget prepared under the direction of the governor; contrasted with a *board-type* budget prepared by an administrative board and a *legislative budget* prepared by a legislative committee.

Grants-in-aid: Program under which the federal government awards funds to state and local governments; the grants are *categorical* (used for specific projects) and the federal government prescribes standards and conditions for their use.

Keynesian theory: Economic ideas associated with government deficit spending during a recession in order to maintain employment.

Property tax: A tax levied according to value on *real* (land, building) and *personal* property; personal property may be *tangible* (household furnishings) or *intangible* (stocks and bonds).

Revenue sharing: Plan under which the federal government returns tax revenues to state and local governments to be spent as they wish; *general* revenue sharing provides grants to be spent on any local project; *special* revenue sharing would be directed to particular areas, such as education or law enforcement.

Regressive tax: A tax in which the burden falls more heavily on low-income groups; it is the opposite of a *progressive* tax, in which the tax rates increase as the ability to pay increases. Typically, property taxes are said to be regressive, while income taxes are progressive or graduated.

It has been one of the themes of this book that politics and economics are interwoven. This has been demonstrated in our analysis of such state and local functions as transportation, education, health, and welfare. In some cases, a political decision may be dictated by economic considerations. But the reverse may also be true: political decisions very often have important economic consequences. In this connection, the reader is referred back to the discussion of these kinds of relationships in Chapter 1.

Though the effort is not to separate economics from politics, for purposes of the present chapter the focus is on the substance and machinery of public taxing and spending. The first section of the discussion deals with how states and localities raise revenues through taxation and bond issues. The second section analyses the principal objects of state and local expenditures. In order to make the relationships as clear as possible, several tables are reprinted from official Bureau of the Census compilations.

The pie chart—Figure 17.1—shows the sources and the expenditures of the state and local government dollar for the year

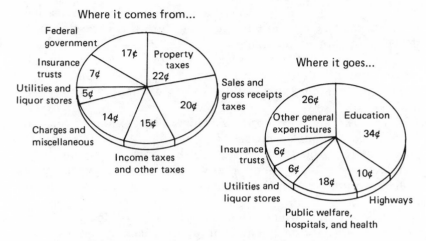

Figure 17.1
The state and local government dollar, 1972.
Source: U.S. Bureau of the Census.

1972. A historical overview of state and local finances is provided by Table 17.1.

REVENUES

The Taxing Power

A tax is generally defined as a compulsory contribution for the support of government, exacted without regard for individual benefit. That is, you cannot refuse to pay a tax simply because you as an individual receive no particular benefit from it. The power of the states to tax is very broad and is subject only to limitations imposed by the federal and state constitutions. On the other hand, local governments possess only such taxing power as has been conferred on them by the states. State governments can and do pass statutes restricting the taxing powers of local governments. In short, a state legislature may levy any tax which it is not forbidden to enact, but local governments may only impose those taxes which the states permit them to levy.

Because over the decades there has been a feeling that state legislatures could not altogether be trusted to levy taxes wisely, all state constitutions impose certain limitations upon the

Table 17.1
State and Local Government Finances, 1950–1972

Item	1950	1955	1960	1965	1970	1971	1972 Total	1972 Percent
Revenue	25,639	37,619	60,277	87,777	150,106	166,090	189,724	100.00
From Federal Government	2,486	3,131	6,974	11,029	21,857	26,146	31,253	16.5
Public welfare	1,107	1,423	2,070	3,098	7,574	9,766	13,251	7.0
Highways	438	596	2,905	3,997	4,608	4,987	5,108	2.7
Education	345	512	950	1,677	5,844	6,802	7,941	4.2
Social insurance administration	168	209	325	413	664	721	756	0.4
Other and unallocable	428	382	724	1,844	3,167	3,870	4,197	2.2
From State and local sources	23,153	34,489	53,302	76,748	128,248	139,945	158,471	83.5
General, net of intergovernmental	18,425	27,942	43,530	62,971	108,898	118,782	135,100	71.2
Taxes	15,914	23,483	36,117	51,243	86,795	94,975	108,801	57.3
Property	7,349	10,735	16,405	22,583	34,054	37,852	42,133	22.2
Sales and gross receipts	5,154	7,643	11,849	17,118	30,322	33,233	37,488	19.8
Individual income	788	1,237	2,463	4,090	10,812	11,900	15,237	8.0
Corporation income	593	744	1,180	1,929	3,738	3,424	4,416	2.3
Other	2,030	3,125	4,220	5,521	7,868	8,567	9,527	4.8
Charges and miscellaneous	2,511	4,459	7,414	11,729	22,103	23,807	26,299	13.9
Utility and liquor stores revenue	2,712	3,688	4,877	6,355	8,614	9,359	9,975	5.3
Water supply system	705	1,092	1,529	2,004	2,687	2,980	3,165	1.7
Electric power system	574	870	1,307	1,833	2,385	2,644	2,912	1.5
Transit system	468	544	581	776	1,135	1,213	1,235	0.7
Gas supply system	61	104	196	295	401	439	475	0.3
Liquor stores	904	1,079	1,264	1,447	2,006	2,083	2,188	1.2

Table 17.1—*Continued*

Item	1950	1955	1960	1965	1970	1971	1972 Total	1972 Percent
Revenue	25,639	37,619	60,277	87,777	150,106	166,090	189,724	100.0
Insurance trust revenue[2]	2,016	2,858	4,896	7,422	10,736	11,804	13,398	7.1
Employee retirement	606	1,180	2,099	3,423	6,493	7,451	8,438	4.4
Unemployment compensation	1,180	1,329	2,323	3,244	3,101	3,096	3,601	1.9
Direct expenditure	27,905	40,375	60,999	86,554	148,052	170,766	188,825	100.0
By function:								
Direct general expenditure[2]	22,787	33,724	51,876	74,546	131,332	150,674	166,873	88.4
Education[2]	7,177	11,907	18,719	28,563	52,718	59,413	64,886	34.4
Institutions of higher education[3]	1,107	1,570	3,202	5,863	12,924	14,785	15,946	8.4
Local schools[3]	5,906	10,129	15,166	21,966	37,461	41,766	45,658	24.2
Highways	3,803	6,452	9,428	12,221	16,427	18,095	19,010	10.1
Public welfare	2,940	3,168	4,404	6,315	14,679	18,226	21,070	11.2
Health	364	471	559	836	1,806	2,119	2,574	1.4
Hospitals	1,384	2,053	3,235	4,525	7,863	9,086	10,293	5.5
Police protection	776	1,229	1,857	2,549	4,494	5,228	5,976	3.2
Local fire protection	488	694	995	1,306	2,024	2,303	2,577	1.4
Natural resources	670	793	1,189	1,730	2,732	3,082	3,110	1.6
Sanitation and sewerage	834	1,142	1,727	2,360	3,413	4,087	4,729	2.5
Housing and urban renewal	452	499	858	1,250	2,138	2,554	2,781	1.5
Local parks and recreation	304	509	770	1,104	1,888	2,109	2,323	1.2
Financial administration				1,267	2,030	2,271	2,480	1.3
General control	1,041	1,452	2,113	1,506	2,652	3,027	3,407	1.8
Interest on general debt[4]	458	838	1,670	2,490	4,374	5,089	5,963	3.2
Utility and liquor stores expenditure[4]	2,739	3,886	5,088	7,058	9,447	10,300	11,414	6.0
Water supply system	849	1,479	1,881	2,505	3,211	3,432	3,732	2.0
Electric power system	534	819	1,244	1,983	2,486	2,816	3,346	1.8

Transit system	570	600	750	1,127	1,753	2,018	2,186	1.2
Gas supply system	52	125	191	272	370	410	433	0.2
Liquor stores	734	863	1,022	1,172	1,627	1,625	1,717	0.9
Insurance trust expenditure[2]	2,379	2,764	4,031	4,950	7,273	9,793	10,538	5.6
Employee retirement	361	722	1,265	2,298	3,629	4,155	4,757	2.5
Unemployment compensation	1,849	1,784	2,364	2,008	2,723	4,708	4,741	2.5
By character and object:								
Current operation	15,948	23,186	36,318	53,929	97,915	111,829	125,630	66.5
Capital outlay	6,047	10,706	15,104	20,535	29,650	33,137	34,237	18.1
Construction	5,169	9,048	12,352	16,413	24,252	26,970	28,107	14.9
Land and existing structures	415	925	1,560	2,471	2,631	3,203	3,012	1.6
Equipment	464	733	1,192	1,652	2,768	2,965	3,118	1.7
Assistance and subsidies	2,918	2,660	3,518	4,127	8,090	10,104	11,527	6.1
Interest on debt (general and utility)	613	1,059	2,028	3,012	5,123	5,904	6,893	3.7
Insurance benefits and repayments	2,379	2,764	4,031	4,950	7,273	9,793	10,538	5.6
Expenditure for personal services	10,043	15,539	24,445	36,095	62,998	70,561	78,679	41.7
Debt outstanding at end of year	24,115	44,267	69,955	99,512	143,570	158,827	174,502	100.0
Long-term	23,056	42,272	66,801	94,204	131,415	143,617	158,781	91.0
Short-term	−1,060	1,995	3,154	5,309	12,155	15,210	15,722	9.0
Net change during year	3.116	5,336	5,845	7,290	10,022	15,243	15,675	9.0

(In millions of dollars, except percent. Prior to 1960, excludes Alaska and Hawaii.
[1] Includes all local revenue received directly from Federal Government.
[2] Includes amounts not shown separately.
[3] Prior to 1960, amounts for locally administered institutions of higher education are included in "Local schools."
[4] Interest on utility debt included in "utility expenditure."

Source: U.S. Bureau of the Census, *Historical Statistics on Governmental Finances and Employment* and *Governmental Finances,* annual. From *Statistical Abstract,* 1974, Table No. 408.

taxing powers of the states. Ordinarily these provisions take the form of exempting certain classes of property from taxation. It is common, for instance, to exempt from taxation all publicly owned property, as well as property used for educational, religious, or charitable purposes. Most states provide exemptions of one sort or another for veterans. Other forms of exemption include "homestead" exemptions (under which owner-occupied homes are wholly or partially nontaxable), certain kinds of industrial and agricultural properties, and, though it is not very common, some degree of tax exemption on the property of the elderly.

Because of these numerous exemptions, in many urban areas a very substantial proportion of real estate does not appear on the tax rolls. As a result, property-tax revenues are severely curtailed unless the rates on nonexempt property are increased. Obviously, such rate increases are not likely to be especially popular with those property owners whose taxes go up.

The tax problems of local governments are further compounded when their power to levy property taxes is subject to percentage or millage limitations upon the rates that may be imposed for stated purposes. As illustration, a municipality may be authorized to levy up to five mills on each dollar of assessed valuation for street purposes, three mills for parks, two mills for health work, and so on. Practice, of course, varies from state to state, but it is not uncommon for the local voters to be allowed through the use of referenda to exceed these maximum rates. Another limiting device, employed in several states, is to set an overall limitation on property taxes. Under this plan, the combined tax levies on a single piece of property may not exceed a maximum total rate. As we have noted earlier, the way local governments attempt to circumvent limitations of this type is to make increasing use of the special district.

Property Taxation. From colonial times to the present, taxes on property have constituted the principal source of local revenue. Until recent decades, such taxes were also the chief source of state revenue. There are two broad categories of the property tax, real and personal. Real estate includes land, buildings, and improvements of a permanent nature. Personal property (personalty) includes all property other than real estate. For purposes of convenience, it is divided into two categories, tangible and intangible. Household furnishings, cars, livestock, and machinery are tangible personal property. Intangible personal property consists of such things as stocks and bonds, promissory notes, and bank accounts.

Originally, the property tax in this country took the simple form of a tax on land. After about 1815, in an effort to expand the tax base, taxes on land and on certain types of personalty were expanded into the *general* property tax. This is defined as an *ad valorem* levy on all property not specifically exempted. By the time of the Civil War the general property tax was accepted as the primary form of state and local taxation. Implied in this concept is that the owner of any type of property—real estate, tangible personal property, and intangible personal property—ought to contribute to the support of government in proportion to the total value of the owner's property.

Property-tax administration. As in many other areas of state administration, the practices of the states in property-tax administration vary a good deal. Everywhere, there is a high degree of decentralization, although the trend is for increasing state supervision. Every state has a state tax commission or its equivalent which is given some supervisory and advisory authority over local tax administration.

In principle, the administration of a property tax is not complicated. In practice, the matter may become considerably complex, and severe inequities may occur among local jurisdictions. The initial step in the administrative process is that of assessment. This merely means the listing and valuation of the taxable property of each owner. Personal property is usually assessed annually, but real estate is normally assessed at greater intervals—up to several years.

A second step is for the assessment rolls prepared by local assessors to be turned over to a local administrative board for review and for equalization. The review process involves the corrections of errors and the handling of complaints. Equalization involves taking action to order horizontal increases or decreases throughout the taxing jurisdiction so that similar properties will receive similar tax treatment.

When the review and equalization agencies have performed their tasks, the assessment rolls are given to a designated local officer, such as the county clerk, who makes "the extension of taxes" by multiplying the property owner's assessment by the sum of all rates imposed on the owner's property.

The final step, of course, is the actual collection by local authorities of the taxes which have been extended. It is customary, though not universal, to provide that a single collecting officer, normally the county treasurer, will collect all property taxes. This official then makes the appropriate remittances to the various levying units, including the state if the state has a state property tax.

Weaknesses of the general property tax. Though the property tax has proved a lucrative and relatively elastic course of revenue, it has serious deficiencies. To start with, it is based on the assumption that the property produces income. But, as we all know, some properties produce no income at all, even though the taxes must be paid. Other properties, which produce a very high income, are taxed at the same rates.

Another weakness of the general property tax we have previously noted is that a great deal of nonexempt property escapes any taxation. It is easy to tax rural land, but it is almost impossible to tax jewelry. Persons whose property is in the form of intangibles find it relatively simple to avoid the general property tax.

In addition to these criticisms, the administration of the property tax has come under fire. In some cases, the assessment districts are simply too small to make much administrative sense. This means that the assessors serve on a part-time and, probably, semiamateur basis. Furthermore, most local assessors are popularly elected. This encourages political hacks and discourages professionals.

As a consequence of these shortcomings, various states have come up with classified property taxes as an alternative to the general property tax. What this amounts to is the elimination of the uniformity requirement (provided for in most state constitutions at the start of the century) and the segregation of property into groups or types, each group or type taxable at different rates.

The present status of the property tax is shown in Table 17.2. The table also compares the revenue of the state and local governments on a per capita basis.

Major Nonproperty Taxes. As we have seen, other levies have supplanted the property tax as the major sources of state revenues. The major nonproperty taxes in recent years have been a state sales tax and, increasingly, a state income tax.

But the state legislatures are ingenious, and they have devised other new measures as well. A brief description of these taxes follows.

Sales tax. Sales and gross receipts taxes were used by all fifty states in 1973. The total revenues raised amounted to $37 billion.[1] A general sales tax is defined as one which has a very broad coverage, as distinct, for example, from selective levies on specific commodities, such as tobacco.

Beginning with New York city in 1934, a substantial number of municipalities and counties have imposed local sales taxes. Since then, the use of this type of tax has spread widely.

The chief criticism of the sales tax is that it is regressive: the tax falls most heavily upon those least able to pay. Nonetheless, the yield on a sales tax is very high, and some states seem to prefer it to the most obvious alternative device, the state income tax.

Income tax. Forty-four states employed individual income taxes by the end of 1973. In all, this second-ranking source of income produced $16 billion for that year. In some states, the tax is progressive, or graduated. In others, as in Pennsylvania, it is a flat percentage of earnings. The simplest way of setting up a state income tax is to adopt the so-called piggy-back system, under which the state tax is determined as a percentage of the federal income tax.

A large number of municipalities and other local governments now are permitted by state law to impose income or payroll taxes. First to establish a wage tax was Philadelphia, in 1938. The tax is based on what is earned through wages or salary, it is calculated on an across-the-board percentage, and there are no exemptions. Obviously, the tax is regressive, and the burden of it is carried by those in the lower income groups. On the other hand, the tax is easy to collect, for most of it is deducted from employees' pay checks. For this reason, it is possible to foster the illusion that the tax does not really exist.

Gasoline tax. Again, all fifty states impose a motor fuel tax. In 1973, the proceeds amounted to $8 billion. Commonly, the revenues derived from this tax are diverted for highway purposes. In this respect, the tax may be considered to be a use tax. This tax is extremely easy to administer. It runs into difficulties only when the price of gasoline discourages consumption, as happened immediately after the Arab oil boycott of 1974. It remains problematical, however, whether Americans will be

Table 17.2
General Revenue of State and Local Governments — States: 1972

State	Revenue (mil. dol.)						Revenue Per Capita (dollars)					
	Total	From Federal Government	From own sources				Total	From Federal Government	From own sources			
			Taxes							Taxes			
			All taxes	Property tax	Other	Charges and miscellaneous			All taxes	Property tax	Other	Charges and miscellaneous
U.S.	166,352	31,253	108,801	42,133	66,668	26,299	799	150	522	202	320	126
Ala.	2,150	601	1,094	149	944	455	613	171	312	43	269	130
Alaska	518	174	149	35	114	195	1,594	536	459	107	352	599
Ariz.	1,501	266	989	382	607	246	772	137	508	196	312	127
Ark.	1,141	314	618	148	471	209	577	159	313	75	238	106
Cal.	21,110	4,148	14,064	6,692	7,372	2,898	1,031	203	687	327	360	142
Colo.	1,958	413	1,181	481	700	364	831	175	501	204	297	155
Conn.	2,600	371	1,945	948	996	284	843	120	631	308	323	92
Del.	525	98	324	56	268	104	930	174	573	99	474	183
Dist. Col.	1,069	506	458	141	316	105	1,429	676	612	189	423	140
Fla.	4,852	733	3,184	1,036	2,148	935	668	101	439	143	296	129
Ga.	3,235	730	1,833	565	1,268	672	685	154	388	120	269	142
Hawaii	837	191	515	98	416	131	1,034	236	636	121	515	162
Idaho	524	124	309	107	201	91	693	164	408	142	266	120
Ill.	9,359	1,838	6,472	2,662	3,809	1,049	832	163	575	237	339	93
Ind.	3,505	485	2,350	1,163	1,186	670	662	92	444	220	224	127
Iowa	2,096	300	1,428	659	769	368	727	104	495	229	267	128
Kan.	1,618	282	1,041	507	534	296	717	125	461	225	236	131
Ky.	2,028	489	1,168	244	925	371	615	148	354	74	280	112
La.	2,746	601	1,563	287	1,276	582	738	162	420	77	343	156
Me.	743	172	484	210	274	87	722	168	470	204	267	84

Md.	3,249	499	2,222	709	1,513	529	801	123	548	175	373	130
Mass.	5,144	925	3,696	1,875	1,821	523	889	160	639	324	315	90
Mich.	7,807	1,296	5,171	2,024	3,147	1,339	860	143	569	223	347	147
Minn.	3,484	573	2,252	904	1,348	659	894	147	578	232	346	169
Miss.	1,466	402	779	177	601	286	648	177	344	78	266	126
Mo.	3,102	617	2,021	752	1,269	464	653	130	425	158	267	98
Mont.	620	164	367	185	182	89	862	228	511	257	254	123
Nebr.	1,102	177	691	348	344	234	722	116	453	228	225	153
Nev.	521	91	320	111	209	110	989	172	607	210	397	209
N.H.	493	88	329	191	138	76	639	114	427	248	179	98
N.J.	5,813	907	4,083	2,286	1,797	823	789	123	554	310	244	112
N.M.	901	268	445	92	353	188	846	252	417	86	331	177
N.Y.	20,566	3,349	14,485	5,322	9,163	2,732	1,120	182	789	290	499	149
N.C.	3,087	625	1,964	493	1,471	499	592	120	377	94	282	96
N.D.	495	110	272	112	160	114	783	173	430	177	253	180
Ohio	6,831	1,020	4,516	1,944	2,572	1,296	634	95	419	180	239	120
Okla.	1,801	444	974	263	711	383	684	169	370	100	270	146
Ore.	1,739	413	1,011	486	525	316	797	189	463	223	241	145
Pa.	8,836	1,439	6,272	1,731	4,541	1,124	741	121	526	145	381	94
R.I.	732	153	498	194	303	82	756	158	514	201	313	84
S.C.	1,509	320	902	209	693	287	566	120	339	79	260	108
S.D.	533	115	313	168	145	105	785	170	461	248	213	154
Tenn.	2,415	550	1,426	381	1,045	439	599	136	354	94	259	109
Texas	7,277	1,441	4,476	1,714	2,763	1,360	625	124	384	147	237	117
Utah	848	225	481	168	313	142	753	200	427	149	278	126
Vt.	420	103	259	99	160	58	908	222	561	215	346	126
Va.	3,086	583	1,994	562	1,432	509	648	122	419	118	301	107
Wash.	3,016	557	1,824	666	1,159	635	876	162	530	193	336	184
W. Va.	1,213	350	697	145	552	165	681	197	391	82	310	93
Wis.	3,779	517	2,721	1,167	1,554	542	836	114	602	258	344	120
Wyo.	355	96	176	87	89	82	1,028	279	510	252	258	238

¹ Based on estimated population as of 1 July 1972.

Source: U.S. Bureau of the Census, Governmental Finances in 1971–72. From Statistical Abstract, 1974, Table No. 412.

discouraged from using petroleum products for automobiles, airplanes, and heating purposes simply by increasing prices and by increased taxes. On the other hand, a shortage which necessitated a shift to other sources of energy than oil would profoundly affect the tax structures of the states.

Other taxes. Other taxes which bring in considerable revenues are motor vehicle and operators' license taxes, tobacco taxes, liquor taxes, corporation net income taxes, death and gift taxes, and document and stock transfer taxes. It is of interest that state parimutuels (based on horse and dog races), supposed at one time to bail the states out of any financial problems, netted only $588 million in 1973. As more and more states jumped on the presumed bandwagon to easy riches, the returns per state declined during the mid-1970s.

Different kinds of license fees produce additional state and local revenues, as do such diversified taxes as those on utilities and severance taxes based upon income from natural resources in the earth such as oil or coal. But the outstanding development of recent decades has been the growth in intergovernmental aid, in this case, grants by the federal government to the states, and by the states to the local governments.

Revenue Sharing

Though President Nixon seemed to suggest in an address on 20 October 1972 at Independence Hall in Philadelphia that his program to provide new aid for the states and local governments was unique, this was not really the case. Thomas Jefferson made a somewhat similar recommendation in 1805. The big difference was that nobody followed up President Jefferson's proposal, while Congress did establish a General Revenue Sharing plan in a 1972 act at the insistence of President Nixon.

The legislative history of the statute, the State and Local Fiscal Assistance Act of 1972, need not detain us. What President Nixon hoped for was a plan to help the states and communities strengthen their fiscal foundations while lessening dependence upon the federal government. The federal government, from general funds, would simply give monies to the states and to the local governments, which would decide, within limits, how these funds would be spent.

Eventually, the plan as approved called for giving to the

state and local governments $30.2 billion during a five-year program. Very few strings were attached to the grants. The idea was to extend the general revenue-sharing scheme until the end of 1976, at which time Congress could reappraise it.

Related to this concept of general revenue sharing was one of special revenue sharing. The idea here was to replace some seventy categorical grant programs currently in existence with special grants to be used in the four areas of urban community development, education, manpower training, and law enforcement. Because of some dissatisfaction with the idea of abolishing categorical grants, the subject of special revenue sharing has generally been disassociated from the general revenue sharing plan.[2]

No matter in what form revenue sharing survives, federal assistance to state and local governments may be expected both to continue and to increase. Especially insistent on the need for massive federal aid are the large cities, led by New York. In May 1975, Mayor Beame of New York city and Governor Carey of New York state descended, amid much publicity, on Washington to demand assistance. Without an immediate federal grant of $1.5 billion, they said, New York city would not be able to meet its payroll by the end of June 1975.

Though President Ford talked to the New York dignitaries, the assignment to handle the matter was given to Treasury Secretary William E. Simon. When asked if he thought the president and Congress would bail out New York city as they had bailed out the Penn Central Railroad in 1970 and Lockheed Aircraft in 1971, Simon, a Wall Street broker, said with a note of sarcasm: "We're going to sell New York to the Shah of Iran. It's a hell of an investment."[3] The responses of the mayor and of the governor were, as it turned out, thoroughly predictable. New York city engaged in massive layoffs of civil servants and a lowering of standards of municipal services.

As it turned out, the day before D (for Default) Day, the state imposed a temporary solution on New York city in the form of the Municipal Assistance Corporation. Big Mac, as it was called, was set up to transform $3 billion in city short-term debt into state long-term debt. But strings were attached. Big Mac was to receive stock transfer and sales tax revenues (more than $1 billion) that previously had gone to the city. In addition, Big Mac was instructed to impose its own auditing procedures on the city and to audit city agencies. Exasperated by what it

Officials of New York city's Patrolmen's Benevolent Association and Uniformed Firefighters' Association hand out "Welcome to Fear City" pamphlets at New York's Kennedy Airport. The action was part of their campaign to halt budget-crisis layoffs of city workers. (Wide World Photos.)

considered a long train of city fiscal abuses, the state of New York felt it necessary to force financial controls on New York city as a condition for assistance.

Although both Governor Carey and Mayor Beame insisted that the bonds to be issued by Big Mac would prove irresistible to the financial community, doubt persisted as to whether New York city would be able to meet its long-range fiscal commitments. But the setting up of the Municipal Assistance Corporation did spare the city the humiliation of defaulting on some of its debts. It did not, however, even remotely resolve the city's long-range fiscal crisis.

Tables 17.3 and 17.4 indicate state tax collections by type of

Table 17.3
State Tax Collections and Excise Taxes, by Type of Tax — States: 1973

State	Total[2]	State Tax Collections[1] [mil. dol]							Excise Taxes		
		Sales and gross receipts					Individual income	Corporation net income	General sales and gross receipts (percent)	Cigarettes (cents per package)	Motor fuels (cents per gal., gasoline)
		Total[2]	General sales or gross receipts	Motor fuels	Alcoholic beverages and tobacco products	Motor vehicle and operators' licenses					
States using tax	50	50	45	50	50	50	44	46	45	50	50
U.S.	67,939	36,992	19,709	8,018	4,930	3,639	15,598	5,435	(x)	(x)	(x)
Ala.	931	630	289	146	100	33	142	41	[3]4	12	7
Alaska	109	25	(x)	12	8	6	43	7	(x)	8	8
Ariz.	682	420	267	88	38	30	109	37	[3]3	10	7
Ark.	523	336	168	95	53	36	89	38	[3]3	17.75	8.5
Cal.	7,324	3,612	2,189	747	366	301	1,886	866	[3]4.75	10	7
Colo.	667	368	220	93	30	32	186	39	[3]3	10	7
Conn.	1,122	800	447	138	94	54	51	139	6.5	21	10
Del.	287	62	(x)	25	16	17	110	19	(x)	14	9
Fla.	2,488	1,875	1,041	349	314	179	(x)	148	4	17	8
Ga.	1,358	886	477	227	141	43	285	114	[3]3	12	7.5
Hawaii	433	275	211	20	17	[4](z)	135	13	4	[5]	[6]5
Idaho	225	116	61	36	12	19	58	16	3	9.1	8.5
Ill.	3,676	2,113	1,196	374	237	303	895	229	[3]4	12	7.5

Table 17.3—Continued

State Tax Collections[1] (mil. dol)

State	Total[2]	Sales and gross receipts Total[2]	General sales or gross receipts	Motor fuels	Alcoholic beverages and tobacco products	Motor vehicle and operators' licenses	Individual income	Corporation net income	Excise Taxes General sales and gross receipts (percent)	Cigarettes (cents per package)	Motor fuels (cents per gal., gasoline)
Ind.	1,190	769	484	185	69	59	285	10	4	6	8
Iowa	854	433	244	114	53	94	243	47	3	13	7
Kan.	610	364	200	106	41	42	114	54	³3	11	7
Ky.	1,015	625	317	170	33	37	179	69	5	3	9
La.	1,166	593	288	147	91	29	100	88	3	11	8
Me.	304	222	118	51	39	17	31	10	5	14	9
Md.	1,456	700	326	172	57	70	516	80	4	6	9
Mass.	2,052	737	230	184	173	57	876	259	3	16	7.5
Mich.	3,528	1,733	1,092	351	206	181	925	364	4	11	9
Minn.	1,638	709	299	145	122	89	586	171	4	18	7
Miss.	661	497	317	115	37	21	70	26	5	11	9
Mo.	1,190	666	359	196	79	91	314	63	³3	9	7
Mont.	187	63	(x)	36	18	10	77	12	(x)	12	7
Nebr.	375	231	109	79	29	33	85	14	³2.5	13	8.5
Nev.	203	171	70	32	18	12	(x)	19	³⁷3	10	6
N.H.	156	90	(x)	36	27	18	8	171	(x)	(⁸)	9
N.J.	1,919	1,288	682	272	218	161	26	171	5	19	8

N.M.	387	243	153	52	18	19	50	15	[3]4	12	7
N.Y.	8,170	3,244	1,734	474	478	274	3,212	875	[3]4	15	8
N.C.	1,657	873	370	264	95	84	431	139	[3]3	2	9
N.D.	180	113	70	25	13	18	27	10	4	11	7
Ohio	2,676	1,640	808	370	254	218	374	168	[3]4	15	7
Okla.	695	361	125	109	73	81	105	35	[3]2	13	6.58
Ore.	596	136	(x)	85	33	64	301	51	(x)	9	7
Pa.	4,367	2,148	1,109	445	329	180	1,011	497	6	18	8
R.I.	317	187	96	32	25	16	68	31	5	13	8
S.C.	825	525	286	121	74	23	183	64	4	6	8
S.D.	151	129	64	36	14	12	(x)	1	[3]4	12	7
Tenn.	1,006	698	403	171	88	76	15	103	[3]3.5	13	7
Texas	2,819	2,004	926	385	340	205	(x)	(x)	[3]4	18.5	5
Utah	359	203	136	48	10	15	89	30	[3]4	8	7
Vt.	175	90	25	22	20	15	50	8	3	12	9
Va.	1,400	712	292	232	58	78	442	97	[3]3	2.5	9
Wash.	1,287	1,024	688	160	109	57	(x)	(x)	[3]4.5	16	9
W. Va.	568	417	246	69	42	34	88	12	3	12	8.5
Wis.	1,868	760	432	156	115	82	728	136	[3]4	16	7
Wyo.	105	75	44	23	5	11	(x)	(x)	[3]3	8	7

(Collections include local shares of State-imposed taxes. Excise taxes as of September 1

X   Not applicable.
Z   Less than $500,000.
[1] Preliminary.
[2] Includes amounts for types of taxes not shown separately.
[3] Excludes State-collected supplemental local sales taxes imposed by local governments under State enabling legislation, as well as locally administered taxes.
[4] Motor vehicle licenses only.
[5] 40 percent of wholesale price.
[6] State rate per gallon in Hawaii County, 8 cents. Combined State and local rates per gallon, in cents: Honolulu, 8.5; Kauai, 9; and Maui, 10.
[7] Includes a mandatory State-imposed 1 percent county sales tax.
[8] 34 percent of retail sales price until 1 July 1971; 42 percent thereafter.
Source: Statistical Abstract, 1974, Table No. 418.

Table 17.4

City Government Revenues, 1972: 25 Largest Cities

City	Total revenue¹	General Revenue — Total	Intergovernmental revenue — From state and local governments	From federal government	Property	Taxes — Sales and gross receipts	Other	Charges and miscellaneous	Gross debt outstanding
Total, 25 cities	19,613.1	16,688.0	5,310.5	1,399.5	4,381.3	1,613.6	1,838.0	2,145.0	22,918.5
New York, N.Y.	100,006.7	8,729.2	3,858.0	232.4	2,131.4	820.0	879.2	808.3	11,279.0
Chicago, Ill.	933.2	787.6	94.2	95.1	296.8	136.8	47.8	116.9	1,384.8
Los Angeles, Cal.	1,052.7	644.4	97.4	28.2	190.1	113.0	65.1	150.7	1,736.2
Philadelphia, Pa.	777.3	721.2	94.7	82.7	118.0	2.6	289.7	133.5	1,163.6
Detroit, Mich.	692.5	581.4	90.2	132.1	151.8	16.7	100.4	90.2	752.6
Houston, Tex.	218.5	183.1	1.8	12.5	80.4	42.1	4.1	42.2	502.5
Baltimore, Md.	755.4	703.8	379.8	43.8	169.3	17.2	42.8	51.0	625.0
Dallas, Tex.	217.2	155.5	3.7	4.8	80.9	32.7	1.4	31.9	382.0
Washington, D.C.	1,014.5	976.3	23.1	408.7	141.4	152.0	164.5	86.7	685.5
Cleveland, Ohio	224.9	158.5	15.7	16.8	39.3	1.0	40.9	44.8	352.0
Indianapolis, Ind.	167.4	166.9	31.9	15.5	87.0	–	2.0	30.4	236.0
Milwaukee, Wis.	221.6	184.9	60.3	10.0	82.4	.4	2.3	29.7	255.4
San Francisco, Cal.	692.6	583.6	161.9	75.1	163.3	52.5	23.4	107.4	468.5
San Diego, Cal.	172.3	137.9	22.6	20.4	30.7	21.5	4.8	38.9	137.9
San Antonio, Tex.	188.2	84.3	2.6	20.9	25.5	10.8	1.0	23.4	233.1
Boston, Mass.	498.1	470.1	65.8	61.2	277.0	–	3.2	62.9	385.0
Honolulu, Hawaii	172.8	157.7	14.9	18.4	80.4	9.3	12.3	22.3	238.2
Memphis, Tenn.	383.2	233.9	128.7	1.3	38.6	9.4	8.3	47.6	451.0
St. Louis, Mo.	209.3	189.2	14.9	14.1	37.1	38.2	49.8	35.2	173.4
New Orleans, La.	147.0	136.3	20.4	14.8	26.0	35.2	5.9	34.1	249.6
Phoenix, Ariz.	123.8	102.4	18.6	9.0	17.0	31.9	3.3	22.7	207.3
Columbus, Ohio	112.7	95.9	12.2	9.4	7.4	.5	37.1	29.3	277.5
Seattle, Wash.	227.6	142.0	26.1	12.7	25.7	21.5	11.6	44.4	342.2
Pittsburgh, Pa.	148.4	131.9	15.8	32.5	46.1	5.1	26.1	6.4	119.2
Denver, Colo.	255.4	229.8	56.4	27.3	37.8	43.4	10.8	54.1	281.3

All figures in millions of dollars. For fiscal year closed in the 12 months ending 30 June 1972. Cities ranked by size of population as of April 1970.

Source: *Statistical Abstract, 1974*, Table No. 423.

tax in 1973, and also the revenues of the nation's twenty-five largest cities in 1972. The purpose of presenting these tables is to indicate the relative proportions of the different sources of income in the total revenues obtained by the states and by the selected city governments.

EXPENDITURES

The Rising Cost of Government

In ordinary times, government receipts and government expenditures tend to balance out. In times of recession, when resort is had to heavy borrowing, the key figure to examine is that of government indebtedness. Though the federal government can and sometimes deliberately does operate "in the red," the Keynesian theory on which this practice is based does not apply to state and local governments. In other words, the maintenance of the national economy is a federal responsibility. The responsibility of the state and local governments is to raise adequate revenues to meet the expenditures incurred in providing the services and functions which their residents demand.

Direct general expenditure of state and local governments has steadily increased. For example, the combined totals rose from $51.9 billion in 1960, to $74.5 billion in 1965, to $131.3 billion in 1970, to $166.9 billion in 1972. While this rise in part represents inflation, it mostly represents demands for new, improved, or extended services. As would be expected, the number of state and local government employees has also risen during the period, from 6.4 million in 1960 to 11.4 million in 1973.

The best way to obtain an overview of the spending of state and local governments is to examine Table 17.5 with care. The two succeeding tables, 17.6 and 17.7, deal, respectively, with a composite view of city finances and a summary of expenditures in the twenty-five largest cities. What all three tables illustrate is the order of priorities in expenditures as established by state and local governments. This should tell one a good deal about American society and its finances.

Budgeting

Until the beginning of this century, public finance in the United States was handled in a haphazard manner and with

Table 17.5
Direct General Expenditure of State and Local Governments — States: 1972

| | Expenditure (mil. dol.) | | | | | | Per Capita[2] (dollars) | | | | | |
State	Total	Ed-uca-tion	High-ways	Pub-lic wel-fare	Health and hos-pitals	All other[1]	Total	Ed-uca-tion	High-ways	Pub-lic wel-fare	Health and hos-pitals	All other[1]
U.S.	166,873	64,886	19,010	21,070	12,867	49,040	801	312	91	10.	62	236
Ala.	2,104	780	296	260	216	551	599	222	84	74	62	157
Alaska	698	237	126	34	20	281	2,147	728	389	105	62	863
Ariz.	1,523	712	185	79	88	458	783	366	95	41	45	236
Ark.	1,014	397	163	142	79	233	512	200	82	72	40	118
Cal.	20,052	6,937	1,560	3,853	1,336	6,366	980	339	76	188	65	311
Colo.	1,920	871	233	226	131	459	815	369	99	96	56	195
Conn.	2,546	973	274	277	160	863	826	316	89	90	52	280
Del.	571	265	69	47	25	165	1,010	469	121	83	43	292
Dist. Col.	1,069	248	71	145	140	464	1,429	332	94	194	187	621
Fla.	4,771	1,918	589	350	454	1,460	657	264	81	48	63	201
Ga.	3,197	1,213	349	400	424	811	677	257	74	85	90	172
Hawaii	940	307	83	91	62	397	1,161	380	102	112	76	491
Idaho	512	203	88	43	40	138	677	268	117	57	53	182
Ill.	8,935	3,524	1,075	1,215	549	2,572	794	313	96	108	49	229
Ind.	3,457	1,711	413	265	290	778	653	323	78	50	55	147
Iowa	2,108	969	409	179	131	420	731	336	142	62	45	146
Kan.	1,551	687	260	112	122	369	687	304	115	50	54	164
Ky.	2,063	796	424	228	118	497	625	241	129	69	36	151
La.	2,691	975	385	310	229	793	723	262	103	83	61	213
Me.	704	247	133	95	32	197	684	240	129	92	32	192
Md.	3,392	1,384	308	344	245	1,111	836	341	76	85	60	274
Mass.	5,166	1,838	381	957	383	1,607	893	318	66	165	66	278

Mich.	7,799	3,241	694	1,085	588	2,192	859	357	76	119	65	241
Minn.	3,528	1,618	450	377	223	861	906	415	116	97	57	221
Miss.	1,427	513	246	188	157	323	630	227	109	83	69	143
Mo.	3,156	1,318	406	333	229	869	664	277	85	70	48	183
Mont.	587	231	139	45	24	148	816	322	194	62	33	205
Nebr.	1,052	444	179	91	76	262	690	291	118	60	50	172
Nev.	543	178	74	31	48	211	1,030	338	140	60	91	401
N.H.	526	201	94	55	33	144	683	261	122	71	43	186
N.J.	5,911	2,225	706	723	350	1,907	802	302	96	98	48	259
N.M.	823	377	121	80	48	196	773	354	114	75	45	184
N.Y.	22,750	7,488	1,486	3,320	2,567	7,890	1,239	408	81	181	140	430
N.C.	2,938	1,254	408	291	223	761	563	240	78	56	43	146
N.D.	475	202	92	38	17	127	752	320	145	60	27	201
Ohio	6,867	2,852	813	710	528	1,964	637	265	75	66	49	182
Okla.	1,767	667	227	306	125	442	671	253	86	116	48	168
Ore.	1,766	727	265	147	83	544	809	333	122	68	38	249
Pa.	8,840	3,624	1,011	1,147	529	2,530	741	304	85	96	44	212
R.I.	699	262	50	126	50	211	722	271	52	131	52	217
S.C.	1,512	672	172	97	164	407	567	252	65	37	61	153
S. D.	521	249	104	41	19	108	767	366	154	60	28	159
Tenn.	2,446	920	337	241	247	702	607	228	84	60	61	174
Texas	7,246	3,089	1,064	741	508	1,844	622	265	91	64	44	158
Utah	821	411	127	70	38	175	729	365	113	63	34	155
Vt.	411	154	82	54	19	103	890	333	177	117	40	223
Va.	3,037	1,314	428	269	188	838	638	276	90	56	39	176
Wash.	3,070	1,223	406	314	153	974	892	355	118	91	44	283
W. Va.	1,250	447	384	106	76	237	702	251	215	60	43	133
Wis.	3,757	1,635	494	376	249	1,003	831	362	109	83	55	222
Wyo.	368	161	79	15	33	81	1,068	466	229	43	95	235

[1] Includes police protection, fire protection, natural resources, sanitation, local parks and recreation, financial administration, general control, and interest on general debt as well as miscellaneous lesser functions.

[2] Based on estimated resident population as of 1 July 1972.

Source: U.S. Bureau of the Census, *Governmental Finances in 1971–72.* From *Statistical Abstract, 1974,* Table No. 413.

Table 17.6

City Government Finances, 1960–1972

Item	1960	1965	1968	1969	1970	1971	1972
Revenue	14,915	20,318	26,521	29,673	32,704	37,367	42,196
General revenue	11,647	15,884	21,276	24,153	26,621	30,575	34,937
Taxes	7,109	9,289	11,291	12,349	13,647	15,090	17,058
Property	5,197	6,537	7,769	8,331	9,127	10,041	10,988
Sales and gross receipts	1,217	1,795	1,837	2,017	2,422	2,780	3,185
General	797	1,184	1,090	1,256	1,479	1,658	1,866
Selective	420	611	747	761	943	1,122	1,319
Licenses and other	695	957	1,686	2,002	2,098	2,270	2,885
Intergovernmental revenue	2,321	3,534	5,971	7,346	7,906	9,697	11,434
From State governments only	1,868	2,745	4,730	5,811	6,173	7,401	8,377
Charges and miscellaneous	2,217	3,061	4,014	4,458	5,068	5,788	6,445
Current charges only	1,342	1,951	2,418	2,753	3,113	3,579	3,944
Utility and liquor store revenue	2,861	3,852	4,482	4,710	5,168	5,728	6,085
Water system	1,253	1,651	1,888	2,026	2,201	2,436	2,552
Electric power system	1,006	1,441	1,663	1,706	1,883	2,082	2,275
Gas supply system	162	215	244	266	292	319	339
Transit system	370	453	565	578	671	743	760
Liquor stores	71	92	121	134	121	150	159
Insurance trust revenue	407	582	763	810	915	1,062	1,174
Expenditure	15,251	20,680	27,007	30,451	34,173	39,061	43,584
By function:							
General expenditure[1]	11,818	16,012	21,563	24,500	27,682	31,947	35,697
Police protection	1,275	1,739	2,261	2,604	2,994	3,471	3,942
Fire protection	885	1,146	1,400	1,565	1,762	1,996	2,208

Highways	1,573	1,807	2,142	2,288	2,499	2,664	2,768
Sewerage and other sanitation	1,332	1,774	2,051	2,211	2,553	3,010	3,298
Public welfare	608	927	1,739	2,145	2,215	2,688	3,031
Education	1,801	2,489	3,405	3,978	4,548	5,242	5,827
Libraries	185	267	341	370	407	445	465
Health and hospitals	799	1,115	1,541	1,704	1,944	2,324	2,773
Own hospitals	569	796	1,049	1,091	1,232	1,500	1,727
Other hospitals and health	229	319	492	613	712	823	1,046
Parks and recreation	551	775	1,003	1,133	1,306	1,439	1,571
Housing and urban renewal	464	686	948	991	1,154	1,442	1,475
Water transport and terminals	63	73	84	104	121	157	164
Airports	189	182	276	360	435	461	534
Financial administration	598	291	361	408	457	515	565
General control	598	468	592	670	776	867	982
General public buildings	182	329	350	422	430	489	531
Interest on general debt	431	603	817	928	1,098	1,308	1,527
Other and unallocable general expenditure	883	1,341	2,252	2,618	2,983	3,429	4,036
Utility and liquor store expenditure	2,975	4,044	4,622	5,068	5,489	5,932	6,587
Water system	1,424	1,820	1,928	2,169	2,337	2,436	2,622
Electric system	859	1,291	1,571	1,644	1,811	2,012	2,346
Gas supply system	143	193	212	231	260	285	300
Transit system	489	662	809	911	974	1,070	1,183
Liquor stores	60	78	102	114	107	129	136
Insurance trust expenditure	458	624	822	883	1,002	1,182	1,300
By character and object:							
Current operation	9,874	13,564	18,021	20,188	22,895	26,263	29,786
Capital outlay	3,691	4,750	5,664	6,452	7,103	7,845	8,237
Construction	2,884	3,808	4,307	5,050	5,649	6,131	6,525
Land and existing structures	436	553	795	796	733	902	876
Equipment	372	389	562	607	722	812	837
Intergovernmental expenditure	158	255	332	343	381	440	510
Assistance payments	386	530	966	1,243	1,245	1,531	1,664
Interest on debt	684	957	1,202	1,342	1,547	1,800	2,086

Table 17.6—*Continued*

Item	1960	1965	1968	1969	1970	1971	1972
Insurance benefits and repayments	458	624	822	883	1,002	1,182	1,300
Total personal services²	6,772	9,075	11,596	13,105	14,784	16,377	18,091
Debt outstanding at end of fiscal year	23,178	31,862	37,505	39,996	43,773	48,961	52,511
Long-term	21,904	29,280	33,942	36,274	38,870	42,140	45,833
Full faith and credit	14,473	18,477	20,185	21,100	22,005	23,988	27,261
Nonguaranteed	7,430	10,803	13,757	15,174	16,863	18,152	18,572
Short-term	1,274	2,582	3,563	3,721	4,903	6,821	6,678
Net long-term debt outstanding	20,103	26,774	31,331	33,871	36,087	39,254	42,759
Long-term debt issued	2,420	3,347	4,035	4,230	3,810	5,336	6,294
Long-term debt retired	1,318	1,776	2,093	2,186	2,310	2,500	2,711

All figures in millions of dollars. Represents all municipalities and their dependent agencies; excludes other local governments overlying city areas. Includes sample-based estimates for cities of less than 25,000 for 1960, and less than 50,000 beginning 1965; thus subject to sampling variation.

[1] Includes intergovernmental expenditure.
[2] Included in items shown above.

Source: U.S. Bureau of the Census, *City Government Finances,* annual. From *Statistical Abstract,* 1974, Table No. 422.

Table 17.7

City General Expenditures, 25 Largest Cities: 1972

City	Total expenditure[1]	General Expenditure							
		Total[1]	Education	Highways	Public welfare	Health and hospitals	Police protection	Fire protection	Housing and urban renewal
Total, 25 cities	20,560.5	17,081.1	3,091.4	707.1	2,775.3	1,904.3	1,756.6	799.5	833.2
New York, N.Y.	10,711.7	9,085.1	2,306.4	160.4	2,215.5	1,243.6	624.0	279.6	485.3
Chicago, Ill.	971.4	856.3	26.1	64.3	10.1	39.6	208.2	70.3	19.8
Los Angeles, Cal.	1,129.6	599.3	—	67.8	.3	2.8	147.5	62.7	14.4
Philadelphia, Pa.	803.7	734.1	6.2	29.6	30.0	84.5	112.2	39.8	43.0
Detroit, Mich.	646.7	489.6	8.7	19.8	4.7	49.6	91.7	28.8	33.2
Houston, Tex.	221.1	180.8	1.5	16.7	(z)	8.2	28.2	25.5	1.1
Baltimore, Md.	770.7	724.3	221.1	42.1	132.4	47.3	53.5	28.1	65.9
Dallas, Tex.	208.7	172.3	—	24.5	—	2.8	27.6	17.1	—
Washington, D.C.	1,194.6	1,115.1	248.2	70.6	145.3	140.0	76.4	22.0	56.5
Cleveland, Ohio	230.0	159.8	(z)	12.5	(z)	4.5	38.6	20.6	5.5
Indianapolis, Ind.	180.7	175.4	1.2	23.3	23.8	26.5	17.5	10.6	1.9
Milwaukee, Wis.	191.0	169.3	10.1	21.2	—	5.9	29.9	12.9	12.6
San Francisco, Cal.	631.3	518.3	1.0	17.8	151.5	63.6	39.3	29.5	32.5
San Diego, Cal.	175.7	141.7	—	14.8	(z)	(z)	17.2	10.2	—
San Antonio, Tex.	173.5	65.9	—	6.1	.8	3.2	11.9	6.5	2.8
Boston, Mass.	529.9	493.2	139.9	17.3	7.8	62.0	45.8	27.3	18.9
Honolulu, Hawaii	162.3	148.4	—	16.9	.3	1.7	23.3	11.5	2.5
Memphis, Tenn.	405.8	260.5	116.0	7.9	.3	30.2	16.9	17.1	4.0
St. Louis, Mo.	203.9	180.8	.2	12.7	2.7	43.5	32.7	11.3	.1
New Orleans, La.	137.3	121.1	.4	6.4	2.8	4.9	17.6	10.7	1.1
Phoenix, Ariz.	140.6	113.9	3.5	10.3	(z)	.2	19.1	7.5	1.3
Columbus, Ohio	111.2	92.3	—	9.8	(z)	2.0	15.1	11.2	.8
Seattle, Wash.	261.4	158.2	—	16.9	—	5.3	24.6	15.4	2.7
Pittsburgh, Pa.	123.3	107.3	(z)	8.6	(z)	(z)	21.3	12.2	15.4
Denver, Colo.	244.6	218.3	.5	8.9	47.3	32.6	16.5	11.1	11.6

— Represents zero.

Z Less than $50,000.

[1] Includes amounts for categories not shown separately.

Source: U.S. Bureau of the Census, City Government Finances in 1971–72. Adapted from Statistical Abstract, 1974, Table No. 423.

little planning. In part, except in wartime, this probably reflected the prevailing philosophy of very limited government performing only the most essential of services. In part, it probably also reflected the fact that the governmental structure itself was poorly adapted to the planning function.

It is interesting to note that systematic if still rudimentary budget procedures were adopted first by cities and states and lastly by the federal government. In the first decade of the century, New York city established a budgetary system, and the states of California and Wisconsin did so in 1911. The national budget system was not approved by Congress until 1921. In the meantime, every state had set up some kind of budgetary machinery.

Budgetary Procedures. Budget making is an extremely complex process, and in any given jurisdiction only a few experts will understand its intricacies. Yet the ordinary citizen need not be a fiscal expert to comprehend the general operations of the system.

First, there is a budget-making authority. This varies according to where the responsibility for preparing the budget has been placed. Under the executive budget (that used by the federal government), the responsibility is assigned to the chief executive. Under the board-type budget, this responsibility is given to an administrative or to an administrative-legislative board. Lastly, there may be a legislative budget, which, as the name implies, is prepared by a committee of the legislative body of the government in question.

At the state level, the executive budget has triumphed, and it is the prevailing type in strong-mayor and council-manager cities. In the counties, the story is different. Since most American counties lack a principal executive with overall administrative authority, budgets are usually prepared by boards or by finance committees. With the exception of counties and of some small towns, the executive budget has been increasingly perceived as a means to strengthen the managerial authority of the chief executive officer of the jurisdiction.

When the budget has been prepared, it is submitted as a formal document to the legislative body. Ordinarily, it consists of three parts: a budget message, a budget summary, and a detailed financial plan. Budgetary proposals are, of course, recommendations only. Yet in practice most of the budget will not be changed in any drastic fashion by the legislature. This is because most of the items in the budget are continuous and not really subject to much tinkering. To put the matter differently, while a budget will contain new items, it will mostly continue to honor past programs and commitments made by the state, county, or municipality.

Different states deal with the budget in different ways. But the crucial stage is committee consideration. Usually, state legislatures have separate appropriations and revenue committees. There is the further complication that financial matters usually must be ironed out by conference committees consisting of members designated by both chambers (except, of course, in unicameral Nebraska). On the other hand, many local bodies have a single finance committee, which means that the machinery exists for integrating legislative action on budgetary matters.

An appropriation act may be of the lump-sum type, or it may be itemized. Under the lump-sum plan, each spending agency is granted its funds in a single amount. While this approach encourages flexibility, which is desirable, its successful execution depends on the ability of department heads and their financial officers to plan carefully and competently.

In contrast, itemization of appropriations furthers administrative planning, but it may result in undue rigidity. Generally, highly segregated appropriations—how much may be spent for what—are looked on with disfavor by fiscal experts. One device they do favor in order to maintain administrative control while keeping a good deal of flexibility is the allotment system. Under this plan, each department head is required to divide the total appropriation into four or twelve parts, depending upon whether the allotments are quarterly or monthly. Expenditure controls are thereby established, in that the accounting officer will not approve expenditures during a particular quarter or month in excess of the allotment. Of course, the expenditure pattern may be revised from time to time if the department head can make a good enough case to the chief executive.

The Execution of the Budget. Though the adoption of the budget is a legislative task, its execution is a responsibility of the administrative branch. In the larger units of government, it is customary to have a principal accounting officer, usually known as the comptroller. The assignment of this official is to make sure that funds have been spent in accordance with the intent of the legislature.

Since no one is likely to expect perfection when it comes to finances, it is also customary in the larger governmental units to provide for a postaudit of expenditures after disbursement. The agency to perform this function should be outside and independent of the administration. The head of this agency is usually called the auditor, and in most cases is popularly elected. An alternative, however, is appointment by the legislative body. This approach, which is the one the United States government uses, is based on the theory that postauditing is basically a function of the legislative process. In any case, the auditor, by whatever title he or she may be known, is expected to report irregularities in expenditures to the legislature for appropriate action. In some states this also takes the form of personal warfare, waged through the mass media, between the governor and the auditor, both independently elected officials and not responsible to each other. A charge that a particular administration has misspent public funds is guaranteed to receive media coverage and to enhance the public image of the auditor who made the charges.

Other Financial Matters

Other aspects of government finance may be dealt with briefly. In many states and cities expenditures for capital improvements are separated from expenditures for day-to-day operations. The advantage of capital budgeting is that it makes possible some measure of long-range planning. Capital and operating budgets may be distinct parts of the same budget document, or they may take the form of separate documents. This distinction has been made in the financial operations of large corporations for many decades, and governments have tended to imitate corporate practice in this and other fiscal areas.

Governmental purchasing is obviously closely related to budgeting, as is borrowing. As we have noted earlier, state constitutions tend to place severe restrictions upon the borrowing power of the states. The subunits of the state governments possess only such borrowing authority as has been positively conferred on them by the states.

Why do governments borrow? The most common purposes

are: (1) in anticipation of revenues; (2) for expenditures arising from emergencies; and (3) for construction of public improvements—most of which will last a long time. There is nothing immoral about a government's borrowing of money. Almost all governments find it necessary or desirable to do so at one time or another. It is when the debt ceiling, imposed by a constitution or statute, has been reached that the real problems begin. When in the summer of 1975 the banks of New York city refused to buy a bond issue proposed by that city, everyone knew that New York city was on the brink of fiscal collapse. It survived, of course, but only at the sacrifice of numerous public services and the discharging of thousands of municipal employees.

INDEBTEDNESS

It is said that in 1912 the total state and local debt in this country amounted to less than $5 billion and the federal debt to only a little more than $1 billion. Both World Wars increased federal indebtedness dramatically, as did the war in Vietnam. In 1973, the gross outstanding federal debt was $468.4 billion. At the end of 1972, the outstanding debt of all state and local governments stood at $174 billion. The breakdown by states as of the end of 1972 is shown in Table 17.8.[4]

EFFECTS OF THE MID-1970s RECESSION ON STATE AND LOCAL FINANCE

The national recession of the early and mid-1970s, coupled with the unparalleled combination of inflation and massive unemployment, created severe financial problems for states and localities. But the impact was uneven. According to a survey by the Joint Economic Committee of Congress, an estimated $3.6 billion in new levies were added in the fiscal year that ended on 30 June 1975.[5] Of forty-eight states responding to the survey, twenty said they were raising existing taxes or imposing new ones—and some were doing both. These states added a total of $2.1 billion to their tax collections. Nearly 40 percent of the additional state taxes came from boosting levies on personal income.

Of 140 local governments surveyed by the committee, 52

Table 17.8
General Debt Outstanding of State and Local Governments — States: 1972

State	Total Amount	Per capita¹	Long-term amount	State	Total Amount	Per capita¹	Long-term amount
United States	174,502	888	158,781				
Alabama	2,700	769	2,574	Missouri	2,532	533	2,462
Alaska	739	2,272	716	Montana	272	379	269
Arizona	1,204	619	1,198	Nebraska	1,541	1,011	1,511
Arkansas	1,033	522	987	Nevada	492	934	490
California	18,088	884	17,691	New Hampshire	441	572	395
Colorado	1,408	597	1,365	New Jersey	6,490	881	5,685
Connecticut	4,087	1,329	3,306	New Mexico	444	417	444
Delaware	841	1,488	804	New York	31,246	1,701	23,824
District of Columbia	820	1,096	642	North Carolina	1,962	376	1,801
Florida	4,545	626	4,433	North Dakota	251	398	245
Georgia	2,939	623	2,797	Ohio	6,865	637	6,017
Hawaii	1,093	1,351	1,040	Oklahoma	1,760	668	1,739
Idaho	188	249	180	Oregon	1,769	811	1,719
Illinois	8,418	748	7,289	Pennsylvania	11,033	925	10,490
Indiana	2,466	466	2,327	Rhode Island	836	863	703
Iowa	1,107	384	1,076	South Carolina	1,291	484	1,243
Kansas	1,265	560	1,183	South Dakota	148	219	142
Kentucky	3,368	1,021	3,296	Tennesee	3,061	759	2,847
Louisiana	3,704	996	3,677	Texas	8,384	720	8,200
Maine	517	503	483	Utah	464	412	460
Maryland	3,872	955	3,786	Vermont	443	958	413
Massachusetts	5,533	956	4,917	Virginia	2,781	584	2,623
Michigan	6,389	703	5,981	Washington	4,730	1,374	4,670
Minnesota	3,518	903	3,357	West Virginia	1,004	563	963
Mississippi	1,372	606	1,334	Wisconsin	2,805	620	2,756
				Wyoming	235	680	235

All figures in millions of dollars, except per capita. As of end of fiscal year.
¹ Based on Bureau of the Census estimated total population, excluding Armed Forces abroad for 1 July 1972.
Source: U.S. Bureau of the Census, Governmental Finances in 1971–72. From Statistical Abstract, 1974, Table No. 415.

raised taxes during the same fiscal year by a total of $850 million. Nationwide, local tax increases were reported to have gone up by a total of $1.5 billion, mostly on property and sales. While they were increasing taxes, states and localities were also cutting back on services. The committee estimated that service cutbacks would save $3.3 billion. In addition, up to $1 billion in capital construction was delayed or cancelled.

Strapped for cash, the states engaged in vigorous warfare against tax dodgers. Particular targets were corporations that pay far less in taxes than the law demands, cigarette smugglers (who cheat Connecticut, for instance, out of an estimated $15 million annually), individuals who are supposed to pay sales taxes but refrain from doing so, and landlords who abandon properties in order to avoid property taxes. Especially in the Northeast, it was reported to be increasingly difficult to collect property taxes. In New York city, for example, the delinquency rate in 1975 stood at 7.6 percent, which meant adding $220 million to the $320 million in delinquencies already outstanding.

A survey was made in mid-1975 by the National League of Cities of sixty-seven cities.[6] The results underlined the findings of the Congressional study. Forty-two cities planned to hike taxes or cut services, or both, and thirty-six had delayed capital improvement programs. What this amounts to is a reversal of a trend toward bigger budgets, new services, and expanding payrolls that has gone on for nearly thirty years in most cities.

Some examples illustrate the nation-wide character of the crises. Detroit withdrew guards from public-housing projects. Cleveland cut its city payroll from 13,000 in 1970 to 10,800 in 1975. Baltimore cut its budget so drastically that the city payroll in 1975 was 25 percent less than it had been in 1972. Bridgeport, Connecticut, fired 15 percent of that city's entire payroll. Boston reduced the city subsidy to hospitals by 20 percent.

Chicago followed a different route. It made no cuts in services and fired no city employees. But it drastically raised taxes. Atlanta did the same thing. San Francisco cut its school budget, ruled out pay hikes for teachers, and eliminated half of the fringe benefits. Dallas deferred purchasing equipment needed for its parks and recreational areas. Newark, New Jersey, simply fired large numbers of police and fire fighters. Hartford began to phase out its famous children's zoo. Berkeley, California, cut its library from twenty-six thousand to nineteen thousand volumes between 1972 and 1975, and reduced operating hours. The list could go on indefinitely.

Yet there was one big city which had lots of money to

Participants in the 1975 U.S. Conference of Mayors discuss urban problems. From left: Mayor Richard G. Hatcher of Gary, Indiana; Mayor Janet Gray Hayes of San Jose, California; and Mayor Albert Hofstede of Minneapolis, Minnesota. (Wide World Photos.)

spend—Houston. In nearly every way, it was expanding. It undertook to spend $422 million in a two-year capital improvement program. Included in this expansion were forty-five hundred streetlights, a massive sewer-building and reclamation project, twelve new fire stations, three new branch libraries, and five neighborhood multiservice centers. It also planned to expand many departments, including the police. In addition, Houston purchased the local bus system in 1975 with federal help and ordered one hundred new buses. Not only were there no tax increases: property taxes were *decreased* in 1975. In 1975 the city was running a small surplus. Needless to say, its bond rating was increased to AAA—the highest.

Default and Bankruptcy

The financial difficulties of New York and scores of other cities in the mid-1970s naturally raised questions regarding the possibilities of default and bankruptcy by municipalities. A distinction must be made between the two terms. Under default, the payment of bills is deferred (as happened in the case of New York state's Urban Development Corporation). Under bankruptcy, a court supervises the affairs of a debtor, deciding who should get paid for what.

In the Depression years before World War II, 140 cities defaulted on bond issues. But most recent cases of so-called municipal defaults deal with such things as toll-bridge authorities that can sell tax-exempt securities. These are known in the trade as *municipals*.

In 1946, Congress amended the bankruptcy laws by setting up a procedure for a court-supervised municipal bankruptcy. But most experts on the subject believe that federal bankruptcy laws simply would not have any practical application to New York or other large cities. For example, the law requires a city to file for court supervision, with the written consent to a payment plan of holders of 51 percent of the city's debt. But as one lawyer noted, "City debt is all over the place. Nobody knows who holds it." In addition, few politicians want their cities to be run by the courts.[7]

IN CONCLUSION

We have tried to make the case that state and local finance is an integral part of the political process. The budget sets political, as well as economic, priorities. Revenue policy and expenditure policy both reflect the values of the society as perceived and understood by the political branches of government. From time to time, one or another emphasis may shift in response to changes in demands made upon the decision-making agencies. From a systemic perspective, fiscal policy is to be considered a policy output. Yet the process does not end there, for there almost always is a feedback from decisions about fiscal policy to conditions in the socioeconomic environment. In turn, these new conditions may generate new inputs into the total political process. In this fashion policy outputs have an influence, which social scientists are beginning to measure, on policy inputs. Paradoxically, we seem to be returning, albeit in a form different from that of a century ago, to an integrated conception of political economy. This is a development devoutly to be welcomed.

Items for Discussion

1. In your local area, what has been the record of success for school bond issues during the past few years? What factors account for this pattern?

2. Why do state and local governments continue to rely so heavily on regressive measures such as property and sales taxes? How can these taxes be made less regressive?

3. Is it fair to the general population that income earned from municipal bonds is tax-free?

4. How do you evaluate the future of revenue sharing? Do you know how your local governments have spent their revenue-sharing funds?

5. If you were the mayor of New York, what actions would you take to relieve the city of its financial burdens? How much responsibility should state governments accept for protecting the financial position of their cities?

Chapter Notes

1. This, and the other tax figures for 1973 in this section, come from *The Book of the States*, 1974—75 (Lexington, Ky.: The Council of State Governments, 1974), pp. 244—245.

2. See Murray S. Stedman, Jr., *Urban Politics*, 2nd ed. (Cambridge, Mass.: Winthrop, 1975), pp. 102—108, for the initial impact of revenue sharing on cities.

3. Fred Ferretti, "Ford Rejects a Plea by Beame for Help." *New York Times*, 15 May 1975. Also, editorial in *The Wall Street Journal*, "New York City Must Meet Its Own Crisis," reprinted in *Philadelphia Inquirer*, 15 May 1975. A survey made by the *New York Times*, released by that paper on 18 May 1975, showed that New Yorkers were currently subjected to twenty-two different kinds of taxes. To meet the expected deficit, Mayor Beame was reported to be looking into additional types of taxes as well as increasing many of the existing ones. The article, by Peter Kihss, was entitled "New Yorkers Subjected to 22 Different Kinds of Taxes."

4. For more detailed information on this subject, one should consult *Governmental Finances,* an annual publication of the United States Bureau of the Census.

5. "Strapped for Cash, States Go After The Tax Dodgers." *U.S. News & World Report,* 23 June 1975, pp. 66—68.

6. "How Slump is Hurting Cities." *U.S. News & World Report,* 30 June 1975, p. 18.

7. Maurice Carroll, "Panel to Explore What Happens if City Defaults." *New York Times,* 23 July 1975.

Index

Page numbers in *italics* indicate figures and tables.